1/4/88

Dissent and Reform
in the Early Middle Ages

With a New Preface by the Author

AMS PRESS
NEW YORK

Publications of the
CENTER FOR MEDIEVAL AND RENAISSANCE STUDIES
1. Dissent and Reform in the Early Middle Ages

Dissent and Reform
in the Early Middle Ages

Jeffrey Burton Russell

Berkeley and Los Angeles

UNIVERSITY OF CALIFORNIA PRESS

1965

Library of Congress Cataloging in Publication Data

Russell, Jeffrey Burton.
    Dissent and reform in the early Middle Ages.

    Reprint. Originally published: Berkeley: University
of California Press, 1965. (Publications of the Center
for Medieval and Renaissance Studies; 1)
    Includes index.
    1. Heresies and heretics—Middle Ages, 600–1500.
2. Christian sects, Medieval. I. Title. II. Series:
Publications of the Center for Medieval and Renaissance
Studies; 1.
    BT1319.R87   1982   273'.6   78-63178
    ISBN 0-404-16196-0   AACR2

MANUFACTURED
IN THE UNITED STATES OF AMERICA

FOR MY PARENTS
Lewis and Ieda Russell

Preface To The AMS Reprint Edition

Seventeen years after its publication, *Dissent and Reform's* argument that dualism in Western Eurpoe before the 1140s is indigenous, rather than imported from the East, has now been accepted by most scholars. On the other hand, I must make a retraction: the heretics I places at Liège in 1048–1054 in the reign of Leo IX are actually to be placed in the reign of Lucius II (1144–1145). Professors Bonenfant and Silvestre demonstrated that I was wrong on this point. In fact, the emended dating helps the argument on eastern influence, since the heretics in question appear to be under Bogomil influence and would thus be an anomaly in the eleventh century. I am grateful for the many responses to my work over the years and call particular attention to two fairly recent works: Malcolm Lambert, *Medieval Heresy* (London: Edward Arnold, 1977) and R. I. Moore, *The Origins of European Dissent* (London: Allen Lane, 1977). In 1981 I published (with Carl T. Berkhout) *Medieval Heresies: A Bibliography, 1960–1979* with the Pontifical Institute in Toronto.

Preface

There are many to whom I owe a debt of gratitude. I should like first to thank those who have read the manuscript of this book, either in whole or in part: Ernst Ekman, Robert Herschler, Donald Howard, and Norman Ravitch of the University of California, Riverside; Gerhart Ladner of the University of California, Los Angeles; and Walter Wakefield of the State University of New York, Potsdam. Their criticisms, and Mr. Wakefield's great knowledge of the sources, were immensely helpful. The students in my seminar at Riverside, particularly Edward F. Little, were also helpful. I am grateful, too, for a year in Europe provided by a Fulbright grant and for a year at the Widener Library made possible by the Society of Fellows of Harvard University. While in Belgium I enjoyed the extraordinarily generous help of Professor Léon-E. Halkin of the University of Liège, of Gérard Moreau, then his assistant, and of the students in his seminar. I am grateful to George P. Cuttino, Francis Benjamin, and the other members of my doctoral committee at Emory University for their supervision of the dissertation from which parts of this book are derived. I owe much, also, to three rigorous teachers: Lola F. White, Robert Brentano, and Henry F. May. Finally, I deeply appreciate the long-standing encouragement of my parents and the long-suffering patience of my wife.

The subject I have elected to deal with is a broad one, and I am certain that this work contains many errors of omission and commission. I am of course alone responsible for these.

In the matter of the spelling and the form of personal and place-names, I have generally used the common vernacular form, but I have used the Latin form when the vernacular is unclear, and the English form when it is firmly established by usage (as Cologne instead of Köln).

Contents

May those be angry with you who do not know with how much anguish truth is sought.
—

SAINT AUGUSTINE

1. Introduction

One winter's day in 1077, as Bishop Gérard of Cambrai arrived in the course of an inspectional tour at the little village of Lambres, about a mile from Douai in the county of Flanders, he was warned by certain zealous people that a notorious heretic was lurking in the neighborhood. In the nearby village of Scherem a man by the name of Ramihrd was professing unorthodox doctrines and had converted many good people of both sexes to his way of thinking. The bishop ordered him apprehended and brought before him at Lambres, so that he might personally investigate the matter. Gérard tarried long enough that gray January or February day to hear Ramihrd's story and then ordered him sent under guard to the episcopal seat at Cambrai, where his ideas might be examined at leisure upon the prelate's return to his cathedral.

When the bishop's tour was over and he was able to assemble a number of abbots and clergy at the episcopal palace, he undertook the examination of the heretic. Ramihrd, angry and wounded at the accusations leveled against him, professed the most loyal orthodoxy and must have satisfied the bishop that he was free from overt doctrinal error. In the course of his impassioned speech, however, he cast aspersions upon the morality of the local clergy. In his anger he may have carried his attack so far that it did border upon heresy, but the violence he met at the hands of his clerical enemies indicates that they were incensed less at the fallacy of his doctrines than by the truth of his accusations. Some of the bishop's assistants and others of the clergy interrupted his defense, seized him, and, over the ineffective and perhaps not very insistent protests of the bishop, dragged him from the palace and outside the town walls. There they forced him into a peasant's hut, barred the door and windows, and set the structure on fire. Ramihrd refused to make any recantations or even supplications and, stretching himself upon the earthen floor of the hut, awaited his death in prayer.

Ramihrd died nearly nine hundred years ago, but his execution is no less a judgment upon all man than if he had died yesterday. The torment suffered by human beings in the struggle between orthodoxy and heresy places both the dissenters and their opponents in the dock. Medieval Catholics were often inclined to liken the orthodox to the wheat of Matthew's parable, which will be gathered into the barn, and the heretics to the tares, which will be delivered to the flames.[1] In fact, though both the medieval Catholics and the dissenters claimed to be true Christians, the number of individuals on either side fulfilling Paul's conception of the Christian who has emptied himself out and become Christlike was probably, as in most ages, small.

In one sense the dissenters held a moral advantage over the orthodox. Some merely drifted into heresy, but others were deeply transformed in a real process of conversion. The spirit that stands at the edge of the abyss and makes the leap into darkness may be justified by the leap itself. By the mere fact of his dissent he is obliged to fulfill Paul Tillich's definition of faith as "participation in the subject of one's ultimate concern with one's whole being."[2] The faith that is the abandonment of self to God may be valid whatever its intellectual matrix, and it is possible that God is sometimes less concerned with the valid proposition than with the willing heart.

Enthusiasm for reform and intellectual independence were the chief motives of dissent in the early Middle Ages, though superstition was frequently as important. Social discontent was less often a factor. A chief reason for the existence of heresy lies in the nature of Christianity itself. Christianity differs from Judaism and many other religions in being credal as well as moral. It has always been concerned with right belief as well as with right conduct. The Christians' interest in abstract truth led them to try to define it in a system of orthodoxy, and since no definition of truth ever goes unchallenged, the inevitable companion of orthodoxy is dissent.

As orthodoxy generates dissent, so dissent generates repression. It was inevitable that medieval society should have treated dissenters unsympathetically. Revering tradition and suspicious of novelty, medieval Catholics believed that the heretics, cut off from the mystical body of Christ, had become limbs of Satan. Further, there was a large number of clergymen who, living corrupt lives, could not tolerate the prospect of reform and who treated dissent, quite correctly, as a threat to their personal positions. Sometimes the attack upon heresy sprang from love of God and sometimes from pride and greed, just as heresy itself sprang sometimes from love and sometimes from pride. Wheat grew in both fields, as did tares.

The term "heretic" is itself somewhat difficult to define in the early Middle Ages, as the precise denotations of scholasticism were still in the future. Medieval writers were often inclined to ascribe heresy to the devil. Modern writers have usually been more sophisticated in their bias, but they too have often—depending upon their points of view— seen medieval heresy as the epitome of all that was bad, or all that was good, in the Middle Ages.[3]

Though medieval men treated heresy, whatever it might be, with suspicion and scorn, they did not often use the term promiscuously, so what is called "heresy" in the sources usually really is dissent of one sort or another.[4] For the purposes of this study, dissent is taken to include not only heresy in the theologically strict sense but all explicit and many implicit deviations from the religious norms of medieval Catholicism. Since our concern is not with metaphysical definitions but with historical movements, the criteria used for distinguishing dissent must be the criteria of the times. And since our concern is with the Church in western Europe in the Middle Ages, the best criterion for orthodoxy at any given time is the position of the pope. These definitions at least satisfy the requirements that they be convenient and that they work.

Using these criteria, one can distinguish a variety of types of dissent in the early Middle Ages. There were *Reformists,* whose enthusiasm for the reform of the Church led them to extremes; *Eccentrics,* whose odd and peculiar doctrines took them far from orthodox traditions; *Catharists,* who defended doctrines that the Church had long before condemned. There were *Reactionaries,* who, like the nicolaitists, were overeager in their devotion to the past and refused to go along with the development of newer Christian doctrine and practice. The *Intel-*

lectuals, dissenters whose deviations were philosophical, took a variety of positions. Those who attacked the authority of the pope and leveled accusations of heresy against the apostolic see itself may be somewhat arbitrarily classified as *Reverse heretics.*

The conceptual boundaries of this study, therefore, include all varieties of religious dissent, nonconformity, and tension. The chronological limits are from about 700 to about 1150. Before the eighth century dissent was, in the tradition of the heresy of the early Church, theological and priestly. After the middle of the twelfth century the increasing influence of Eastern dualism under the name of Catharism changed the whole emphasis and style of medieval dissent. Between 700 and the mid-twelfth century, however, dissent was typically medieval in its moral and popular emphasis without yet being adulterated by currents from the East. In this period it was closely connected with the growing intensity and diversification of movements of moral and intellectual reform. With these movements and as part of them, dissent was one of the elements shaping medieval civilization.

2. *Heretical Enthusiasm*

Before the Twelfth Century

The story of medieval dissent is inseparable from that of the Great Reform Movement. This movement, the single most important element in the Christian early Middle Ages, emerged in the eighth century[1] with the mission of Saint Boniface and his associates and culminated in the work of the reform papacy in the eleventh century. A manifestation of the perennial need, and the perennial ability, of the Church to reform itself in the context of its tradition, the movement resembled tendencies of the contemporary Church in its emphasis on *renovation,* the effort to restore the Christian community to its original likeness to what Christ desired.

Centering in northwestern Europe[2] between the Seine and the Rhine, and in northern Italy, the reform movement was the chief dynamic force, throughout the period, not only of moral reform itself, but of intellectual ferment, of the political programs of the reform papacy, of the Crusades, of pogroms against the Jews, of the repression of dissenters, and of dissent itself. Dondaine's suggestion that it helped do away with heresy by removing the impurities to which the heretics objected is true only in a limited sense. The Great Reform Movement generated warmth, vitality, and enthusiasm which sometimes spilled over the dams of orthodoxy. It was a mother, not an undertaker, to dissent. This was an age of reform, and of this age the dissenters were enthusiastic members. Between the great revolutionary reformer and the great revolutionary heretic there is little difference. Robespierre, Lenin, Calvin, Hildebrand, Valdes, Tanchelm, Claudius of Turin—

enthusiasts all, puritans all, fanatics all, and all revolutionaries and reformers. Call men of this spirit orthodox or heretic as you please; the same fire dwelt within them all.

It has always been recognized that the Reform dissidents were spurred by the desire for perfection, and the various names by which they have been known indicate this fact. They were called evangelistic or *bibelgläubig* because of their attachment to the teaching of the Gospels, but this appellation is inexact. It is vague and gratuitously assumes that the teaching of the Gospels is what the dissenters supposed it to be. Further, though most of these dissenters were firmly attached to the authority of the Bible, the same is true of the orthodox. The term "apostolic" suffers, in addition to identical disabilities, from having been the name of certain specific sects like the Apostolici of Italy and so open to even greater misinterpretation. The name "neo-montanist" has often been used but is even less precise, for it implies a continuity between the ancient Montanism of the third century and the medieval dissidents. Even when direct affiliation is disavowed, the assumption that the motivation, the response, and the context were similar in ancient and medieval times is unacceptable. Tanchelm and Valdes were not avatars of Montanus and Tertullian. The term "pre-Waldensian" suffers from similar drawbacks. While the Waldensians, unlike the Montanists, were at least medieval and their motivation and principles were similar to those of the dissidents of earlier centuries, there was again no affiliation between them. In addition, the term has certain unjustified teleological implications, like the designation of the Waldensians themselves as "precursors of the Reformation." The protest of the Waldensians was meaningful for their own time: for Valdes, the Kingdom of God was at hand to be won or lost in the twelfth century, not realized in the person of a future Luther. In the same way, Claudius, Ramihrd, and Lambert sought the salvation of Christendom in their time, not in a Waldensian future. One might with some justice call these heretics "pneumatics" in view of their great devotion to the Holy Spirit. But perhaps the best designation, one that identifies their motivation and places it both ideologically and chronologically in the context of the Great Reform Movement whence it sprang, is "Reformist."

Unlike Catharism, a dualist heresy imported from the East, Reformism is understandable within the tradition of the Church and especially in the context of orthodox reform. The enthusiasm of the dissenters that propelled them beyond the bounds of orthodoxy was an unselfish zeal for the reform of the Church. Traditional Christianity has always harbored the germs of dualism and fanatical puritanism. The monastic rules of poverty, chastity, and obedience were always visible as standards. The attitude of some of the greatest orthodox saints toward sex, for example, was extreme. Throughout the eleventh and twelfth centuries the attacks of orthodox reformers upon sin were particularly intemperate, and this extremism encouraged heresy on the part of others. Saint Peter Damian wrote a *Liber Gomorrhianus* in which he compared papal Rome to the cities of the plain and called for a return to the morality of the primitive Church. Humbert of Silva Candida attacked simoniac clergy with such abandon that he did not hesitate to call them minions of Satan, and the whole litertaure of papal polemic against the Empire was marked by vituperation and violence. The willingness of the dissidents to attack the clergy was encouraged by the statements of the polemicists that ordinations made by heretics were invalid, or that people ought to be prevented from hearing masses said by sinful priests. All sacraments administered by heretical priests—even baptisms—were declared invalid. In such circumstances, the people's faith in their pastors could not have been strengthened.

The papacy and the bishops were willing to support such extremism. Gregory VII forbade priests guilty of fornication to say mass,[3] and similar prohibitions were common.[4] The ecumenical council of the First Lateran in 1139 attacked simony, the rendering of tithes to laymen, condemned the clergy for taking money for the sacraments, and forbade the people to attend the masses of married or concubinary priests. The Church was not, of course, taking the donatist position that sacraments administered by unworthy priests were invalid, but simply that such priests ought for disciplinary reasons not to be encouraged; but it is no wonder that some people were encouraged by this view to mount an attack upon the entire hierarchy. Dissidents cannot be blamed for finding fault with the opulence of the Church as a whole when Saint Bernard spoke so heatedly in condemnation of the wealth of Cluny: "The walls of the church are indeed resplendent, but her poor go needy. She clothes her stones with gold and leaves her children to go

7

naked. The eyes of the rich are flattered at the expense of the poor. The delicate find the wherewithal to gratify their taste, but the miserable find nothing to satisfy hunger." [5] No accusation lodged by Tanchelm or by Albero of Merke could have been more bitter.

Reform Dissidence begins with the mission of Saint Boniface and the reform movement. But like all chronological boundaries this is in part a convenience. Before Boniface's mission there were rumors of popular discontent with the Church. Gregory of Tours indicates that such unrest was common throughout sixth-century Gaul. [6] Precedents for Reform Dissidence can be found before 716, just as precedents for the reform movement can be found before that period, but it is with Boniface's mission that they begin to marshal widespread support. On the other hand, it is not easy to fix an end date for the history of the Reformists, who certainly continue after the end of our period in 1160. Valdes and Saint Francis at the end of the twelfth century are the archetypes of the Reform heretic and the Reform saint; the Waldensians, the Apostolics, the Lollards, the many other sects, bear the marks of Reform Dissidence, as of course do Luther and Zwingli. Fortunately this is not a problem that we are obliged to solve, for the story of early medieval dissidence as we have defined it comes to an end when, in the middle years of the twelfth century, Catharism was introduced and Reform Dissidence ceased to be the single dominating form of heresy.

Reformists from the eighth to the twelfth century shared certain common characteristics. First was their emphasis upon simplicity and purity and their desire to return to the virtuous life of the golden age of apostles and martyrs. With this went a belief that purity was a sign of authority. Authority derived from God, particularly from God the Holy Spirit, and the presence of the Holy Spirit was evidenced by the cleanliness of the temple in which He dwelt. Sectaries who led a pure life, therefore, much more clearly possessed authority than did the often corrupt hierarchy. The marks of such authority were poverty, simplicity, and purity. The authority of the spirit was thus raised over visible authority, and the right of the visible Church to feed Christ's sheep was denied.

Devotion to the Holy Spirit has often not occupied a central position among Catholics, perhaps for the very reason that the emphasis upon internal illumination which it involves is so dangerous to the Church.

With their emphasis upon the internal illumination of the Spirit, the Reformists were, ironically enough, moving away from the practice of the primitive Church, with its strong sense of community, and toward the Protestant ideal of the individual alone with his God. Both the medieval dissidents and later the Protestants frequently labored under the misconception that the earliest Church preferred individual to community worship. The only indication of this was the existence of the "prophets" of the earliest Christian communities, who went about preaching the good news at will, but even before the end of the first century these prophets had begun to disappear to be replaced by the more reliable, if less inspirational, institutional structure of bishops, priests, and deacons.

The individualism of the dissenters, however, together with the courage of their refusal to conform to the norms of society, led them in their simple way back in the direction of a true understanding of Pauline faith. As the Church had developed, it had confounded two concepts that originally had had different denotations, faith and belief. Whereas to Paul faith was essentially an action, an affirmation of the whole being, an existential throwing of oneself upon God with abandon, to the Church it gradually became an unqualified affirmation of certain intellectual propositions. Thus faith came to mean a degree of belief, of intellectual assent. Lack of sophistication is certainly not to be praised in itself, but the simple courage of the dissidents which enabled them to feel an "ultimate concern" put them close to a Pauline idea of faith which had been somewhat neglected.

While the old idea that the Catholic Church in the Middle Ages neglected the Bible has long been known to be false, it is true that the Reformists tended to be more devoted to Scriptures than did the orthodox. The reason for this is simple. Their rejection of the authority of the Church, their contempt for the laxity of the clergy and the pomp of prelacy, meant that they needed to seek authority somewhere else. It is true that the Holy Spirit within provided them with authority, but they were not completely antinomian. More concrete guidance was needed, and this they found close to hand. It was Scripture, after all, that provided them with the ideal of the apostolic Church which they set over against the imperfections of the Church they knew. So it was that they always appealed to the Bible. Neither Protestants nor Catholics have ever completely resolved the question of the true preeminence of Scripture or tradition. The naïve Reformists of the Middle Ages, like many naïve Protestants after them, believed simply that all authority came from the Bible. They did not trouble with the complexities of interpretation: this problem the Holy Spirit would resolve for them.

In particular terms, the Reformists attacked the immorality of the clergy, the hierarchy, and the authority of the Church; usually they also attacked the sacraments as unnecessary to salvation and as supposing the necessity of a mediating clergy between a man and his God. Sometimes their enthusiasm led them into an unhealthy belief in their own sanctity, even to the extent of assuming the name of saint and attributing special supernatural powers to themselves.

In fine, the Reformists were extremists, but they presented a creative challenge to the elements of moral sluggishness in the Church and thus performed a creative role in the dialectic of Church history.

The eighth century.

In the eighth century, the Great Reform Movement was still embryonic; correspondingly, Reform Dissidence had not yet developed to maturity. In many respects, the eccentricity and wildness of this kind of dissent still resembled the chaotic heresies of the days of Gregory of Tours. Eighth-century Reformists had yet to work out anything like a consistent program of reform.

Aldebert, an Eccentric, also exhibited some of the characteristics of a reformer.[7] Preaching apostolic simplicity, he passed himself off as a man of surpassing holiness; he scorned the clergy and impugned the authority of the pope. His followers among the people venerated him, owing to his championship of the apostolic life.

The age of Boniface produced other Reformists. In a letter[8] from Boniface to Bishop Daniel of Winchester, written between 742 and 746, the English missionary told his friend that his task in Germany had been made difficult by false priests and hypocrites teaching false doctrines. The doctrines were curious indeed. Some of the heretics abstained from foods "ordained by God for our use"; some partook of nothing but milk and honey. Thinking of the purported African Manichees in Thuringia, one might leap to the conclusion that here were more dualists with a distaste for procreation. This would be an error. In the first place, if the heretics consumed milk they were not likely to have been Catharists, as the dualists shunned milk as well as meat owing to its connection with the reproductive process. Further, the "milk and honey," if it does not make us think of the Land of Cockaigne, may remind us of John the Baptist, who ate locusts and wild honey in the wilderness. The German dissidents may simply have substituted milk for locusts, finding it less difficult to procure. This seems to be an instance of the exaggerated asceticism associated with Reform Dissidence.

A hint of Reform Dissidence appears in a couple of the rules in the Penitential of Theodore, current in the eighth century.[9] For example, if one prayed with a heretic as if he were a priest, a week's penance had to be done. If anyone ordered a mass for a dead heretic and preserved his relics "on account of his piety, and because he fasted much," penance was to be done and the spurious relics burned. It is clear from this that there were heretics abroad leading the faithful astray with feigned (or real) piety.

At the time of the Adoptionist controversy in Spain, then theologically more sophisticated than the still barbarous north, Migetius[10] made his appearance. The apostolic see had, in order to combat the Adoptionism of Archbishop Elipand of Toledo, put Archbishop Wilichar of Sens in charge of a program of reform in Spain, which was to accomplish the closer union of the eccentric Spanish Church with that of Rome. Wilichar delegated his authority to one Egila, whom he appointed bishop without a fixed see and sent into Spain to combat Elipand's influence. Egila decided to center his activities in Granada, where he found sentiment already warm for an assault upon Elipand, sentiment that Egila later was to find too enthusiastic for his taste. A party devoted to the papacy and opposed to the Adoptionists had been formed by Migetius, a native of the area, and it was with this Migetius that Egila became associated. But just as the extremism of the Nestorians encouraged the pendulum to swing to the opposite extremism of the Monophysites, so the extremism of the Adoptionists was matched, or more than matched, by the fanaticism of Migetius, and Egila by his association with the man gave the Spanish clergy a ready weapon with which to belabor Rome.

Rubbing his hands with pleasure, Elipand did not tarry in calling a council at Seville in 782 to condemn Migetius. Elipand may well have exaggerated the heresies of Migetius in order to make his point against Egila and Rome more firmly, and no reply from either Migetius or Egila exists to correct any exaggerations. Migetius was accused of teaching that there were three corporeal persons in the Trinity, the Father incarnate in David, the Son incarnate in Jesus, and the Holy Spirit incarnate in Paul. Migetius himself claimed to live a life completely disembarrassed of sin. He also stated that the *confiteor* was unnecessary in the mass, because a priest should be without sin and have no need for confession, and if he was not free from sin he should be prevented altogether from saying mass. The fatihful Christian was not to eat with infidels or even with sinners. Rigid asceticism and intolerance of failure were prescribed. Certain foods were prohibited and fasting was enjoined. And whereas Elipand maintained that the term "Catholic Church" applied to the entire Church, Migetius held that it referred to the Roman Church alone.

The origins of Migetius' opinions are unknown. Certainly there was a tradition of extremism in Spain which prepared the ground for him. The Priscillianists, condemned at the council of Braga in 563, had been characterized by an extreme asceticism. Migetius' name was also linked with Sabellianism and with "Cassianism" (Hefele-Leclercq suggest the connection lies in Cassian's attack upon predestination). Whatever his roots, Migetius, convinced of his own holiness and preaching an intolerant puritanism, typifies the Reformist. The fact that he upheld the authority of Rome indicates merely that he was invoking a distant and therefore less threatening authority against a nearby and dangerous one, much as the Frankish bishops of the time of Charles the Bald preferred the authority of the pope to that of the king. Rome was not pleased by support from this quarter, which embarrassed it in its efforts to win back the Spanish Church, and Pope Hadrian I upbraided Egila in no uncertain terms for having associated himself with the heretic.[11] Amann properly suggests[12] that the most extraordinary of Migetius' supposed errors, his doctrine of the Trinity, was an exaggeration on the part of Elipand. Migetius had probably said that the man Jesus was the Second Person of the Trinity and that Jesus was "a son of David," and of this the archbishop drew a gross caricature. The ultimate outcome of Migetius' case is unknown, though his influence seems to have continued in Spain into the ninth century.[13]

The ninth century.

The heretics condemned by Raban Maur in his commentary upon Joshua, if they were not Catharists—and it is not likely that they were —were probably Reformists. Their objection to the Book of Joshua, on the grounds that Joshua lacked humility, implies puritanical zeal. Clearer indications of Reform Dissidence come from the national German council held at Mainz[14] in 852, whose twentieth canon says, "Whoever shuns a priest who has been married and refuses to receive communion from his hands shall be anathema." Here is a clear example of a position being condemned for being ahead of the times. Gregory VII would, in the eleventh century, positively order the faithful to avoid masses said by married priests; in the eighth century, the Reform Movement had not yet progressed that far, and what was later to be considered a mark of obedience to the apostolic see was still deemed a sign of rebellion.

As Spain produced the most egregious example of Reform Dissidence in the eighth century, so Italy produced the outstanding example of the ninth. Claudius of Turin[15] was born in Spain and studied, if the hostile sources may be believed, under Felix of Urgel the Adoptionist. Whether or not he was a pupil of Felix, he was most definitely not an Adoptionist himself, nor did his ideas bear the slightest resemblance to either ancient Adoptionism or the Spanish variety. Indeed, Claudius specifically stated that Christ was to be considered the natural Son of God, not a son of God by adoption. His opponents no doubt intended to smear him by linking him with the Spanish heretics, or else they were at least culpable of making the facile assumption that any Spaniard with unusual ideas must by that fact stand condemned of being an Adoptionist. Neither was Claudius an Arian, as his accusers, eager for epithets, also claimed.

Claudius eventually left Spain and became master of a school in Frankish Aquitaine, where he met and gained the confidence of Louis the Pious. Some time after the death of Charlemagne in 814, but no later than 820, Louis appointed Claudius the bishop of Turin, which see he occupied until his death (between 830 and 839). Claudius defended Turin against Moslem raiders and ruled his see with ability and strictness. His strictness eventually became too severe, and opposition grew among his flock.

Claudius was a learned, though not particularly original, thinker, who wrote biblical commentaries, including works on the Epistles, the Gospel of Matthew, and the Books of the Kings. His works demonstrate a thorough knowledge of both the Old and New Testaments and a devotion to the thought of Saint Augustine, who was his chief intellectual guide. As bishop of Turin, his puritanical tendencies became increasingly pronounced, and he finally came to hold some very exaggerated views. Among these was a dislike for and disapproval of the use of images in Christian worship, and from this it has been suggested that Claudius was an Iconoclast. Iconoclast he was in a sense, but there is no evidence to connect him directly in any way with the Eastern Iconoclastic movement. If Claudius' Iconoclasm, which is by no means the salient point of his doctrine, is taken in context rather than placed in exaggerated relief, a different picture of the Spaniard emerges. Claudius, like other Reform Dissidents, was motivated first by a distaste for the imperfections of the Church and second by a devotion to the apostolic life, a devotion he had learned from his studies of the Gospels and of Paul. Iconoclasm appears in Claudius' doctrine for the same reason that it appears later in that of Peter of Bruys: images were believed to stand in the way of a true spiritual conception of God. If Iconoclasm stood out more prominently in Claudius' thought than in that of some of the later dissidents, it was not because of connection with the East. He had closer examples to follow: At Barcelona around 490, one Vigilantius attacked the use of images, as did Serenus of Marseille toward the end of the sixth century. He also had more recent examples: The council of Frankfurt in 794 and the synod of Paris in 825 had both condemned the Second Council of Nicea for what the Franks considered extreme iconoduly. Agobard, bishop of Lyon from 814 to 840 and an exact contemporary of Claudius, wrote a book against the superstitions of the iconodules[16] which was only a little less intense than Claudius' condemnations. "Whosoever," said Agobard, "adores a picture or a statue, whether carved or cast, does not worship God, nor does he worship angels or saints; he is an idolater." Rejection of images was not unpopular in lands ruled by the kings of the Franks. With Claudius, a mind already committed to extreme puritanism readily championed the puritanical cause of iconoclasm. If in this he was intemperate, it is not surprising—temperance does not appear to have been one of his ruling characteristics.

Claudius, like most enthusiasts, was convinced of the rectitude of his own position and does not seem to have realized that there were those who might consider it ill-advised. He accordingly sent, in all good faith, a commentary on Leviticus to Theodemir, the abbot of Psalmodi in the neighborhood of Nîmes and a friend from the days when Claudius was a schoolmaster in the Midi. Theodemir replied by warning his friend that his lack of caution was leading him into perilous waters. Claudius answered in turn by addressing an *Apologetic* to Theodemir. This defense of his own doctrines has unfortunately been lost in its original and has come down to us only in passages cited by his adversary Jonas of Orléans for the purpose of refutation. Jonas may therefore have exaggerated Claudius' errors, but the emotional tone of the Spaniard's reply to Theodemir is easily explicable in terms of his hurt feelings and injured pride at a supposed friend's readiness to condemn. Theodemir does not in fact seem to have been much of a friend, for, not content with warning Claudius, he circulated the reply that he had received from his erstwhile companion and thereby occasioned the summoning of a synod and Claudius' condemnation by no less a person than his former protector, the emperor Louis.

The defenders of orthodoxy now attacked the bishop. Dungal, an Irishman teaching in Pavia, in 827–828, wrote a reply to Claudius' defense of himself—the *Replies against the Perverse Opinions of Claudius of Turin.* This was followed by *On the Cult of Images,* dedicated to Charles the Bald and written after Claudius' death by Bishop Jonas of Orléans (*ca.* 821–843). It was a bombastic and intolerant little work, in which the good bishop buried his deceased colleague in derision. The butt of polemic, condemned by councils and kings, Claudius did not, so far as we know, ever reply to the bitter attacks launched upon him. Neither did he in any way recant, for Jonas tells us that he died in his errors and left his nefarious books behind him to cause more trouble.

It is fortunate from our point of view that much of Claudius' work was preserved. Ironically, it was Jonas and Dungal themselves who, by replying so fully to Claudius' *Apologetic* to Theodemir, preserved that document from oblivion. Impassioned and immoderate as their polemic may have been, there is no reason to suppose that they misrepresented Claudius to any great extent. Jonas in particular thought that the Spaniard's arguments were so preposterous that they would perish most quickly when exposed to mockery.

Claudius was heavily influenced by Saint Paul and the Fathers, particularly Augustine, and from them he had adopted that intolerance of the world, that rejection of things material, which characterizes Christian dualism. Claudius stated this puritanical dualism in exaggerated terms, betraying a distaste for things material which was almost disgust. Whether this amounted to a pathological fear of the "dirtiness" of the world, as was true of Marcion in the second century, for example, is uncertain. Poole saw Claudius as a precursor of Protestantism, a brave man standing up against the materialism of the Church of his day, but he was, perhaps, more the type of Reformist who, informed by internal illumination, can tolerate no compromise with the world and is in any age and country unhappy with the Church as a human institution.

Emphasizing faith and the importance of the spirit within, Claudius objected to corporeal concepts of religion and to the use of material objects in the worship of the Church. He considered that such corporeal notions derived from a Jewish sense of Scriptures and that true Christianity rejected any physical symbol of Christ. He ordered the destruction of the images in his diocese, much to the horror and rage of his people, and forbade any kind of adoration of the cross. Not hysterical about matter, he admitted the use of the water of baptism, the oil of chrism, and the bread and wine of the eucharist, but beyond these he could find nothing of spiritual value in things material. The cross was particularly distasteful to him, and, in a passage of the *Apologetic* where he allowed his anger to run away with him, he suggested that if Christians wished to venerate the cross they might just as well also venerate all virgin girls because Christ was nine months in the womb of a virgin and only six hours on the cross, or all old cloths because Christ was wrapped in swaddling clothes, or all asses because Christ had ridden an ass into Jerusalem. Jonas of Orléans did not delay in seizing upon this unfortunate attempt at irony to point out that it ignored the position that the Passion, and with it the cross, hold in the very center of the Christian religion. Denying the use of any material symbols, even lamps, in Christian ceremony, Claudius viewed images of the saints with particular disdain, and from this he passed to a denial of the communion of saints as a whole. No one can profit from the virtues of another, he said, and the whole cult of saints, including the celebration of their feasts, ought to be done away with. He dismissed pilgrimages as useless, though he granted that they might not do positive harm, and characterized the popular pilgrimage to Rome as folly. Here at his most extreme, Claudius denied the apostolic authority of the pope. As the synod of Paris in 825 had accused Pope Hadrian I of acting indiscreetly in the matter of Iconoclasm, so Claudius accused Paschal I of similar incompetence and held that the pope had no authority unless he led a truly apostolic life. Peter's primacy had ceased with his death; the measure of a man's apostolicity was the purity of his life, not his institutional position.

Claudius himself was a man of fervor, of apostolic warmth, of an extraordinary longing for that world of ideals that in this world we can see only through a glass darkly. But he was also impatient, intolerant of human failings. Yet he could not see his own failing; like most puritans, he permitted his love for the ideal to obscure his love for those who, like most human beings, share only imperfectly in the ideal. The story of Claudius is another installment in the scandal of Christendom: the hatred and schism provoked when the arrogant intolerance of orthodoxy meets the intolerant pride of heresy and Christian smites Christian for the love of Christ.

A century of silence.

The century from the death of Louis the Pious to the coronation of Otto the Great, though by no means as uncreative as used to be thought when it was characterized as an Age of Iron, was a century of troubles in western Europe, a time when empire and papacy both collapsed under the double assault of barbarians from without and political weakness from within. The Great Reform Movement, well under way when Charles and Louis ruled the Franks and Hadrian I ruled the papacy, lost its momentum and faltered as society changed step. The monastic reforms of Gorze, Hirsau, and Cluny, and the restoration of some degree of order by the Ottos, began to impart renewed vigor as the tenth century progressed, but it was not until the beginning of the eleventh century that the Great Reform Movement swept again into full strength. And it was not until then that significant instances of Reform Dissidence again appeared.

The eleventh century.

The opening years of the eleventh century produced a number of Reformists. The peasant of Champagne, Leutard, is discussed later as an Eccentric,[17] but many of his doctrines bear the marks of Reform Dissidence: his rejection of crucifixes and images and his belief that marriage was immoral betray the excesses of puritanism associated with this tradition.

Another indication of Reform Dissidence appears in a letter[18] written to Archbishop Heribert of Cologne (999–1021) by an immigrant citizen from Speier about the year 1000. The identity of the citizen is unknown. Only his initial, A, appears in the letter. He was probably a layman, or he would have referred to himself as *monachus* or *presbyter* rather than *civis*. Though he speaks of "the brothers," this reference is vague, and it is unlikely, though possible, that he included himself among their number. On the other hand, for a layman of the period he seems extraordinarily learned. His identity and walk of life must remain a mystery.

His purpose in writing to the bishop was to protest what he considered the abuses of the sacrament of penance. Many Benedictines, he claimed, though erudite and otherwise upright, had fallen into the lax habit of remitting sins in the confessional with less concern than they would have over spending three farthings out of their own purses. This laxity gave people false assurance and induced them to commit new sins with the confidence that they were as easily forgiven as the old. As was common with dissidents, A went from this simple statement to a condemnation of the whole system of penance. In the first place, he said, only God can forgive. The priest has not the power in himself, but forgives only so far as he is dispensing God's will. The priest has no right to any such formula as *Ego te absolvo*. Even Christ himself did not say, "I forgive you," but rather, "Your sins are forgiven you." For the priest to say "I forgive" is the height of pride, for he is imputing to himself sufficient holiness to judge the sins of others. Thus A did not admit the interpretation that the priest is speaking with the voice of God when he says "I forgive," and so fell into an error close to the donatist supposition that the efficacy of the sacrament depends upon the virtue of him who administers it. A made the mediating power of the clergy appear greater than the clergy would ever affirm, as if the power lay in them by their own virtue rather than as representatives of God. He did not go so far as to deny the power of absolution, but he insisted that it should be exercised only in the spirit of proper humility and, further, only after the proper careful investigation. The priest should be fully informed about the sin, and he should assign a fitting penance.

A considered the laxity surrounding the sacrament of penance an innovation. "The new absolutions should more properly be called public deceptions," he said. The key to his indignation lies in the change that was taking place at that time in the penitential practice of the Church. The early Christians had no system of penance, since it was considered that the Church had no authority to remit sins committed after baptism. A subsequent general relaxation of rigor in addition to a reaction against abuses of the system gradually led to the institution of a sacrament whereby such postbaptismal sins might be forgiven. Even then, the system was at first strict, for only one serious sin, followed by penance, was allowed until extreme unction was administered on the deathbed. Further, the penance done was a public one and usually of considerable severity, such as a pilgrimage, flogging, or severe fasting.

Relaxation of standards then took place on two fronts. On the one hand, the number of times one was admitted to the sacrament of penance was increased and finally became unlimited. On the other hand, public penance was gradually supplanted by a private system, the severity of the penances was reduced, and the system of indulgences developed. During the eighth through tenth centuries, partly through the efforts of the Irish, who championed private penance, these new practices came to predominate and gradually won the day. Frequent confessions were permitted, and the penitent, instead of being obliged to wait until he had performed his penance to receive absolution, was granted it in the confessional directly after his confession. In the eighth century, the clergy were admitted to penance for the first time. In the ninth and tenth centuries there was much debate on the form of penance, but by 950 the ideas of recurring confession and private penance had gained control of all northern Europe, and by 1000 they were universal.

Another change occurred at the same time. The verbal expression of absolution on the part of the priest in the early Church was in the form of a prayer or supplication. "No indicative form of absolution, as *'Ego te absolvo,'* is known to have come down from the early centuries." [19] A period of mixed forms, including a supplication and an indicative form concomitantly, may have intervened, and by the eleventh century, the indicative form had come to prevail.

Citizen A now appears as a defender of the old ways, a reactionary who has not kept up with the development of the Church and who views novelties as noxious. One can understand his position. The medieval Church was innocent of a doctrine of development and was wont to look upon innovations as heretical. In this instance, when the innovations seemed to promote laxity, they may well have seemed harmful. Whether the new system actually did encourage spiritual laxity is doubtful. By providing for frequent confessions, it permitted the pastors to give more effective spiritual guidance to their congregations. By refusing to make too rigorous demands, it saved people from despair on the one hand or defensive indifference on the other. It reduced the danger that people would lead immoral and desperate lives, relying upon a last deathbed penance to save them from hell. But none of this was apparent to A, who, the typical puritan, had only contempt for human frailties. He did not hesitate to draw the ultimate conclusion from his attack upon the new practices. They represented a hidden heresy: *latentem istam haeresim.*

A declared the now commonly accepted practice of the Church heresy, but in effect it was A himself who was a heretic. In his pride, he set himself up in opposition to the Church; he deemed himself holier than others. His attack upon the sacrament of penance, which would have been acceptable in the fifth century, was no longer so in the eleventh. The Church had moved ahead and left A behind. It was he who wandered into heresy, not those he accused. The radical reactionary nature of Reform Dissidence is patent in A. Puritan and zealot, he looked back to what he imagined was the purity of the early Church for his ideals. He ignored the principle of *reformatio in melius,* of progress in the historical development of the Church.

His arrogance is most evident in the peroration of his letter. Writing to his archbishop, Citizen A concludes, "May Almighty God grant you the faculty of understanding and executing his will." Pride and lack of charity are sometimes the keys that open the door of heresy.

The *Corrector* of Bishop Burchard of Worms, written around 1008–1012, offers another glimpse of enthusiasm in the early eleventh century. Chapter 78 asks, "Hast thou fasted on the Lord's day on account of abstinence and religion? Thou shalt do penance for twenty days on bread and water." [20] Here were men who in their zeal could not refrain from works of supererogation, who in their puritanical asceticism could not resist fasting on the day of the Lord's Resurrection, when to do so was irreverent if not blasphemous. Chapter 89 [21] asks, "Hast thou despised the Mass or the prayer or the offering of a married presbyter, so, I say, that thou wouldst not confess thy sins to him or receive from him the body and blood of our Lord for the reason that he seemed to thee to be a sinner? If thou hast, thou shalt do penance for thirty days on bread and water." This is again the enthusiasm of the zealot, though here, curiously, the reform papacy itself was to take precisely the same position in the latter part of the century. Here the zealot's enthusiasm was dissidence only so far as it was ahead of its time.

Reform Dissidence at Liège and Arras in 1025.

Though the first inroads of heresy in the diocese of Liège at the beginning of the century were apparently made from the direction of France, the next are supposed to have come from the direction of Italy. Sometime before January, 1025, a group of heretics arrived at Liège,[22] led by one Gondolfo from Italy, where instances of purported Catharism had already occurred.[23] These heretics dwelt awhile within the borders of the diocese and made a number of converts by preaching among the simple folk. Finally the dissenters sent some of their original group to Arras to make converts there. Bishop Gérard of Cambrai-Arras, arriving at this town shortly after the Epiphany of 1025, was apprised of the existence of the heretics in town, and ordered them arrested.

When they were brought before him he questioned them and, finding them in fact heretical, sent them to prison for three days to ponder their iniquities. They were given ample encouragement to muse in the form of torture provided by order of the good bishop.

Brought back into the prelate's presence in the synod of January 10 or January 17, they admitted that they were followers of the heresiarch Gondolfo. They were asked to confess their doctrines and began to do so, but they were interrupted by Gérard, who was evidently convinced that he understood their doctrine much better than they, for he discoursed upon it for what must have been several hours. Indeed, the worst torture that the heretics had to undergo was the prolonged harangue of the bishop himself. When the bishop paused, the writer of the account, doubtless some sycophant at the episcopal chancery, informs us that those present, marveling at the piety and truth of Gérard's words, could not refrain from praising him and weeping with joy. The heretics, however, refrained from such manifestations of pleasure, much to their sorrow, for the bishop recommenced his sermon. Finally, either convinced by the skill of his monologue, or wearied to death, they professed repentance. An abjuration was drawn up and read in Latin, but the heretics, being simple folk, were unable to understand that tongue, and it was necessary to have it read in the vernacular. The heretics then accepted it by making their marks in the form of a simple cross. They were then allowed to go their way with a warning, and everyone rejoiced.

The harsher treatment beginning to be meted out to heretics is here evident. Réginard of Liège freed the colleagues of these heretics without much ado, but at Arras they had to undergo torture and were let loose only after abjuration. Had they persisted in their error, it is possible that they might have met the same fate as their brothers burned at Orléans in 1022 and at Goslar in 1051.

We may assume that the doctrines held by the heretics at Arras were the same as those of their colleagues in Liège. To begin with, the heretics of Arras were sent there from Liège by the heretics of that town. Then, the letter of Gérard to Réginard gives a brief sketch of the heretical doctrines of Arras, implying that Gérard expected Réginard to find the same errors in his own diocese. When one examines closely the letter and the account of the synod to determine what exactly were the beliefs of these heretics, one notices a curious division. In his discourse, Bishop Gérard accuses them of abhorring baptism, at least the baptism of infants, rejecting the eucharist, rejecting penance, abominating marriage, and venerating no saints except the apostles and martyrs. Prayer for the dead they believed useless, according to the bishop, and a church was no more holy than the stones and mortar of which it was made. The heretics were said to reject holy orders and to maintain that the ministry was secretly imposed upon men of their sect. They were held to be indifferent to Christian burial, because priests took money to perform it; they were said to despise psalmodizing and the offices, to contemn the hierarchy, to shun the cross and images. In place of the Church order, they were accused of setting up their own order, a simple one based on the Gospels and the teaching of the apostles, and regulated by the *justitia* that the dissenters possessed.

With the exception of the last accusation, all the above suggest possible Catharism. Certain of the doctrines, such as rejection of the hierarchy and dislike of the offices of the Church, might come from a broader and a vaguer impetus to revolt, but rejection of marriage and of infant baptism, despising of the cross, rejection of the eucharist, dispensing with prayers for the dead, all bespeak the complex and ramified dogma usually associated with Catharism. Their rejection of marriage, of baptism, and of the eucharist is also testified to by the letter of Gérard to Réginard. Were this information the sum total of what we possess, we might imagine that the heretics had fallen under Catharist influence of a sort.

The heretics themselves, when allowed to speak, which was admittedly not often, gave a somewhat different account of their tenets. According to their own testimony, they had been thoroughly taught in the precepts of the Gospels and of the apostles by their master Gondolfo, and they would accept no other authority than this, to which they adhered tenaciously. The doctrine they derived from Scriptures prescribed that they must renounce the world, restrain the flesh from lust, prepare food by their own hands, seek to do ill to/on one, and manifest charity to the others of their sect. It need hardly be said that such standards may very readily be drawn from the New Testament. Thus far, their doctrines could be deemed heretical by no one. They went on, however, to admit that they rejected the baptism of children, but for the following reasons. First, because the child did not understand what was happening and so could not profit by it; second, because the minister performing the rite was often a man of reprobate life; third, because whatever sins were renounced at the font were resumed later in life. Anyway, there was no need of baptism when the life of justice according to the New Testament was followed. Out of their own mouths, then, these heretics were condemned of heresy, but of a heresy in which not the slightest trace of dualism can be found.

At any rate, at the end of their arduous day of questioning, the heretics had assented to an abjuration that affirmed the orthodox doctrine on marriage, the holiness of churches, penance, the eucharist, and baptism, but that omitted the other points on which the followers of Gondolfo were accused of heresy.

There were thus three testimonies. The first was that of the bishop, which accused the heretics of doctrines apparently dualist in nature. The second was that of the heretics themselves, in which they admitted to doctrines that were heretical but contain no trace of dualism. The third was that of the abjuration, in which the accused joined with the faithful in condemning a number of unorthodox doctrines. Of these, only one, the rejection of baptism, was admitted to by the heretics in the testimony we possess. On the other hand, not all the points Gérard raised against the accused were included in this final abjuration.

It is possible that the discrepancy can be explained by the nature of the document. If the account of the synod is really more a polemic, as Professor Sproemberg believes, than a simple and straightforward résumé of events, the polemicist may have embroidered upon fact at his will. He may have refrained from reporting the heretics' own admission of dualist doctrines in order to avoid repetition. His obvious desire to build up the character of Bishop Gérard would have led him to reproduce or embellish the rounded periods of his hero in exposing the iniquities of dualism, rather than to report the heretics' stuttering confessions. Yet the extraordinary length of the document refutes such an assumption. In the face of so many pages, so many apostrophes, so many labyrinthine phrases and extended discourses, it is impossible to imagine that the composer of the account was in the slightest interested in brevity. On the other hand, he may have made up the entire dualist part of the affair out of whole cloth. If the document is a polemic at all, it is a polemic against the dualists, and it is surely more likely that the author inserted matters pertaining to dualism than that he subtracted them.

This explanation, however, also seems unlikely, and on two counts. First, the author's incessant and compulsive desire to magnify Gérard probably means that he was a sycophantic contemporary of the bishop. He would, therefore, hardly have circulated abroad a fraudulent and impossible account of the synod, which all those who had been present would recognize as such and which would therefore make the bishop ridiculous and bring discredit upon the author. The fact of the account's contemporaneousness with the synod it describes is also witnessed by the letter that accompanies it. It was written in Gérard's lifetime and was sent to another bishop introduced by a personal letter from Gérard. The polemic could neither be very falsified nor very mistaken. The same letter provides the second reason why such an explanation is unlikely, for it too mentions the rejection of marriage, baptism, and the eucharist.

Since it is impossible to believe that the account of the synod is in any major way false, other explanations of the discrepancies among the three testimonies must be sought. It is possible that Bishop Gérard was himself in error as to the doctrines held by the heretics. Certain words today, such as "liberal" or "radical," when applied to a given individual cause people to attribute to that individual a complex of beliefs he may or may not actually hold. In the same way, Gérard may have attributed to all heretics the complex of beliefs he had learned to associate with one kind of heresy, the Manichaean, which was well known to literate Churchmen of the day. It is possible that Gérard lectured the unfortunate heretics of Arras on Manichaeism in the same manner that in years not long past people lectured trade unionists on Communism. That the accused are not reported to have denied the accusations may mean simply that they were intimidated by imprisonment, torture, and the hostility of the assembly, or that the author of the report thought it useless to reproduce denials he took to be manifestly false. That they assented to the abjuration may be owing in part to a willingness to repudiate doctrines most of which they did not hold anyway. It is, then, not only likely that the heretics of Arras were not, as has always been thought, Catharists, but that they showed no trace of any kind of dualism at all.

It must be remembered, however, that the accused were questioned once by the bishop when they were first arrested and brought before him, and that he had received reports of their doctrines from others before ordering them arrested. Moreover, they were tortured and interrogated in prison, so that it must not be supposed that the bishop spoke in the synod without having previously inquired into the beliefs of the accused. It is therefore barely possible that the heretics deliberately and cleverly hid their dualism from the synod, perhaps knowing what fate had befallen their brothers at Orléans in 1022. The fact that Gondolfo originated in Italy has always seemed good reason for supposing his followers to be Catharists, once the theory of the transportation of dualist doctrines from the Balkans to Italy and then into northern Europe has been accepted.

But these heretics were simple folk, unable to understand Latin, doubtless intimidated by the assembly of ecclesiastical dignitaries in whose power they found themselves, terrified by three days in jail and by torture, overwhelmed and friendless. It is unlikely that they would have had the wit or the presence of mind to disguise any dualist doctrine. It is unlikely even that they would have been aware of the distinction between dualist and nondualist doctrine. They argued their case for what they believed to be the truth with ingenuousness. Convinced of the righteousness of their cause, they stated their doctrines frankly and attempted to justify them with reference to the Gospels and to the apostles. Believing that they were guilty of no error, they would not have understood why it was necessary to hide some of their beliefs from the assembly. One can imagine them, dazed by the harsh treatment they had received, bewildered by the lengthy discourses upon doctrines of which they had never heard, frightened and bullied, only too happy to affix their marks to a formula with which they could find little fault anyway so that they would be allowed to go home. One can imagine their puzzled comments to one another as they left the rejoicing assembly. They doubtless thought they had fallen into the hands of a group of madmen.

The dissidents of 1025, then, were Reformists rather than dualists. In most respects they were entirely orthodox, basing their beliefs upon the

Gospels and upon the admonitions of the apostles. They desired, in accordance with evangelical teaching, to leave the world, to restrain the flesh from lust, to do ill to no one, to prepare food by the labor of their hands. In all this one can find nothing heretical; indeed, quite the contrary. Their tenet that charity was to be manifested to their brothers in the sect is perhaps not so comprehensive a virtue as possible, and it demonstrates moreover that they viewed themselves as somehow apart from the rest of Christianity. In this they were probably correct, for they appear to have led lives more blameless than usual at the time. Only in their rejection of baptism were they obviously heretical, and here the reason given was the children's lack of comprehension of the words said over them and the fact that sins renounced at baptism are always repeated. More significantly, it was rejected because of the impurity of the priests who performed the sacrament. This is evidently the old donatist error, but it would be absurd to suppose that these heretics were learned in donatist lore. Rather, the error springs from virtuous men's natural horror of impure and sinful men controlling the access of others to the Deity. This position is one that frequently appears among the doctrines of reform heretics. Not only the baptism of children, however, was to be rejected. Indeed, no baptism was necessary for those who possessed *justitia,* and it is clear that these sectaries conceived of themselves as possessing it. *Justitia* consisted, in their definition, of following the precepts of justice which they deduced from Scriptures.

Relying upon personal righteousness, then, the heretics rejected the necessity of baptism. It is therefore conceivable that some of the other accusations made against them by Gérard were true. They may, for example, have rejected the eucharist and the sacrament of penance. If baptism was not necessary in their minds, neither would be the other sacraments. The heretics of 1025 seem to have been spiritual individualists, enthusiasts in the Reformist tradition.

Orléans.[24]

An active group of Reformists existed at Orléans, beginning in about the year 1015.[25] The chroniclers of the time linked their activities to those of heretics in Aquitaine, Auvergne, and Toulouse, and the label "Manichaean" was attached to them, as it was to so many of the dissident groups. Though they were few in number, their influence reached beyond Orléans itself. Their heresy had been introduced from the south, one source imputing the responsibility to an Italian woman who brought the pestilence into Gaul, another laying the blame at the feet of a certain "simple" of Périgueux who was supposed to have carried the plague northward to Orléans. Once there, the heresy spread along the Loire and infected neighboring towns. As far away as Thérouanne, Bishop Baldwin (*ca.* 989–1030) trembled lest the error should make its way northward into his diocese. Shortly after the events at Orléans, Baldwin wrote to warn his people to ward off the noxious influences of the south, and he feared that the family connections of the count of Boulogne with the count of Auvergne might make the road of heresy northward an easy one. With the help of Fulk, a deacon of Paris and the brother of Count Eustace of Boulogne, he undertook to fortify his people against the menace.

The terror felt by the orthodox was enhanced by the knowledge that the sect had been permitted to flourish for some years before it was ultimately detected, the detection itself making a peculiar story. It had come to pass in this way. There was a knight named Aréfast, a vassal of Duke Richard of Normandy and a man in favor at the court of King Robert. This Aréfast, a man of action and political experience, was also a man of exceptional piety, and he ended his life as a monk at the house of Saint Pierre in Chartres. In Aréfast's household dwelt one Héribert, a priest, probably chaplain to the good knight and scholasticus of the school of the same Saint Pierre in Chartres. In the year 1022, probably during the summer, Aréfast sent Héribert on an errand to Orléans, where he fell in with two other priests, Etienne and Lisois (Lisoius). Lisois was a revered official of the collegiate church of Sainte Croix in Orléans, and Etienne, now associated with Lisois, had been the confessor of Queen Constance herself. Etienne and Héribert had perhaps met each other at court and the more readily became friends now; in any event, Héribert found them at the center of a little group of devoted followers whom they had attracted, not so much owing to their learning and influence as to the outstandingly holy and simple life that they both lived and preached. In this little group were at least ten canons from the church of Sainte Croix, a number of nuns and other women, a man named Foucher, who seems to have been one of the principals in the group, and a number of the "better clergy" and "more noble laity." [26] The piety of Lisois and Etienne could attract the simple, while their education and refinement won over the literate and the well-to-do. The dissidents of Orléans were no unlettered group of peasants like the followers of Eudo or Aldebert. We do not know the exact size of the group, but the sources tell us that they were "many," and this may well be believed, especially in the light of the fact that their influence was feared in neighboring towns and as far away as Thérouanne. In any event, Héribert became a humble disciple and ardent follower of Etienne and his companions.

All in the Orléans group was not simple piety, and if any of the reports of the later trial can be believed, the doctrines taught by Etienne were, though learned, far from orthodox, and Héribert, like the other sectaries, seems to have received them all with equal enthusiasm. Héribert returned to Aréfast's castle dazzled by the "resplendent wisdom" [27] of what he had learned and ingenuously reported what had transpired in the hope of converting his master. The upright Aréfast, sensing heresy in what his chaplain said, argued and remonstrated with him, with what success we do not know, for Héribert now passes out of the picture. Greatly disturbed by what he had heard, Aréfast wrote to King Robert for advice, and the monarch replied that it might be a good idea for Aréfast to accompany his chaplain to Orléans and investigate this matter for himself. The king, therefore, was forewarned, so that swift action might be taken when the truth of the matter was revealed. Aréfast did not immediately make up his mind to act upon the king's suggestion. He journeyed to Chartres to ask the advice of sage old Bishop Fulbert, only to find that he was away at Rome. Encountering a clerk of Orléans named Ebrard, Aréfast confided in him, and Ebrard suggested that Aréfast go to Orléans as an *agent provocateur*. This advice was similar to that Robert had given, and Aréfast determined to make the journey. Evidently feeling that Héribert was not yet to be trusted, he left him at home and went by himself.

The pious Aréfast, arming himself with quantities of prayer, fortifying himself by continually making the sign of the cross, and bearing in mind Ebrard's suggestion that daily communion during his journey would protect him from the snares of the heretics, traveled to Orléans completely at his own expense and with the sole purpose of serving

God by unmasking the heretics. Such vigor in the defense of orthodoxy was new in the history of dissent. It inaugurated a long and baleful history of intolerance and was the immediate prelude to the first official execution of heretics in the history of the church.

Arriving at Orléans, Aréfast inquired as to the whereabouts of Etienne and Lisois and, having discovered them, identified himself as a friend, very likely offering Héribert's name as a reference and pretending that their recently acquired companion had converted him. Having been received in a friendly manner, Aréfast asked for a closer instruction in their doctrines, which they did not hesitate to give him. Meanwhile, at least according to Aréfast's testimony, the sectaries performed a strange liturgy. Initiating the knight into their group, they told him that as a member of the sect he was to rise above the weeds and thorns to become a great, stately fruit tree fertile in good fruit. He was to put off the thorns and weeds of this world, so that he might remove from this evil age into their fellowship. There he would receive wisdom, he would learn how to protect the word of God from the thorns that threatened to injure it, and, with senseless doctrines put aside, would receive with pure heart the doctrines that the Holy Spirit had revealed to the sectaries. Aréfast, doubtless muttering in his heart supplications to all the saints, contrived to convey to the dissidents the impression that he supported them wholeheartedly. They now hastened to reveal to him all the secrets of their teaching. He listened attentively, asking for full explanations whenever something seemed unclear, taking care that nothing escaped him so that when the time came no detail would be missing from his report.

Autumn was now at an end and the Christmas season approaching. King Robert, who had foreknowledge of the plot and who no doubt wished to enhance his own reputation for piety and to offer the Church the present of a few heads to weigh in the balance against the censure his irregular marital activities had brought down upon him, arrived at Orléans. Accompanying him was his third queen, Constance, whose confessor Etienne had been, and who, vacationing from the countless intrigues with which she was troubling the kingdom, had chosen to spend the feast of Christmas with her husband. Assembling at Orléans at the behest of the king were a number of prelates, including, besides Bishop Odolric (1021–1035) of Orléans himself, the archbishop of Sens,

Leotheric (*ca.* 999–1032), and the bishop of Beauvais, Guarin (1022–1030).

When the notable company was all lodged in town, Aréfast arranged for himself and his supposed coreligionists to be captured by the king's men. Bound and put in chains, he was led before Robert who recognized him and set him free. This was Aréfast's moment of triumph. He reported the success of his mission and accused his erstwhile associates.

Early in the morning on Christmas Day, after mass, Etienne, Lisois, and the other dissenters were brought before the King and his bishops for questioning. The interrogation lasted until about three in the afternoon, while the city mob, eager for an entertainment suitable to the anniversary of the Incarnation, gathered outside the episcopal palace. Confronted with their accuser, Etienne and Lisois admitted to holding doctrines that the Church considered heretical and as steadfastly refused to recant. Ten canons of Sainte Croix stood by their leaders throughout, but most of the sectaries seem to have deserted rapidly, and at the last moment one clerk and a nun who had hitherto stood firm yielded. All in all there were thirteen or fourteen who remained loyal to their beliefs to the end. The clerks among them were defrocked and excommunicated. Meanwhile, the mob had succeeded in making a way to the doors of the chamber in which the synod was being held. Forcing the doors open, they attempted to lay hands upon the condemned in order to bring them to a quick and, if possible, painful end. At this point Queen Constance showed the mettle and determination that frightened her subjects and helped bring her husband to an early grave. Forcing the populace back, she barred the doors—taking advantage of the confusion, however, to revenge herself upon Etienne who, once her confessor, had now embarrassed her by being a heretic: she put out his eye with her stick. When order was once more restored, the king elected to do the job the mob had been unable to complete. He sentenced the culprits to death at the stake. This first bloody repression of dissidence was scheduled, appropriately enough, for the Feast of the Holy Innocents following, on December 28, 1022. It was much to the taste of the chroniclers, who felt that it was a salutary measure that would by its example discourage the heretics of Gaul and Belgium; Radulf Glaber went so far as to say that the Catholic faith shone everywhere the more strongly owing to the witness to piety borne by the Christian king and his spouse and their aide, the stout knight Aréfast.

On the appointed day, Etienne and Lisois with their companions were led outside the walls to the place of execution. It was still the fourth day of Christmas, and the crowd was doubtless on hand in holiday mood. The heretics imagined that the Holy Spirit would protect them from the flames, and went to the stake laughing. When the torch was set to the faggots, pain banished illusion, and they began to scream and cry out that they had been deceived by the devil. Taking this as a sign of repentance, some of the more charitable bystanders ran up in an attempt to rescue them, but the flames burned too hot and high, the rescuers were unable to free them from their bonds, and the sentence of death was executed as planned. Not content with punishing the living, King Robert also wreaked vengeance upon the dead. Théodat, a former chantor of Sainte Croix who had been a member of the sect but was now dead these three years, was disinterred and his bones were expelled from consecrated ground.

Unfortunately the sources differ so radically in what they say as to the doctrines held by these dissenters that it is difficult to determine exactly what they believed. As already shown, there is no good reason for supposing them to have been Catharists. According to Radulf Glaber, whose value as a primary source is questionable, they said that they had long been heretics and expected everyone eventually to join their sect, that the Trinity is a delirium; heaven and earth are eternal; good works are supererogatory; and lust will not be punished. Another source, however, the *Miracula Sancti Benedictini,* contradicts Glaber's statement in regard to the Trinity; certainly the idea of the eternity of the world is strangely out of place, and in view of the purported holiness of the heretics the doctrines on good works and the punishment of lust seem unlikely. Glaber's evidence may therefore be discounted.

A few among the dubious doctrines reported by other sources were that the heretics scorned the cross; they rejected the authority of the bishop, penance, marriage, and the foods that God has created (probably meat). So they may actually have believed,[28] but one of the most reliable sources contradicts this testimony on at least one important point: Baldwin of Thérouanne said that the heretics believed that one might eat meat at any time without fear of sin. An accusation of magical activity comes from at least two sources, one of which is fairly reliable. Adhémar of Chabannes sets forth their activities as follows. While pretending to be Christians, he said, they practiced the most abominable things in secret. They had sex orgies. They spat upon the image of Christ. They adored the devil, who appeared to them first in the form of a Negro and then in the form of an Angel of Light. The devil appeared to them daily and presented them with great heaps of money. They carried the ashes of dead boys around with them, which they made into cakes, utilizing this unusual dish as communion wafers. One might be inclined to dismiss all this as the product of Adhémar's diseased imagination, were not similar excesses also reported by the *Deeds of the Synod of Orléans*. The *Deeds* tell us of secret conventicles, of the same sexual orgies, but go Adhémar one better. In this version, the children who result from the promiscuity of the secret meetings are sacrificed to the devil and burned, and it is their ashes that the sectaries carry around with them. When, after the judgment, the sectaries were burned at the stake, the nefarious powder of ashes was consigned to the flames along with them. The ashes serve as a viaticum. Paul of Saint Père of Chartres, the author of the *Deeds,* also describes the conventicles in closer detail than Adhémar. Assembling in private homes, he said, the sectaries gathered in the darkness carrying lighted lamps in their hands. They recited a litany of demons, upon which Satan appeared among them in the form of a great beast. Then all the lights were extinguished, and every man seized the woman nearest him, whether it were his mother, his sister, or a nun, and had his will of her. And this they called the essence of holiness.

In addition, the strange liturgy that was revealed to Aréfast had a pagan flavor. A third source, Baldwin of Thérouanne's letter, contains a cryptic phrase that may possibly be further evidence of pagan practices: the heretics were said to have taught that *cultum divorum exsibilandum,* which probably means that "the cult of the saints is to be sneered at," but might conceivably mean that "the worship of the pagan gods is to be whispered secretly." [29]

The existence of magical practices at Orléans is thus possible—but it is unlikely. The rites ascribed to these heretics are far too diabolic to be written off as mere survivals of ancient magical practices, while most other evidence indicates that the witch cult did not appear until the later Middle Ages. The evidence for magic at Orléans must therefore be regarded as very dubious.

Fortunately, the *Deeds of the Synod* offers a rare indication of what the heretics themselves said. Etienne and Lisois, accused of heresy before the tribunal, admitted believing certain doctrines, and it is these admissions, and these alone, which can be admitted as incontrovertible evidence of their real teaching. They said that Christ was not born of the Virgin, that he did not suffer for men, that he was not really placed in the sepulchre, and that he did not really rise from the dead. At first sight this looks like Catharist dualism. But when asked *why* they believed those things, they replied that they could not believe in the virgin birth because it was contrary to reason. Immediately we recall that both the leaders of the sect and a good number of their followers were learned men, intellectuals as it were, and we seem to be in the presence of intellectual skepticism. This is confirmed by their statements in regard to the resurrection. When asked why they denied it, they replied simply that they had not been there, they had not seen it, and unless with their own eyes they had seen a thing contrary to reason and experience, they were unable to believe it. They further held that baptism was incapable of cleansing from sin and that the eucharist was useless, as were prayers to martyrs, confessors, and saints. Finally, and this is what identifies them as enthusiasts, they answered arguments adduced against them from Scripture with a contemptuous dismissal: "*You* believe the fabrications of mortal men written upon the skins of animals (that is, parchment); *we,* on the other hand, believe what has been written in our hearts by the Holy Spirit. We believe nothing that God has not so revealed to us." (Aréfast had testified that they had told him that after his initiation he would be purified of his sins and would receive the Holy Spirit, who would reveal to him the true meaning of Scripture. With them he would now see angelic visions, and—this is very likely an embroidery of Aréfast's—he would be able to move from place to place with the angels whenever he liked.)

Their piety and holiness of conversation also mark them as apostolically oriented. Héribert was first attracted to Etienne and Lisois on account of their preeminent virtues; the people of Orléans thought highly of both Lisois and Etienne on account of their wisdom, holiness, and generosity with alms. And Théodat, whose body was exhumed by the zealous after the trial, had been revered by the people as a saint in the three years following his death.

There is much in the story of the heretics of Orléans that remains obscure and will always remain so. But the most likely portrait that we can draw depicts them as neither Catharists nor witch cultists, but as men both intellectual and enthusiastic, combining intellectual skepticism with a faith in the guidance of the Spirit within, dissidents with a unique cast of mind that set them off from other heretics of the period, but that leaves them still in the broad tradition of Reform Dissidence.[30]

The Midi.

In 1018 or shortly thereafter heresy began to appear again in the south of France. During the reign of Bishop Gérard (1012-ca. 1023) of Limoges, a group of dissidents designated by Adhémar of Chabannes as Manichaeans was active proselytizing among the population. They denied the validity of baptism and rejected the use of images and crosses. Feigning piety "as if they were monks," they fasted and simulated a life of chastity while secretly practicing every kind of lecherous excess.[31] Adhémar told of other heretics, whom he also described as Manichaeans but whose doctrines he unfortunately failed to specify, who made their appearance around 1026–1028 in Charroux, not far from Limoges, on the march of Poitou and Aquitaine.[32] Owing to the proximity of time and place, it seems likely that the sectaries of Charroux and Limoges had some connection. Finally, Adhémar noted that around 1022 "Manichaeans" were found at Toulouse; they held secret conventicles and exerted themselves to convert whatever men and women they might lure into their erroneous ways.[33]

Since the accusations of sexual immorality may probably be discounted as stemming from the bias of the chronicler, all these heretics, if we may judge from the Limoges group, were Reformists.

Monteforte (ca. 1028).[34]

Archbishop Ariberto of Milan (1018–1045) was on a tour of visitation of his suffragan dioceses when he heard that heresy had broken out in Monteforte and ordered one of the sectaries to be brought to him for interrogation. One was found, a man named Girardo, who seemed positively eager to inform the prelate as to his beliefs, perhaps in the hope of converting him. Having subjected him to a thorough inquisition, Ariberto learned that the entire population of the castle, including the countess and the nobles, subscribed to these beliefs. The heretics even claimed to have brothers dispersed throughout the world. The archbishop needed to hear no more; he immediately dispatched troops to make wholesale arrests. His orders were quickly obeyed, and the inhabitants of Monteforte were brought to Milan so that the learned clergy of that town could convince them of the error of their ways. Yet even as the Milanese clergy argued with them and preached to them, the brave and confident enthusiasts did not hesitate to preach their own doctrines to the peasants and other simple people who had come to town to be in on the excitement. Seeing that words were having little effect, the clergy lost patience and elected to employ sterner measures. They ordered a cross and a stake raised and told the heretics to choose between them. Some found their courage unequal to the ordeal and gathered around the cross, but much to the surprise and annoyance of the archbishop, more chose the stake. Faggots were gathered and torches brought, and the second official execution of heretics in the western Church was effected.

Owing to a relatively full account of the archbishop's examination of Giardo, the beliefs of these dissenters can be clearly described. With his usual unfailing inaccuracy Radulf Glaber informs us that the town of Monteforte worshiped idols and made sacrifices "in the manner of the Jews." The precise account offered by the Milanese chronicler Landolfo is fortunately able to correct this nonsense by presenting a complete picture of the Reformists in Italy in the early eleventh century. Their teaching was centered on the belief that the Holy Spirit dwelt within them and led them into the ways of truth and righteousness. Girardo, who was clever enough to know that he was in danger, was never quite frank during the interrogation until forced by the archbishop's probing questions to reveal himself more fully, at which times he never flinched from telling the truth. Thus, when he was first asked about penance, he said that "we believe that we are bound and loosed by those who have the power of binding and loosing"; but it later became evident that Girardo did not believe that the Catholic hierarchy had such powers. When asked whether the group believed that a priest or a prelate could remit their sins, Girardo answered that they recognized no priests or prelates. "We have a pontiff, but not the one at Rome, another one who daily visits our brothers wherever in the world they may be dispersed." Girardo meant, not an earthly prelate other than the pope, but the Holy Spirit himself.

Their lives were lived in accordance with the indwelling of the Spirit. They refrained from eating meat. They praised virginity and, like Saint Paul, deplored marriage. For those who could not resist marriage, toleration was prescribed, in the manner of Saint Paul, though the rigor of the enthusiasts went the apostle one better—Married men were to treat their wives like mothers or sisters and to refrain from all carnal intercourse with them. When the archbishop scornfully asked in defense of the ancient institution of sex how Girardo proposed that the human race perpetuate itself without recourse to those things he found distasteful, Girardo replied that when human beings had rid themselves of corruption, they would produce their children without sexual intercourse in the manner of the bees.

They fortified their spirituality by continual prayer and fasting. The "elders" (*maiores*—it is uncertain whether this is an official title indicating a special function or merely a term of respect) kept up a chain of prayers that never ceased, replacing one another in their orisons day and night. They also held the peculiar doctrine that, to gain salvation, they must end their lives in torment. A violent death was deemed so desirable that if one of the sectaries was dying a natural death he would call upon his fellows to dispatch him. The rationale seems to have been an *imitatio Christi,* a desire to suffer as the Lord had suffered, with an eye to the blessing accruing to one who suffers for Christ's sake. Also, in obedience to the demands of charity, and with apostolic fervor, they held all their goods in common. They assiduously read the Scriptures, both the Old and the New Testaments, and even were familiar with the canons of the Church.

When asked about the Trinity, Girardo was somewhat evasive. He affirmed that they believed in the Father, the Son, and the Holy Spirit. But Ariberto could not so easily be put off and ordered Girardo to explain exactly what he meant by these terms. Girardo replied that the Father was he who is eternal, who created all things, and in whom all things subsist (*consistunt*). Except for a possible hint at pantheism, this seemed all right. But by "the Son" he meant the human soul loved by God, and by "the Holy Spirit" he meant "the understanding of the divine wisdom, by which all things are properly regulated." This seemed to imply a kind of Sabellianism lightly disguised by an allegorical interpretation of the Trinity. The Holy Spirit that dwelt within them they would then consider the divine wisdom of God in which they participated. Their doctrine, that the Son was a human soul beloved of God, Borst and others have taken to mean that to them Jesus was the son of God not in that he was part of God himself, but rather in that he was only a beloved human soul. They seemed to have meant that *any* human soul beloved by God might be considered "the son of God," and that Jesus, therefore, was only one of a number of just men who could claim that title.

Ariberto did not fail to note the difficulties for Christology in Girardo's doctrine of the Trinity and asked him point-blank what he would say of Jesus. Again Girardo's reply was evasive: "Jesus is a soul sensually born of the Virgin Mary, that is to say, of Holy Scripture." The meaning of this folderol is not patent, but it seems to imply, again, that Jesus was merely a man, and that he was born of the Holy Spirit and the Virgin Mary only in the allegorical sense of being a child of divine wisdom (the Holy Spirit) and Holy Scripture (the Virgin).

There is at least one happy note in the story of these unfortunate enthusiasts. Those who had the courage of their convictions were able to fulfill in their demise one of their tenets: not to end one's life without torment.

Gerhard of Czanád (*ca.* 1045).

Saint Gerhard, bishop of Czanád in Hungary, reported the presence of heretics in his diocese shortly before his death.[35] These Reform Dissidents, sometimes mistaken for Catharists, rejected the Church, the clergy, and prayers for the death; they denied the resurrection of the body.

Châlons, Liège, Reims, and Goslar (1046–1054).

In the first volume of his *Corpus documentorum inquisitionis*, Paul Fredericq published a letter found in Anselm's *Gesta* and written by Wazo of Liège (1043–1048) to his colleague Roger II of Châlons-sur-Marne in reply to the latter's questions about how to deal with the heretics in his diocese.[36]

According to Anselm's report the heretics were peasants, as were the followers of Leutard, in the diocese of Châlons during the reign of Roger I, and the heretics arrested at Arras in 1025. Whether or not they were native to Châlons is not certain, as Anselm noted only that Roger said that in "a certain part of his diocese there were certain rustics," not specifying their origins. Anselm himself refers to them, curiously, in almost the same terms that Egbert used in the title of his poem *De Malis Francigenis,* calling their heresy the "madness coming from France." In any event, they were probably local, as there was a tradition of peasant heresy at Châlons, and it is probable that such rustics would not have wandered far from home. It is very likely that they came from the neighborhood of Montwimers, for it was from that village of the diocese of Châlons that Catharists arrived in Liège around 1048–1054.

According to Anselm's report of Roger II's letter, the heretics met in furtive conventicles and held obscene rites. That they met furtively is probable in view of the unsympathetic attitude of the authorities toward their activities, but the accusation of obscenity is stock-in-trade for orthodox writers on heresy. That they preached that Mani was the Holy Ghost is the fantasy of either Roger or Anselm. One of them felt impelled to engage in some of that pedantry so common in orthodox writers familiar with the works of Saint Augustine. The heretics were also accused of detesting marriage, of abstaining from meat, of refraining from killing animals, and of using the imposition of hands among themselves to confer the Holy Spirit. In his reply to Roger, Wazo terms the heretics Manichaeans, noting that their error had been refuted in antiquity by the Fathers. His designation of their heresy as Arian is unnoteworthy, since medieval writers often mistakenly called dualists Arians.[37] In fact they were Reform Dissidents of the ordinary variety.

The importance of the letter of Wazo and of Roger's request for advice in the history of heresy at Liège is twofold. First, the letter of Wazo demonstrates that the attitude of that bishop was one of extreme leniency toward religious dissent, and since this opinion was highly praised by Anselm in his commentary of Wazo's letter,[38] we may take it, with Réginard's attitude toward the heretics of his time, as indicative of a possible tradition of leniency at Liège. The advice that Wazo gave Roger was this: You know what to do with heretics. Excommunicate them and make it clear to your flock that they are to be shunned, lest others be soiled in touching the pitch. But as for harsher measures, they are not justified.

In condemning harsh practice toward heretics, Wazo relied upon the parable of the tares.[39] It is not correct, however, to take the parable, at least in the way Wazo used it, as a text of religious liberty, as Bainton does.[40] The tares were to be left among the wheat only till the time of harvest, and only because, in an attempt to pluck them out beforehand, much of the wheat would go as well. It was for the sake of the innocent that it was unwise to pursue religious persecution. Moreover, Wazo insisted that the pious hope should be entertained that the heretics might eventually be brought to see the light. Sometimes, he noted, the greatest persecutors of the truth have become in aftertimes its greatest defenders. Had Saul been destroyed, there would never have been a Paul. Though not a plea for religious liberty, Wazo's letter presented a sensible and convincing case for religious toleration, and it is a pity that it was not more widely heeded. Whether the bishop of Châlons was induced to stay his hand or not is unknown.

The second reason for including these texts in a history of heresy in the Low Countries is one of which Fredericq was ignorant. Heretics of the same variety as these are known to have existed at Liège only a year or two after the writing of this letter. It is quite possible then, that they existed there during the reign of Wazo himself, for the presence of heterodoxy seems to have been frequent at Liège from the time of Notger. The possibility is enhanced by the presence of Roger's letter. Why, indeed, would the bishop of Châlons write to another bishop, one living at some distance, in another kingdom, suffragan of a different archbishop, to ask him his opinion on heresy if that bishop had not had some experience in the matter at hand? There is, unfortunately, no means to resolve the question. It seems quite likely, from all the facts, that Wazo did have to do with heretics in his diocese, but this must remain merely a supposition. As Wazo was also highly thought of as an intellectual, and we know that Henry III asked his advice at least twice, once in the affair of Wiger of Ravenna and once in the affair of Sutri, it is possible, although no other bishop is known to have addressed a plea for advice to Wazo, that Roger II wrote him as an intelligent and learned man whose judgment could be trusted.[41] Whatever the reason, if Wazo did not have to deal with heretics himself, his successor was not spared the difficulty.

Bishop Théoduin (1048–1075) found himself in much closer contact with the heretics of Châlons than did his predecessor Wazo. Wazo had only had to answer a letter of inquiry from the bishop of Châlons, but in the course of the next year or two the heretics from the village of Montwimers journeyed northward and began preaching at Liège.[42] Théoduin mistook them for followers of the eucharistic heretic Berengar of Tours, but it is quite evident they had nothing to do with him. They were, like the heretics of whom Bishop Roger II had complained to his northern colleague, enthusiasts of the Reform variety, denying the efficacy of Catholic sacraments and the authority of the Catholic clergy. They held that Catholic bishops had no power to confer grace by the imposition of hands, the eucharist was of no use for salvation, the baptism of children was likewise of no avail, and a Catholic church, was no more holy a place than the house of an ordinary citizen. The Liégeois heretics seem to have boasted an organization of their own in opposition to the Catholic hierarchy. They were divided into *auditores* and *credentes,* and they had "faithful, priests, and prelates, just like" the Catholics. They entertained Christological heresies as well as Reform doctrines, betraying the usual distaste for matter: the body of Christ was not a real body at all, but a shadow or "form" of a body.

During his tour of northern Europe in 1049, at the same time that Reformists were troubling Roger II, Wazo, and Théoduin, Leo IX or his aides held a council at Reims.[43] Of the bishops of northwestern Europe, Adalbero of Metz, Thierry of Verdun, and Guy of Reims were present. Simony and nicolaitism were dealt with in this council, but another "heresy" was also mentioned in terms that exclude the possibility that simony or nicolaitism were meant. This heresy must have been Reform Dissidence. The council excommunicated the "new heretics" who had emerged all over Gaul,[44] and the heresies "pullulating in these parts."[45] There seems to have been, then, widespread activity of Reform heresy throughout Gaul, especially in the north, and so in the diocese of Liège.

Twenty-nine years after Robert the Pious had first put religious dissidents to death, another saintly ruler passed the Christmas season in striking down enemies of the Church. The old Henry III, together with a number of bishops, including Archbishop Liutpold of Mainz (1051–1059) and Bishop Azelin of Hildesheim (1044–1054), came to Goslar as the winter season was approaching and there sat in judgment upon a group of heretics who had come into the town.[46] There can be no doubt that these were the same kind of Reformists who were causing trouble in France and the Low Countries.[47] They had been discovered by Duke Godfrey II the Bearded, of Upper Lorraine, and brought to Goslar before the king, a token of Godfrey's eagerness to please his suzerain after his long years of rebellion. The duke probably considered that the gift of a few heretics on Christmas Day would be the most thoughtful present possible for the emperor.[48]

The connection of these heretics with those of France also appears in their doctrines. For the most part typical Reformists, they also professed an unwillingness to kill animals; and this was one of the more striking teachings of the heretics of Châlons a few years earlier. When Duke Godfrey brought them in, the king and bishops assembled and examined them at some length. They were finally condemned when one of the bishops, more zealous in his prosecution of the case than mindful of the dignity of his rank, presented them with a live chicken and ordered them to wring its neck. They refused to kill the bird, and were deemed beyond hope of redemption. Ignoring the arguments and threats of the assembly, they refused to recant and were hanged upon a gibbet.

Though one of the chroniclers, as is usual, could not refrain from calling them Manichaeans, there is little that we know about their doctrine except that they were vegetarians and interpreted the commandment "Thou shalt not kill" in an exaggerated fashion. The Liégeois chronicler Anselm, in commenting upon the Roger-Wazo correspondence, wrote angrily about the judgment of Goslar—an indication that Christian charity toward the heretics was not everywhere lacking.

Ramihrd (1077).

Another atrocity occurred in the eleventh century, this time at Cambrai, where the reformer Ramihrd was put to death by an angry mob.[49] Ramihrd had attracted many followers by virtue of an alliance of his apostolic teaching with the social unrest that prevailed in the region of Cambrai in his time. One of the first communal insurrections in the Low Countries took place at Cambrai in 1077, the year that Ramihrd was arrested, and among the supporters of the insurrection were the probably poorly paid weavers. It was from among the weavers that much of Ramihrd's support came, according to the chronicler, and it was of course against the established classes, among them the beneficed clergy and particularly the politically powerful bishop, that the insurrection was directed. Both the popular support of Ramihrd's program and his savage murder can be explained in part by the social antagonisms that were abroad. The enthusiasm of his followers, who thought of him as a martyr, is proved not only by the fact that they went to the hut in which he was burned and gathered up his ashes as relics, but by the even more significant fact that his doctrines persisted for many years among the people of the area, presumably including the weavers, and in many of the small towns and villages around Cambrai.

Though his specific doctrines are not known, it is certain that he preached a reform puritanism, attacking the abuses of the Church. He affirmed that he was an orthodox Catholic in every way, but it was his refusal to seal this affirmation by receiving the eucharist that led him to his doom, and the reason he gave was that he could not in conscience take communion from the hands of a clergyman tainted by simony or avarice of any kind. Ramihrd may, as did so many, have crossed the line that separates reform from enthusiastic heresy, but we cannot be sure of this from the evidence we have. He may simply have been an especially devout and holy defender of the Reform Movement. Certainly Gregory VII (Hildebrand) was shocked and horrified to hear of the burning, in the provinces, of a man who was professing the same sort of apostolic zeal that characterized the pope. Indeed, Ramihrd was burned for refusing to take the sacrament from a sinful priest when Gregory himself had ordered the faithful—for disciplinary purposes—to shun masses said by such priests. Little could have separated the enthusiastic Ramihrd from the fiery pope whose puritanism his acquaintances satirized by calling him "Saint Satan."

Nor was Cambrai a city loyal to the pope in the incipient struggle between Gregory and the Emperor Henry IV. Ramihrd's was the sort of cause to engage the fiery Hildebrand's attention, and engage it it did. Having heard of the atrocity, he wrote an angry letter to Geoffroi of Boulogne, bishop of Paris (1061–1095), demanding that the bishop investigate the events at Cambrai. If he found the reports of Ramihrd's assassination true, Geoffroi was to order the immediate excommunication of the perpetrators of the outrage and to report back to Gregory himself, who would take further action. The final chapter of this, like so many medieval stories, is missing, so that we do not know whether Geoffroi was willing or able to follow the orders given him; but there is no doubt that the pope's indignation was genuine.

Ramihrd was burned, then, by the local clergy for teaching doctrines sympathetic with those taught by the pope himself. Substituting for burning the more subtle pressures of the twentieth century, we find that this is not a situation with which Catholics of the present day are unfamiliar. It raises the question of who were the real heretics. We have said that the only viable criterion for orthodoxy in the Middle Ages was the doctrine of Rome. The Reform policies of Gregory VII must be considered the policies proper to the Church. Yet these policies were by all standards radical, and they were only quantitatively, not qualitatively, different from those of the Reformists. To the conservatives of Cambrai, whose lax and unenlightened way of life was threatened by reforms, and whose conception of the Church as an unchanging, comfortable kind of shelter was outraged, Ramihrd was a troublemaker; to some he was nothing less than heresiarch. Who then was the heretic? As we shall see in chapter 5, it is possible to fall into heresy by an excess of phlegm as well as by an excess of the sanguine humor. The Church had passed by the clergy of Cambrai in its journey of reform and development. Whether or not Geoffroi ever carried out his investigation and excommunicated the culprits, they had been left behind by the progress of the Church in its journey of development. Moreover, as the murder they committed indicates, while the Reformists erred through excess of charity, the clergy of Cambrai erred through want of it.

The Patarini.

The Patarini of Milan have been the subject of a great many studies, particularly in recent years. I do not presume to offer even a brief summary of the whole complicated question, which is to an unusual degree bound up with social and economic considerations.[50] I wish only to indicate the ways in which the Patarini stood in the tradition of Reformist heresy.

It is shown later that the Patarini were not Catharists and had nothing to do with Catharism. Père Dondaine recognized this, maintaining that Catharism did not appear in Italy until the middle of the twelfth century.[51] Insofar as the movement was religious, it was in the Reformist tradition, a fact that was recognized by some imperialist contemporaries, who blamed the policies of Gregory VII and the Reform Movement for encouraging Reformist excesses like those at Milan.[52] Nor was the blame, if blame it was, ill-placed. No Reform dissidents received so much protection from high sources as did the Milanese heretics, whom the pope protected and supported for both political and religious reasons. Indeed, because of Gregory's support they were never officially condemned as heretics, though their enemies did not hesitate to call them so, and since our criterion for medieval orthodoxy is Rome, we include them in our study simply because their motivation and doctrines so closely resemble those of the other Reformists.

Led by Erlembaldo, a layman, they attacked the political authority of the archbishop over Milan: episcopal administration was, they felt, economically harmful to the town. Archbishop, nobles, workers, pope, and emperor changed alliances with kaleidoscopic rapidity, but, persisting through all these changes, the chief aim of the Patarini was the political and economic liberation of the Milanese workers from the inhibiting control of prelate and nobles. In addition to this political goal, they formulated religious goals upon the basis of apostolic purity. Many Milanese priests, like their colleagues throughout Europe, were corrupt simoniacs or nicolaitists, and the attack upon the authority of the archbishop opened the door to an attack upon the clergy as a whole. From criticizing the clergy for their laxity, the Patarini went on to question the authority of the clergy and the hierarchy as a whole; from refusal to accept the sacraments at the hands of unworthy priests they went on to question the efficacy of the sacraments in general. The chronicler Landolfo attempted to link them with the heretics of Monteforte,[53] though this has generally and correctly been regarded by historians as an attempt on Landolfo's part to blacken the name of the Patarini by associating them with a group already condemned as heretical. Landolfo was at least more accurate than some modern historians who persist in linking them, or at least their intellectual contingent, with the Manichaeans or the gnostics.[54] Morghen was correct when he placed them in the same tradition as the northern enthusiasts. The Patarini were Reformists.

Guibert of Nogent (ca. 1065–1070).

As the attacks by Rome upon married and simoniac clergy mounted,[56] there were bound to be excesses, and some of those whom the Reform Movement encouraged were not of as blameless a life or as apostolic inclinations as Ramihrd or Girardo. Guibert of Nogent describes in his *Autobiography* the conduct of a cousin who must have been of the less admirable variety:

There was at that time a fresh attack being made by the Apostolic See upon married priests, followed by an outburst of rage against them by the people who were zealous for the purity of the clergy, angrily demanding that they should either be deprived of their benefices or should cease to perform their priestly duties. Thereupon a certain nephew of my father, a man conspicuous for his power and sagacity, but so bestial in his debauchery that he had no respect for any woman's conjugal ties, now violently inveighed against the clergy because of this canon, as if exceptional purity of heart drove him to horror of such practices. A layman himself, he refused to be bound by a layman's laws, their very laxity making his abuse of them more shameful. The marriage net could not hold him; he never allowed himself to be caught in its noose. Being everywhere in the worst odor through such conduct, but protected by the rank which his worldly power gave him, he was never prevented by the reproach of his own unchastity from thundering persistently against the holy orders.[56]

In some ways human nature is wont to change very little. Guibert's cousin would find many ready table companions today. Most of us have seen such a corpulent gentleman, highball in one hand, the other hand tapping the table with a large class ring. He is outraged by the business practices of some of the large labor unions and indignant at government wastage; but he has neglected to declare all his income to the internal revenue people and has not shrunk from employing a little graft to get a municipal contract for his firm. He is a strange kind of reformer, just as Guibert's cousin was a strange partner of Hildebrand and Ramihrd in the struggle for clerical purity.

Perversions of the Reform spirit.

The enthusiastic mentality of the Reformists did not, unfortunately, generate a uniformly charitable spirit. It is undeniable that the golden moon of reform had a dark side explored alike by the orthodox Reformers and the heretical Reformists. The puritanical reform spirit often errs by perceiving the mote in another's eye more readily than the beam in its own. This was true with Guibert of Nogent's cousin. Regrettably, intolerance was not limited to the grumblings of an old man at the dinner table.

The spirit of Reform, awakening the religious fervor that had burned low in the preceding centuries, began to flame up in people's hearts in the course of the eleventh century, and with increasing religious awareness new forms of devotion appeared. Besides concern for the moral renovation of the Church, an increased devotion to the Virgin and to the saints was apparent. Pilgrimages increased in both popularity and length. Soon the gates of popular piety opened to intemperance. Sometimes intemperance caused those excesses of charity mingled with pride that created Reform Dissidence; but sometimes the results were more violent. The Crusades, a popular movement growing out of the pilgrimages and receiving approval and support from both lay and religious leaders, was in essence such an excess. The Crusades were particularly popular in northwestern Europe, where the Reform spirit was strongest. Since the Crusades were wholeheartedly supported by the papacy until the Fourth Crusade, at which time Innocent III began to entertain well-founded doubts, they cannot be characterized as heretical. Though the concept of a holy war could scarcely be deduced from the teachings of Christ, there was no lack of precedent for spreading the Gospel by the sword: Charlemagne's war against the Saxons was the most notable previous example, and the sanctioning of force against King Harold II and Stigand by Alexander II and against Henry IV by Gregory VII were more recent precedents. The Crusades were not heretical, but they represented a channeling of Reform energies into warlike passions that at first had some semblance of nobility but quickly degenerated into lust and greed.

Another excess of the Reform spirit was the persecution of heretics, which was another passion of the people often encouraged by the authorities. Ironically enough, it was often Reform dissidents against whom this anger was turned. Robert II and Henry III were both men noted for their piety; they considered the execution of heretics a pious practice pleasing to God and the Church.

The most shocking perversion of religious zeal in the eleventh and twelfth centuries was the persecution of the Jews. The attitude of Christians toward unconverted Jews was never unusually friendly, and there are instances of strong anti-Jewish sentiment among the Fathers. These were relatively uncommon, however, and much less in evidence than was the great veneration for the people of the Old Testament. In the early Middle Ages in particular, Jews and Christians usually lived together in western Europe in mutual tolerance and even some amity. They cooperated in business, sometimes formed personal friendships, and even on rare occasions converted to each other's religion. Though the Visigothic rulers passed restrictive laws against the Jews, Louis the Pious was so favorably inclined toward them that he provoked resistance from some Christian leaders, notably Agobard Archbishop of Lyon (814–840) and his successors Amulo (841–852) and Rémy (919–926). Agobard was provoked at least as much by a personal enmity for the king as by dislike of the Jews, and there was no general attack upon the Jews at that time.[57]

Religious opposition between Jew and Christian was natural, and bitterness against the religious beliefs of the other was expressed in the writings of each. There was before the eleventh century little visceral reaction against the Jews as a people; it was only with this century that the widespread persecutions of the Jews began. The ground had been prepared. The Jews had always chosen to live apart from the Christian community in order to preserve their own identity, nor did they cease to believe that they were a specially chosen people. This aloofness brought resentment. Further, and most important, the Jews had made enemies by their skill in trade, and under Louis the Pious they were already disliked for their economic power and consequent political advantages. The Middle Ages were, after all, like all cultures before our own, a closed society, in which the Jews were the most visible outsiders.

On the Christian side, justification for anti-Jewish sentiment was sought in the tradition that all Jews were cursed for the part their people had played in the crucifixion. With economic resentment, the rising influence of the Great Reform Movement was a decisive factor. Christians, informed by new zeal against infidelity as well as immorality, concluded that it would be pleasing to God to remove these infidels from the face of Christian Europe. Precedents had been set as far back as Charlemagne's reign for the use of force in religious conversion, and the crusading spirit turned against Jews almost as readily as against Moslems. In 1012, Emperor Saint Henry II was at Mainz, where he took action not only against some heretics who were active there but also against the Jews, ordering their expulsion from the city. Though the Jewish community at Mainz was not permanently broken by this order, it survived only to meet harsher treatment later in the century.[58] Jews were killed at Rome in 1021 [59] and at Orléans in 1031.[60]

When the Crusades began, the gates were opened for savage attacks upon the Jews, attacks that centered in that northwestern area of Europe where the Crusades were the most popular and where the Great Reform Movement was always at its strongest. The First Crusade was proclaimed in 1095, and the following year witnessed attacks upon the Jewish communities along the Rhine.[61] Undisciplined contingents of peasants gathered in France, Lorraine, and Flanders, and, motivated by the desire for adventure and plunder and even by a degree of religious zeal, began their rowdy march in the direction of Constantinople. Lacking the guidance of responsible nobles or clergy (although at least one count and three priests were involved, it would be too great a compliment to pay the parish priests of the day to imagine that they were too intelligent to participate in the massacres), the peasants were unrestrained from plundering the countryside as they went. Christian and Jew alike were prey to their lust and greed, but, with the Jews, the Crusaders mixed religion with sadism, the result being agony for several thousand unfortunate Jews whom they encountered on their way to rescue the Holy Sepulchre. Rouen, Prague, and Regensburg were the scenes of wholesale slaughter of Jews, but it was the Jewish communities of the Rhine and neighboring areas which suffered most. One Count Emmerich led an attack on the Jews of Speier, Worms, and Mainz; other bands attacked Cologne, Metz, and Trier. Offering the Jews a quick choice between conversion or death, the rabble did not delay in dispatching those who elected the latter, and the desperate Jews, especially women and girls, not infrequently took their own lives to escape a crueler death at the hands of the Christians. The course of these holy pilgrims' progress has fully been described by James Parkes and others, and it is useless as well as distasteful to repeat the story here. No one will doubt that religious enthusiasm here showed itself in its worst light.

The attitude of the authorities toward the massacres is of interest in uncovering traces of the dividing line made in the Middle Ages between what was tolerated in the way of perverted enthusiasm and what was not. It must first be observed that none of the disciplined armies led by the feudal seigneurs placed at the head of the crusading movement was involved in the atrocities, although it has been suggested that Godfrey of Bouillon was tempted by the thought and was persuaded to change his mind only by a large bribe offered by the Jewry of Cologne. The bishops usually acquitted themselves as well as they could, though they proved unable to curb the savagery of the mobs. Johann I (1090–1104) of Speier sheltered the Jews in his palace and punished a number of his citizens—who had joined the crusading mob and had succeeded in murdering eleven Jews before they could be stopped—by ordering their hands cut off. At Worms, both Bishop Adalbert (1070–1107) and the communal authority of the burghers tried to protect the Jews, but their efforts were unsuccessful and the mob succeeded not only in doing to death the Jews who had taken refuge in the homes of leading citizens but also in forcing those who cowered in the episcopal palace to take their own lives in despair of succor. At Mainz, Archbishop Ruthard (1088–1109) undertook to protect the Jews and gave them refuge in his palace, though he proved himself an unworthy occupant of the see of Saint Boniface when, as the rioting grew violent, he prepared to flee and was persuaded by the Jews to remain in the city only through the means of a not inconsiderable bribe. Even after receiving the bribe, the cowardly prelate was unable to restrain himself from flight once the crowd had gained entrance through the city gates. Taking refuge across the river in Rüdesheim, now the Old Orchard Beach of the Rhine, he attempted to rescue some of the Jews by bringing them across in boats; but the mob detected the attempt and followed the archbishop's men. Faced again with the frenzied mob, the archbishop's conscience once again proved unequal to his terror, and he turned the Jews out into the countryside, where they were hunted down by the Crusaders. The count, meanwhile, had showed more courage and ordered his soldiers to protect the Jews who had fled to him for refuge, but the crowd overpowered his men and killed these refugees as efficiently as the others. At Cologne, Archbishop Hermann (1089–1099) attempted to save the Jews by sending them out of the city into the neighboring villages, but the mob discovered their hiding places and slaughtered those who had fled to the country as well as those who had elected to take shelter in the homes of Christian acquaintances. The archbishop of Trier, Engelbert (1079–1101), though less brave than some of his colleagues, was more effective in his defense of the Jews in that he persuaded them to allow discretion to be the better part of valor. Engelbert, seeing the mob approaching with murderous intent, gave a sermon in defense of the Jews, which nearly occasioned his own death. He fled before the angry mob and hid himself in a secret chamber of the cathedral, while the Jews took refuge in his palace. Communicating with them secretly, he admitted that he was incapable of defending them and warned them that their only hope was to convert; with one exception they agreed and were spared. In Prague and Regensburg, the bishops and city authorities attempted unsuccessfully to protect the Jews, but there the Crusaders, less cruel than their brethren to the west, administered only forcible baptism rather than the sword.

The higher authorities were no less willing than the local authorities to exert whatever power they could command to restrain the mobs. The emperor Henry IV promised protection to the Jews when the atrocities first began; unfortunately he was in the south and unable to prevent the outbreaks of 1096, but afterward he took the Jews of Germany under his special care. Though Urban II was silent in 1096, perhaps because he wished to take no action that would cast a shadow upon his beloved Crusades, Alexander II had condemned the anti-Semitic violence in

Spain in 1063, and Urban's successors in later crusades also worked for the defense of the Jews. The atrocities were committed by the mob, often abetted by the worst elements of the urban population, and sometimes, unfortunately, by the local clergy. But the authorities, both lay and religious, condemned the outrages in no uncertain terms. It remained for writers of the next century to bestow upon the persecutors of the Jews the title of heretic.

Although the horrors perpetrated against the Jews during the First Crusade were never again equaled in the Middle Ages, subsequent crusades also were occasions of danger. At the time of the Second Crusade (1146), the Jewish communities in France and Germany, notably at Würzburg, suffered persecution. Official reaction was as condemnatory as in the First Crusade, and now that most redoubtable of Christian polemicists, Saint Bernard of Clairvaux, mounted the pulpit of denunciation. Writing to Archbishop Henry of Mainz (1142–1153) in condemnation of a monk named Radulf who had led a pogrom, the saint was obviously infuriated by the perversion of the Crusade that he himself had done most to promote.[62] There were three chief errors in the actions of Radulf, according to the Cistercian; first, that he had abused his responsibilities as a preacher; second, that he had showed contempt for the bishops who had condemned pogroms; third, that he had taken the liberty of approving murder. We pray for the conversion of the Jews, Saint Bernard reminds us, and once dead they are beyond the powers of persuasion. To all appearances, the saint was more indignant than usual in his choleric attack upon Radulf. "Your doctrine isn't your own," he exclaimed, but "that of your father [the devil] who sent you . . . O most impure of heresies! O wanton sacrilege!"

The Church never formally condemned persecution of the Jews as a "heresy," but Saint Bernard did not use the term idly. To preach the extermination of the Jews was to preach the desirability of murder and to do so in defiance of the explicit and repeated orders of pope, emperor, and bishops. This frenzy proceeded from the same zeal that motivated the Reformists and the orthodox Reformers. In its refined forms, this spirit, quickening arid souls and making religion central in the lives of people to a greater degree than since the days of the early Church, produced the monastic reformers of Cluny, the orthodox reformers surrounding Hildebrand, and apostolics like Ramihrd or the Reformists of Liège. These, orthodox and dissidents alike, occupied the bright side of the moon. On the dark side raged the mobs. On the one side, enthusiasm, and on the other, fanaticism. It is part of the curse of Adam that the medieval Church was unable to produce the one without the other.

3. Heretical Enthusiasm

The Twelfth Century

Reformist Dissidence waxed even stronger in the twelfth than it had in the eleventh century, for now the Great Reform Movement was in full flood. Pneumatic enthusiasm would continue to dominate medieval religious dissent until, in the middle decades of the century, Catharist dualism arrived from the East to transform its nature.

The Reformists of Ivois.

On the River Chiers, a tributary of the Meuse that joins the great river about halfway between Verdun and Namur, stands a village called Carignan or Ivois. In the French-speaking area of the Ardennes, not far from Bouillon, Ivois was within the borders of the medieval archdiocese of Trier and in the duchy of Upper Lorraine. Once again the Fertile Triangle, between Rhine, Seine, and sea, produced dissidents, this group being discovered during the reign of Archbishop Bruno (1102–1124).[1]

Of the heretics discovered, four were apprehended and brought before the bishop. Two of them, Dominic William and Frederick, were priests, and the other two, Durand and Hamelric, were laymen. While Bruno was discussing their case, Hamelric escaped and was not heard from again. Durand made a great show of confessing and abjuring his error with the aid of holy relics. The priests were more resolute in their error. Frederick willingly confessed to the heresy but maintained that he was justified in having preached it, inasmuch as it was the simple truth. When Bruno had lectured him, drawing upon Saint

54

Augustine as an authority, he still refused to yield. Confusion followed. The clergy who were present rushed upon him and demanded his degradation and condemnation, and Frederick took advantage of the chaos to escape, after which he was degraded and condemned *in absentia*. It may be debated whether for the sake of his soul he should have escaped or not, but for the sake of his hide there seems little doubt that he took the right decision.

The fourth heretic, the priest Dominic William, appears to have been the wiliest, in evidence of which the *Gesta* note that he affected two names. Dominic William steadfastly denied that he had had anything to do with the heresy—until he was confronted by two witnesses, who had evidently brought the original charges against the heretics, and who now affirmed that they had personally seen him addressing a secret meeting of the sect. The accused then offered to undergo an ordeal, and it was decided that he should say mass in affirmation of his innocence, so that if he lied the reception of the host under such circumstances would be his ruin. The mass was said without untoward event until time came for communion, at which point Archbishop Bruno rose and sternly addressed Dominic from the congregation, forbidding him to receive if it were true that he had professed the heresy. Dominic received and, since no heavenly thunderbolt obliterated him on the spot, was adjudged innocent and set free. For the story to have a moral, the chronicler adds that he returned immediately to his former heresy, doubtless fortified in his zeal by his success in defrauding the bishop and high heaven to boot. Going from heresy to heresy, sinking from vice to vice, he was at last caught in adultery and "done to death in a manner suitable to his unworthiness." [2]

Little is known of the doctrines of these dissidents, because the chronicler unfortunately thought it best to refrain from passing them on to posterity. He does inform us, however, that they rejected the eucharist and the baptism of infants, while the testimony of their accusers before the bishop reveals that they had secret conventicles. Brouwers[3] makes the mistake of believing them to have been followers of Berengar of Tours, because of their denial of transubstantiation, when there is actually no evidence for a popular Berengarism, and when their rejection of the baptism of infants implies something rather different. Fredericq was surprised [4] at the term, but did not make the obvious deduction that Brouwers did not know what he was talking about. These dissidents were exactly the same sort of Reformists that were active in Lorraine in the preceding century. If the story of Dominic William's adultery and general immorality be dismissed as a fabrication or exaggeration on the part of the chronicler, as it most probably is, there can be no question but that this is what they were: the rejection of the eucharist and of infant baptism and the "secret conventicles" are by this time very familiar to us.

Poland (1110–1118).

If the creed that appears engraved upon the sepulchre of Bishop Maurus of Cracow (1110-1118) is evidence for the existence of heresy in Poland at this time, it might indicate the excessive repugnance for the flesh sometimes evinced by hysterical Reformists, or it is always possible that it does represent, as David thought, Bogomil influence from the south.[5] David discovered that the creed, which consists of initial letters only, omits the initials of the words "hell" in "he descended into hell," "dead" in "he rose from the dead," "dead" again in "the living and the dead" and, finally, of all the words in the phrase "the resurrection of the body." If David's observations were correct, this does seem, as he says, too striking to be coincidental, but our information on Maurus' reign is far too meager to allow us to do more than speculate on whether the bishop or one of his followers was a heretic, or to be able to judge accurately whether the heretic was a Bogomil or a Reformist.

Tanchelm.[6]

Meagerness of sources is not the problem with Tanchelm, one of the best-studied dissenters of the early twelfth century.[7] A native of the Netherlands, probably of Utrecht, Tanchelm may have been a renegade monk.[8] Having encountered difficulties in the diocese of Utrecht, possibly at the hands of Bishop Burchard (1099–1112), a man not insensitive to Church reform, Tanchelm fled to the county of Flanders, where he came to the notice of Count Robert II (1093–1111). It so happened that Robert was very willing to welcome anyone with a grudge against the diocese of Utrecht, and very shortly the crafty baron worked out a scheme by means of which Tanchelm could be revenged and his own power strengthened at the same time. The exact relationship between Tanchelm and the count is not clear, though it is too much to assume, as Borst does, that Tanchelm became one of Robert's "councilors," let alone to follow Pirenne in making him a "notary" of the comital court. On the contrary, Tanchelm's residence in the county of Flanders was only temporary, though his literacy and oratory were qualities that recommended him to his host. It is impossible to date the future heretic's sojourn in Flanders with any exactitude, though it probably occurred very shortly before the death of the count in 1111, as Tanchelm was preaching heresy as early as the next year. It is not likely that he let his animosity toward the Church of Cambrai cool for very long after the failure of his plot with Robert.[9]

Robert's plot was a simple one, but one worthy of his reputation as a political fox. Both he and Louis VI of France, whose vassal he was, were interested in weakening the ecclesiastical power of the German emperor in the Low Countries. Henry V and Louis VI were enemies; they were shortly (in 1124) to approach fighting the closest thing to a national war that the twelfth century could produce. Count Robert was interested, as always, in furthering his own political power at the expense of anyone who stood in his way, and in the Low Countries this was likely to be the emperor. Thus there was an opposition of Franco-Flemish and German interests. The power of the emperor rested to a great extent upon the support of the bishops, with whom he was bound in a close alliance. As was previously noted, Liège, Cambrai, and Cologne were particularly close to the emperor, and he could also count Utrecht fairly reliable. The Franco-Flemish interests succeeded in reducing the imperial influence in 1094, when the see of Arras was separated from that of Cambrai. The French forces, separatist in the case of Cambrai and Arras, were equally ardent for union in the case of Noyon and Tournai, where the see of Noyon, firmly in the French camp, dominated the more northern see. In this instance, they turned out to be less successful, and Tournai achieved its independence in 1146 as Arras had done fifty years earlier. Count Robert saw in the determined and skillful agitator of Utrecht an excellent tool to use in yet another diocesan gerrymander: he would use the rhetoric of the brilliant and persuasive Tanchelm to convince the pope to partition the diocese of Utrecht and bestow a portion of it upon a diocese under Franco-Flemish control.

Since Pirenne's article upon the proposed partition appeared in 1927, the subject has aroused interest among Belgian and Dutch historians, the latest study having appeared in 1961. Pirenne believed that the diocese to which Robert and Tanchelm wished to annex parts of Utrecht was Tournai, his argument being that this diocese was contiguous with Utrecht, while that of Thérouanne, the other possibility, was not. His judgment in this particular matter has long been questioned. The only source, the letter of the canons of Utrecht to Archbishop Frederick, gives *Teruwanensi* (Thérouanne), and from the paleographical point of view the possibility of this being a scribal error for *Tornacensi* is very small: the words simply do not look that much alike. Also, it is a general rule of criticism that a familiar or likely name is more apt to be substituted erroneously for an unfamiliar or unlikely name than the other way about. The very fact that Tournai is in closer conjunction with Utrecht makes it unlikely that a scribe would have replaced the word Tournai with the word Thérouanne, particularly if the scribe were himself Dutch and therefore more familiar with Tournai. Further, in terms of Count Robert's motives, Thérouanne is the more likely choice, for his control over that diocese was much more secure than his control over that of Tournai.

There remains the problem of the contiguity of the dioceses. It is of course true that dioceses were usually geographically continuous and that the annexation of a noncontiguous portion of Utrecht to Thérouanne would have been an unlikely project. Unlikely, but not impossible: the diocese of Münster had jurisdiction over a strip of the Frisian coast separated from the episcopal see by the entire breadth of the diocese of Osnabrück. Then, too, it is not absolutely certain that the dioceses of Thérouanne and Utrecht did not actually have a common border in the twelfth century. Jurisdiction over the constantly changing coastline of Flanders was indubitably in the hands of the archdiaconate of Bruges in the diocese of Tournai in the later Middle Ages, but it is possible that it lay in the hands of the bishop of Thérouanne in the earlier Middle Ages. Finally, as De Smet suggests, it may well be that this was no formal project of annexation at all, but an attempt on the part of the Hildebrandine party to strike a blow at the imperialists by *temporarily* approving the extension of the power of a Hildebrandine bishop, Jan van Waasten of Thérouanne, over a portion of the territory of a diocese that had remained stubbornly imperialist. We may conclude with reasonable certainty that it was with Thérouanne and not with Tournai that Tanchelm's project had to do.

It was probably about 1109 or 1110 that Count Robert sent Tanchelm and the priest Everwacher, pastor of Voorne (as De Smet has shown), to Rome to lay the scheme before Paschal II. Frederick I, archbishop of Cologne, hearing of the plot, intervened and prevailed upon the pope to reject the scheme, and Tanchelm and Everwacher were obliged to return to Flanders and to report the failure of their mission to their employer.

It is at this point that Tanchelm began to take the road that led him into heresy. We have no direct knowledge of his motivations, but they are not hard to guess. Pirenne suggested that, while at Rome, Tanchelm absorbed the principles and spirit of the Reform Papacy and that these, when he had pondered and assimilated them, awoke in him that intemperate enthusiasm we have learned to associate with the Reformists. One might add that it is possible that the sight of the luxuries of Rome shocked him, as it would Arnold of Brescia and Luther, and so drove him to revolt. On the other hand, there was plenty of opportunity to imbibe the reform spirit in the Fertile Triangle as well, and De Smet may be right that Tanchelm had a reformer's conscience long before his trip to Rome.

The attitude of Count Robert must also be considered. The ambitious count must have been not a little displeased by the failure of his scheme, and the welcome he bestowed upon the returning emissaries could not have been characterized by great warmth. Had he retained Tanchelm and Everwacher in his pay, or bestowed upon them some substantive mark of favor, it is not likely that Tanchelm would have taken to preaching heresy in the county of Flanders even after Robert's death in 1111. But here was a proud and ambitious man, his rhetoric rejected by the pope, and his self-esteem damaged by the contempt of Count Robert for his failure; very likely embittered, Tanchelm put his skills to other work and again proved the persuasiveness of his oratory, this time as an heresiarch.

Whether or not he was a monk, Tanchelm had had some clerical training; he was literate and proud of his oratorical abilities. A failure at his one political venture, he turned naturally to preaching. Since he had no license to do this, he was, in the very act, setting himself up against the Church, and his tendency to dissent was reinforced by the fact that prelates had given him little cause to love them. He therefore began to preach anticlerical doctrines. The clergy was corrupt, and the people were clamoring for apostolic purity; an enthusiastic audience was already prepared for any Reformist willing to walk upon the stage, and Tanchelm was willing. Returning to his native diocese, he began preaching in Flemish to the inhabitants of Walcheren and the other islands that lay low at the mouths of the Meuse and the Scheldt. In this quiet rural area with its enormous skies and flat lands merging almost imperceptibly with the sea, Tanchelm, dressed in a monk's habit to demonstrate his sanctity, taught the people the doctrines of Reform Dissidence. Archbishop Frederick of Cologne, hearing of this activity, had both Tanchelm and the ironmonger Manasses, now the heresiarch's follower, arrested and imprisoned. How long this detention lasted is unknown, but Tanchelm was shortly on the loose again, this time determined to carry his doctrines back to his home town. It was this tour at Utrecht that occasioned the indignant letter of the canons of that church to the archbishop, asking him to take action against Tanchelm now as he had done before. "We beg and plead with you in the Lord not on any account to let [Tanchelm and his supporters] slip out of your hands. If they escape, we assure you and state uncategorically that the future of our church will be irrecoverably thrown away."

In spite of the dire warnings of the chapter of Utrecht, Tanchelm succeeded in slipping through Frederick's hands and returning once again to Flanders, where he preached at Bruges (1113?). Passing on to Brabant, he taught at Louvain and at Antwerp. It was in Antwerp that he made his deepest mark. There he found the people disgusted with the pastor of Saint Michael's, at that time the one church in town. This man was living in sin with his niece and was of such disreputable a life that the people were left "like a flock without a shepherd." Under such circumstances the citizens of Antwerp were ready to follow anyone who offered them purer and more responsible leadership. It was a natural stage upon which Tanchelm might display himself; by this time his Reformism had been drowned in the same kind of unbounded egotism that had characterized the Eccentric, Aldebert, four centuries earlier. His pretensions knew no limits; as they grew, so did the number of his enemies. One day in 1115, after Tanchelm had been preaching, he was out in the river in a small boat with a number of other people, including a priest. Seizing the opportunity to launch a violent attack upon the clergy, Tanchelm succeeded in enraging the priest to such an extent that he struck Tanchelm heavily on the head and killed him. So departed from this life one of the more colorful of twelfth-century heretics.

During his lifetime, Tanchelm's appeal was enormous. The people at Antwerp and the neighboring regions were disgusted with the morals of their spiritual guides, invigorated by the moral reform that was quickening northern Europe, and aroused by the first stirrings of social discontent against the feudal privileges of prelate and noble. Under the gray skies of the north and in an age that provided little in the way of popular entertainment, they longed for excitement. Tanchelm seemed to fill all their needs. Of his associates two are known by name, the ironmonger Manasses and Everwacher. The latter is described by the letter of the canons as an apostate priest. There is no record that Everwacher was ever formally defrocked, but there can be no doubt that he vacated his priestly functions to serve his unruly master. Besides these two, all the chroniclers agree that Tanchelm had many other followers. Standing in the flat, green fields in cold and mist, Tanchelm, like Aldebert, like Eudo, like George Whitefield and John Wesley, preached in the open air to great throngs. Women were the first to flock to him, drawn no doubt by his compelling personality and an oratory the chroniclers described as mellifluous. The women eventually brought their husbands, and all together stood rapt by the power of his words as "if he were the angel of God." Few in the throng could have spoken against him, else a riot would have ensued.

From his audiences Tanchelm chose a smaller band of disciples, men he kept near him, allowed to entertain him, to carry his emblems, and to protect him. For the last function, he apparently formed a bodyguard that grew until it reached paramilitary proportions. Even if the figure of three thousand "brawlers" reported by the *Vita Norberti* is certainly an example of the tendency of the ancients to exaggerate numbers, there is no reason to doubt that he mustered, during the time he preached at Antwerp and perhaps before, a large force. No duke or prince could stand against him, the *Vita* tells us; again, the biographer of Saint Norbert must be pardoned for exaggerating the strength of his hero's foe, but the anguish of the good orthodox people of Utrecht and Antwerp indicates that the heretics were no mean antagonists. Whatever the size of Tanchelm's force, it was armed and presented both a danger to public order and a threat to constituted authority.

It is difficult to believe that Tanchelm often used his mob to terrorize. Trithemius says that much slaughter of the clergy was perpetrated by Tanchelm's armed bands, but Trithemius is a much later writer, and none of the earlier sources speaks of such carnage. Robert de Monte says that the people of Antwerp in their terror of Tanchelm hid the eucharist away in the nooks and crannies of their homes for ten years. But he also adds that later they returned to the faith, implying that they were Tanchelmists, so that the story seems somewhat inconsistent. Neither tale demonstrates that complete terror reigned at Antwerp during Tanchelm's residence, else the neighboring authorities would have taken sterner measures, and more chroniclers would have referred to what would have been a most extraordinary situation. Our sources have simply exaggerated an already dramatic situation. Tanchelm was very powerful at Antwerp, but not so powerful as to have completely disrupted constituted government.

Though Antwerp came to be the center of his power, he had already made converts on the islands, in Bruges, and in Brabant. In the area around Antwerp almost all the villages and localities counted his followers, who would come from miles around to hear him preach. Nor did his sudden death silence the heresy; for at least a decade thereafter the Tanchelmists were active, and it was no easy job to stamp them out. The tale of how Saint Norbert of Xanten, a countryman of Tanchelm's and founder of the Premonstratensian order of canons, came to Antwerp town to root out the still virulent remnants of the heresy indicates its continuing importance. Saint Norbert's visit to Antwerp in 1124 has been discussed at length by other writers, and the details of his journey need not detain us. The essential point is that the church of Saint Michael's in Antwerp, which had originally been under the cure of one priest and had been turned into a collegiate church with twelve secular canons and a provost in 1119 by Bishop Burchard of Cambrai, had become infested with Tanchelmist errors. In 1124 the provost was one Hildolf, who, finding himself unable to control the heresy at Saint

Michael's, sent a plea for help to Saint Norbert. Saint Norbert heeded the call and went to Antwerp that year, where the twelve secular canons who had been infected with Tanchelmist errors were transferred to the church of Our Lady, while Saint Michael's was given over to a group of Premonstratensian canons to purify it from all error. The regular canons were presumably successful in this endeavor, but the college of Our Lady seems to have given them some trouble, as the two colleges were still quarreling as late as 1148, though there is no indication that Tanchelmist sentiments persisted that long. Be this as it may, nine years after Tanchelm's death these sentiments were causing enough trouble to warrant the intervention of a man as important as Saint Norbert.

Nor was Saint Norbert the only one in authority to be concerned with Tanchelm's influence. The heresiarch was known as far away as Paris and Rome, and we have seen that Archbishop Frederick I of Cologne had at one time imprisoned Tanchelm and was later besought by the cathedral chapter of Utrecht to do so again. Yet there was no general intervention on the part of either the secular or lay authorities, nor did Paschal II, though he had seen Tanchelm at the time of his mission to Rome, ever formally condemn the Dutch dissident. The response of the Church to Tanchelm's challenge can only be described as moderate.

The challenge itself was firmly in the Reformist tradition, though it was overlaid with Eccentricity. A great deal of grotesque mummery was attributed to Tanchelm by the hostile clerics upon whose information we must depend. At least some of these accusations are false, as we shall see, and others are very likely exaggerated. Yet, remembering Aldebert and Eudo, among others, not all these accusations are impossible. At the peak of his influence he is supposed to have glorified himself beyond all sanity, dressing in golden clothes purchased with the tribute of his followers, entwining strands of gold in his curled and beribboned hair, and bedecking his clothing with precious ornaments. He is supposed to have lived in a luxurious house and entertained frequently in enormous splendor, realizing as a heresiarch the power and affluence deprived him as a politician. When he preached he went out to the open fields, since the churches were closed to him by order of the bishop. He would go to the fields in state, accompanied by followers bearing his standards (*vexilla*) and his sword in imitation of imperial state.

The cult that came to surround Tanchelm at Antwerp, while it originated in the feverish imagination of his followers, was hardly discouraged by the heresiarch himself. Besides carrying his emblems in procession, the sectaries gathered what they could of his personal effects and effluvia, in the tradition of contagious magic and of the strange fetishism that in all times grips admirers of great men (this was Schiller's footstool!), and stored them up as holy relics. They chanted to him, they venerated him as a saint or even as the Son of God, and they built a temple to him. (Aldebert's followers had constructed churches for him and dedicated them in his name.) All the sources agree that they obtained samples of his bathwater, which they drank either as a benediction or even—so the chapter of Utrecht says—as a sacrament. Borst found this difficult to believe,[10] as indeed it is in an age that pays more attention to hygienic matters than the twelfth century did, and suggested the unlikely alternative that this was simply a scornful way of speaking of watered wine. But in the light of other excesses of his cult, and remembering that Aldebert distributed his nail parings as relics, it is not impossible to believe, especially since this is something upon which all the sources agree.

According to the sources, Tanchelm proclaimed himself the Holy Spirit and "married" the Blessed Virgin Mary in the form of an image. He called upon the people to pay for his wedding, ordering the men to lay their offerings to the right of the image, the women to the left. His followers hastened to obey, vying with one another in an insane contest with gifts and oblations, the women throwing down their necklaces and earrings, the men "an infinity of money." One is inclined to believe that this mummery proceeded from Tanchelm's brain: the chapter of Utrecht no doubt possessed the rancor, but scarcely the imagination, to invent anything so preposterous. The activities of Manasses' guild also bear the stamp of validity. Twelve members of the guild were designated as the twelve apostles. To their number was added a woman who took the name of the Blessed Virgin whom the apostles led about on display, one at a time.

How many of these activities really occurred and how many were an invention of Tanchelm's enemies is difficult to determine. Much more dubious are the tales of sexual debauchery that here, as in all instances of dissidence, accompany the reports. The chapter and other sources were perfectly capable of inventing sexual revels in the grand tradition: the "apostles" had intercourse with the "Virgin" as a kind of confirmation ceremony; Tanchelm approved fornication and debauchery, going so far in his perverted revels as to deflower young girls in the presence of their mothers, while the sectaries gladly offered their wives and children as immolations to Tanchelm's lust. There can be no question but that these monstrous doings proceeded from the imagination of the authors of the sources, perhaps drawing on a knowledge of the practices of witch cults. Though many writers, modern as well as ancient, have not declined to accept such delicious tidbits, we must reject them as fabrications. As Borst points out, anyone would have a difficult time passing himself off as a defender of apostolic purity if he were at the same time indulging in public debauchery. It is also difficult to believe that any large number of people would be so caught up in their frenzy of devotion to their leader that they would permit, even encourage, him to ravish their wives and daughters. The verdict of most recent historians has properly been to exonerate Tanchelm from the charges of overt sexual corruption.

If the cult surrounding Tanchelm was open to excesses, his doctrines were purely Reformist. So in the tradition of the Reform Movement did he stand that not only have historians suggested that he learned his doctrines at Rome but even that he was not a heretic at all. Philippen raised the question of whether he ought to be called a heretic, noting that Gregory VII himself was branded as heretical by his enemies and suggesting that it is inconceivable that Robert II would have sent a heretic to plead his cause in Rome. The latter point is easily disposed of when one notes that the most sensible chronology of events places Tanchelm's heretical preaching after the failure of his mission to Rome. Philippen finally agrees to the appellation of heretic, noting that even Reformers like Norbert did not hesitate to describe Tanchelm so in later years. Most recently, Josef-M. De Smet has revived Philippen's argument, suggesting that Tanchelm's mission to Rome occurred toward the end of his life and that this is a proof of his basic orthodoxy. De Smet believes that the enmity Tanchelm had provoked on the part of the clergy of Utrecht caused the blackening of his character in the letter sent out by the chapter of that city.

While admitting that the charges against Tanchelm were exaggerated and that, rather than a monster, he stands revealed as a Reformist who let his pride get the better of him, it can scarcely be maintained that he was not a heretic at all. To do this would be to fly in the face of all the evidence. He did permit, if not actively encourage, the excessive cult that sprang up around him, and the doctrines ascribed to him by the sources fit the pattern of Reformist Dissidence perfectly. He rejected obedience to bishops, priests, and possibly the pope (only the chapter of Utrecht includes this point and it may be one of their exaggerations designed to strike horror in the minds of their readers, though of course if priests and bishops are done away with, the pope is likely to be dismissed as well). The hierarchy was not only not to be obeyed, but its pretensions to authority were empty, since holy orders were "nothing." The eucharist was of no value; he urged the people not to take it. This may provide credibility to the story of the Tanchelmists' hoarding of the eucharist. Forbidden by their leader to consume the host, they may yet have feared to desecrate it and, taking it in their mouths at communion, removed and taken it home to hide rather than swallowing it. Meyerus' statement that Tanchelm taught that it should be vomited up when taken at Easter may be true. It would indicate that the Tanchelmists still presented themselves in church in the effort to preserve the appearance of orthodoxy.

Not only the eucharist but all the sacraments were rejected. Saying that they were better named pollutions than sacraments, Tanchelm urged the people to eschew them entirely. On the other hand, the chapter of Utrecht also tells us that he took a donatist position and said that the virtue of the sacraments depended upon the virtue of the minister and that polluted priests administered only polluted sacraments. Since the chapter is more likely to have erred on the side of exaggerating his heresy than of minimizing it, we may deduce that Tanchelm probably did not object to the sacraments as such but merely taught a Reformist doctrine that since all priests were corrupt the sacraments were thereby all corrupted. The chapter also reported with horror that Tanchelm had said that "the churches of God are to be considered whorehouses." Again it is likely that what Tanchelm really said was that since the priests were so impure they had turned the churches into houses of ill-repute. That the true Church was not the Catholic, but consisted instead of the sectaries, was a doctrine so common to Reformists, for example those at Liège in 1025, that it is readily believable that Tanchelm held it as well. According to the chapter of Utrecht, and on this point there is no reason not to believe them, Tanchelm said that the Church existed among "the Tanchelmists alone." Like many other enthusiasts, his pride overcame him; he not only permitted the outrageous cult to grow up around him, but claimed that he was God, asserting "that if Christ is truly God because he has the Holy Spirit, [I] am not inferior nor less similar to God, because [I] have received the plenitude of the Holy Spirit." Here again the pneumatic quality of Reformist enthusiasm reveals itself: so filled with the Holy Spirit did Tanchelm deem himself that he felt in no way dissimilar to Christ.

A final doctrine of Tanchelm, who "preached what he knew would please the people," was one that we shall find also with Leutard the Eccentric: he urged his followers not to pay tithes to the clergy. The Tanchelmists were "easily persuaded" to accept this doctrine, and Tanchelm's follower Everwacher, always a loyal follower of his master, seized the tithes of the church of Saint Peter's in Utrecht and drove out the priest. Things had come to such a pass, the chapter of that city moaned, that people were reputed the holier the more they despised the Church.

With the heresy of the Patarini and Leutard, that of Tanchelm is one of the first that seems to have social implications. This was a period in the Fertile Triangle when social unrest was common. There had been communal uprisings as far back as that of Cologne in 1074, and bishops, clergy, merchants, and artisans frequently found themselves at cross-purposes. Some of Tanchelm's followers were artisans, as we have seen—but Tanchelm was no particular representative of the artisan class. Though his greatest successes were at Antwerp, a relatively large and industrious city where many of his followers must have been artisans, he had equal success with the peasants, who flocked from the neighboring villages to hear him, and with the clergy itself, as witness the canons of Saint Michael's who, as late as 1124, were still tainted with his doctrines. Tanchelm did preach the abolition of tithes, but aside from this and the general resentment of the hierarchy, there was no social content in his preaching. Marxist historians consider this sort of movement utterly naïve: there was no attempt to utilize the enormous forces of popular discontent and enthusiasm for reform to political ends. Having no clearly defined class support and no specific social or political program, Tanchelm's was not a social, but a religious, movement.

Henry the Monk, Peter, and Ponnus.

At the beginning of the twelfth century there appeared in the north of France a preacher with an unusual ability to sway souls.[11] He preached penitential sermons in France and Lausanne, though the traditional interpretations that make him a native of that city or even of Italy lack firm support from the sources.[12] The only real key to his origin is that, as Manselli suggests, his popularity as a preacher would be explainable only if his native tongue were French. His original kerygma, while somewhat flamboyant, seems to have been orthodox, for when he later returned to Le Mans he was at first received without hesitation. Whether Henry was ordained or not is uncertain, but he was a monk, possibly a Cluniac, and he was able to read and write. It is impossible that at the time of his entrance into Le Mans he was already a "renegade," as Borst describes him, following attacks leveled later by Saint Bernard, for in that event his reception by the learned Bishop Hildebert would be inexplicable.

Yet the manner of his arrival in town should have presaged trouble for a cautious person—and probably the only reason that he was allowed to preach there was that the good bishop was too preoccupied with a projected journey to Rome to take many pains in evaluating Henry's credentials. On Ash Wednesday in 1116 a small but extraordinary procession was seen approaching the walls of Le Mans. Henry was coming to offer the Manceaux hell-fire sermons for their lenten fare. Two of his disciples preceded him into the town to announce his presence, as Christ had sent two of his disciples to precede him into the village of Bethphage (Matt. xxi:2) in preparation for the Palm Sunday procession into Jerusalem. If Henry himself did not enter Le Mans in the guise of his Savior, he came in illegitimate pomp nonetheless: his disciples bore a cross before him as if he were a bishop. The people, who had previously enjoyed his powerful sermons, rushed to welcome his followers "as if they were angels."[13] In spite of this unusual furore, the bishop received Henry tolerantly and gave him license to preach a series of lenten sermons in the hopes that his eloquence might stir the conscience of the people. It was, after all, as Manselli says, not unusual for wandering preachers to offer their services as evangelists in this period.

Henry began his mission with the accustomed success, stirring the emotions of the people until many of his auditors were moved to tears. The bishop, fancying that things were in good order, took leave of his people and set off upon the road to Rome. When he was gone, Henry's sermons soon passed from the fiery to the inflammatory, and the Manceaux kindled readily. In spite of the efforts of a good bishop, Hildebert of Lavardin (bishop of Le Mans 1097–1125, archbishop of Tours 1125–1133)—a good poet and one of the first medieval humanists, a conscientious shepherd of his flock promoting reform and founding new religious houses—Le Mans had deep political and social problems, as did many other northern French towns at this time. The usual venality and licentiousness prevailed among many of the clergy. Geoffrey, abbot of Vendôme, for example, was a wordly and powerful feudal politician, and Bishop Hildebert himself, a man with many connections among the nobility, showed an interest in politics and played a considerable role in the union of Maine and Anjou.[14]

The people were engaged in a long-term struggle against the count, and the bishops had put their weight behind the feudal nobility. In 1092, Bishop Hoel had even placed an interdict upon the town. Thus the people had reason to resent bishop and clergy as well as the count. With the bishop now away at Rome, there were two religious forces in Le Mans, the relatively prosperous, sometimes venal, and thoroughly unpopular clergy, and the eloquent Henry, and the odds in any struggle were not difficult to predict. If the chronicler may be believed, Henry preached in the garb of a wild man. A young man and tall, he stood before them on the bare ground in the open air, even in the midst of a storm, unshaven and dressed only in a hair shirt. A wild man, perhaps, but wild with the same fire that sent John the Baptist to wander in the wilderness dressed only in skins, and the people braved the elements to hear Henry as they had done to hear John. Against this powerful man with his "terrible voice" [15] the clergy had little chance of retaining their influence over the people.

Seizing the opportunity of Hildebert's absence to translate words into action, Henry first advised ostracism of the clergy and their servants. When he saw that this failed to crush the priests, he was willing to tolerate more violent action. The mob was eager to take any hint in this direction and began to attack clergymen in the streets. When at last three priests were beaten black and blue and rolled in the mud, they and their outraged colleagues determined to take action. Presumably they had already written the bishop, though any such letter has been lost. There is, however, a letter of Hildebert dating from this period and addressed to a heretic named Henry, and it is likely that this was a response of the bishop to an earlier communication from his embattled clergy.[16] This epistle expresses surprise and regret that "Henry" was preaching that prayers to the saints were useless and orders him to stop teaching such heresy. The peremptory tone suggests that this Henry was at the time under Hildebert's jurisdiction and therefore probably was the fiery preacher of Le Mans. But Hildebert was far away, and the Manceaux priests were obliged to cope with the problem themselves. Not daring to face the terrible preacher in public, they diffidently sent him a letter forbidding him to preach any longer under the pain of excommunication of himself and his supporters. Henry refused to obey. One brave clergyman, Willus Musca (Guillaume Mouche?), encouraged by the fact that the Count of Anjou had now expressed his own desire to be rid of the troublemaker, summoned up the nerve to go to Henry and present the threat of excommunication in person. Henry received him and, having heard his message, replied succinctly, "You lie." Had the count's seneschal not been present, Henry's mob would probably have fallen with murderous intent upon the rash priest.

Henry continued to preach openly. What we now say of his conduct will depend upon whether we are willing to believe the hostile and outraged chroniclers, who, as usual putting the worst construction upon all of his actions, issued the standard accusations of impurity against him. To believe the Manceau author of the *Vita Hildeberti*, Henry seduced matrons and little boys and luxuriated in foul perversions. He had women stripped naked in public while he looked on pruriently; he took large contributions from his followers and squandered them upon his own evil delights. In short, he was a depraved and slavering monster. But the *Vita Hildeberti* is incautious enough to report the words of the people of Le Mans on the occasion of Hildebert's return: the priests, they said, are lying to you about Henry, for they fear lest he bring their sins into the light. Clerical authors had reason to blacken Henry's character. It cannot be doubted that Henry was injudicious and violent, moved by the Reformist spirit to reprehensible excesses, but, as in the case of Tanchelm, it seems best to reject the charges of licentiousness as fabrications or exaggerations on the part of his enemies. These accusations were clichés to begin with, and it is difficult to imagine that the Manceaux would have continued to be enthusiastic over Henry's attack upon the morals of the clergy if he were himself wallowing in lust.

On the other hand, his activities were unusual enough. It is probably true that he induced women to strip themselves of their rich clothes and ornaments, for, like Savonarola in aftertimes, he had fires lit to consume "vanities." It may charitably be assumed, however, that the ladies were not obliged to take off their clothes, or at least not all of them, in public. Another of his ideas that readily permitted misconstruction was that of encouraging his followers to take prostitutes to wife. These overdressed ladies were encouraged to consign their cosmetics to the flames and thenceforth to lead chaste lives with their new husbands. It is again charitable to see in this a work of mercy, if a bit priggish, rather than of lust. ("The naked shall marry the naked," said Henry, "the weak the sick, and the poor the needy.") Their husbands had to receive them without dowry, and new and simpler clothes were provided them from the funds contributed by Henry's followers.

Henry was no libertine, but his enthusiasm had clearly passed normally permissible bounds. When the bishop returned, as he eventually did, he found his city in an uproar. Henry had retired to the church of Saint Calais, which he established as a strategic headquarters while he planned and waited for the bishop to make the first move. It was clearly necessary for Hildebert to take immediate action to control the popular preacher. Where the priests and canons had feared to face Henry in public, the learned and experienced bishop showed no such hesitation. He determined to interview him in order to judge the merits of the accusations and counteraccusations darting like birds through the streets of Le Mans. The meeting was soon arranged, and the bishop inquired—one wonders why, even in his haste, he had not done this before departing for Rome—what orders Henry claimed to be in. Henry replied that he was a deacon. The bishop then tried to ascertain the extent of Henry's learning, and was shocked to find that the preacher had not attended mass that morning, that he was ignorant of the office of matins, that he did not know the psalms. Hildebert was astonished that out of such ignorance a man would dare preach to the people, and he quickly decided the case in favor of his clergy, ordering Henry to leave the diocese. Henry, humiliated by his defeat, went away with as much dignity as he could muster and followed by a faithful few who would not abandon his cause.

It remained to quiet the Manceaux themselves, who were not pleased with the banishment of their hero. The learned Hildebert found this a difficult task. When he had first entered the gates of the town upon his return from Rome, he had found the disaffection of the people evident. Wishing to bestow upon them the wonted episcopal benedictions, he was buffeted with jeers and clenched fists. "We don't want your benediction!," they shouted. "Go bless the mud! Sanctify that if you like. We have a father, we have a bishop, we have an advocate whose authority, honesty, and wisdom are far greater than yours!" Now, in the flush of their rage at the banishment of Henry, the people were even more incensed. Hildebert was, however, no mean rhetorician himself, and by using all his art and skill he was able at last to restore good order and proper obedience to his city.

But the career of Henry was not over. The bishop of Le Mans had solved his problem with Henry in the same way the monks of Sint Truiden solved theirs with the fantastic weavers' ship (see chap. 4): he sent him on to make trouble somewhere else. Upon leaving, Henry took with him a number of Manceaux, including two priests, who, however, left his train before 1125. Taking the road southward, he preached at Bordeaux and Poitiers and attracted enough attention in the south of France to cause Archbishop Bernard of Arles to have him arrested and brought before Pope Innocent II at the council of Pisa in 1135. It is possible that the synod of Toulouse in 1119 aimed its condemnations particularly at Henry.

Before Pisa, sometime between 1132 and 1135, Henry debated publicly with a monk named William, probably the famous William of Saint-Thierry, native of Liège and companion of Saint Bernard. An account of this encounter was recently discovered and edited by Raoul Manselli. It is clear that Henry's ideas had not progressed in the direction of orthodoxy since his sojourn at Le Mans. He no longer recognized the authority of the church and claimed that he owed no obedience to men, that is, the clergy, but to God alone. God had given him a special mission to go out and preach. His message was based upon the evangelical precept of love of neighbor. He rejected the baptism of infants on the grounds that conscious belief was prerequisite to the sacrament. Original sin, he said, affected Adam and Eve alone and was not transmitted to their descendants, for it is not just that we should be penalized for the sins of others. Children, therefore, are all saved if they die before attaining the age of reason. Much of the meaning of baptism was lost in this view, but Henry was willing that the sacrament continue to be given, but only as an external sign of belief and in the simple form with water, discarding oil and chrism as useless trappings. In this Henry departed from Peter of Bruys, who did not deny original sin. Henry went on to deny all sacerdotal power to unworthy clergy. They had no power to consecrate the host, to give absolution, or to preside at marriages. And not only were unworthy priests devoid of spiritual power, but the whole hierarchy was useless. The visible Church did not constitute the real Church of Christ; the true Church consisted of the faithful who obeyed the mandates of Scripture. The believers might confess to and bestow absolution upon one another rather than having recourse to the clergy. Marriage was a mutual consent between two people and the presence of clergy was unnecessary (Catholic doctrine on marriage itself still envisages the priest as witness more than participant). Henry condemned luxury as unapostolic, attacking the hierarchy for its pomp, and set aside Church buildings as useless. A man, he said, could pray anywhere as well as he could in a church. The communion of saints was an illusion. The essence of Henry's beliefs at this stage was clearly a thoroughgoing rejection of the authority and spiritual power of the hierarchy. For Henry the true Church was characterized by apostolic simplicity rather than by power and glory.

As Manselli points out, this is already a mature and well-thought-out doctrine. Manselli holds that Henry had encountered Peter of Bruys at some point before this disputation with William and that he had absorbed some of Peter's ideas, though expressing them in a more organized and more refined manner. A previous suggestion was that Henry came into contact with Peter's teachings only later, when, condemned for Reformist enthusiasm at Pisa in 1135, he was ordered to return to his home monastery and remain there. He contrived to get permission to leave, go to Clairvaux, and join the Cistercian order, but he never gained that refuge or, if he did, he quickly left it and returned to preach again in Provence. Before Manselli's work, the idea of Henry as a disciple of Peter was generally accepted, but Manselli emphasizes Henry's independent contributions. Most historians, however, agree that Peter exerted some kind of influence upon Henry. This belief rests in part upon the testimony of medieval opponents of both, notably Peter the Venerable, whose *Tractatus contra Petrobrusianos* ("Treatise against the followers of Peter of Bruys") is the chief source for the ideas of this dissident.

This Peter of Bruys, probably a native of what is now the village of Bruys in the canton of Rosans in the French Alps, had been a priest. For unknown reasons, he had been expelled from his church and had begun preaching in the south at the beginning of the century, about the same time that Henry had begun his work in the north.[17] Like Henry, he wandered about from place to place, unshaven, dressed in rags, barefoot, and preaching the doctrines of enthusiastic Reformism. He claimed to be preaching the true message of the Gospel. He attacked the immorality of the clergy. He taught that the eucharist was useless and that the priests were defrauding the people when they claimed that they were transforming the elements into the body and blood of Christ. The body of Christ was made only once, he said, at the time of the Incarnation. The words of consecration spoken by Christ at the Last Supper, "This is my body" and "This is my blood," had meaning only at the Last Supper and not thereafter. Peter held that since the true Church consisted of the faithful, a church building was no better a place to worship God than a tavern, a marketplace, or a stable. Churches therefore ought not to be built, and those already standing ought to be pulled down. He doubted the authority of the Bible beyond the Gospels, but the Gospels he claimed to interpret more truly than did the Church. He scorned prayers for the dead, and he condemned the baptism of infants on the typically Reformist grounds that the sacraments were invalid if administered to those who did not understand them and that the merits of one person could not be transferred to another. Crosses, rather than being venerated, should be burned, for it was not seemly to venerate the instrument of the Savior's death.

Peter seems to have taught a doctrine of justification by faith alone, as indicated in his rejection of churches, clergy, and sacraments.[18] He must have had considerable success as a preacher, for he was notorious enough to attract the attention of the powerful abbot of Cluny, Peter the Venerable. The fact that the abbot's tract against Peter was issued *after* the death of the dissident and that it aimed at "Petrobrusians" indicates that he had followers in some number and that they were loyal enough to continue his teaching after his death. Addressed to the bishops of Embrun, Arles, Die, and Gap, the treatise also indicates that Peter's success was greatest in Provence. However great his success, Peter was finally brought down by the mob that had so often followed him. In 1132 or 1133 he was seized by the people near the abbey of Saint Gilles in Provence, a town that would shortly become important in the annals of Catharism, and burned to death.[19]

Though Peter died in the flames, his influence lived after him, and no one was more fit to take up the mantle of his heresy than Henry, who had left his monastery ostensibly to go seek Saint Bernard at Clairvaux. He bent his steps away from Bernard as quickly as he could, little dreaming that he would soon have to deal with the terrible Cistercian under less favorable circumstances. For Henry did not go to Clairvaux, but rather sought the far south, Provence and its neighboring lands, the territory where Peter of Bruys had recently taught. The influence of Peter upon Henry, assumed by Lea, Borst, and other historians, cannot be proven. The doctrines that Henry taught in the south were common to many of the Reformist Dissidents and might even have developed in Henry's own mind without outside influence. The persistence of Petrobrusian influence in the Midi, however, makes such influence likely. Manselli (*Studi,* p. 62) calls Henry a *"discepolo . . . ma autonomo,"* asserting his cultural superiority to his purported master. Manselli's position that any contact between the two was brief is undoubtedly correct. At any rate, Henry now used his considerable talents as a demagogue to convince his audiences that churches were no more holy than other buildings; indeed, he referred to them as synagogues. He denied that the sacraments were efficacious or holy, and he spurned feast days. Under his influence, infants were not baptized nor were the last rites administered to the dying. The secret of his success lay in his persuasive manner and in the Reformist spirit with which he spoke and which the people longed to hear. Even Saint Bernard saw that it was the impulse to apostolic holiness that made the people accept Henry's heresies, for, said he, "He doubtless had the appearances of piety." [20]

Such were the inroads being made by heresy in the south at this time that the bishops were unable to cope with them, and they called upon the papal legate, Alberic of Ostia, to come to their aid. Alberic in turn enlisted the services of Saint Bernard, who agreed to come, as Diego of Osma and Saint Dominic were to come sixty years later, to give missions for the purpose of restoring orthodoxy. Bernard took an extended tour of the south in 1145, in the company of Alberic and Bishop Geoffrey of Chartres, debating with heretics, exhorting the people to reform and to regeneration.[21] Not only Petrobrusians and Henricians, but also the vanguard of the Catharists, were now infesting the south of France, and Bernard and his companions found the condition of the Christian religion in that area in an appalling state. Successful in some towns and less successful in others, the companions made their way through the countryside preaching and debating. They found Toulouse in a particularly shocking state of disaffection to the Church. Henry had been preaching there with great success; when Bernard arrived the dissenter went into hiding. The heretic who in his youth had been sure enough of his charisma to challenge the bishop of Le Mans now refused to meet Bernard in public debate and abandoned the field to him. This may, as Lea suggests, have marked a turning point in his career. His followers must have been disappointed in his failure to confront the Cistercian, for Bernard enjoyed considerable success in restoring the faith at Toulouse. At any rate, Henry now disappears from history. He may at last have been captured by the bishop of Toulouse. The story that he was brought before Pope Eugenius III at Reims in 1148 derives from a confusion of Henry with Eudo.

Henry's life and doctrines were those of a typical Reformist, though he had perhaps refined his ideas more than most. The most noteworthy characteristic of his program was his emphasis upon the individual nature of man's relationship with God. Like many Protestants after him, Henry seems to have misunderstood the nature of the primitive Church and to have ignored its strongly communal spirit.

The influence of Henry persisted after him, but the Henricians as a group did not long preserve their identity. Saint Bernard and his companions had already confused the Henricians and Petrobrusians with the Catharists, a confusion understandable in view of the fact that Catharism was a new and unfamiliar doctrine in the twelfth-century West and in view of the similarity of the ascetic doctrines of the Reformists to those of the Catharists. Modern historians like Vacandard have less excuse for confusing the two. Peter, Henry, and their followers were Reformists, not Catharists. But the rapidly increasing strength and influence of Catharist dualism in the south succeeded in quickly assimilating indigenous heresies, and those of Henry's followers who remained heretics after his death must have become Catharists. At Toulouse, at Albi, in Provence, in all the regions where Henry and Peter had been most successful, Catharism now took vigorous root. Some small indications of the continuation of Henrician ideas apart from the Catharist flood do exist, however. An inspired young virgin is said to have converted some Henricians in 1151,[22] and heretics found at Périgueux between 1155 and 1160 may conceivably have been under Henry's influence.[23] Lea was mistaken in believing that the heretics with whom Evervinus of Steinfeld had to deal were Henricians; they were simply Rhenish Reformists with ideas common to all Reformists including Henry and had no direct connection with the heretic of Le Mans and Provence.

As in the instance of the evidence binding Henry to Peter, there is no proof that the heretics of Périgord were followers of Henry. Their proximity to his time (they appear around 1140–1147) and to his neighborhood, in addition to some similarity of doctrine, are the only bonds that tie them together. But Reformist views were widespread and Périgord is not particularly close to the Midi, where Henry was preaching in these latter years of his life. The doctrines of the Périgourdins are dissimilar enough from those of Henry to make affiliation unlikely. With the heretics of Périgord we are dealing with an independent Reformist group, not with disciples of Henry.

Like Reformists everywhere, these dissidents, whose leader's name was Ponnus, gained many followers from all classes. Nobles, clerks, priests, monks, and nuns were attracted to their preaching, as were illiterate peasants. They taught Reformist doctrines of apostolic purity, claiming that members of their sect led good Christian lives. Like the Catharists, they ate no meat, but unlike the Catharists they also drank no wine and took no money. They genuflected a hundred times a day. Giving alms bestows no spiritual benefits upon the donor, they said, since no one ought to possess anything at all. They forbade the adoration of the cross or of images of Christ, calling them graven images and saying to the image of Christ, "Oh how wretched are they who adore you." The mass they held worthless, nor did they go to communion. If, for the sake of safety, they were obliged to pretend to be Catholics, they would go to mass and receive communion but hide the host in their mouths and throw it away when the opportunity arose. Heribert the monk, upon whose letter we rely for our information about this sect, adds that they practiced magic and worshiped the devil, who obligingly assisted them whenever they fell into any difficulty. "Thus if one should be fettered hand and foot and placed under an inverted hogshead watched by guards, he would disappear until it pleased him to return." [24] It is possible to doubt Heribert on this score. Whether or not Satan preserved them from harm, their influence does not seem to have spread. And there were other dissidents who, if they could not command such powerful help, had considerable influence of their own.

Soissons (1114-1130).

Soissons was the scene of Reformist Dissidence in the early twelfth century. In his autobiography, the monk Guibert of Nogent launched an attack upon his contemporary Count John of Soissons, whom he accused of favoring Jews and heretics and to whom he referred as a "Judaizer." [25] It is more than doubtful that John was ever converted to the Jewish religion; his relationship to the dissidents is clearer, though whether he subscribed to their doctrines or not is unknown. Clement and Ebrard, two brothers who had farms in the little village of Bucy-le-Long near Soissons, began preaching Reformist doctrines about 1114 and received protection from the count. They believed that the body of Christ was an illusion and that the baptism of children was valueless. They found the mass so repugnant that they were accustomed to call the mouths of priests "the maw of hell." They rejected the eucharist, and if they, like the heretics of Périgord, were obliged to receive communion in order to deceive, they did penance for this crime by partaking of no food for the remainder of the day. They denied the holiness of sacred ground, including cemeteries. They condemned marriage and propagation. They ate no food produced by sexual generation. The chronicler naturally tells us that they held secret conventicles, practiced obscene rites including homosexuality and lesbianism, and murdered little boys, from whose ashes they baked bread for their own macabre communion service. If the last accusations are rejected as typical clichés, Clement and Ebrard can be recognized as extreme ascetics, radical Reformists of the variety who would later readily accept Catharist teachings. They believed that God dwelt with them, that the Word of God was theirs, and that they, practicing the true apostolic life, were the true Christians.

Bishop Lisiard of Soissons (1108-1126), having heard of the activities of these heretics, ordered them brought before him. He examined them in the presence of Guibert of Nogent, who reported their interrogation as an eyewitness. At the interview, Clement, claiming to be a Christian, defended himself in an extraordinary fashion. Taking the words *Beati eritis* ("Blessed shall you be") from the Beatitudes, he translated them as "Blessed are the heretics" and attempted to demonstrate from this that God smiled more fulsomely upon him than upon the bishop. Lisiard was not impressed. He ordered witnesses summoned who had heard the brothers preach, and a woman and a deacon appeared to bear witness against them. The bishop then decided to put Clement, the leader, to the test of an ordeal. He ordered the sacrament brought and distributed it with the words, "May the body and blood of the Lord judge your case today." This done, the bishop and Peter, the archdeacon, proceeded to lead the heretics on to the ordeal by water. "With many tears" the bishop intoned the litany and then formally exorcized the suspects. He then proceeded to the ordeal proper. Clement was thrown bodily into a large tub of water. When it was seen that he floated rather than sank, the entire church broke out in jubilation: the Lord, present in the sacrament Clement had consumed, had made the facts clear. Clement was guilty in accordance with the legal tradition that stipulated that if the accused sank he was innocent, for if he floated it meant that the water refused to accept the guilty.

The people, always loving a spectacle, the more brutal the better, were meanwhile crowding into the church and massing outside in such numbers as had never before been seen in Soissons. Their noisy calls and jeers could not have added dignity to the already grotesque proceedings. Clement, having been rejected by the water, was put in chains, and his brother Ebrard was now led before the bishop. At once less devious and more courageous than his brother, Ebrard did not deny that he had been preaching in Clement's company, and by so confessing he spared himself the ordeal. However, he refused to abjure and remained firm in his convictions, so that he also was put in chains by order of Bishop Lisiard. Two other heretics from the nearby village of Dormans were also forced to undergo the ordeal and we e judged guilty. The bishop now decided to take the matter before a synod meeting in Beauvais in December, 1114.[26] The fathers there in turn called a synod to meet at Soissons the following month to study the heresy on the spot.

In accordance with the decision of Beauvais, a synod met at Soissons on the Epiphany, January 6, 1115,[27] but it was unable to interview Clement and his companions. They were dead.

Soissons had had a long history of popular unrest and violence. As far back as the ninth century the people had rioted for the confirmation of one bishop and the exclusion of another. In the course of the eleventh and twelfth centuries, however, the influence of the people in episcopal elections had gradually been eliminated as the choice fell more and more into the hands of the king of France. At Soissons as in other episcopal cities the people had come to be dissociated from their government. Meanwhile, economic growth, increased commercial and agricultural activity, were effecting changes typical of those in other developing northern towns, and the people came to have economic expectations they had lacked before. Yet they found the Church supporting the oppressors rather than the oppressed, and unrest and anger built up steadily from the end of the eleventh century, while heat was added by the news of successful communes in nearby cities like Noyon. Popular unrest finally forced the bishop to grant a charter of liberties and to permit the establishment of a commune. The first charter was dated 1115 or 1116, precisely the period when Clement and his friends underwent their ordeal.[28] The mob, always ready to lynch helpless and terror-stricken men, was particularly aroused that December of 1114 by the agitations that led eventually to the establishment of the commune. The people had not yet been provided with a specific, realistic program into which to channel their wrath, such as the limiting of the bishop's power. They were still a leaderless mob, a mob that would vent its anger wherever it found the opportunity.

It was December of 1114. Bishop Lisiard was away at Beauvais attending the synod. The mob proclaimed that the milksop clergy would treat these wicked heretics too leniently and streamed on toward the jail. The jail was stormed and the frightened prisoners dragged out. Pushed and kicked, mocked and ridiculed, they were led outside the walls of town. There, as Guibert tells us, "the people, lest the cancer of the heretics spread, exercised against them the just zeal of God." [29] The people of Soissons defended the Church and expunged the blot on their orthodoxy by burning all four dissenters to death.

An illuminating note to the study of Reformist Dissidence is found in the creed of Bishop Joscelin of Soissons, issued about 1130,[30] which demonstrates that a revulsion against marriage and propagation such as that expressed by Clement and Ebrard was by no means unusual. The opinions of the Fathers of the Church are well known, and they did not exceed those of Bishop Joscelin in violence. "All that is conceived as a result of intercourse between male and female is conceived in sin," said the good bishop. The pleasure (*voluptas*) of sex is a punishment deriving from original sin. Fortunately the Blessed Virgin did not have to suffer this when she conceived her Son, for Christ was born in Mary as the worm is generated from the mud when the sun heats it (an accepted item of natural history in the Middle Ages)—without sexual action. When an orthodox bishop was thorough in his rejection of sex, it is small wonder that, when Catharism appeared in the West, Reformists often found it congenial.

Toulouse (1119), *and the Second Lateran Council of 1139.*

A synod was held in Toulouse in 1119, the third chapter of which dealt in a general way with dissent. Demanding that heretics and their defenders be driven from the Church, the synod said that the heretics rejected the eucharist, the baptism of infants, holy orders, and legitimate matrimony—in fine, all the sacraments of the Church. Whether this was a condemnation of Reformists in general or of a particular group at Toulouse is uncertain. They may have been followers of Henry, but they were probably not Petrobrusians, as some historians have suggested, for their doctrines are much more similar to Henry's than to Peter's. The condemnation issued at Toulouse was repeated twenty years later at the Second Lateran Council of 1139, and at that earlier time it was clearly meant as a warning for the Church as a whole.[31]

Cambrai, Liège, and Milan (1135–1140).

In the meantime, unrest was spreading in the Low Countries. Cambrai, in the midst of social struggles over the commune, produced religious dissent at the same time. Under the rubric, "Evils perpetrated by the citizens," the author of the *Deeds of Nicholas Bishop of Cambrai* (1137–1167) composed a bit of doggerel informing us that the citizens were no longer able to control themselves. They vilified the Church and profaned the law of God. They seized the consecrated host from the tabernacle and cast it upon the ground, and they smashed crucifixes and holy pictures. Whatever was holy they profaned. Clearly connected with the agitation for social change, these outbursts illustrate the deep wrath of the people against the venal clergy.[32]

Two summary references on the part of the chronicles reveal the presence of Reformists at Liège in 1135.[33] In that year an unspecified number of dissenters was apprehended. They were probably natives of the city, since no mention is made of their origins and the chronicler is so well informed on the history of their religious practices. There is no positive evidence to connect them, as some historians have done, with Henry the Monk. Their way was to lead a holy and apostolic life and to feign devotion to the Catholic Church. Some orthodox watchdog must have decided that there was a discrepancy between these two devotions, and the dissenters were accused of error, apparently in a public square or a church, since the populace was present. The dissidents did not deny the doctrines of which they were accused, and the people of Liège, like the people of Soissons outraged at this insult to their conformity, wanted to stone them. The authorities were, however, able to prevent this, and the heretics were not imprisoned immediately, since many of them, rightly fearing for their lives, fled the town under cover of night. Three unfortunates did not make their escape. Two returned to the bosom of the Church, under what pressures one may suspect, but the third refused to recant and was burned at the stake. What authority ordered and carried out the execution we do not know.

The chronicles reveal only four of this group's doctrines and practices: they denied the legitimacy of marriage; they purportedly believed that women should be shared in common (though it were better to dismiss this indictment on the grounds that medieval chroniclers always put the worst possible constructions upon the Reformists' rejection of marriage); they held the Reformist doctrines of opposition to the baptism of infants, and to prayers for the dead.

Because of the modest scope of the information provided by the chronicles, it is difficult to hazard an interpretation of the causes of the outbreak of 1135. Schism in the episcopate and intermittent feuding between the two candidates, Albero I of Louvain and Alexander of Juliers, had recently begun. Alexander finally secured his election after the death of Albero in 1128 but continued to scandalize the Church by his intemperance and immorality, finally causing Innocent II to depose him at the council of Pisa in 1135, the very year the dissidents were discovered. Schism, civil war, murder, simony, excommunications, and depositions, all these provided the spiritual background at Liège at this time, a situation against which people concerned with religious purity and simplicity might well have revolted. That Reformists appeared and gained support is not surprising.

There are vague indications of Reform Dissidence at Milan in 1135: Archbishop Robaldo was obliged to issue orders that one John, "called a priest," stop preaching to the people that laymen were not obliged to pay tithes to the clergy,[34] a position similar to that of Leutard and bound up with the general Reformist distrust of the clergy as well as aimed at enlisting enthusiastic popular support. The dissidents burned at Utrecht and Trier in 1135 were also probably Reformists.[35]

Toul (ca. 1130's–1140's).

In the 1130's or 1140's Hugh Metellus, a native of Toul who had become a noted student of Aristotle and an Augustinian canon, is thought to have written a letter to Henry, bishop of Toul (1126–1165), in which he warned the bishop that there were "pestilential men" in his diocese who detested marriage, abominated baptism, derided the sacraments of the Church, and abhorred the name of Christian.[36] The date and authenticity of the letter being in doubt, it is difficult to say whether these heretics were Reformists or Catharists.

Evervinus of Steinfeld and Eckbert of Schönau.

Cologne, as well as Cambrai and Liège, was the scene of Reformist Dissidence at this time. Archbishop Arnold I interviewed a number of dissenters at the church of Saint Peter in Cologne in the year 1143, of whom some were burned at Bonn by order of Count Otto of Rheineck. Evervinus, the canon of Steinfeld, engaged in correspondence with Saint Bernard on the subject of these dissidents, and from his letter we see that there were actually two opposing groups of heretics active around Cologne at that time, one dominated by newly arrived Catharist doctrine, the other, more conservative, still identifiable as Reformist. The Catharist group and its infiltration into Rhenish dissidence will be discussed later;[37] it is the Reformists who concern us here.

The Reformists were completely at odds with the Catharists, and both groups had been detected because of their constant warfare with each other. The Reformists had a well-worked-out program. They began with a general attack upon the corruption of the Church. The Chair of Peter had been so defiled, they said, that its occupants had lost all apostolic powers. They were therefore unable to consecrate validly; hence the entire hierarchy of the Church was a false show, a fact amply demonstrated by the condition of the hierarchy's morals. For this reason, the bread and wine of the altar were not transformed into the body and blood of Christ. This argument was unnecessarily and irrelevantly reinforced by a donatist appeal to the unworthiness of the priests who consecrated the elements.

From there they went on to claim that none of the sacraments of the

Church was valid. They did believe in baptism, however, with two qualifications. First, baptism should not be administered to children. This might represent influence from the Catharist side, since the Catharists, too, denied the baptism of infants, reserving their baptism, or *consolamentum,* to those adults near death or desiring to be *perfecti.* On the other hand, it was more likely, as with the heretics of 1025, merely disbelief in the efficacy of a rite performed over creatures who cannot understand it. Their belief that priests had no real power of transmitting grace, owing to the lapse of apostolic authority, would reinforce such a belief. Second, they believed that anyone could at any time be the minister of the sacrament of baptism, a tenet approximating the belief in the priesthood of believers associated with the later Waldensians and Protestants.

They believed that fasts and penance were useless, for remission of sins was obtained by the sinner's simply and privately confessing his sin to God and resolving to correct it. They rejected prayers to the saints as useless and denied the existence of purgatory. These two doctrines might be Catharist influenced, since the Catharists believed in predestination and the transmigration of souls, but a closer examination rules out this possibility, since these heretics maintained, rather than a doctrine of metempsychosis, a belief that souls went immediately after death to eternal bliss or to eternal damnation. They believed that all marriage was fornication, unless contracted between two virgins. This peculiar doctrine may or may not bear the traces of a Catharist repugnance to the marital state, but it does betray a puritan zeal considerably in excess of the Pauline position. Finally, and most proto-Protestant of all, they maintained that all observances of the Church that Christ, and his apostles directly following him, did not personally and specifically found were superstitions.

Not content with a donatist view of the sacraments, they proceeded to a rejection of the hierarchy, to a doctrine resembling that of the priesthood of believers, and to an extreme puritanism. Manselli considered them Henricians,[38] that is, followers of Henry the Monk, who held similar doctrines. He noted two differences: first, that the Cologne dissidents seem to have lacked the great spiritual fervor of Henry (this objection seems unfair in that we have only the brief and indirect testimony of Evervinus in this regard), and second, that, while these heretics believed that baptism was truly a sacrament, though ministered by Christ through the believer, Henry maintained that it was a mere rite. It is doubtful that the Cologne dissenters were Henricians, for there is no evidence that Henry had followers in Germany, and it is more likely that indigenous Reformist Dissidence might have developed spontaneously, or with the aid of Catharist influences, into this extreme form. The existence of another extreme Reformist, Albero of Mercke, in the area shortly afterward, strengthens the supposition that these heresies were indigenous.

By 1163, when Eckbert of Schönau reported the continuing activities of the Rhenish dissidents, the Catharist inroads had gone deeper. Instead of two hostile sects there was now only one, in which the Catharists dominated and formed the elite inner core while Reformist doctrines were preached for the general public to introduce people gently to dissidence and prepare them for the eventual reception of the dualist doctrines that formed the core of the sect's belief. The Catharists had captured the Reformist movement at Cologne.[39]

Reims (1148).

The synod of Reims in 1148 under the presidency of Pope Eugenius III issued a general condemnation of the heretics in "Gascony, Provence, and elsewhere." [40] Besides the Catharists, who were now making their first inroads upon southern France, the synod also doubtless aimed its attack at the heresiarch Henry. The eccentric Eudo was condemned here and consigned to the custody of the archbishop of Reims, where he shortly died. But before Eudo succumbed to delusions of grandeur, he taught doctrines in the tradition of Reformist Dissidence, attacking the authority of the hierarchy and drawing his inspiration directly from Scripture for the conduct of an apostolic life.

Albero of Mercke.

Around the year 1150 a priest of Mercke, near Cologne, was brought before the authorities and condemned of heresy.[41] Very little is known of the facts of the case and nothing is known of Albero's background except that he was in holy orders. He lived an exceptionally pure and ascetic life and attracted many followers by virtue of this apostolic life and the zeal of his preaching. He was a man of some learning, a fact that appears from his erudition in defending himself with references to Scripture and to the Fathers. In addition, he possessed the high courage often associated with Reformists. He refused to recant or even to admit that the doctrines he held were heretical. Steadfastly maintaining that what he preached was the true Christianity of the apostles, he offered to submit his innocence to the test of the ordeal by fire. The clouds of time have obscured his end. Whether he perished as a result of the ordeal, by order of the authorities, or at the hands of the mob, is unsure, but it is certain that in one way or another he died in the defense of his beliefs. His kerygma and the following he won indicate that Catharist dualism had not eliminated all traces of Reformist Dissidence in the Rhineland and that a man could still win over the people by teaching simple doctrines unelaborated by the arabesques of dualism.

A *Pamphlet against the Errors of Albero* is the source for his case. The unknown author, a contemporary, is good enough to state Albero's positions and to elucidate them fairly and at length, citing the arguments and authorities that bolster the Reformist's position, then countering with arguments and authorities on the other side. The origin of Albero's dissent was his disgust with the corruption of the clergy. In his zeal against sinful priests, he fell into the donatist error that often followed. The eucharist might not be performed by an unworthy priest, he maintained, and bolstered his arguments by Scriptures and by the decrees of Nicholas II, Alexander II, and Gregory VII against nicolaitist and simoniac priests. Thus far he was orthodox, but the author of the *Pamphlet* cautions us against what follows. The papal pronouncements against the ministrations of unworthy priests, the polemicist notes, were disciplinary in nature and did not deny the priestly powers of such clergy. Simoniac and nicolaitist priests were to be deprived of benefices and congregations wherever possible, not because they had no powers to confer the sacraments, but because when it was made unprofitable for priests to be simoniac or nicolaitist these abuses would presumably die out.

Albero evidently did not understand papal policy on this point and held that immoral priests lost their sacerdotal powers. He then went on to a refinement of his own. If an unworthy priest consecrated, he maintained, the sacrament would be invalid for those who knew that the priest was in sin, but valid for those in ignorance of it. Here the validity of the sacraments began to depend in Protestant fashion upon the state of men's minds rather than on priestly powers conferred at ordination, powers not heightened or lessened by the state of mind of either priest or communicant. More curious than the heterodoxy of the statement, however, is the source from which Albero probably drew it. At the council of Piacenza in 1095 it had been decided that, although simoniac bishops were to be deprived of their functions, they were, nonetheless, validly consecrated prelates. If, therefore, a priest came to be ordained at their hands and did so in innocence of their crime, his ordination would be valid. If, however, he was ordained while aware of their suspension, his ordination was not valid.[42]

Here again it was a question of discipline, and the ruling of the council was designed as an alleviation of intolerable difficulties experienced by those who had been ordained in good faith and now saw their orders questioned. The denial of orders to those not in good faith rests upon the lack of proper intention on the part of the ordinands, not upon the lack of episcopal power on the part of the prelates. In making this fine distinction the Church was very close to the no-man's-land separating heresy from heterodoxy, and it is little wonder that an Albero might easily make the transfer from ordination to the eucharist and maintain that the lack of proper intention on the part of the communicant voided the validity of the sacrament, whereas the Church would maintain that in such an instance the sacrament was valid but caused the condemnation rather than the healing of the communicant. It need hardly be said that Albero can scarcely be blamed for his misconception of this point.

Nor was his next belief, that the dead cannot be aided by the sacrifice of the wicked priest, very far along the highway into heresy. Donatist it is, for, once again, the Church's position concerning sinful priests was purely disciplinary, and had not gone so far as to deny the validity of the sinful priest's sacraments for the dead. Albero may have been thinking of the profits made by priests from those pious people asking them to say masses for the repose of their relatives, but in any event he was falling over the edge into donatism by maintaining that once that request was made and accepted, however much at fault the applicant to the sinful priest might have been, the dead could not profit by the priest's sacrifice. There is evidently in this instance no question of lack of proper intention on the part of the dead.

From this tentative step into donatist error, Albero took the full plunge. More often than not, he maintained, demons rather than angels were to be found at the altar during mass. Here again, the mass was valid however depraved the priest, and it was clearly heresy to maintain that a valid mass, the Son's offering of Himself to the Father, was attended by throngs of demons. Such a violent statement on the part of a learned man like Albero was probably either made unguardedly in anger or else was meant somehow figuratively—bad priests, for example, perhaps being meant by "demons."

Finally, and most radical of all, Albero seems to approximate his predecessor heretics at Cologne by hinting at a sort of priesthood of believers. He drew a distinction between priests who were in sin and his own group of heretics. The sinful priest, he said, has the *appearance* of having the sacraments, but the heretic has the *real* sacraments. In this belief the established priesthood of the Church was in effect dismissed and replaced by the dissenting priesthood. The implication that moral purity rather than the sacrament of orders itself was the essential tended toward the elimination of the priesthood altogether and leaned in the Protestant direction of the priesthood of believers.

While condemning the excesses of Albero's doctrine, the writer of the pamphlet against him made an admission unusual for the time, placing the blame for these errors ultimately upon the corrupt and immoral clergy that provoked them. "Upon you, evil priests," he concluded, "the entire weight of the aforementioned error lies, for he who prepares the way for error is more wicked than he who errs." Here the Reformer spoke with unusual understanding of the Reformist.

Arras (1153).

A bull of Eugenius III to the clergy and people of Arras on February 5, 1153 called upon them to rally to their bishop in the time of his need.[43] Bishop Godescalc's (*ca*. 1149–*ca*. 1163) position was insecure in any event, and he was beset by heretics as well. Eugenius had recently received a visit from Godescalc in Rome, where the pope was shocked to hear of the presence of heretics in the diocese of Arras. Godescalc had issued a strict condemnation of them, and the pope specifically approved this measure. These heretics had recruited many disciples; unfortunately, the bull tells us nothing specific about their doctrines. They were probably Reformists, but it is possible that Catharism may have spread into the diocese by this time.

Lambert le Bègue.

If we may slightly transgress the chronological limitations of our study and return to Liège in the years following the midpoint of the twelfth century, we find still another reformer on the verge of heresy. With Lambert le Bègue the historian exchanges the embarrassment of lack of materials typical of the study of medieval heresy before the twelfth century for the embarrassment of wealth usually encountered by historians of more modern eras. Not only are the sources abundant,[44] but, what is more, they include the writings of the dissident himself, the first time we have been so blessed. Moreover, the amount of secondary writing about Lambert is copious. For the history of Liège, if not for the history of heresy, there is need of a book examining at length all the evidence and dealing with the several problems involved.[45]

The date of Lambert's appearance is fairly easy to fix. He was born about 1131,[46] and although Gilles of Orval and Jean of Outremeuse fix the date of Lambert's commencement as a preacher at around 1170, he was certainly active earlier. He was cited before a synod held by Bishop Alexander II of Liège (1164–1167),[47] and Daris sets the synod in the year 1166.[48] It is probable, then, that Lambert was preaching from at least the year 1160. His troubles came to a head in the reign of the antipope Calixtus III (1168–1178) to whom he made his appeals and Fredericq fixes the date of most of the correspondence between 1175 and the end of Calixtus' regin.[49]

Very briefly, the train of events involving Lambert is as follows. Originally a simple parish priest with a benefice in Liège, he was already taking a strong stand for reform at the council that Alexander II held in 1166 when Lambert and his followers demanded that canon law be followed and sons of priests not be admitted to holy orders. Between that date and 1175 he preached openly and violently against the abuses of the local clergy, thereby gaining their love no more than Ramihrd had done at Cambrai. In 1175 he was hailed before a council presided over by Bishop Radulf and found guilty of heresy. He was imprisoned, and five friends who supported him were deprived of their benefices and exiled from the diocese. Immediately both he and his friends petitioned Calixtus III for a hearing, and the antipope accordingly ordered Lambert to be freed and his friends restored to their benefices until such time as Lambert should come to Rome to present his case. Difficulties were still experienced with the Liégeois authorities, however, for Lambert was eventually driven to escape from his prison, upon which he made his way *ad limina*. Lambert defended himself with skill, and it is probably that Calixtus III would have justified him, had not his own luck at that time run out. Following the defeat of Frederick Barbarossa at Legnano in 1176, the emperor abandoned Calixtus in favor of the legitimate pope, Alexander III, and at the Peace of Venice in 1177 Calixtus was definitively shorn of the tiara. The ultimate upshot of Lambert's case is unknown. It fades into obscurity with the antipope before whom it was brought. It is for us, then, to judge where Calixtus could not, and to determine whether Lambert was in fact a heretic.

To begin with, neither Lambert nor his friends ever admitted to a point of heresy. Lambert made one confession: that he did not receive holy orders with an entirely pure motive. What this means is uncertain, but it is probably a reference to a not uncommon desire for the fruits of a benefice. At any rate, this was more in the nature of a confession to a sin than of an admission of heresy, and it was, moreover, a sin of which Lambert later repented. This point was not raised by the opponents of Lambert, at least as reported by the writings of the Lambertine group, and since the bishop allowed him to exercise his ministry for a decade at the very least before he was accused of heresy, it may be assumed that there was no question of adjudging him heterodox on those grounds.

The majority of writers of the history of Liège in the past have tended to accept the interpretation of Lambert as a heretic almost *a priori*, because Lambert appealed his case not to the legitimate pope, Alexander III, but to the imperialist pope, Frederick I's appointee, Calixtus III.[50] These authors are guilty of making the papal-imperial conflict into much more a black and white affair than it actually was, as if the Gregorians had a monopoly on virtue and the imperialists a monopoly on vice, and, what is more, of assuming that people living in the midst of the conflict were able to discern this pattern as clearly as nineteenth-century historians did. It must be remembered that it was the Frankish kings and emperors and their successors who, from the eighth century, took Constantine as their model and themselves assumed the burden of reforming the Church. It can hardly be supposed, then, that every person, even every sincere Christian, of the eleventh and twelfth centuries should immediately and thoroughly have grasped the new principles and seen the faults of the imperialist tradition.

It is true that the succession of energetic pontificates under Gregory VII, Urban II, and Paschal II had, along with the development of the canon law in the twelfth century, put Gregorian theory far in the lead of imperialist by the time Lambert le Bègue was having his difficulties. It is also true that the efforts of Frederick I and Henry VI to restore imperial leadership were quickly overwhelmed by the triumph of the papacy under Innocent III. In the face of this general truth, however, is the fact that many areas of Christendom remained faithful to the imperialist conception long after the Gregorian position and been accepted by the majority. Such an area was the diocese of Liège. The imperialist tradition of the emperor's heading the Church was a long and established one; it was particularly strong at Liège, had brought the church of Saint Lambert many advantages; and the pope of Frederick Barbarossa's choice sat in Rome with the relics of the apostles, while his opponents roamed in exile. No one in the diocese, so far as can be ascertained, denied the right of Calixtus to sit there. Had Lambert le Bègue recognized in Calixtus the antipope it would have been a miracle of which the Gregorian partly could justly have been proud. The fact that he did not does not establish him as a heretic.

The actual accusations made against Lambert were wide, far-ranging, and lacking in doctrinal cohesion, which permits us to suspect from the beginning that at least some of them were false. Moreover, Lambert's tone in replying to the accusations was one that inspires respect and induces belief: instead of hysterically denying them out of hand, he explained in each instance how his enemies chose, from either ignorance or malice, to misinterpret his true beliefs. However, it must be noted for the sake of caution that we have here to deal only with the writings of Lambert and his friends, apart from a short and uninformative note from Calixtus III and the account of Gilles of Orval, which is sparse and was written nearly a century afterward. Whereas in most of the other cases we have studied the accusers have had the last word, here that honor goes to the accused, and once again we are deciding a case on the basis of the representations of one side alone.

Both Lambert[51] and his friends[52] admitted with pride that Lambert had preached aganist the abuses of the clergy, and indeed there could scarcely be any heresy in this. He preached against the practice of priests taking money for the administration of the sacraments,[53] but this was no heresy either and was shortly to be the official position of the Church: the Fourth Lateran Council of 1215 forbade the taking of money in return for the sacraments.[54] At the council held by Alexander II in 1166, Lambert demanded that the canons against priests wearing gaudy clothing and against the promotion of the sons of priests to holy orders be enforced.[55] His requests were rejected by the synod, but can hardly be said to have been heretical. As we have seen, the first step into heresy for those who were overzealous in their condemnation of the failings of the clergy was usually to adopt a donatist view of the sacraments, but nowhere do we hear in Lambert's case that he denied that a sinful priest could validly administer the sacraments. Since this is one accusation that would have been easily credible, its absence is a strong point in favor of Lambert's orthodoxy. It is undeniable, however, that Lambert was often violent in his attacks on the priests. Immoral priests were wolves, he said; they were priests of Baal rather than of Christ. They were despoilers of the people, dominated by women, and concerned only with amassing personal fortunes, demanding payment of tithes in addition to selling the sacraments.[56]

The accusations brought against Lambert concerning his teachings upon the sacraments are bizarre, and his indignation in rejecting them is great. The clerks at Liège who were his enemies were apparently not only immoral but lacking in subtlety as well. To begin with, Lambert admits with pride to teaching that divinations and other occult practices should be barred from the celebration of mass.[57] He was accused of teaching that milk could be mixed with wine and offered up at the mass as Christ's blood.[58] To this he replied to the antipope in the same tone of patient asperity with which more recent unfortunates answered some of the more improbable suggestions of Senator McCarthy. He had, he explained, been replying to someone who suggested that, since water as well as wine poured forth from the wound in Christ's side, it would be possible to use water as one of the elements of consecration. Not approving this doctrine, but as a *reductio ad absurdum,* he had replied that one might just as well use milk, and his enemies had immediately seized upon the statement as heretical. Of like provenance was the accusation that he had maintained that the mass could be celebrated without water and wine.[59] Finally, the accusation that he maintained that the eucharist was not truly Christ's body[60] he flatly denied, and there is nothing else in the case to indicate that such a belief on his part was likely.

Lambert was also accused of stating that the sacraments were not necessary to salvation,[61] and that the human race could be saved without baptism.[62] Depending upon one's interpretation of it, the latter might be taken as heretical, but Lambert denied ever having maintained it. Both accusations derive from his teaching upon baptism, wherein he held that the reception of baptism by water was not absolutely necessary to salvation.[63] Now, the Church has generally held that baptism of fire (martyrdom) and baptism of desire (for those who are unable to receive baptism by water) are sufficient in themselves without the use of water. Lambert's teaching that the mercy of God is extended to those who do not receive the normal priestly ministrations was, therefore, far from heretical.

Lambert further denied that he had maintained that confession was unnecessary[64] and that he had condemned pilgrimages.[65] He said that in the latter instance he had indeed condemned the fraud, theft, and debauchery that often accompanied pious pilgrimages, but that he had not meant to condemn the practice itself. In like manner, he denied that he had said that servile labor was permissible upon Sunday,[66] for what he had really said was that servile labor on the Lord's day was less sinful than refraining from such labor only to turn to lascivious reveling and debauchery. As to the accusation that he, in accordance with his purported teaching, forced the good people of Liège to work in his garden on Sunday, he thought it shameful and ridiculous that such an absurd report should have gone halfway across

Europe and over the Alps to be laid at the feet of the Holy Father.[67] In answer to the indictment that he and his sectaries did not attend church, he said that, first, he was not aware that he had any "sectaries," second, he did not want any, and third, he and his friends worshipped God regularly and piously both within and without church.[68]

Lambert was also rather fantastically accused of trampling the body of Christ underfoot.[69] The source of this calumny was a remark that Lambert had made to the effect that it was no worse to trample Christ's body underfoot than it was to hear His word preached inattentively. Since this sentiment originated with Saint Augustine, Lambert argued reasonably that if it were true, it ought to be accepted, but if false, it was Augustine who was to blame and not he.

It was objected that Lambert had translated parts of the Scriptures into the vernacular;[70] to this he willingly admitted, scorning the lack of initiative of others for having failed to do so and inquiring why others who had made translations were not equally persecuted. Far from being a heresy, this was a deed that was not yet forbidden even for disciplinary purposes.

It is evident from all this that Lambert was not a heretic, but instead a sincere, zealous, and outspoken reformer. Yet the same qualities that commend him as a reformer could not have made him an easy or tractable person. His outspokenness doubtless was often carried to the point of tactlessness, as was true with Ramihrd. The one point on which Lambert was certainly at fault was one of discipline and restraint. Taken aback by the ruthless virtue of the reformer, Alexander III had, at the synod of 1166, not only refused to implement the program of reform that Lambert demanded, but also had ordered him to cease preaching for the time being. Lambert did not obey this order, and on this point alone his justification of himself [71] is forced and unconvincing. If he had been guilty, he asserted, then he should have been formally condemned (as he was, later, in 1175), but if he had not been guilty, why was he prevented from preaching? Tenable on the grounds of abstract morality, perhaps, this excuse does not obviate the fact that as a priest he had disobeyed the orders of his bishop. On the other hand, that he disobeyed his bishop in a matter of discipline does not prove that he was a heretic, as Daris believed. Lambert may not have been obedient, he may not have been tactful, he may not have been cautious, but he was not a heretic. More clearly than any other figure in our period,[72] Lambert's career illustrates the narrow margin separating the Reformer from the Reformist dissident.

Arnold of Brescia.

Perhaps the best known dissident of our period, sung in fiction and drama as well as in history, Arnold of Brescia was born to a noble family in that Lombard town near the turn of the twelfth century. A younger son, he was soon sent to a monastery to study. The boy showed intelligence and was permitted to undertake a journey to France in 1115 to pursue his theological studies. In Paris, Arnold encountered Abelard and sat for a while at the feet of the great challenger of authority. There is no evidence that Arnold ever adopted the intellectual propositions that caused Abelard to be accused of heresy, but he could not have learned from his master inordinate respect for the Church. Arnold was morally rather than intellectually oriented, and a man of action rather than a contemplative. An idealistic young man, he was wounded by the differences that he perceived between the way the Church was and the way it ought to have been, and when he returned to his native town in 1119, he began to preach apostolic poverty.

Arnold's career began, like many Reformists', in loyalty to the Church; as with many other impatient men, the slowness of the Church to respond to pleas for reform gradually drove him away. Moreover, Arnold's homeland was one that offered political and social inducements to revolt. Lombardy was the center of communal agitation in the south; it had been the scene of the Patarini controversy of the century past, and it would shortly be a battleground between empire and papacy. When Arnold returned from Paris he found Brescia in a turmoil. The bishop, Manfred (1133–1153), a reformer himself, had stirred up a hornet's nest in an attempt to raise the morals of the clergy. Rather than loyally supporting the bishop in an attempt to achieve moderate reforms, Arnold chose to propose such extreme measures that he alienated him. Maintaining that the Church ought to divest itself of all its wealth and live in apostolic poverty, Arnold stood against both bishop and the generality of the clergy, though he achieved a measure of popular support. While bishop and clergy were at odds, the people, as was usual in economically advanced areas at this time, were more interested in the formation of a commune and the limitation of the political and economic power of the clergy than in religious disputes. As a result, when Arnold raised an anticlerical banner, they followed it for their own purposes. Manfred set out on a journey for Rome in 1138, and it was then that Arnold and his allies raised the standard of revolt. The commune was proclaimed, and Arnold proceeded, like Savonarola after him, to use the commune's authority to enforce apostolic reform. Manfred, however, was able to persuade Innocent II to condemn Arnold at the Second Lateran Council in 1139, and the young zealot was obliged to leave Italy and cross the Alps into France once more.[73]

Having visited with his old teacher Abelard, Arnold returned to Paris and began to teach, resuming his attacks upon the clergy. As he had turned against Manfred, he now launched shafts at a greater reformer, Saint Bernard himself, whom Arnold disliked especially for his attacks upon Abelard. Saint Bernard in turn used his influence to persuade King Louis VII to banish Arnold from the realm, and Arnold was obliged to take refuge first in Zurich and finally in Bohemia (1143). In Bohemia he made friends with Guy, the papal legate, who at length persuaded him to make his submission to the pope. This was accomplished in 1146, when Arnold went to Viterbo to meet Eugenius III and beg pardon for his previous indiscretions. In an excess of confidence, the pope ordered Arnold to come to Rome after having completed his penance, so that he might be kept under surveillance, and Arnold readily obeyed.

The sight of Rome enraged Arnold to the point where he resumed his apostolic preaching with greater vigor than before. Like Peter Damian before him and Luther after him, he was scandalized by the luxury, pomp, and venality of the Roman clergy, and he now leveled open and violent attacks upon pope, curia, and clergy. His fame had followed him from Brescia, his fiery rhetoric had not deserted him, and he was soon able to inflame the wrath of the Roman people against their clerical masters. Fed by economic and political conditions similar to those prevailing at Brescia, the flames quickly became a conflagration. Eugenius III was driven from Rome in January, 1146, and a commune was established with Arnold as leader and with the middle classes forming his chief support. Only July 15, 1148, Eugenius excommunicated Arnold[74] and was able in November of the year following to regain his capital with the help of Sicilian arms. His hold on the city was only military, however; the people did not relent in their support of Arnold, and in 1150 the commune revived and drove the Vicar of Peter once more from his see. Eugenius could not return again till December of 1152, and he died the following July.

Arnold's program of 1150, after Eugenius had been driven out the second time, was so extreme as to lose him some of his previous support, particularly among the Roman nobility, and even Eugenius' mortal enemy Frederick Barbarossa would not underwrite Arnold's policies. It was left to Hadrian IV to break the back of Arnold's power in 1155, and to cause him to be arrested. Resisting, Arnold was imprisoned and strangled to death. His body was burned and his ashes thrown into the Tiber. His party does not seem to have survived his death, and his influence, except among the students at Paris, was always limited to Italy. Yet his name has continued as that of no other medieval dissident. He has been seen as a saint, a proto-Protestant, a fighter for democracy, and a leader of a class struggle. He was perhaps to some degree all of these, but he is most realistically seen as a Reformist, one of the medieval dissidents whose zeal for apostolic purity led him to excess.

In Brescia he had already moved across the borders of heresy in his dispute with Bishop Manfred. Arnold himself led a totally apostolic life, practicing asceticism, wandering about, and begging. He attacked the morals of the clergy and the monks, but would tolerate no half measures, maintaining that priests and monks who had personal possessions could not be saved. The only hope for salvation in the Church was the abandonment of property and reliance solely upon the providence of God. His attempt to use the commune to enforce these extreme ideas led to his banishment; when he returned to Italy and went to Rome after his brief reconciliation with the pope, he advocated an even more extreme program. His shock at the pomp of the Roman clergy induced him to proclaim that they should abandon not only their personal property but their regalia. He now carried his doctrines to their logical conclusion. If individual clergymen were in danger of damnation because of their personal involvement with goods, then the entire Church was in danger of ruin because of its temporal concerns. He demanded the abolition of the temporal power of the pope and advocated the superiority of the emperor to the pope in temporal matters.

It would be wrong to imagine that Arnold's motives here were political. First of all, as a political program his was largely unsuccessful. Though the supporters of the Roman commune were naturally in favor of the abolition or at least the reduction of papal political power, the emperor was not induced to lend his support to Arnold. And though the political environment was such as to encourage support for some of his policies, these originated not in political ambition or even in social conscience, but in the religious desire to purify the Church. Arnold's ideas are too similar to those of other Reformists to permit us to think otherwise.

Arnold, like other Reformist dissidents, questioned the value of the sacraments along with the value of the priesthood. He attacked any manifestation of concern with the things of this world on the part of the Church and resented churchly dabblings in things temporal. For example, he condemned Crusades and executions. His main concern was with apostolic poverty. Not only the pope, but the Church as a whole was to abandon its possessions, give up all its land, all its wealth, all its political influence. Bishops were to give up their feudal immunities and to extricate themselves from political commitments by extricating themselves from the feudal land system.

It is curious in all this to compare Arnold to other zealots for Reform in his period—Saint Bernard, for example. Had Saint Bernard and Arnold not been at odds over Abelard, it is possible that the saint might have recognized a kindred spirit in the heretic. Had not Bernard condemned wealth and luxury in the Church? Was he not an ascetic? Did he not preach apostolic purity? And even in the matter of the papal temporal authority, Bernard once remarked that it would be better if the pope would leave the *urbs* and dwell more in the *orbis*.[75] But Bernard was a monk. If Arnold's program was not far removed from that of the general monastic point of view in the eleventh and twelfth centuries, it was radically different from that dominating the reform papacy from Gregory VII onward. It was Gregory's design to increase the independence and spiritual influence of the Church by increasing its political and economic power. It was Arnold's contention that it was precisely this worldly power that was the source of corruption. Both Reformer and Reformist desired to remold the Church in the image of Christ but differed in their notions of how to go about it.

Conclusion.

That Rome under the rule of a responsible pope like Hadrian IV could execute Arnold of Brescia and scatter his ashes upon the Tiber is an indication of how deep the animosities caused by these differences over method could go. The animosity was strong on both sides. Neither the orthodox in their desire to defend existing truth nor the dissidents in their desire to promote purity suffered from an excess of charity toward the other. The orthodox often suffered from sluggishness and lack of sympathy; the dissidents often suffered from impatience and lack of sympathy. If charity without truth is dangerous, truth without charity is barren.

Enthusiasm and Reformist Dissidence were to continue long after the twelfth century. They will doubtless be with the Church until the end of her days. But from the middle of the twelfth century on the Reformists ceased to dominate dissent so completely. Other actors, notably the Catharists, began to upstage them, and if the Waldensians are important for the latter years of the twelfth century, the Catharists are even more so. The Reformists, who became important in the West with the mission of Boniface, and central in importance in the eleventh century, no longer held the center of the stage after 1160.

From Claudius of Turin through the Liégeois of 1025 to Henry and Arnold, the Reformists kept in their hearts three central principles: the pure life, the example of the apostles, and the inspiration of the Holy Spirit. In their enthusiasm they offered programs that were often ill-conceived and ill-prepared, programs the Church could not assimilate. But their banner, flying far to the left, encouraged as well as repulsed; because it was there, more moderate reformers within the Church pressed forward themselves with more vigor. The role of the Reformists in the Church was a role often played by heretics. They aided in the development of Christian doctrine by raising questions that needed to be answered and taking positions that needed to be debated. The tradition of assent as well as the tradition of dissent is the stronger and perhaps the purer for their presence.

4. The Eccentrics

In the fields and villages of Europe in the early Middle Ages men occasionally appeared who preached strange doctrines rooted in superstition, whimsy, and fantasy. Sometimes these men gathered an unlettered following and succeeded in causing such a disturbance that the authorities were obliged to take action against them. Had they not been so successful in gaining converts, the extravagance of these heretics would often have made them objects of ridicule, rather than of fear, for the Church. Ignorant of philosophy, theology, or any of the refinements of thought, they taught doctrines in which the holy was mingled with the grotesque. Elated by the reception they received among the people, their self-esteem swelled, and they spread their doctrine abroad. The young man in a small village who has an unusual facility of speech and a compelling personality, who has absorbed from sermons and from popular stories and hagiologies some of the notions and vocabulary of religion, sometimes gets it into his mind that the Holy Spirit is calling upon him to preach. He may be met at first by jeers and mockery, but if his eloquence is great enough, the ridicule of his audience turns to curiosity, and if he is exceptionally skillful, curiosity will in turn yield to enthusiasm, and the career of the young prophet begins.

The very early Church encouraged prophets whose enthusiasm spread the Good News rapidly through the countryside, but before the first century of Christianity had passed the Church became more tightly organized. When this happened, the prophets were asked to be silent, for their enthusiasm might get out of bounds and disturb, rather than nurture, the growing Christian community. And so prophecy made way for sober teaching and apostolic succession. But though the office of prophet was no longer tolerated in the Church, the prophetic spirit remained, ebullient and undisciplined. Usually it was repressed; often it was harnessed and diverted to more socially acceptable methods: Saint Bernard and his fellow monks of the eleventh and twelfth centuries often played the part of prophets, urging popes, kings, and bishops into the ways of holiness. When the prophetic spirit broke forth unbridled, however, the Church was always obliged to suppress it.

Some of the Eccentrics were bumpkins whose heads were turned by the adulation of their followers; some were not free from the taint of charlatanism and turned their kerygma into a means of material support. All had in common an extravagant enthusiasm that they allowed to run unbridled. Sometimes this enthusiasm was for ideas that were simply grotesque or absurd, but sometimes, too, their doctrines were rooted in the legitimate grievances of the people, grievances against tithes or against the ignorance or worldliness of the clergy. So it was with Leutard or Eudo, for example. The people would not, after all, have followed these men if they had not answered some spiritual needs that were not being fulfilled elsewhere.

Some of the Eccentric dissenters, therefore, occupy a place in the history of medieval nonconformity not far from that of the Reformists, while some of the Reformists—Tanchelm, for example—seem to have shared many of the extravagances of the Eccentrics. The Eccentrics were characterized by a spiritual pride and rebelliousness that often prevented them from making the proper submission to the religious authorities. But they also represent one form of protest against the materialism, ignorance, and indifference of the medieval clergy to the needs of the people. Wild as their ideas sometimes were, the Eccentrics were part of the mainstream of early medieval dissent.

Among the dissenters with whom Saint Boniface dealt, the sources reveal none more clearly than Aldebert, the first Eccentric heretic in the Western tradition.[1] He was born of simple parents, had no education, but at some point in his life discovered that he had the talent and the personal appeal to launch a career as a prophet. Affecting apostolic humility in gait, speech, and dress, he impressed the people with his holiness and began to preach. Whatever his place of origin, we first find him wandering in the villages near Soissons and gathering rural congregations. It is questionable whether Aldebert was in holy orders, but, since he had preached in churches, he must have acquired at least a modicum of education.

The bishop, however, did not seem much impressed by his credentials, for he forbade him to preach in churches. Aldebert obeyed the letter of the bishop's prohibition but refused to observe the spirit and set up crosses in the countryside, much in the manner of the Christian missionaries to the Anglo-Saxons. He was enormously successful at this outdoor evangelism, and in some localities the crosses were replaced by little oratories built with the contributions and the labor of the peasants who believed in him. Eventually the oratories were replaced by churches, which Aldebert himself consecrated, so that his support among the population must have been wide and enthusiastic. Their need for what Aldebert preached must have been great for them to have dedicated so much from their pitiful store of wealth and time, liened already by lord and parish priest, to the construction of even modest chapels for their prophet.

Nothing could be more indicative of the failure of the Church of that time to provide adequate instruction and inspiration to the people. Like the Reform Dissidents, Aldebert expressed, in his teaching of a simple, apostolic life, the people's resentment of the increasing remoteness of religion. The people wanted to hear that it was the meek and the humble who walked more directly in the steps of the Lord than the great and the wealthy, and this he taught them.

But Aldebert's pride did not permit him to stop there, and pride engendered mania. He was not merely a reformer or a prophet, he claimed, but a holy saint and worthy of veneration. If the people wished an example of how perfectly to live the apostolic life, he said, they need only look at him. As a living saint, he could perform miracles, and his followers ascribed many prodigies and cures to his ministrations. As is usual in these cases—so Saint Paul observed in the very beginning of the Church—great numbers of women flocked to him and formed the nucleus of his cult. Whether or not he took advantage of their adoration to induce them to participate in licentious revels with him is difficult to say. Pope Zachary tells us that he did, and such initiative is by no means uncommon among religious charlatans, whether medieval or modern. On the other hand, Aldebert seems to have been more an enthusiast than a charlatan, and, moreover, accusations of immorality were so often levied against heretics in the Middle Ages that they prove nothing.

Though we recognize two strands in Aldebert's life, one of the reformer and the other of the madman, it was the mad side of his character that was the stronger. Not only was he a holy man and a living saint, he said, but he was endowed with many mystical powers. While still in his mother's womb, he was filled with the grace of God, and he was born a saint *ex electione Dei*. Before his birth, his mother had dreamed that a calf emerged from her right side, indicating that her child had received grace while yet unborn. In this claim there is more than a hint of blasphemy. The calf is very close to the lamb, and the story inevitably reminds one of the Annunciation to Mary that she was "full of grace" and that the fruit of her womb was blessed. The analogy was all the sharper in view of the popular belief that Christ had been born through the right side of the Blessed Virgin, nor is it uncommon for the religious madman to pass from the illusion of saintliness to the illusion of divinity.

These special favors remained with Aldebert all his life, so that he was, in his own words, "solemnly crowned with the grace of God." He dedicated no churches to apostles or martyrs but only to himself, for he claimed he was the equal of the apostles. In this position of particular favor with the Deity, he received many special favors. An angel of the Lord brought him relics of great efficacy from the ends of the earth, through the virtues of which he was able to obtain for himself and his followers whatever he requested. His own merits were such that they were of great service to those who prayed to him in the communion of saints. His supernatural powers endowed him with great wisdom. It was not necessary to confess to him, he told his followers, since he already knew all their sins: "To me all things that lie hidden are revealed." To his eager and credulous sectaries he distributed his nail parings and hair clippings as talismans of great virtue, in a manner similar to that in which the later Tanchelm bestowed samples of his bath water. Willibald, Boniface's biographer, reports that Aldebert sold these purported spiritual benefits, and this must have been true since he had no other means of support than that offered him by his followers. Yet Boniface himself says that he used apostolic dress and manners, and though Boniface judges this hypocrisy, this is not a necessary interpretation: Aldebert was more lunatic than charlatan.

Pope Zachary noted that Aldebert claimed to know the names of the angels, and it has on account of this been suggested that he may have been a member of some esoteric, possibly gnostic, cult. Boniface's messenger Denehard reported a prayer of Aldebert to the synod of Rome in which God was described as sitting on the seventh throne above the cherubim and seraphim. The prayer went on to say that God the Father had promised Aldebert whatever he desired and concluded with a most peculiar peroration—a plea for support from the angels Uriel, Raguel, Tubuel, Michael, Adinus, Tubuas, Sabaoc, and Simiel.[2]

No less strange than his attachment to the eight odd angels was a letter that he claimed to have received from Jesus Christ himself, a claim that smacks of charlatanism but that, in view of Aldebert's character as a whole, was probably more the result of delusion. Possibly he was himself duped by one of his followers or someone else who may have passed the letter on to him. Or Aldebert may have meant it as a pious fraud, attributing to Christ the teachings he felt it necessary to propagate. The letter was sent by Boniface to Rome as part of the evidence against the heretic, but, unfortunately for the historian, only the introduction is reported in the accounts of the council; we do not have the letter itself. The introduction began: "In the name of God. Here begins the letter of our Lord Jesus Christ, the Son of God, which fell from heaven in Jerusalem." It would be valuable to know what Christ was purported to have said in the letter, for Denehard, Boniface's messenger, said that Aldebert made use of it in his own teachings. This fraud is part of a long tradition of letters falling from heaven, so that in this respect Aldebert was, if an Eccentric, not an innovator.

The people followed Aldebert not only as a prophet but as a reformer. In addition to his more Eccentric beliefs, he cherished ideas similar to those of the Reformists. He dressed humbly, carried himself humbly, and preached the apostolic life. Like many later reformers, he attacked the authority of the pope and discouraged people from visiting Rome. It is true that he suffered delusions about his own holiness, but it was the apostolic life and not dualism or gnosticism that he preached, and the people followed him for this reason. Whether or not he was a charlatan, whether or not he was mad, it was his championing of apostolic simplicity that attracted them, and attracted them in large quantities. When Boniface wrote to the council of Rome, he asked the pope to help him "lead the Franks and the Gauls back into the right path," which indicates that a good many were involved, and later he said that Aldebert "led astray a multitude of the ignorant." Of the nature of the people who followed him, little is known directly. Everything leads us to believe that they were unlettered people of simple life, peasants from the villages of northern France, as the term *rusticus* used in the sources would indicate.

Aldebert's bizarre activities inevitably brought down upon him condemnations stronger than that of the bishop who forbade him the use of churches for his preaching. In the sources, his name is linked with that of Clement, a heretic of a totally different variety, one whose dislike of orthodoxy arose from dislike of its rigors rather than from disapproval of its laxness. These two heretics, the mad reformer and the disobedient libertine, were both active before 741, at which date we first hear of them through a letter of Pope Gregory III. With the approval of Pope Zachary, and under the aegis of kings Pepin and Carloman, Saint Boniface held a synod at Soissons on March 3, 744, to check the spread of Aldebert's activities.[3] This synod decided to condemn him formally and to burn the crosses he had set up in the countryside. He was taken into custody, and later that year Zachary wrote to take note of the fact that Aldebert had been suspended from the functions of the priesthood, which it is dubious that he ever legitimately assumed.

These measures proved ineffective. Aldebert managed to escape and to resume his teaching, and this new display of defiance occasioned the summoning of the German council of 745, presided over by King Carloman and Saint Boniface. This council went farther than that of Soissons. Officially describing Aldebert as a heretic, it ordered him not only deposed but also excommunicated; he, with Clement, was singled out as one of the chief authors of the errors growing among the Franks. But even this action was not effective. Aldebert continued to teach, and a synod was convoked at Rome itself on October 25, 745, in the Basilica of Theodore on the Latern. Remarkably, neither Boniface, the chief accuser, nor Aldebert and Clement, the defendants, were present. Boniface was doubtless too occupied with the press of business north of the

Alps to consider coming himself, but he sent Denehard, a priest of the archdiocese of Mainz, who acted as his messenger on other occasions, as his representative.

Zachary introduced the twenty-four assembled bishops to the problem and noted that the two heretics had already been condemned at northern councils. He called upon Denehard to read three items: (1) Boniface's letter detailing their errors, (2) the so-called-*Vita* of Aldebert (a biography officially approved by the lunatic), and (3) the prayer he had composed. The council agreed with the pope that he was a madman and therefore meted out to him a lighter sentence than that visited upon his fellow heretic, Clement. Aldebert was invited to recant and was stripped of all priestly dignity. If he refused to repent and persisted in his error, he was to be anathematized. Boniface had demanded a harsher sentence, involving immediate excommunication and imprisonment, and many of the bishops at the council also favored severity, asking that the writings of Aldebert be consigned to the flames, but, the pope wished to moderate the zeal of the other prelates and ordered the condemnation toned down and the writings placed in the papal archives for further consideration.

Boniface could not have been satisfied with the results of the synod, and if its goal had been the silencing of Aldebert, events proved the missionary's dissatisfaction justified. The lenient policy of the pope did not succeed in suppressing the Eccentric preacher. An embassy of King Pepin sent to Rome in 746 was obliged to report that Aldebert was still active. Zachary, still inclined to moderation, suggested a new council which Aldebert and Clement would be forced to attend. Whether or not this council was ever held we do not know; Aldebert and Clement now escape the eye of history. There are vague reports of Aldebert's murder shortly afterward, and in any event he ceased to trouble the Church.

The spirit of prophecy, which had never been expelled from the Church and which had found utterance in Aldebert, spoke again in the following century, this time through the lips of one Thiota or Theuda, a woman who in 847 or 848 upset the neighborhood of Mainz with her prophetic activities.[4] As with Aldebert, her ultimate origins are unknown, though the *Annales* of Fulda describe her as a native of some region of Germany. She appeared in the villages around Mainz preaching that she had had a special revelation from God and knew some of the secrets of the divine heart, including the exact date of the End of the World, which she said would take place that very year.

It is not difficult to understand Theuda's personality, especially since the preacher of doom with his little band is not unknown today. Theuda had the necessary charisma, and the people followed her as they had followed Aldebert, seeking from the lips of an extravagant madwoman the religious satisfaction they were unable to derive from ordinary religious expression. She was a talented preacher, and many of the common people of both sexes followed her, bestowing gifts upon her and begging her to pray for them as if she were a saint. In this instance, the extraordinary thing is that some men in holy orders seem to have abandoned their posts to follow her as well. It was not until the thirteenth century produced the prophetess Guglielma in Italy and the fourteenth produced Saint Catherine of Siena that a female religious figure with such charismatic qualities appeared again; later there were other examples, like Jeanne d'Arc, the Holy Maid of Kent, or Anne Hutchinson in New England.

Theuda was not allowed to continue her activities for long. She was brought into Mainz under guard and taken before the archbishop, who summoned the clergy in an informal synod [5] and examined her carefully. She made the defense, natural enough in her fear, that she was only doing as she had been told. When asked who had ordered her to go about the countryside preaching nonsense, she replied that it was a "certain priest," but it is likely that this priest was nothing more than a figment of her imagination. Her case was deemed unworthy of long deliberation, and judgment was quickly forthcoming: she was forbidden to preach any longer and received a public whipping to insure that she remembered. Whether she then returned to her home, wherever it was, we do not know, but there is no indication that she continued to cause trouble.

Some of the other assaults upon the dignity of the Church in the ninth century sprang less from spiritual enthusiasm than from brutal violence. One Burgand gathered together a sizable group of followers in the diocese of Bordeaux in the reign of Archbishop Frotaire (860–876) and with their help broke into churches, where they laid hands on the altar and seized chalice and paten as well as the holy oil. Their motive may have been theft or vandalism, or it may have been an explicit challenge to the Church; at any rate, they deliberately desecrated the most sacred utensils of Christian worship.[6] Burgand and his followers were thrown into chains and sentenced to a penance of seven years after which they might be readmitted to communion.

Another man named Liutward, who had come from the humblest origins, rose to a position of influence and power under King Arnulf of Germany (887–899). Directly Arnulf came to the throne in 887 he raised this Liutward to great favor. To begin with Liutward's activities were of a safely carnal nature. Protected by the king's favor and eager to build up his social standing by the time-honored method of making marriages between his family and those of higher quality, he embarked on a program of carrying off the daughters of the German nobility north and south of the Alps in order to marry them off to his friends and relatives. His respect for the Church was so small that he sent some of his bravos to force their way into a nunnery in Brixen, kidnap a young noblewoman, and carry her off to be married to his nephew. The horrified nuns invented their own happy ending to this story: one of them had a vision in which she saw God striking the infamous nephew dead on his wedding night so that the young woman might remain a virgin.

But this extraordinary Liutward did not confine himself to abduction, for he was accused of indulging indiscriminately in rape and theology. He is said to have maintained that the Redeemer was "one in the unity of his substance but not of his person," and the chronicler attacks Liutward for separating the human personality of Christ from the divine. Whatever the reason that Liutward held such an extraordinary doctrine, the emperor was unable or unwilling to resist the pressures against his friend, and at a council at Kirchheim in Alsace, Arnulf declared him stripped of his dignities and expelled from the palace. Liutward fled to Bavaria, where another Arnulf, this one the son the Liutpold upon whom King Arnulf had bestowed the county of Bavaria, was already filled with the ambition of declaring the independence of his county from the rest of Germany and standing in opposition to the authority of the German king. Count Arnulf received Liutward with pleasure, and together they plotted against the throne of the man who had done so much to raise them both to power.

The political machinations continued, but we hear nothing more of the heretical. Indeed, it seems unlikely that a man of Liutward's political and dynastic interests would have interested himself in theology at all, let alone taken a position that would have given his enemies a lever against him. His enemies among the nobles and in the Church were numerous, and it is probable that the heretical charges against him were either completely false or, more likely, that in his ignorance he may have made theologically imprecise statements that his enemies made haste to use against him.[7]

Around 970 a schoolman named Vilgard of Ravenna chose to defend the study of the ancient classical authors against a rising wave of attack on their place in a proper Christian education.[8] Virgil, Cicero, and the other great Roman authors had always been read and valued by Christians, but there was a good deal of suspicion of them also, since they were not, after all, Christians themselves. From the time of Justin Martyr, himself philosophically trained, Christian writers had defended the classics; from the time of Saint Jerome's dream that he was accused before the Bar of Judgment for being a Ciceronian rather than a Christian, other Christian writers had warned against the pernicious effects of overindulging in the pagan classics. Toward the turn of the eleventh century, distrust of the classics was becoming more prominent, and Vilgard's impassioned defense of the ancients put him in a danger-out position. The facts of the case are somewhat obscure. We know that Vilgard was a grammarian learned in the classics, and that he was fond of citing Juvenal, Virgil, and Horace at length—a fault, if it was one, committed by many of the Fathers. Very likely he placed great weight upon their opinions and cited them, as was the wont of medievals, as authorities. This again was nothing unusual, as the *Aeneid* had always been used, next to the Bible itself, as a special source of authority and even of prophecy. Vilgard may have made his points too strongly, however, for he was accused of citing the pagan authors as infallible authorities. The dicta of Virgil and Juvenal were apparently as infallible as the dicta of Luke or Paul. This in itself would place Vilgard in the category of an eccentric schoolteacher, perhaps a bit pedantic, whose enthusiasm for his subject carried him beyond the bounds of prudence, and he was formally condemned by Archbishop Peter VI of Ravenna.

But Radulf Glaber, the source of our knowledge of the schoolmaster's career, tells us that Vilgard had many disciples in Italy and in Sardinia, and that Sardinians infected with the heresy had taken ship and infected a portion of the Spanish people with the error. It is possible that Vilgard would have been able to enlist the support of a few other classical enthusiasts for a doctrine that granted infallibility to classical authors, but it is highly improbable that great numbers would have flocked to such a standard. It is true that there is a modern parallel in the elevation of Victor Hugo to the level of a cult figure by the strange Vietnamese sect, the Cao Dai, but even in the Middle Ages, with their susceptibility to strange doctrines, it is impossible to imagine that large numbers of people in the western Mediterranean would have subscribed to such a movement in favor of Virgil or Horace. When the account adds that many of the heretics were hunted down with fire and the sword the idea becomes ludicrous: one envisions Italian peasants expiring at the stake with a line from the *Odes* on their lips. Clearly there is something wrong. Lea[9] imagined that Vilgard must have been a Catharist, and that this would explain the popularity of his doctrines. Certainly the only people in Italy that we know of from other sources who were pursued with sword and flame were the purported Manichaeans of Monteforte in 1028. But that was fifty years after Vilgard's time, and, as Borst points out,[10] all the evidence is against Vilgard's having had anything to do with Catharism. Radulf himself wrote in the early eleventh century and describes other heretical movements, and it is therefore very unlikely that he would have himself confused the heretics of Monteforte with the followers of Vilgard. Either Vilgard held other doctrines of which we know nothing, or Radulf was simply exaggerating the size of his following.[11]

Shortly after the turn of the century a peasant of the village of Vertu near Châlons-sur-Marne, a town that was more than once to have problems with heresy,[12] began to preach a strange doctrine. This man, Leutard by name,[13] was of the same variety of prophet as Aldebert and Theuda: the spirit of prophecy and truth welled up within him and compelled him to speak. Unlike Aldebert and Theuda, however, he was a native of the area in which he made his reputation. One day, probably while working in the fields, Leutard became convinced that a swarm of bees had lodged itself in his innards and that to rid himself of these unwelcome guests he must set himself to preaching. There is not the slightest suggestion of the charlatan in Leutard, as there may be in Aldebert or Theuda, for there is no indication that he took money from his followers. His conviction that a swarm of bees was active in his belly was a pathological delusion of being filled by the Spirit moving within him.

Pfister, Borst, and Lea,[14] among others, assumed that Leutard was influenced by dualist doctrines. Upon his "conversion," Leutard went home and drove his wife out, preaching that marriage was immoral. He broke crucifixes and images, and he rejected the Old Testament as a source of revelation, saying that some of the prophets were to be believed and others not. None of Leutard's doctrines but the last arouse any arresting suspicion of Catharism. The rest derive from puritanism, for Leutard, like Aldebert, was in the tradition of Eccentricity bordering on Reform Dissidence. Leutard derived his popular support, as Aldebert did and Tanchelm would later, from his attack on the corruption of the clergy and his teaching of the apostolic ideals of the worth of the poor and ignorant. This explains Leutard's teaching that the people should withhold tithes from the clergy. This doctrine, which has nothing to do with apostolic teaching and even less with Catharism, sprang purely from the resentment of the clergy by the people. Some historians suggest that there is a difficulty in explaining the popuarity of this doctrine, since people in the Middle Ages did not as a rule object to paying tithes to the clergy but accepted it as their just and bounden duty. This objection enormously exaggerates the piety of the Middle Ages and ignores the fact that while it is possible that many people did not object to paying tithes to a clergy they respected, they would strenuously object to paying tithes to a not infrequently incompetent and immoral clergy. Finally, one cannot disregard the enormous quantity of capitularies, synodal decrees, and other evidence that refusal to pay tithes and resentment of tithing were very widespread indeed.[15] There can be no doubt that Leutard's attack on tithes, whether calculated for that purpose or not, purchased for him a great deal of popular support.

There is evidence for this support. Leutard was arrested and brought before the aged Bishop Gibuin II of Châlons who, in accordance with the usual procedure, summoned a synod to examine the heretic. The clergy easily refuted the ideas of the simple peasant, and he probably recanted. One can imagine the despair of this unlettered hind who, convinced that the Spirit within was urging him to speak and encouraged by the people to prize his own saintliness, was now totally bested in debate with the bishop's men. Had not Christ promised that the Holy Spirit would speak for the true believer in times of persecution? His faith must have been shaken and his self-esteem shattered by his humiliation before the synod. In the year of grace 1004, totally despairing, he cast himself into a well and drowned. But even after his suicide, his effect upon the peasantry was great. Eleven years later, in October, 1015, Bishop Roger I held a synod at Châlons to take measures to destroy the last vestiges of the heresy. We hear no more of it after this, but a movement that persists eleven years after the death of its master is one that had a good initial store of strength. As in the time of Aldebert and of Theuda, the people had rallied to a charismatic popular leader.

Leutard was a reformer as well as a madman, but the people participated indiscriminately in religious activities that were aimed at reform and those that were purely lunatic. Alberic, a priest of Fougères in Brittany during the pontificate of Bishop Silvester of Rennes (1076–1096), engaged in numerous immoral activities.[16] This rascal had robbed another priest, Reginald, and was further addicted to stealing the collection money in his own church by the expedient of taking the coins offered him into his hand and surreptitiously letting them slip down his sleeve into his garments. Our witness, a monk named Fulk of Saint Martin's of Tours, claims to have watched the performance with his own eyes. And this scoundrel was not only a thief but a madman. He laid the cross (presumably of his own church) upon the altar and smeared it with human excrement; the outrage was discovered by a priest named Geoffroi and a scribe named Eudes, who brought other witnesses to confirm what they had seen. At first they planned to hale Alberic before the bishop in Rennes, but for some reason they were unable to do this and satisfied themselves with reporting him. The bishop took it seriously enough to send the archdeacon of Rennes, Arnulf, to investigate. Arnulf uncovered a number of scandals, among them that Alberic had for three or four years refused absolution in confession to many of the women in his parish unless they agreed to share his bed.

Thus far Alberic appears as nothing more than a revolting lunatic;

his other actions are even more revealing. Alberic poured animal blood [17] all over the altar of his church and over the altar cloth and all the coverings, letting it run down and then capturing it again in a vessel. He maintained that the blood had been rendered holy by this process and he took it as a gift to a neighboring monastery, where the monks accepted it with thanks, probably tricked into thinking that it was a valuable relic. The sacred blood was displayed, and the people came in large numbers from all around to venerate it as a thing of great virtue. Neither Fulk nor Albert, the narrators of this episode, tell us what ultimately became of Alberic, but we can have little doubt that his frauds were exposed and that he received due punishment. In any event, the credulity of the people had again been demonstrated.

An extraordinary example of bizarre demonstrations took place at Sint Truiden in the diocese of Liège between 1133 and 1136.[18] Sint Truiden began to be developed economically in the twelfth century, when it found itself on the new route from Cologne to the coast,[19] and a cloth industry arose, nothing like the vast enterprises shortly to appear in Flanders,[20] but sufficient to support a vast number of weavers. These weavers were paid workers, extremely poor, and formed a kind of proletariat.[21] The local peasants began to resent them. Some of the weavers were strangers to these localities and disliked by the natives for this reason, and the cloth industry was generally feared as an innovation and therefore a disruptive influence in the community.

In this instance, popular indignation against the weavers chose to manifest itself in an unusual manner. A peasant from a village called Inda, in which there was a monastery known as Kornelimünster, near Aachen, seems to have detested the weavers for personal reasons. This dislike must have bordered on the pathological, for he went to enormous pains to play a gigantic trick on them. In a nearby forest, with the help of some friends, he constructed a wooden boat, placing it on wheels. Having secured the connivance of the authorities, he and his companions rounded up as many of the local weavers as was feasible and somehow forced them to draw the vessel behind them from Inda to Aachen. The choice of this extraordinary method of humiliating the weavers has been examined by Paul Bonenfant. Since the conceit of the "Ship of Fools," the *Narrenschiff,* does not appear in literature until the fifteenth century, there is little possibility of any connection here. Bonenfant notes that the weaver's spool was called a *navette,* or *Weberschiffchen,* because of its fancied resemblance to a boat, and the fact that on the first stage of its journey the boat had no sail made it resemble the spool all the more.[22]

At Aachen the strange cortege was joined by huge crowds of both sexes and all ages. Bonenfant believes that the entire episode was nothing more than a cruel joke upon the weavers. It is possible to view the trip from Kornelimünster to Aachen as a mere amusement, but at Aachen the character of the episode changed. It was no longer a question of one man's revenge upon the weavers, no longer a question of a few unfortunates pulling a rolling bark up and down the slopes west of the Rhine. The boat was now followed by a throng, growing daily, which seemed willing to continue to follow wherever it went. From Aachen it was drawn to Maastricht, where it was fitted out with a sail. On from Maastricht to Tongeren it went, from Tongeren to Bergloon, and from Bergloon to the walls of Sint Truiden, a mad ship sailing up the green slopes and rolling down into the valleys, pulled by sweating human oxen and steadied by the ready hands of a mad crowd. Fifty miles it is from Kornelimünster to Sint Truiden, and how long it took the weavers' ship to make its voyage we do not know, but it must have been several days at least. At night when they paused to rest, one might have seen the weird bulk of the ship looming up in some nighttime meadow, illuminated by the flickering light of the campfire around which strange revelers danced. What had perhaps started as a spoof was becoming a major demonstration. By the time the boat reached Sint Truiden, a huge crowd surrounded it, shouting and reveling. The abbot of Sint Truiden, Rodulf, pleaded with the citizens of his town to ignore the boatmen's saturnalia which would, he said, bring ruin upon the whole town. But the townsmen, no more immune to the lure of the madness than the inhabitants of Bergloon or Maastricht, refused to heed his admonitions and poured forth from the gates to add their efforts to the general confusion. Completely abandoning themselves to revelry in a frenzy like that of the later manic dancers of the Middle Ages, the people circled the craft and began to worship it. How sincerely this worship was meant, and how much it was part of a carnival that knew no limits, is open to question, but it is clear that this was no longer an economic or social demonstration against the weavers, but instead indication of the willingness, even eagerness, of the people to give vent to an enthusiasm, an ebullience, that everyday religion and everyday life blocked.

The assertion of the chronicler that the affair represented a reversion to ancient paganism is scarcely credible for the twelfth century, at which late date overt paganism would not have occurred. Such a statement must have been an embellishment of the imagination. Medieval chroniclers had a passion for discovering ancient origins in anything they touched, and the chronicler of Sint Truiden's classical bent is revealed in his frequent references to the authors of the Golden Age and in his plagiarism from their works. This was no recrudescence of ancient polytheism, either Roman or Germanic. Nonetheless, the willingness of the peasants to participate in what soon became rites of a highly questionable nature reveals that underlying lack of real understanding of Christianity which persisted throughout the early Middle Ages. Their religious Eccentricity was the product of grossness and ignorance, but it was religious Eccentricity nonetheless. Bonenfant's assertion that the chronicler exaggerated his report because of the clergy's sympathy for the weavers as well as their fear of social tensions created by the attack upon them is not brought out by the text, which affirms first of all that the weavers were more overweening and full of pride than anyone else and then, later, that the weavers had brought upon themselves the just punishment of God for leading people away from the hallowed life of labor on the soil. Aside from the misplaced classical allusions, there is no reason to doubt the testimony of the chronicler, who was an eyewitness to those of the events he could bring himself to watch.

For the revelry soon became an orgy. The weavers were forced to work day and night packing the boat with provisions and treasures, as though it were an errant shrine. By the light of day, and at night by the light of the flames, the crowd danced and sang blasphemous songs. A strange rite, recalling the magical powers attributed to the Ark of the Covenant, was invented, whereby anyone except the weavers who touched the ark was forced to leave a gage with them until it was redeemed, presumably with money. The weavers seem thus to have been transformed into religious Janissaries, a variety of Levite slaves to the jesting crowd. Perhaps in some strange fashion the weavers were turning the affair to their own account. As night fell upon the ship's first evening at Sint Truiden, the women of the town issued forth from their dwellings "dishevelled, some half-naked," to join the throng in their wild processions and choruses around the ship. The blasphemous caroling continued until the middle of the night, at which time the revelers broke up into small groups or pairs of either sex and gave themselves up to a debauchery whose description our chronicler modestly leaves to "those who desire to watch and participate."

The orgies at Sint Truiden continued no less than twelve days, a longer period than peasants could usually claim as a holiday. The news of the spree must have spread about the countryside and lured many a hind and his wench to the scene, so that we must image a carnival whose population is continually shifting as some tired and went home to their duties while others arrived and refreshed the assemblage with their vigor. After twelve days—one wonders why not earlier—the authorities of town and monastery gathered to decide what measures would have to be taken. The soundest counsel, so the chronicler says, suggested that the boat be set afire, but the majority insisted that this would provoke a riot and that the best course was to persuade the revelers to move on with their precious ship. This counsel prevailed, as it doubtless had at Aachen, Maastricht, Tongeren, and Bergloon.

The weakness of the authorities induced them to tolerate more than modern authorities ever would, though they acted similarly in attempting to get criminals out of town and sending them on to the next community. Nonetheless, finally following the decision of these authorities, the disordered procession set out from Sint Truiden for the neighboring town of Léau, still in the diocese of Liège but within the domains of the count of Louvain. Getting wind of what was afoot, the count, less tolerant than the other authorities, arranged to meet the wild band and destroy the ship. The count also used this opportunity not only to disperse the revelers, but to invade and ravage the territory of the abbey of Sint Truiden. With this violence ended the episode of the weavers' ship, another of the popular manifestations of the disorderliness of medieval religious life. What proportions the madness might have attained had not the count of Louvain put an end to it with the sword may only be surmised by considering later popular movements, greater in both madness and might, such as that of the *Pastoureaux* in thirteenth-century France.

Another and better known movement of popular madness arose in Brittany in the fourth decade of the twelfth century.[23] It was there that the spirit that had moved Aldebert, Theuda, and Leutard appeared again, in the person of a fanatical and crazed man named Eudo,[24] a native of Loudéac in Brittany. It is possible that he was of noble birth, though the evidence for this derives from a source composed fifty years after his death, so that one would be tempted to dismiss the notion and to suppose that he was, like his predecessors, of humble birth, if it were not for the extraordinary fact that he was able to read and write. By the most reliable sources we are told that he knew his alphabet and even circulated mandates and written instructions to his followers. All the sources agree that Eudo was not in holy orders, but he must have attended a monastic or cathedral school for a while to have obtained what education he had. It is possible that he sprang from a poor family and was awarded a free education owing to his promise as a scholar; this was common practice in medieval schools, and certainly his fertile imagination, if it manifested itself at an early age, would have given indications of intelligence to his preceptors. In the last analysis, the question of his origins is insoluble, but perhaps the best guess makes him a younger son of an impoverished noble family who had first been sent to receive an education in preparation for a career in the Church and who somewhere went off the track.

Like Aldebert and Theuda, Eudo began to preach his own message to the people. Very likely he wearied of the rigorous course of studies preparing him for the priesthood and elected to set himself up as a preacher on his own. He began to preach some time around 1145[25] and found that he had the requisite skill with words and attractiveness of personality to make a success of it, for he began to attract large crowds, and many were those who abandoned home and field to follow his charismatic leadership. As usual, his followers were drawn from the peasantry and the simple folk. The chroniclers heap scorn upon their stupidity and gullibility. But Eudo was preaching what they wanted to hear; from his lips they heard expositions of the Scriptures, and he did not hesitate to reinforce their loyalty by appealing to their ignorant pride. Upon them he bestowed the names of angels, of prophets, or apostles, or names of virtues like "Wisdom," "Knowledge," and "Justice," and though he had never completed the training required for the reception of holy orders himself, he consecrated his followers bishops and even archbishops. Even Aldebert had not gone this far, or he had not been clever enough to. Aldebert had emphasized his own dignity; Eudo emphasized that of his followers as well, and this in turn made them the more eager to believe in his. These pathetic Bishops and Archbishops, Principalities and Powers, were so devoted to their master, whom they came to consider divine, that they followed him everywhere, even to death itself. Numbers preached his doctrine in various areas and, persecuted by the authorities, suffered torture. Refusing to recant, many were put to death, one deluded fellow on his way to the stake calling upon the earth to fulfill Eudo's promise by opening and swallowing him up. Such was the faith that Eudo instilled in the minds of his devotees.

With what doctrines had he won over such a large body of loyal followers? Some of his practices and doctrines are hidden from our view by the reluctance of the chronicler of Gembloux to reveal them lest the reader be scandalized or, worse, converted. Though not an ordained priest, Eudo celebrated masses and preached to the people. These are actions common to his predecessors and represent, as they did with them, a willingness to challenge the established Church, a feeling that the spiritual gifts dispensed by the Church were inadequate, and a disregard for the whole system of apostolic succession upon which the Church based her claim to authority. Though we cannot ascertain the exact nature of his kerygma, we know that he used the Scriptures, quoting from them, expounding them, and engaging in disputes over their meaning. In this he was like the Reformists in their desire to draw inspiration directly from the Scriptures rather than through the medium of the teaching Church, and it is very likely that, like his predecessors and successors in this tradition, he taught something like apostolic poverty. He would be unusual among medieval dissidents if he had not, and the fact that he began his career by living an eremitical life in the forest is a positive indication. The large following he commanded suggests that he made successful use of the apostolic commandment to "leave all that you have and follow me."

But, like Aldebert before and Tanchelm after, Eudo passed from teaching the apostolic life as a follower of Christ to maintaining his own preeminent holiness. Indeed, he went further than Aldebert had ever done and proclaimed that he was the Son of God himself. This he announced in explicit terms, and claimed that it was his name that was meant in the phrase used at the end of prayers, "per *eundem* Dominum nostrum Jesum Christum." "Through *the same* Jesus Christ our Lord" was translated as "Through *Eudo,* Jesus Christ our Lord." [26] At the council of Reims he made such a statement and followed it up by revealing to the assembled prelates another token of his divinity: he had a stick forked in the shape of a Y, which represented the Trinity—Father, Jesus-Eudo, and Holy Spirit. When the two ends of the fork were pointing up, two-thirds of the universe belonged to the other Persons of the Trinity and the remaining third to Eudo; when the stick was reversed, Eudo had dominion over the two parts and left only one part to the Father and Holy Spirit.

Several chronicles assert that Eudo engaged in incantations and spells, and though this is by no means impossible in the light of his other deranged activities, such charges are bandied about in too many cases to be very convincing in this one. A more serious charge is the one that would make of Eudo a gnostic or a dualist. Runciman, Borst, and others have considered this likely. There are two bits of evidence that have been adduced to support such a position. First, he gave his followers names of angels and virtues, and this has a gnostic ring to it. But we must remember that Eudo made bishops of them as well, and the assigning of these extraordinary names seems to have been part of his program of flattery rather than an attempt to spread gnosticism. Next, there is the use of the word *Eon,* which Eudo may have adopted as a second name. Runciman speaks of a "paraphernalia of *eons,*" and relates this choice to gnostic teaching in which the term is frequently employed with a number of connotations. But it is by no means certain that Eudo ever did take another name.[27] And, if he did take such a name, it was more probably *Eun* than *Eon,* since one of the two most reliable sources, the Gembloux Continuation, has *Eun.* Finally, we must remember that Eudo was a Breton, and if he had taken another name, he was likely to have drawn it from the Breton language. Now, in Breton, there are two words that would fit his case:

one is *eon* itself, with the meaning of *froth* or *foam,* this being an unlikely appellation for anyone to adopt for himself, and the other being
eeun or *eun.* We must remember that the Gembloux Continuation
refers to Eudo as *Eun,* not Eon, and in Breton this word means
straight or *direct,* a name that he or his followers might very likely,
in view of their apostolic inclinations, have used. Eudo was *Eun,* the
straight one, the upright one, in contrast to the twisted followers of
the false orthodoxy. At any rate, the connection with the gnostic *eon*
must be ruled out and with it any suggestion that Eudo was tinted
with gnosticism or dualism.

It was therefore an evangelical teaching combined with a charismatic personality that convinced the simple of his saintliness or even
his divinity that acquired for Eudo his great following. The famine,
poverty, and dearth of the years 1144 to 1146 may also have had something to do with provoking popular unrest, even a popular desperation
that would cling to such a fragile straw as belief in the divinity of a
madman. With this group of disciples Eudo was able to give much
annoyance to the authorities. With what must have been at first a
small entourage, he took up residence in the forest of Brecilien in
Brittany, and from there migrated to other woods, leading a semi-
eremitical life of poverty and mortification. There his reputation grew,
his band expanded, and at last they left the Breton wilds to spread
their word abroad. They preached in many areas with increasing success, using force to effect conversions when eloquence failed. Appearing
before monasteries, convents, and isolated churches, they would demand that the inhabitants leave all behind them and come away to
follow Eudo the Christ. On several occasions, having been met with
refusals, they invaded monasteries by force and dispersed the monks.
Pillaging and riot marked such events, for even where the leadership
of such an undisciplined band is sincere, there are always ill-inten-
tioned followers or hangers-on, and the sources indicate that there
were acts of destruction in many a diocese.

It would be helpful to know how far, geographically, Eudo's efforts
were extended. There are some strange but hardly credible indications
that his heresy penetrated all the way to the south of France. The
Annales of Magdeburg state that the band was active in Gascony, of
all places, and the *Annales Casinenses,* which were geographically re-

moved from the scene of action, place them in Spain. These annals, however, depend upon the Breton chronicle, and the statement about Gascony must have been derived from the Breton chronicler's remark that the followers of Eudo were particularly active in the diocese of Alet,[28] which is in Languedoc, not far from the Spanish border and relatively close to Gascony, close enough for a German chronicler to make a geographical mistake.

There are three possible explanations of this remark. One is that it is true. The sources all indicate that the heresy pullulated in a number of dioceses. But it is hardly likely that Alet, at the other end of the kingdom, would have been mentioned erroneously by the sources when no other area in between is specifically cited as a theater of Eudo's activity. The route between Brittany and Alet is not and was not that direct; it is not at all likely that any doctrine would have flourished on a Breton-Aletian axis, and when the connecting points on that axis are lacking, we are inclined to dismiss its possibility. The second explanation is that the chronicler erred and wrote Alet when he meant to write Angers or Avranches, which are closer to Brittany. The fact that the word "diocese" was used in connection with Alet, when that town was in the twelfth century not yet an episcopal see, is evidence in favor of this theory. Yet it is scarcely likely that a Breton chronicler would err in writing the name Alet, a far and to him obscure town, in place the names of towns much more familiar and close at hand. The third and best solution is that the chronicler confused the followers of Henry the Monk with those of Eudo. Henry was a heretic who had appeared in the north, at Le Mans, and then gone south to preach in sunnier climes. He was active at the same time as Eudo, he preached apostolic doctrines, and his activity would have been known to a northern chronicler. Other chroniclers mentioned the two together, though they had no overt connection, and the council of Reims condemned both. Hearing of the rise of such heresy in the south, a Breton chronicler might well, out of local pride, ascribe the movement to the efforts of a Breton heretic. Though heretics are undesirable, he might have thought, if one is going to have notoriety, then let it be a Breton.

We must limit Eudo's influence to the north, then, and it was great enough there so that such a limitation need not detract from his importance. Archbishop Hugh of Rouen induced the apostolic delegate Bishop Alberic of Ostia to preach against the heretics, followers of either Eudo or Henry of Lausanne, and Alberic had a speaking engagement to this end at Nantes, where popular enthusiasm for the heretics was so great that attendance at his speech was very small and the champion of orthodoxy accomplished little.

When it was announced in 1148 that Pope Eugenius III, on a tour of the north, would hold a general synod at Reims that year, the Breton authorities elected to seize the opportunity to put an end to Eudo's disruptive activities. A Breton bishop, which one we do not know, had Eudo and a number of his followers arrested and brought in custody to the great council, which opened March 21, 1148. The council dealt with a number of cases involving dissidents, among them Henry of Lausanne, Arnold of Brescia, Gilbert de la Porrée, Peter of Bruys, and the defunct antipope, Pierleone (Anacletus II). In such a context the trial of one more heretic fitted nicely. Eudo was examined before the council and interrogated carefully. The sophisticated bishops were less horrified than amazed at his insane doctrines and, when he produced his forked stick, were unable to refrain from laughter. Their hilarity did not prevent them from adjudging him guilty of heresy, however, and it is possible that a severe penalty would have been visited upon him had not the Breton bishop who had arrested him pleaded for leniency. Dumbfounded and intimidated by the august assembly, mocked and made sport of by all, Eudo was no more successful in keeping his composure than Leutard; he recanted, admitted his error, and threw himself upon the mercy of the assembly. The Breton bishop had no difficulty, it may be imagined, in convincing the assembled prelates that Eudo was more lunatic than vicious, and the pope indicated that he was prepared to be lenient. Eudo was remitted to prison, in a tower belonging to the Archbishop of Reims,[29] where he was treated with the ordinary courtesy offered a prisoner in a medieval jail—that is to say, he was treated like an animal, exposed to the jokes and cruelties of his jailers, and given improper food and insufficient warmth. Before the year was up, he died, never more to see his native forests.

Eudo was mad, he was a troublemaker, he was dangerous, and his followers had done damage to property and perhaps even to life. Yet he had given something to the people that they wanted and needed, hope perhaps, and the illusion of dignity. He may have deserved a kinder fate; in any event the manner of his death must have atoned for much.

Among medieval Eccentrics, we have seen acts of superstition and violence which indicate that Christian principles had not altogether penetrated society. Most important, we have seen many dissenters, from Aldebert to Eudo, who possessed the conviction of internal fire, and combined the extravagance of the fanaticism of inner light with a popular program of opposition to the established Church. These dissenters were both pathetic and noble, pathetic in that their immoderate pride and self-esteem led into strange and devious ways and brought down upon them the censures of both reason and society, and noble in that their love and fervor could not be contained within conventional limits. From a religious context that was increasingly cold and distant they plunged into the warm and enveloping waters of commitment. Whatever their madness and their errors, theirs was not the shady trail of indifference but the burning path of concern.

5. *The Reactionaries*

In the same way that the Reformists were drawn into heresy by their overeager zeal and their exaggeration of the orthodox position on reform, that is to say, by their advance too quickly and too far, there were others who were left behind in the movement toward reform. These too were relegated by orthodoxy to the category of heretics. They were those who held to the old ways, to the buying and selling of offices, to the marriage of priests, to the imperialist position on lay investiture. When the battle lines were drawn up, they often took their stand as schismatics and supporters of antipopes. Their beliefs and practices had existed in the Church for a long while, but now the Church had moved beyond them and, looking back in her path, she castigated them as heretics for their failure to move as fast and in the same direction as she did. There was no "rise" of this sort of dissent. It is the reform movement that "rose" and inspired the advance of doctrine that left these heretics behind. They were conservative in their opposition to reform; when it triumphed, they were reactionary in their efforts to resist it.

Writers dealing with heresy have not often considered these simonists and nicolaitists as heretics. The hesitation has been owing to the confusion between intellectual and moral fault. In the argument of those who would not classify simonists and nicolaitists as heretics, a cleric's living in sin with a woman or taking a bribe is a question of moral fault, or sin, not of rejection of Christian doctrine, or heresy. This would be true if it were only the overt actions of individuals who were under consideration. But it is more. If a man has two wives, it is his sin. If he maintains that it is in accordance with Christian doctrine to have two wives, or, more, that it is permissible for everyone to have two wives, then he is in heresy. In like manner, if a priest sells or buys an office, he is in sin, but if he advocates such a trade or justifies it as Christian, then he is in heresy. The point is not that some few priests bought offices or took wives, but that a good many people, priests and otherwise, maintained that it was permissible to do so and that priests doing so could virtuously exercise their ministry. As Humbert of Silva Candida said of simoniacs:[1] "If however *they believe,* they are manifestly heretics." Gerhoh added that persistence in the error is necessary for it to be called heresy,[2] a stipulation that Aquinas would later use in his general definition of heresy.

In dealing with simonists, nicolaitists, schismatics, and givers and receivers of lay investiture, we are, then, sometimes dealing with heretics—but not always. Here as elsewhere the contemporary orthodox writers were sometimes careless in the profusion in which they scattered epithets. The term "nicolaitist," for example, was often applied to any priest who happened to be living with a woman; it was not restricted to those who maintained that it was in accordance with Christian doctrine for a priest to be living with a woman. This confusion, however, does not mean that true heresy of this sort did not exist. Another mitigating factor is the ability of the human mind to rationalize. It is not necessary to accept Abelard's position that sin lies only in the intention, rather than in the deed, to realize that most people who advocated simony or schism had probably convinced themselves that they were doing the right thing. No one who reads the impassioned and sometimes cogent arguments of Sigebert of Gembloux in favor of the married clergy could doubt that he was as sincere in the defense of his position as Humbert of Silva Candida was in his attack upon the simonists. One might conceivably argue that the simonists and their companions could be convicted only of material heresy and not of formal heresy, since they believed that they were holding the traditional doctrine of the Church against heretical innovations. If however, this argument were pursued it would lead directly into quicksand, because the solution could only be found once one had established what the legitimate authority in the Church was. For the purposes of this study, I have defined heresy as that held to be heresy by Rome at a given period, and Rome clearly condemned the simonists and nicolaitists. Those who disagreed persisted in doing so even while they knew full well that they stood against the pope's authority. Their categorization by the reformers as heretics is therefore justified in historical terms.

The situation may be clearly understood if we keep in mind that the criterion for orthodoxy was a changing one. The Church was progressing; Christian doctrine was building. The imperialists and nicolaitists were defending a position that the Church had, if not approved, at least tolerated. The marriage of clergy, speculation in land by clergymen, the interference of secular powers in ecclesiastical affairs, all these formed part of what was once the generally accepted pattern of Church life. The movement of reform came increasingly to question this state of affairs, and when reform captured the papacy in the mid-eleventh century, it was in a position to enforce its demands for change. The accession of Leo IX and his successors, then, represents a crucial point in the history of reaction as dissidence. Condemnations, particularly of simony, had occurred previously, but in the eleventh and twelfth centuries they increased greatly both in number and in vigor. And though the term "heresy" had previously been used in conjunction with these errors, especially with simony, its use became much more frequent under the reform papacy. And in this period of heightened concern for definitions of the Church's position, the popes and theologians must have meant it in a precise sense: the term "heresy" was not often used merely as an insult. When Gregory VII called simony *heresy,* he meant exactly that.

The Great Reform Movement was in a way a "cause" of this reactionary heresy, since it impelled the Church to advance, to leave these people behind, and then to have them labeled heretics because they would not keep up with the movement. While puritans deserted the Church because of its corruption, simonists, nicolaitists, and the other grosser dissidents opposed any movement in the direction of greater purity. That the determined attacks upon the reactionaries mounted by the reform papacy sometimes encouraged Reformist error of a donatist variety was a charge frequently made by the reactionaries and, as we have seen in the preceding chapters, it was a true one. Thus, in an ill-defined manner, the two extremes faced each other in this moral conflict as the two extremes of Monophysitism and Nestorianism once faced each other in intellectual conflict. In the development of Christian doctrine, determined conservatism may easily be transformed into reaction, and stubborn reaction contains as great a potential for heresy as hasty innovation.

These reactionaries deserve a place in the history of dissent, then, for several reasons. First, those of their contemporaries who supported the reform papacy believed that they were heretics, and in the strict sense. Second, they are of interest to the history of Reformist Dissidence because of the close dialectic between their ideas and those of the reformers. Third, they represented an open challenge to the view of the Church that was coming to be increasingly accepted, and our interest, as always, is in dissent as a whole rather than in precise theological definitions of heresy.

Simony.

Of all the reactionaries, the Simonists stirred up the biggest mare's nest. Simony is, generally speaking—we shall return to more precise definitions—the buying and selling of ecclesiastical offices and spiritual benefits. A simoniac is a person who engages in simony; a simonist is a person who advocates simony or maintains that it is licit. The term "neophyte" was often linked with the term "simoniac" from the time of Gregory the Great.[3] In the earlier Church, neophytes, newcomers to the Christian religion or laymen without adequate religious preparation, were occasionally ordained and even consecrated bishops without the proper preparation. Sometimes this was permissible when the candidate was outstanding, as with Saint Ambrose, but more often the office was purchased or gained through undue influence; hence the connection between neophytes and simoniacs.

The word "simony" is probably derived from the name of the seer Simon Magus, a native of Samaria. Simon was a worker of marvels and, impressed by the miracles wrought by the apostles, he offered Peter and John money that they might lay their hands upon him, for he wished thereby to obtain the power of the Holy Spirit. Peter's reply laid a curse upon him and those of his opinion: "Thy money perish with thee, because thou hast thought that the gift of God may be purchased with money."[4] Cursed though it was, the practice of obtaining spiritual office in this way became so common that several varieties of simony came to be distinguished by canon lawyers. There is simony *a manu,* where money or some other tangible object of value changes hands, simony *a lingua,* where influence is exerted or when payment is made in prayers or masses, and simony *ab obsequio,* where some temporal service is exacted from the person receiving office.[5] N. A. Weber offers the best general definition of simony: "the intended or real exchange of a supernatural good, or a natural good annexed thereto, for something that is temporal." [6]

Thus the number of offenses included under the rubric "simony" is great. The Fathers (Basil, Ambrose, and Jerome) commonly used the term, as did Pope Pelagius I and Gregory the Great. Fliche says that Gregory used it with the particular meaning of the sale of priestly office by a bishop. In the ninth century it was applied to the sale of episcopal offices as well, and this new meaning was fixed in the tenth century by Atto of Vercelli. He specified that the sale of bishoprics by lay princes was to be considered simony.[7] In the same century Abbo of Fleury enumerated the forms of simony as three: the sale of priestly ordinations by a bishop, the sale of episcopal consecrations by a metropolitan, and the sale of *any* ecclesiastical office by lay princes.[8] It was generally understood that both the sale and the purchase of spiritual goods were simony, though a distribution was made in regard to the validity of orders of simoniacs. If a man sold a spiritual office, he sinned, but his orders were not thereby annulled, since holy orders were indelible. If he bought his orders, they were invalid, and if he received orders from the hands of a man he knew was a simoniac, his orders were invalid. The nature of simony as a sin was defined with increasing precision as the years went by and the sin became more common. The sin itself was one outcome of the involvement of the Church in secular affairs.

But simony came to be not only a sin, but a heresy as well. Emerton is not wholly correct when he says that the use of the term was nothing more than a weapon that came readily to hand and that there was no theoretical justification for it.[9] One justification lies in the restriction of the term "heretic" to simonists, people who defended the institution, excluding mere simoniacs, who practiced but did not defend. But the line is difficult to draw. Does a great man in the public eye, an archbishop who openly sells offices, not in effect offer a public, though tacit, defense of his action? It is incontrovertible that Gregory VII and his contemporaries were not so judicious as to make the distinction between simonist and simoniac clear. Contemporaries offered other justifications for calling simoniacs heretics. The one that came most often to the medieval mind was that, since the sacraments are gifts of the Holy Spirit, to maintain that they can be sold is in effect to maintain that the Holy Spirit can be sold. Humbert of Silva Candida elaborated an even more tortuous argument. By their activities, Humbert argued, simoniacs in effect attack the Church, and if they do this they are heretics. Further, if they attack the Church they in effect leave her, and anyone who leaves her must deny Jesus Christ. Therefore simoniacs deny Jesus Christ, and no worse heresy (he might better have said apostasy) than that can be imagined. It is conceivable that this argument may have been somewhat disingenuous, but it was advanced nonetheless.

The history of the application of the term "heresy" to simony goes back to the Fathers, including Jerome. Gregory I used the term frequently and established it as a cliché, in which capacity it continued for some centuries. Churchmen often spoke of "simoniac heresy" as absently as they sometimes today speak of "atheistic Communism." No one thought out what the precise implications of the phrase were. In fact, between the death of Gregory I and the time of Saint Boniface, the term seldom appears. With the revival of the Church that began with the mission of the Anglo-Saxon, it appeared again, the first reference that I have found in the eighth century occurring in 744.[10] Following the precedent of Gregory the Great, "simoniac heresy" appeared fairly regularly in the eighth and ninth centuries, declined in the first part of the tenth century when European society was still distressed by the Second Barbarian Invasion, and increased again in the early eleventh. From the accession of Leo IX onward it was used so frequently as to defy tabulation. The conclusion from this is that in periods when the Great Reform Movement was strong, attacks against simony were naturally pressed with more vigor.

The effect of the reform papacy was not only to increase the number of condemnations of "simoniac heresy" but also to use the term more precisely.[11] The idea of simony as heresy was, after the mid-eleventh century, no longer a cliché inherited from Gregory the Great. In the mind of Gerhoh there was no question but that the simoniacs were really heretics;[12] to Humbert of Silva Candida their heresy was as bad as that of Arius or Novatian. To Peter Damian they were not all that bad. He considered them better than the Arians, though as bad as Novatian and the donatists. To Peter, simony was "the first of all the heresies to burst from the bowels of the devil."[13] Humbert, whose huge work in three books, *Adversus simoniacos* ("Against the Simoniacs") was the most sweeping condemnation of all, explored the subject at length. Since heresy is believing about God and his creatures what ought not to be believed, he said, and simony fits into this category, it is to be considered heresy: "It is manifest that the simoniacs have wandered from the faith."[14] Abandoning all moderation, Humbert finally concluded that he could not think of one other heresy that was as bad as simony; it was the most pernicious of all.[15] So great was the determination of the reformers to crush secular influence in the Church. In the period after the flush of battle, theologians continued to call simony heresy but with decreasing fervor, and eventually the term again became the cliché it had once been. In the twelfth century, Peter Lombard defined simony as heresy and calmly classified its variations;[16] Ivo of Chartres accepted his definition.[17] Aquinas and Bonaventure made the distinction between simoniac and Simonist more clearly than anyone in the earlier period. Aquinas said that simony "is called a heresy," but that it is really a heresy only in the sense that the simoniac *protests* that he is master of a spiritual gift and can buy or sell the Holy Spirit. In such an instance he is really a Simonist. Bonaventure likewise held that simony is heresy only if the guilty *believe* that spiritual goods can really be bought. To the Scholastics, simony was more a sin than a heresy, though they recognized its heretical implications.[18]

The violence that surrounded this controversy is seen not only in the fiery works of a reformer politician like Humbert inveighing against the simoniacs, but in the fierce reaction against the preaching of the reformers that the clergy of Cambrai showed against Ramihrd in 1077 when they put him to death. That such heat was generated proves that the question was very important in men's minds. It drew its warmth from the great struggle in Christian society between the ecclesiastical and the secular powers. A curious footnote is that accusations of simony were not leveled only against the imperial party or only by the supporters of the papacy. Before their classic struggle, Gregory VII praised Henry IV specifically because of his great work against simony and nicolaitism; later Henry was to become in Gregory's eyes the greatest of simonists.[19] In his deposition of Gregory VI at Sutri, Emperor Henry III accused the pope of simoniac heresy,[20] and Pope Alexander II was obliged to condemn German bishops who were accusing Hugh the White of simony.[21] Wherever used, the term generated anger. The controversy over simoniac heresy was a symptom of the great upheaval of Christianity that took place in the eleventh century.

Propertied clerks and lay investiture.

In its enthusiasm for the elimination of secular interference, the papal party used the term "heresy" more broadly than before. Gerhoh of Reichersberg even came close to hinting at the deepest problem of the Church, its involvement in material concerns, when he classified "propertied clergy" as well as simonists and nicolaitists as heretics.[22] No one took this definition very seriously, however, and it was not repeated.

More serious was the classification of lay investiture as heresy. Lay investiture and lay proprietorship of churches (*Eigenkirchenwesen*) were manifestations of the same central problem of the Church in the eleventh century, the one on a grand, the other on a petty, level. Though the tendency now in the Church is to encourage the participation of the laity, the situation was then otherwise. On the local level, lords owned churches and appointed their priests. The connection between this lay proprietorship and simony is very close. The candidate for the rectory or vicarate would ordinarily have to pay the lord a certain price to attain his election, or the lord would take the revenues of the land himself and pay the clerks a small percentage. This is simony or something very similar. Or Count X might transfer his holding of Church land to Sir Y in return for goods or services rendered or expected. This again borders on simony. Yet lay proprietorship as such was never condemned as heresy, probably because the leaders of the Church had decided to deal with the major threats from emperors and kings before dealing with petty interference on a local level.

The connection of lay investiture with simony is also close, for by its very nature it tends to simony. Kings and emperors were likely to ask candidates for bishoprics for assurances of material or political support before bestowing investiture upon them. Lay investiture was a violation of the rules against simony; more important, it was the most overt manifestation of the entrenchment of secular power in the Church. The struggle between pope and lay rulers in the so-called investiture conflict over this galling indication of secular power is well-known. In the heat of the controversy, the papal reformers once again brought out the term *heresy,* partly as a polemical weapon and partly in dead earnest.

The history of the variations in the methods of appointing bishops is a long and complicated one. Suffice it to say that, in the early Church, appointment by lay authorities was not recognized. The First Council of Nicea specified that a bishop was to be elected by other bishops and confirmed by the metropolitan.[23] From the time of Constantine on, the increasing power of the emperor led to modifications of this rule, and bishops were often appointed by emperor or king. So common had this custom become that, at the Lateran synod of 774, Hadrian I specifically ordered that no one was to consecrate bishops *until* they had been invested by the king.[24] The practice of the Church had changed. As early as the Second Council of Nicea in 787, however, resistance to the new state of affairs developed, and canon four of that assembly held that according to the "ancient rule" bishops were to be elected only by bishops.[25] In the west, the power of the Frankish rulers and their successors over the appointment of bishops continued, with the result that bishops were often simoniac, often worldly, and often more loyal to their prince than to the pope. This was a situation that Hildebrand would not tolerate. A few months after his election, he wrote to Anselm of Lucca forbidding him to take investiture from Henry IV,[26] and the battle was joined.

In 1075 a formal condemnation of lay investiture was issued, and soon anyone who engaged in this practice was condemned as a heretic. As the heat of battle grew, it was Emperor Henry IV and his creature the antipope Clement III who most often received this title.[27] Lay investiture was never called heresy as frequently as was simony, nor were there as many justifications offered for the usage. With lay investiture, the use of the word "heresy" was intended primarily as a political weapon. There were, however, a few theoretical justifications offered. Geoffrey, abbot of the Holy Trinity at Vendôme, wrote a little book entitled (in translation) *On Simony and Lay Investiture; Why Both Should Be Called Heresy*.[28] After offering the usual argument in regard to simony, that it was heresy because it involved belief that the Holy Spirit could be bought and sold, Geoffrey passed on to lay investiture. Investiture was truly given by Christ, he said. But if you practiced lay investiture, you said that you could give investiture in Christ's stead; in effect you were saying that your authority was higher than Christ's, which was clearly heresy.

This was flinging the syllogistic net a little far; Geoffrey's reasoning did not seem much more convincing then than it does now, and there are few other attempts to bestow the strict theological definition of heresy upon lay investiture. The investiture problem was solved early in the twelfth century; the deeper problem of election and control over bishops continued, and it is somewhat strange that no one specifically attacked the appointment of bishops by secular rulers as heresy. The medieval mind tended to think in terms of symbols, and lay investiture was the symbol of all the deeper dissensions between the papacy and the secular power.

Schism.

Schism in the medieval Church was related to lay investiture and simony. The problem of lay interference was the most embittered of the Church's problems in the eleventh century. It was here that the papacy most consistently and most firmly drew the line, so that simonists and others who would not move along with the new currents found themselves ipso facto in opposition to the authority of the pope and in schism. Schisms and sects had existed from the beginning, and the original meaning of the word *hairesis* was simply "schism." The two terms early became separated, "heresy" referring to doctrinal error while "schism" was applied to those who rejected the proper authority of the Church without necessarily falling into doctrinal error. Now in the course of the eleventh century two things happened. First, it was established more firmly than before that it was the pope who was the legitimate authority in the Church; to reject this authority was to be in schism. Second, the terms "schism" and "heresy," so long distinguished, came to merge again.

Schism was, from the eighth century, on rare occasions described as heresy. In the eighth century, the Eastern emperors and their followers were called schismatics and heretics, but the terms were not quite equated and were brought into conjunction more on account of the doctrinal error of the Iconoclast emperors than on account of their break with the authority of the bishop of Rome. In the ninth and tenth centuries, the terms were rarely used together, an exception being the case of the antipope John XVI, whom Pope Gregory V described as a heretic in 997.[29] Schism and heresy seem to have been equated by Clement II in referring to the recent struggles between three claimants to the papal throne, the struggle that Emperor Henry III terminated in 1046 by placing the triple crown upon Clement's brow.[30] The schismatic bishop Cadalus of Parma, who as antipope took the title of Honorius II, was described as a heretic in about 1063.[31]

Schism came generally to be considered a heresy after the accession of Gregory VII, in that period when the epithet "heresy" came to be applied to an increasing variety of offenses. The citations linking the terms "heresy" and "schism," so infrequent before 1073, multiplied rapidly from 1074 on, particularly in 1076 when the assembly of Worms under the leadership of Henry IV declared Gregory VII deposed. Throughout the Gregorian period and the early twelfth century, schism was commonly described as heresy.

The range of usage was fairly broad. Bishops taking lay investiture and therefore in effect ranging themselves against the papacy were condemned as heretics and schismatics.[32] At the time of the Photian schism of the ninth century, the Greeks were so described, though no overt doctrinal question had been raised at this time.[33] Opponents of the reform papacy, particularly Henry IV, often earned the sobriquet of heretic.[34] The antipopes, imperialist claimants to the papal throne, naturally received the title of schismatic, and that of heretic was usually added. Earlier, in 864, John XII had already condemned Leo VIII as *schismaticus et pseudopapa,* though the term "heresy" was not actually used. Wibert of Ravenna (Clement III), Bordinus (Gregory VIII), and Pierleone (Anacletus II) were all condemned as heretics.[35] The term was less commonly applied to local bishops who usurped their sees from reform bishops with the help of imperialist support.[36]

The heresy here, as with simony and lay investiture, consisted in opposition to the program of the reform papacy, which program came to be established as that of the Church. To call schism heresy was primarily a polemical device to make it seem as black as possible. Nonetheless, a few theoretical justifications were offered for the usage. Though as late as 1097 Deusdedit set a firm distinction between the two,[37] the synod held under the presidency of Paschal II on March 12, 1102, held that it was heresy to "teach and maintain that the (papal) anathema is to be contemned and that the ties that unite the church are to be held as naught." [38] Bruno, Bishop of Segni, writing around 1111, said that "all those are heretics who, deserting the Catholic Church, join Wibert's party and defend and believe his impious heresy." Earlier, Bruno had stated flatly that Wibert was a heretic and zealously went on to maintain that anyone who supported a heretic must of necessity be a heretic himself, a twelfth-century exercise in the art of imputing guilt by association.[39] Theologians generally distinguish between schism and heresy, but the sizable opposition to the papal reform program represented a strong body of dissent from the position that the Church as a whole was coming to occupy.

Nicolaitism and Incest.

The original nicolaitists were an obscure sect mentioned in the Apocalypse (ii:6–15), and by the end of the second century there were in Asia dualist, gnostic heretics called nicolaitists. There may have been little connection between these groups; Maurice Goguel suggests that the common denominator may have been a willingness to go too far in making the relationships between Christianity and paganism easier. Immorality was early associated with nicolaitism, but Goguel believes that this accusation was leveled at their doctrines rather than at improper practices.[40] In any event, the term "nicolaitism" acquired the connotation of immorality, especially sexual immorality, and in the Middle Ages it came to be applied specifically to married priests and to those who defended the marriage of priests.

Nicolaitism in this medieval sense of the word has some connection with simony in that married priests with children have more material concerns and are of necessity exposed more often to the temptation of trafficking in the goods of the Church. In the dialectic of Christian doctrine, the position of nicolaitism is more similar to that of lay investiture. While simony was never permitted by the Church, there was a time when the marriage of the clergy, like lay investiture, was tolerated. Thus the nicolaitists of the eleventh century are clearly reactionaries: they wished to return to a position that the Church had formerly permitted but now condemned. They did not keep up with the march of Christian custom. The theological objection arises that since the celibacy of the clergy has never been proclaimed *de fide* it may be considered a disciplinary injunction rather than a doctrine. Of late the Church has, on rare occasions, even dispensed from the rule in the case of non-Catholic clergy who convert but wish to become priests. But though theologically speaking nicolaitism may not be true heresy, the condemnation of nicolaitism by the eleventh-century papacy was absolute, and resistance to the papacy must be considered a form of religious dissent.

The impetus to celibacy in the clergy comes from the dualist, ascetic strain in Christianity. Primitive Christianity contained both world-accepting and world-rejecting elements derived from eastern dualism through Essenic Judaism and soon reinforced by the influence of Platonic idealism. The attitude of Saint Paul and of most of the Fathers toward the flesh is well known: celibacy and virginity are highly desirable, and one may marry only if one finds oneself unable to overcome one's weakness. The influence of monachism and the emphasis of the ascetic sects of the ante-Nicene Church enhanced the value of celibacy, and, though even Saint Paul had found room for a monogamous clergy, it was increasingly felt that bishops and priests at least ought to remain celibate. Though no formal requirements of celibacy were made in the early fourth century, the ascetic mood continued to increase, and by the time of Saint Ambrose it was considered the ordinary state of the clergy. About the end of the fourth century, local bishops began to pronounce formal condemnations of clerical marriage, and this tendency was reinforced by the example of Saint Augustine.[41]

Ambrose, Jerome, and Augustine all opposed the notion that a man might retain his wife after he had been ordained, Pope Gregory the Great issued general condemnations of married clergy, and the Carolingian dynasty under the influence of Saint Boniface attempted to enforce these rules. In spite of the increasing opposition to clerical wedlock on the part of the leaders of the Church, it is unquestionable that marriage, not to mention concubinage, continued to be common among the lower clergy, particularly in country districts, and was not unknown among the higher clergy as well. The reform papacy under Leo IX and his successors renewed the earlier condemnations and exerted itself to enforce them.[42] The fact that the reformer popes were obliged to exert themselves to a great degree in combating clerical marriage indicates how widespread it continued to be.

The eleventh-century authorities were determined, however, to stamp it out once for all. Previously the punishments meted out to clerical husbands had been relatively light, the most common being that they were overlooked for advancement. But in the eleventh century the penalties became more stringent. Already in 1022 the reform-minded Emperor Henry II had summoned a synod at Pavia in which clerics were forbidden under pain of deposition to wed or to keep women improperly. In addition, the sins of the fathers rested upon the shoulders of the children, for priest's children were declared serfs of the Church.[43] In 1059 the Lateran Council under the presidency of Pope Nicholas II repeated these admonitions and added the strict injunction that priests living with women were not to administer the sacraments or perform any priestly duty.[44] From that time forward, the reform party generally accepted the view that the characters of spouse and priest are irreconcilable, and the prohibition of clerical marriage was renewed from time to time, ever more strictly. The First Lateran Council of 1123 pronounced that marriage was automatically dissolved by holy orders, and that not only could priests not marry but married men could not become priests unless they put away their wives. Innocent II repeated these admonitions at Reims and Liège during his tour of the north.[45] Finally, the Second Lateran Council in 1139 formalized the rule that no one in Christendom was knowingly to hear masses said by nicolaitist priests. The final anathematization of nicolaitism was pronounced by the Fourth Lateran Council in 1215 under the presidency of Innocent III, and from that time to the present sacerdotal celibacy has been the accepted rule in the Catholic Church.

As with simony and lay investiture, it was the program of the reform papacy that connected nicolaitism with heresy. References to the immorality of priests as heresy were almost nonexistent before the Lateran synod of 1059. Clement, a contemporary of Aldebert whose name was linked with his by the letters of Saint Boniface,[46] was described by that worthy Englishman as a heretic. Clement's chief crime was his possession of concubines and at least two illegitimate children, but he also rejected the authority of the Church and spurned the Fathers, particularly Augustine, Jerome, and Gregory, and the canons of the Church dealing with celibacy. This indicates the logical connection between nicolaitism and heresy: if the Church condemns clerical marriage but one overtly defies the Church in practicing it, one impugns the authority of the Church. Clement, however, also held other peculiar doctrines, believing for example that at the harrowing of hell Christ led not only the virtuous but also all other men out of perdition, so that after his visit no man remained, the demons being left in sole possession of hell. Thus Clement was heretical on more than one score, and we cannot be sure that the term "heresy" was meant by Boniface to apply specifically to his irregular sexual activities. In the eighth century, as in the two centuries following, clerical marriage was regarded, when it was considered worthy of attention at all, as a sin rather than as a heresy.

As, also, with simony and lay investiture, it is necessary to make a distinction that escaped most of the zealous reformers of the eleventh and twelfth centuries. Any simple priest who took a wife or concubine could not be considered a heretic. To be actually in heresy, a man would have openly to declare that priests might legitimately be married and continue to perform the sacraments. Thus a bishop who, cognizant of the prohibition of clerical marriage by the Church, did nothing to remove the abuse from his diocese, would be closer to heresy than the simple parish priest keeping his woman, while there was no question as to the heresy of a man who positively proclaimed that clerical marriage was permissible.

Thus there are two separate questions in regard to the development of nicolaitist heresy: first, when and how often the term "heresy" was used to apply to the married clergy; and second, when and how often was the marriage of clergy openly defended against the increasingly clear consensus of the Church against it.

If it was not Clement's sexual activities that earned him the epithet of heretic in the eighth century, the first mention of clerical marriage as heresy appears at the time of Nicholas II's condemnation of 1059. The term "nicolaitism" is revived at the same time. The reasoning must have been somewhat like this: married clergy are heretics; what sort of heretics? immoral heretics; then they must be nicolaitists—for this was the early sect against whom accusations of immorality were most frequently lodged. In 1059 Peter Damian initiated the use of the term "nicolaitist heresy," his justification being that the nicolaitists as well as the simonists were defying the authority of the Church and therefore deserving of the name of heretics,[47] though at another point Peter drew the proper distinction between sinner and heretic, saying that a defense of sin was requisite to heresy.[48] In a letter of 1059 to the bishops of Gaul, Nicholas II explained the decisions of the synod of 1059, describing married clerics as nicolaitist heretics,[49] and after that the term was often used during his reign and those of Alexander II, Gregory VII, and their successors. It was used much less frequently than the term simoniac heresy, however, indicating that Churchmen were less sure of its definition, and often the terms *crimen* or *morbum* would be used in conjunction with nicolaitism rather than the specific *haeresis*.

It was left to Gerhoh of Reichersberg early in the twelfth century to offer the most complete theoretical justification of the use of the term *heresy* in this context. Quoting Nicholas II in his letter to the bishops of Gaul, Gerhoh maintained that it is just to call the nicolaitists heretics, and that this applies to both married and concubinary priests. Gerhoh went farther than Peter Damian and held that it is not necessary for a nicolaitist to defend his position for him to be so classified. The distinction between sinner and heretic holds for all errors, said Gerhoh, except for two, these being the errors of the simoniac and the nicolaitist. Nicolaitists and simoniacs are heretics not only because they defend their error but because of "the deed itself." In raising the question of why, if this were true, they were not condemned as such by the early

Church, Gerhoh stood on the brink of understanding the development of doctrine, but then he withdrew and said only that condemnations did occur earlier, even if the term "heresy" were not specifically used, an observation that is true enough but that misses the point.[50] Gerhoh's arguments are not totally convincing, and his apparent lack of self-confidence here is evidence that no one felt secure in using these terms.

Turning to the other side of the argument, it may be granted that those who overtly defended the marriage of the clergy in the face of frequent and vigorous condemnations in effect placed themselves in the position of dissenters. Extreme conservatives before the Church's position had been finally defined, after the reform position was firmly defined and entrenched these people found themselves reactionary dissenters. Clement, the contemporary of Aldebert, defended his activities, but in the eighth century this could not be considered heretical, since a letter of Pope Zachary to Boniface in 743 specifically tolerated clerical marriage, stipulating only that priests not exceed the measure of one wife apiece.[51] Around 894 a priest named Angelric in the diocese of Châlons-sur-Marne decided to take one Grimma to wife and went to the bishop complaining that people were objecting to this. To his chagrin he found that Bishop Mancion objected too, but what is significant is that the man should have showed so little hesitation in defending his position openly. Evidently the Church's position on clerical marriage had not yet been clearly defined.[52] In April, 967, Bishop Rather of Verona called a synod for the purpose of promoting celibacy in his see; to his horror he found that the majority of his clergy gallantly defended the role of the ladies in their lives, and did so publicly and unabashedly.[53] At Le Mans, no less a person than the bishop himself, Segenfrid (971–996), was openly married and had many children by his wife Hildeberga, upon whom he graciously bestowed the title of *episcopissa*.[54]

It was with the clarification of the Church's position in 1059 that the defenders of clerical marriage came really to be heretics. There had previously been the barest margin for disagreement; now the Church had spoken firmly, and any who did not fall into line were left behind. Orthodoxy had moved ahead, leaving those behind in the position of heretics. Lea held [55] that the election of the antipope Cadalus of Parma in 1061 provided the nicolaitists with a rallying point and permitted them to band together under his banner in resistance to the reform program. It is certain that the antipapal factions from then until well into the twelfth century often did provide a place of refuge for the reactionaries, and it is also true that the majority of the nicolaitist tracts date from this period. Bishop Ulrich of Imola (1053–1063) wrote his *Rescriptum* to Nicholas II around 1060, a treatise in which he argued that it was better for priests to wed lest they form even less savory attachments.[56]

Aiming his arguments at refuting Peter Damian's attack on the nicolaitists, Ulrich permitted himself to go so far as to question the pope's right to legislate such matters for the Church as a whole, a good indication of how the reactionary position could lead easily to schism. Bishop Altmann of Passau (1065–1091) found, in attempting to impose celibacy upon his clergy, that they refused to cooperate and defended their practice on the grounds of "immemorial custom."[57] This defense was a good one. Again the question of development, if people had only been able to recognize it, had been raised. The nicolaitists were correct; their position had been accepted by the earlier Church. But the reformers could not admit this because, innocent of the idea of development, they dared not admit that doctrine had changed. The synod of Paris in 1074 refused to support the papal program of celibacy on the grounds that it was an insupportable burden and opined that the papal commands on the matter were to be rejected as absurd.[58] The Liégeois Sigebert of Gembloux, defender of empire against papacy, was one of the most enthusiastic supporters of the married clergy and the author of *An Argument against Those Who Calumniate the Masses of Married Priests*.[59] Sigebert not only defended the right of priests to wed but also placed the blame for the appearance of Reformist Dissidence upon the reform papacy. The papacy's commands to the people to avoid masses said by married clergy, he said, was to encourage donatist error. Much of this may be true, but Sigebert permitted himself to exaggerate. The reform papacy was itself in danger of donatism, he said, and once this step into heresy was taken, the papacy encouraged the people to profane the sacred mysteries, to use holy oil to baptize and to employ earwax as holy chrism, to trample the eucharist underfoot.

Sigebert was more enthusiastic than others, but the fight against celibacy continued protected by the aegis of antipapalism. Archbishop Siegfried of Mainz attempted in 1075–1076 to induce his clergy to accept celibacy and failed; their pressures helped induce him to throw in his lot with the imperialist party.[60] In 1078 the clergy of the imperialist city of Cambrai and those of Noyon argued from the decisions of the First Council of Nicea that the traditions of the Church permitted clerical marriage. They accused the reformers of undermining the dignity of the clergy by holding them up to the ridicule and blame of the people and suggested that the remedy for this was not that the clergy should reform their ways but that the reformers should stop urging reform upon them. They attacked the papacy violently and called the papal legates impostors.[61] Later, about 1075–1080, another French writer wrote an anonymous *Treatise in Favor of the Marriage of Clerks* which attacked the papal party as hypocritical.[62] A similar defense was issued about 1079 in a letter of the Pseudo-Udalric,[63] and around 1100 a Norman anonymous wrote a *Defense of the Children of Priests*.[64]

The most bizarre use of the term "heresy" in this period dates from 1065 when two councils of Rome solemnly anathematized the "heresy of the incestuous." This lurid title, like the covers on some pocketbooks, covers only a prosaic matter: it seems there were some who questioned the current method of calculating degrees of consanguinity and favored a method that would be more lenient. In the minds of the conciliar fathers, these bold souls could be guilty of nothing less than formal heresy.[65]

Schism, simony, lay investiture, and nicolaitism did not first appear in our period, but they were now described formally as heresies for the first time, and for the reason that Catholic teaching upon these subjects had developed. This development was largely the result of the impetus supplied by the Great Reform Movement, which was thus responsible for the appearance of dissent in two ways: First, in encouraging reform it helped encourage the Reformists. Second, in forcing the development of Christian doctrine on matters such as nicolaitism and lay investiture it propelled the Church ahead on a road that left behind those who held to the old traditions.

Reverse heresy.

Roma locuta, causa finita: "Rome has spoken; the question is resolved." I have assumed that the judgment of the papacy at any given time is the criterion for orthodoxy. There were many in this period who refused to make this assumption. Some of these have already been dealt with under the rubric of schismatics, but some upheld their schism with such vigor that they proclaimed that it was they who were orthodox and the pope who was a heretic. This extreme form of schism I have labeled reverse heresy: by the fact of believing that the pope was a heretic, these technically became heretics themselves.

The roots of opposition to the papacy are as old as Christianity. The authority of the bishop of Rome over the Church was not, except in the most inchoate form, recognized in Christendom until well into the second century. There were always those who resisted the centralization of the Church and defied the central authority, whether that authority lay in the breast of pope or emperor. Donatus and Optatus had early assaulted the imperial authority, and Hilary of Poitiers provoked the emperor Constantius by the following statement: "I proclaim to you, Constantius, what I would have spoken to Nero. . . . You are an usurper, not only of things human, but of things divine." [66]

Resentment of imperial influence was of course increased by the feeling that a secular power had no place in the Church, but the residual dislike of any kind of central authority could be turned against the papacy as well, and would increase in proportion as the power of that institution increased. Thus, attacks upon the papacy become strongest in that reform period that centers in the reign of Gregory VII and that is characterized by a striking assertion of the papal powers. Yet, oddly, it must be noted that heavy criticism of the papacy began a century earlier, toward the end of the tenth century, and continued into the early years of the eleventh, in that period when the papacy was debased and at the mercy either of the emperor, or, far worse, of Roman political factions. The papacy could expect attacks both when it was extraordinarily base and when it was extraordinarily brilliant. The attacks upon Rome at the time of the reform papacy had motives other than the purely moral, of course. The antipapal party became one with the imperial party, and enemies of the pope supported the emperor from desire for gain, from traditional loyalties, or from the suspicion that the emperor's hand might be less heavy than the pope's.

All imperialist writers cannot be classified as reverse heretics, of course, for this would be throwing the net too wide. Only those who openly attacked the papacy as heretical or enmired in error may be considered heretics themselves.

The general impetus to reverse heresy was the traditional distrust of the papacy, whose powers as an institution were even less clearly defined in the eleventh century than they are today and were therefore more open to attack. Again, "when in the barque of Peter, don't go near the engine room": visits to the center of papal power at Rome have disillusioned many people from Peter Damian and Henry the Monk to Luther. Another motivation was one which was in large part justified. Sigebert of Gembloux and other antipapal writers accused the papacy of promoting donatist heresy by their attacks upon the corrupt clergy. Sigebert and his colleagues were correct in seeing a close connection between reformer and Reformist, but what they did not understand was a doctrine of development: the papacy must err, for tradition stands against it. The papal position was not a break with tradition, but it was a development of tradition along new lines, and this the imperialists could not understand. Finally, the antipapal position of the Greek Church is unique. The authority of Rome over the Eastern patriarchates had never been firmly established in the minds of the Greeks, and the schism of 1054 was merely one more event in a long chain of mutual antagonisms. Disputes between Constantinople and Rome often grew heated and angry words were used. Moreover, the Greeks had a number of strange ideas about the Western Church, such as their belief (according to Hincmar of Reims) that at Easter the Latins brought to the altar not only the bread and wine but also a sacrificial lamb, which they sacrificed in the flesh.[67] Whether based on fantasy or on fact, Greek anathemas of the Latin Church cannot be taken as examples of reverse heresy, for the Greeks stand outside the general context of Western civilization that permits the historian to establish the judgment of Rome as the criterion for orthodoxy.

The first hint of reverse heresy in the medieval West is at the synod of Paris in 825, where the intolerant Franks accused the deceased Hadrian I of acting "indiscreetly" and "superstitiously" in approving the actions of the Empress Irene in favor of images.[68] The Reformist Claudius of Turin impugned the authority of Paschal I (817–824), who had reprimanded him earlier. "He is not to be called apostolic who sits in the seat of the apostle," said Claudius, "but he who fills the office of the apostle." [69] Out of the disgraceful controversy at Rome surrounding the ordinations of Pope Formosus (891–896), when popes denied the validity of one another's ordinations with abandon and when Stephen VI, Formosus' successor, had his predecessor's body exhumed from consecrated soil, arose a disgusted attack upon the papal prerogatives. One Auxilius, writing about the beginning of the tenth century, held that "the Father is said to have given all power to the Son, not to Rome, nor did the Son say, 'Thou art Rome and upon this rock I shall build my church,' but, rather, 'Thou art Peter. . . .' A person is not the successor of Peter unless he has the merits of Peter. . . ." [70] The tenth century, perhaps the worst in the papacy's history, did little to revive respect for the institution. With the rise of Ottonian authority, when it became possible again to appeal to an emperor against an incompetent or evil pope, voices were raised in greater number. The enemies of Pope John XII, in bringing about his deposition by Otto the Great in 963, accused him of every heresy and vice their aroused imaginations could invent, including a statement that he had drunk the health of Satan in wine.[71]

Toward the end of the century the papacy continued at such low ebb that one is tempted to speculate about the possibilities of a real religious revolution. Though such a revolution was delayed until the sixteenth century, attacks upon Rome became ever more frequent. On June 17 and 18, 991, the synod of Saint Basle of Verzy near Reims met to consider the condition of the see of Reims.[72] Following the death of Archbishop Adalbero in 989, a dispute had arisen over the succession to the see. Adalbero had been one of the leaders in placing Hugh Capet upon the throne, and his chief assistant in this as in other undertakings had been Gerbert of Aurillac, the future Pope Silvester II. Gerbert expected to be elevated to the see after his master's death, but King Hugh instead appointed one Arnoul, a bastard son of the former King Lothar. Arnoul promptly betrayed Hugh to his Carolingian competitor for the throne, Charles of Lorraine, and when Hugh succeeded in crushing this plot, he immediately demanded that Pope John XV support him in deposing Arnoul. John XV delayed, and the French bishops assembled at Verzy to take matters into their own hands. Active at the synod were, besides Gerbert himself, Bishop Arnoul of Orléans, Archbishop Séguin of Sens, who presided, and a large number of other bishops and abbots including the famous Abbo of Fleury. Abbo led the pro papal party which, relying upon the pseudo-Isidorean decretals, claimed for Rome the right of intervention in such affairs and held that no action should be taken without papal approval; Arnoul of Orléans led the attack upon his namesake and, incidentally, upon the papalists who were delaying the decision; Gerbert quite naturally sided with his colleague of Orléans. The significant thing is the violence of Arnoul's arguments. Outraged that a papacy that could sink to such a level would dare to interfere in a decision over the see of Reims, Arnoul launched a violent attack upon the apostolic see. His anger was perhaps further kindled by the fact that he was a personal enemy of the papalist Abbo and that he was a loyal supporter of the Capetian monarchy, which did not look with favor upon the intervention of Rome in French affairs, especially when that intervention obstructed Capetian policy.

Arnoul's speech comes to us only as edited and published by his ally Gerbert, so that we cannot be sure how much of it is really Arnoul's. There is no question but that Gerbert enthusiastically supported the antipapal position, a fact that is curious, though scarcely unparalleled in history, in the light of the fact that he later became pope himself. It is worth giving a résumé of the speech, because it spells out the antipapal position more clearly than any other document of the period.

Rome had always been honored because of the memory of Saint Peter, so said the speech, but one must not forget the canons of the (First) Council of Nicea, which the Church ought always to obey. Whatever John XV decided to do in this case, it was not enough to set aside the canons, for the canons spoke with divine authority (a glimpse of an embryonic conciliar theory). What good were canons if the pope could suspend or annul them? If this be admitted, the church were in peril. Now, if the pope was a good and intelligent man, his decrees were worthy of attention; otherwise, they were not. Ignorance, fear, and cupidity now ruled at Rome, and under these circumstances neither the pope's opinion nor his silence was to be considered. The opinions of a man who violated the laws of the Church could hardly be taken into consideration in judging their merits. "O wretched Rome," Arnoul (or Gerbert) continued, "who held aloft the clear light of the Fathers to our ancestors, but have shadowed our own time with monstrous crimes that will be notorious in that of our children." The list of popes included some great names, continued the speech, but in recent years one had witnessed nothing but degradation at Rome. Was the Church to bow her head to these monsters, ridden with every vice and ignorant of divine and humane letters? The pope posed (*videri appetit*) as the head of all the bishops; how was it then that he was not more carefully selected? If the pope was enlightened by neither charity nor wisdom he might as well be a statue. The opinion of such popes as one now had was worthless; instead one should rely upon the opinions of the holy bishops of France and Germany.

So Arnoul expressed himself with a violence worthy of Luther. One might be tempted to attribute this to a passing outburst of anger were it not that Gerbert took the trouble to approve, record, and polish it for publication. Nor was the opinion of Arnoul and Gerbert isolated: so little did it shock the assembled clergy that the majority approved it and voted to proceed with the deposition of Arnoul of Reims and the election of Gerbert in his place.

The matter was not closed there. News of Verzy reached Rome quickly, and the papal legate Leo wrote to King Hugh[73] attacking the speech as blasphemous and accusing the perpetrators as schismatics and heretics. Leo summoned the principals to meet him at Aachen to discuss the affair; they refused, and he went eastward to Ingelheim among bishops free from the influence of King Hugh. There he called a synod and asked the German bishops to quash the decisions of Verzy.

Far from being intimidated, the antipapalists continued to act. Gerbert wrote a letter (no. 192) to the pope warning him not to try to excommunicate the French bishops, and then presided over another synod, at Chelles in 994, to reaffirm the position taken at Verzy. "If the pope," said the fathers of Chelles, "should suggest something against the decrees of the Fathers, it shall be null and void in accordance with the apostolic saying, 'Shun the man who is a heretic.'"[74] The affair was finally resolved, to no one's complete satisfaction, when in 997 Gerbert renounced his claim to the see of Reims and was appointed by his friend and pupil the young Otto III to the see of Ravenna.

The earlier years of the eleventh century were not lacking in instances of opposition to the papacy,[75] though their instigators were not usually so explicit in their defiance as were Gerbert and Arnoul. In 1007, however, the corrupt Pope John XVIII received a pointed rebuff from the clergy of Anjou.[76] Count Fulk of Anjou, a notorious reprobate and plundered of the Church, built a monastery—in order, one supposes, to assuage his feelings of guilt. He asked the archbishop of Tours to come consecrate it; the archbishop refused on account of Fulk's reputation, and Fulk promptly sent to Rome to bribe the pope to send up a legate to do the job. The French bishops were outraged at this interference, particularly because of the money involved, and they issued a scathing condemnation of the papacy. Let no bishop, they said, interfere in the affairs of another diocese without the permission of the bishop of that see. It was right that honor should be granted the Roman see, but not that it should transgress the canons. But justice was done at last: God himself intervened during the unholy consecration and caused a huge storm to arise and smash the church down. John XVIII found himself no more popular in the following year, when Fulk, bishop of Orléans, and Liétry, bishop of Sens, burned a papal bull that ignored the proper authority of the bishops.[77]

These conflicts between pope and bishops in. northern France are indications of something more than the long anticentralizing tradition. This was a period when the pseudo-Isidorean decretals were still in the process of becoming established in the traditions of the Church, and the natural inconsistency between the authentic documents of the early Church that favored decentralization and most of the forged documents that (although many of the decretals were originally forged to bolster the position of bishops against the king) favored centralization caused an increase in already existing tensions. No one knew at the time that the decretals were forged, and so each party had some documents to which it could point. The *Decretum* of Burchard of Worms, written about 1008–1012, indicates that the position of the papacy was by no means universally deemed secure. Burchard gives due honor to the see of Peter, but very little more, and in Book I of *On the Primacy of the Church* refers to the episcopacy as a whole rather than to the pope in particular as the cornerstone in the ecclesiastical edifice.[78] The synod of Anse in 1025, judging a suit between the abbot of Cluny and the bishop of Mâcon, elected to prefer a canon of the council of Chalcedon to a papal exemption,[79] and at the synod of Sutri in 1046, Henry III did not hesitate to label Gregory VI a simoniac and a heretic. Peter Damian's *Liber Gomorrhianus* was a stringent attack upon the corruption of Rome.

With the advent of the reform papacy, attacks upon Rome grew more, not less, common, because papal interference in local affairs and papal political activity became more vigorous. People who forgave corruption were unwilling to tolerate commotion. Berengar of Tours dared to accuse Leo IX of heresy,[80] but the real attacks upon the reform papacy came with the reigns of Nicholas II and Alexander II. This is when the controversies over simony and nicolaitism began to generate their heat, and anger against the positions now taken by the papacy sometimes exploded into accusations of error. Benzo of Alba referred contemptuously to Pope Alexander II as "the heretic of Lucca," [81] and the synod of Paris in 1074 called the decrees of the reform popes on clerical celibacy absurd.[82] During the controversy between Gregory VII and Henry IV epithets fell like arrows. To the synod of Worms in 1076, Gregory was, among other things, an intruder, an oppressor, and a violator of divine and human law.[83] The imperialist clerks of Cambrai called their bishop, Gérard II, a supporter of Gregory, a heretic.[84] Wibert ("Clement III"), Peter Crassus, Wido of Ferrara, the synods of Brixen in 1080 and Mainz in 1085, all these deemed that Hildebrand was, among his other sins and crimes, a heretic.[85] Perhaps the fullest catalog was that of Benzo of Alba, who dealt with Alexander II, Gregory VII, and their supporters in words that, in the period between Martial and Henry Miller, have infrequently found their way into literature.[86]

The climate cooled after the death of Hildebrand, but Paschal II was accused of promoting heresy, his party even being identified on one occasion with that of the Manichaeans.[87] Paschal has the distinction of being the only pope accused of heresy by both the reactionaries and the reformers. In 1111, after the emperor Henry V had captured him, thrown him into prison, and threatened him with torture, Paschal capitulated completely on the question of investitures, fearing for the peace of the Church as well as for his own safety. The angry reform party, gathering at the Lateran synod of 1116, accused the unfortunate pontiff of heresy for yielding to Henry. Paschal apologized and declared null the concessions given Henry since they were secured by force, whereupon the assembled fathers granted that it was really improper to call heretical any agreement not voluntarily made.[88] As the limited victory of papacy over empire came generally to be accepted in the twelfth century and as the controversy over the secular power in the Church temporarily faded, such violent polemic became less common. In general the reactionaries fell into line, and the reform papacy was no longer under suspicion of heresy by those to whom tradition—any kind of tradition—was more important than reform.

6. The Intellectuals

Eastern and antique influences.

Juvenal's complaint in the second century that the Orontes was flowing into the Tiber and transporting the eastern mystery cults into Rome and the West might be applied to the history of Christian doctrine in the early Church as well. It was the East that, under the continuing influence of Hellenistic speculative philosophy, produced the heresies and doctrinal refinements of the early Church. Though Rome became an administrative and organizational center of Christendom, Italy and the West were not spawning grounds of theological speculation. From its beginnings, the Western Church emphasized conduct and worship while the Eastern was concerned with metaphysics.[1] This dependence of the West upon the East for its doctrines and its heresies grew less as the political and economic separation between the two sections of the Empire grew wider, and by the eighth century, when the gap was being deepened profoundly, Eastern influences in Western thought came to be increasingly unusual. The channel between Tiber and Orontes was after many centuries silting up.

In that century and the following one, nonetheless, there were a number of controversies that were not only foreign to the West in that they were oriental in origin but also anachronistic at a time when the West was ceasing to be concerned with Eastern problems.

One of these controversies was the Iconoclastic.[2] The central events in the history of Iconoclasm, the doctrine that attacked the veneration of images, took place in the Byzantine Empire, and it had little influence in the West. Pope Hadrian I readily accepted the Second Council of Nicea, which condemned the doctrine. Though Charlemagne and his advisers, especially Alcuin, opposed the decision of the council, there is no trace of any Occidental holding real Iconoclastic beliefs. The only hint of such an attitude is in the case of Bishop Claudius of Turin (*ca.* 820–839). Claudius has sometimes been considered an Iconoclast, but if he were, his isolation from other intellectual and moral currents in the West would be difficult to understand. The West was at once too immature intellectually and too suspicious of the East to respond to Oriental puritanism with an Iconoclasm of its own. Certainly a puritan, Claudius may have incorporated into his teachings some of the ideals of the Iconoclasts, and he must have derived inspiration from the decisions of Charlemagne's council at Frankfurt, but he was at bottom a Reformist dissident in the Western tradition rather than an Iconoclast in the Eastern.[3]

Like Iconoclasm, the problem that arose over the procession of the Holy Spirit created a division between Western and Eastern Churches rather than factionalism and dissidence in the West itself. Like the Spanish stand in Adoptionism, the position of the Greeks on the legitimacy of the *Filioque* clause was, in Western terms, reactionary. This is a good test case for the proper definition and use of the term "heresy," for to the Greeks the Latin position in this matter seemed even more heretical than the Greek position seemed to the Latin, and it is of course tendentious to extend the criteria of the Western Church to that of the East. The Greeks had much on their side in the way of the antiquity of the doctrine they professed. Creeds drawn up before the sixth century held that the Holy Spirit proceeded from the Father but were silent on the relationship between Holy Spirit and Son. It was not specifically stipulated that the Holy Spirit did *not* proceed from the Son as well as from the Father, and it could be maintained, by those who wished, that the Fathers really had a doctrine of double procession in mind. But it is nonetheless clear that the early Church did not choose to affirm such a doctrine. The Greeks could therefore appeal to antiquity, and this had force, since it was generally understood at the time that innovation in doctrine was heretical in the light of Vincent of Lérins' formula *quod semper*. In the eyes of the Greeks, the Latin Church was changing, and it was the Latin Church, therefore, that was in error. The Greek theologians did not at first take violent exception to the theology of the double procession itself, since the East had always permitted the expression of the idea that the Holy Spirit proceeded from the Father *through* the Son. Later Byzantine theologians, in reaction to Western pressures, would assert the single procession, but the chief Greek objection in the eighth century (as later) was that the insertion of any phrase into the Nicene Creed, hallowed as it had been since the First Council of Constantinople, was improper. Thus the Greeks appeared as the defenders of ancient tradition.

Yet doctrine does develop. As the doctrine of the Trinity grew more refined, the double procession came to seem more satisfactory to people in the West: as the Father generates the Son as his Word or Wisdom, so the Father and the Son bring forth the Holy Spirit as their mutual love. By the sixth century, belief in the double procession had become common in the West, and the council of Toledo in 589 affirmed it specifically. From Spain the idea passed to the Franks, who became its standard-bearers, eventually persuading the entire Western Church to add the double procession to the Nicene Creed: "the Holy Spirit, who proceeds from the Father *and from the Son*." [4] By the eleventh century the papacy had also yielded to this popular religious practice, and though Rome had neither led nor opposed the movement in its favor, it now came to adopt it. No similar development occurred in the East, however, and the point of disagreement still remains between the Latin and the Oriental Churches.

An anachronism was Arianism, which, though originally an Oriental heresy, was imported into the West owing to the conversion of the Goths, Vandals, and Lombards by Arian missionaries. Far more than the Greek position on the double procession, Arianism was reactionary, speaking in terms that the whole Church had long since declared impermissible, while the conversion of the Goths and Lombards to Catholicism, together with the subjugation of the Vandals by Justinian, removed it from political power and influence. Yet it is not surprising that the wholesale conversions of Arian peoples to Catholicism effected through the offices of their rulers did not have total effect immediately. Saint Columban had to deal with Arian influences in Burgundy in the sixth century, and in the eighth century traces of Arianism may have been visible in Bavaria.[5] Heinz Löwe postulates that the original conversion of Bavaria to Christianity was not free of Arian influence, and as late as the time of Vergil of Salzburg, both Vergil and Bishop Arbeo of Freising had a fragment of an Arian theological work copied in their scriptoria. The evidence is dubious, however, and it is certain that Arianism had no substantial following in Germany in the period under consideration.

Spain was the center, in the eighth century, of a dispute somewhat connected with the impact of Arianism in the West: a revival of the ancient heresy of Adoptionism that had flourished in the second and third centuries. This extraordinary revival can be explained only against the background of Visigothic Spain which, beset by internal quarrels and always isolated from the practices of the rest of the Church, was effectively disconnected from Christendom by the Moslem invasion of 711. The isolated Spanish clergy fell ready prey to unusual ideas, including a moderate Adoptionism which maintained that although Christ, the Word, was Son of God by nature, Jesus was a man and Son of God only by virtue of his adoption by the Word. The debates on Adoptionism came to the ears of Charlemagne, who had the doctrine condemned at Frankfurt in 794, and after the publication of a treatise on the *Doctrine of the Holy Trinity* by Alcuin in about 802 or 803, Adoptionism, while not disappearing in Spain, ceased to be of importance for the West as a whole.[6]

The Intellectuals.

Though the mainstream of dissent in the medieval West was moral, intellectual heresies appeared with increasing frequency as society grew gradually more complex. The history of intellectual heresies in the West from the time of Boniface to the mid-twelfth century falls into two chronological periods divided at about the year 1050. From the eighth to the eleventh century, intellectual activity and intellectual heresy were less concentrated, more dominated by Platonic thought and the Platonic method of exposition in the form of dialogue. This prescholastic period of dissent ended when, from the end of the eleventh century, heresies arose from the new methods and concepts introduced by scholasticism. Many of these controversies have been studied at length by specialists in the history of doctrine.[7] I offer here only a summary account emphasizing the continuity of intellectual dissent in the period, its varieties, and its relationship to the development of doctrine and to the Great Reform Movement.

The pre-Scholastics.

Among the dissidents of Saint Boniface's own time was Vergil, the Irish Fergil from the abbey of Aghaboe,[8] who had immigrated to the Continent and had risen to become bishop of Salzburg. The Irish for all their missionizing had long been cut off from the Christianity that was taught at Rome and that was being established in northern Europe by Boniface, so that the Irish clergy in Europe had frequent differences with the English missionary. Vergil and Boniface had confronted one another over various problems of administration and organization, and this quarrel helps to explain the severity of Boniface's censures. Since Vergil's relics were venerated at Salzburg immediately following his death, and since he was formally canonized in 1233, it is clear that he was not formally a heretic. But he did teach a doctrine that was strongly disputed: he believed in the existence of the antipodes. Now, if this had meant only that he believed in the sphericity of the earth, there would have been no furore, as this astronomical fact was generally admitted. It is difficult to garner from the meager sources what exactly Vergil did teach, but the best guess is that he held that there was a southern hemisphere and that, if this did exist, there might be other men below, separated from us by a band of fire at the equator. The theological implications of this would be that, since the northern and southern hemispheres are completely separate, the men below would be a different race than we; and in that event one Incarnation would not suffice for all men, which is heresy. If Vergil indeed held such doctrines, the fact that he died in the odor of sanctity is evidence that he came eventually to abjure them.

Another Irish priest, Samson, also irritated Boniface by holding a peculiar doctrine in regard to baptism.[9] He maintained that by the laying on of hands bishops conferred all that was necessary to initiate a person into the Church and that baptism was unnecessary. Pope Zachary, hearing of this, wrote to the missionary saying that Samson ought to be defrocked and excommunicated.

Later in the century, at Volvic in 761, Pepin III took measures against heretics who held unorthodox opinions on the Trinity and threatened them with exile, and a bit later Charlemagne wrote to various bishops in France, Germany, and Italy in regard to a heresy on the nature of the Holy Spirit.[10] In the 780's or 790's an obscure monk named John had a peculiar vision of a being like a man but with dove's wings. In his dream, this being was called the Son of God. As Pope Hadrian I observed to Charlemagne, this was an evident confusion of Christ with the Holy Spirit and therefore merited condemnation.[11] In 790 the Irish Church cautioned against the twisting of the Fathers to obtain support for heretical doctrines, an indication that heresy may even have presumed to make its way to Ireland itself.[12]

The first major controversy in the medieval West occurred in the next century and centered on the person of the monk Gottschalk of Orbais.[13] It raised a fundamental question of theology that the Church had never resolved, the question of free will and grace, in which the basic problem was the reconciliation of the freedom of the human will with the omnipotence of God. Gottschalk, born shortly after 800 in Mainz, was, as a child, pledged to the religious life and educated at Fulda. After trying unsuccessfully to abandon his vows he finally settled at the monastery of Orbais near Reims. After a career in which he challenged many of the leading thinkers of the Western Church and was a center of dispute at nine synods,[14] he died excommunicate in 868–869.

Building upon the position on grace and free will established by Saint Augustine, Gottschalk said, and stated in a treatise, that God doubly predestines, to hell as well as to heaven, since with God to foresee is to foreordain. But though God predestines the punishment for sin, he does not predestine the sin itself. This sensible position, which avoids the predestinarianism of Calvin, was unacceptable to many of Gottschalk's contemporaries, who, failing to understand the subtleties of Gottschalk's position, found double predestination blasphemous. It seemed impossible to them that God should predestine to hell in any sense. Archbishop Hincmar of Reims led the hue and cry against the unfortunate monk, believing that he had said that God predestines to sin, and ordered the author beaten and the treatise burned. The result was that a great controversy arose around the cause of the wretched Gottschalk, his friends and antagonists entering the lists one after the other.

In a sense, both sides behaved badly. The question of predestination is an exceedingly delicate one, and the intellectual instruments of ninth-century thinkers tended to be somewhat blunt. Both parties substituted invective and obfuscation for elucidation. The party of Hincmar was unable to comprehend the distinction between predestination to hell and predestination to sin, while the party of Gottschalk failed to explain its position clearly and had recourse to charging its opponents with Pelagianism. The Church has never offered a definitive solution to the problem, nor did Rome speak then, but since the most powerful forces in France, Hincmar and his associates, were able to secure synodal condemnation of Gottschalk, he was held to be a heretic at the time. For the most part, his beliefs have come to be considered acceptable to a large number of Catholic theologians.

If we discount all the probable exaggerations, not to mention the nonsense, of his adversaries' allegations, it appears (as Aegerter pointed out) that Gottschalk may really have been heretical, in the sense of opposing the general teaching of the Church, on only two points: that Christ suffered only for the elect, and that baptism was ineffective for those not of the elect. Otherwise his ideas should have been acceptable, and were to those who took the trouble to examine them carefully. Hincmar and his allies do not come off well in this game of blindman's buff. In the dialectic of Christian doctrine Gottschalk's career had little influence, provoking no formulation of doctrine in the way that Berengar's did later. The synod of Tuzey in 860 that concluded the debate on predestination made no contribution but to deny double predestination, to affirm that Christ died for all, and to restate the Augustinian position in all its ambiguity. In effect, the quarrel over Gottschalk was a doctrinal dispute that produced no constructive advance in Christian doctrine.

Eriugena, who was involved in the controversy over Gottschalk, himself verged on heresy on several counts.[15] Born early in the ninth century in Ireland, John Scotus Eriugena came in middle life to the court of Charles the Bald, which he graced as one of the leading intellects. Of his works only two known to be authentic have survived, the treatise *On Predestination* and the long work *On the Division of Nature*. Eriugena was heavily influenced by the neoplatonic writers Pseudo-Dionysius and Maximus Confessor, as well as by Gregory of Nyssa, and it was in his application of their ideas to the problems of his day that, on three points, he came close to heresy.

On the first, he attacked Gottschalk on the grounds that the attribution of predestination or anything else to God is merely a symbolic way of speaking. This contradicted Gottschalk, it is true, but it introduced by-the-way concepts with which no one at that time was prepared to deal, and the Irishman's treatise was condemned at the anti-Hincmarian synods of 855 and 859. Eriugena also very likely held a position on the eucharist close to that of Ratramnus of Corbie, denying transubstantiation. If Eriugena did so believe, this would not have been strictly heretical in the ninth century, for it was only in the course of the debate with Berengar in the eleventh that the Church came to define its position.

On the second point, Eriugena's *On the Division of Nature* has been examined for traces of pantheism. Eriugena was never condemned in his own time on such grounds, but in 1225, after his book had been used by Amalric of Bène, a pantheist professor at the University of Paris, it was posthumously anathematized by Honorius III. In point of fact, Eriugena was never a pantheist, but a neoplatonic emanationist. For Eriugena, God is in the world and is its essence. But God is also above and beyond all. The world is totally in God, but God is not totally in the world, and the transcendence of the Deity is preserved.

Finally, the doctrine of emanations implied some other dubious propositions as well, for example that which stated that the devil will eventually be saved and that evil itself will return to God. In the fourth stage of the world cycle, the stage of return, Eriugena held that since contraries are always contained in contraries, darkness in light for example, evil is contained in the good, and in this sense both will be brought back to God in the final stage. Another dangerous implication was one of omission. In precisely the way that in our day Teilhard de Chardin encountered difficulties by creating a system in which the fall of man has no immediately apparent place, Eriugena's doctrine of cosmic emanation and return leaves little room for original sin. When he does come to specifics on the question his answer is somewhat unusual. The sin of Adam consisted of choosing to know phenomena in a carnal rather than in a spiritual sense, and one consequence of the fall is that we are obliged to arrive at knowledge through the cumbersome process of sensory perceptions rather than by direct contemplation of the deity. Eve was not a real woman but represents man's senses in an allegorical fashion. Peculiar in itself, Eriugena's doctrine of the fall and of consequent redemption adjoins his cosmic doctrine like an ill-fitted lean-to. The basic difficulty was in explaining the presence of evil (or illusion, or the absence of good) in a universe consisting of emanations from God.

Eriugena, though his ideas were unusual and his background neoplatonic, was not a religious dissident in the sense that we use the term. He was not condemned during his lifetime and at no time resisted the will of the universal Church. That his work was in part condemned after his death in no way reverses this judgment.

Another Carolingian controversy surrounded the career of Amalarius of Metz,[16] who was appointed by Louis the Pious to the see of Lyon after the deposition of Archbishop Agobard. Interested in the liturgy, Amalarius was handicapped by a propensity for politics as well as for psalms, and his enemies exerted themselves to search his liturgical writings for traces of heresy. When all the preposterous accusations are cleared away, Amalarius emerges as an orthodox Churchman who, however, expressed himself in a florid manner and permitted himself ecstasies of symbolism that could readily be interpreted by a malevolent mind as heretical. That his foes would stop at nothing too petty to calumniate him is seen in an accusation that Amalarius angrily refuted,[17] that he spat too soon after communion.

A synod at Rome on November 18, 862, called to deal with the difficulties created by Archbishop John of Ravenna (850–878), accused that prelate of heresy.[18] John had been a despotic ruler of his diocese and had on many occasions offended the apostolic see. Nicholas I summoned him to Rome to clear himself; he refused on three occasions to come, and at last Nicholas summoned the synod to condemn him in absence. Two theological errors were condemned by articles of the synod. There is no direct evidence that John himself was responsible for them, though it is possible, since the articles follow a general condemnation of John for heresy. At any rate, such doctrines must have existed at the time. Condemned were the doctrines that Christ suffered in his divine person, so that deity itself suffered, and that baptism is not effective for all. The second doctrine probably represents a defense of Gottschalk's position on predestination. The first is the heresy known as the theopaschite, which originated in the sixth century as a corollary of Monophysitism: if Christ has but one nature, the divine, and if Christ truly suffered in his passion, then so must the Deity.

There is no evidence in the ninth century of any Monophysite background to this ninth-century manifestation of the theopaschite heresy, though it must be observed that Ravenna was still a window on the East, whence John might have obtained Monophysite literature. It is perhaps more likely that the doctrine was simply stumbled on anew, which, granting that Christ is believed to be divine, is not difficult to imagine. John finally confessed to his crimes and was conditionally restored to his see. Whether or not it was he personally who was responsible for these ideas, theopaschitism vanished thereafter.

Toward mid-century, according to Cantù, a group appeared at Padova with fanciful ideas about the Redemption,[19] and in the wilds of the diocese of Utrecht, only recently claimed from paganism, a group in Staveren and the outlying districts held a belief on the Trinity that appeared Sabellian or unitarian. Bishop Frederick I (*ca.* 825–*ca.* 835), with the help of Odulf, canon of Saint Martin's, went north to preach the true faith in the affected area. They were successful in restoring orthodoxy, and Frederick, leaving Odulf to keep things in order, returned to his see where he asked his clergy to say a special prayer stressing the equal eternity of the three persons of the Trinity, their unity in power but trinity in name, and the generation of the Son by the Father and the procession of Holy Spirit from both. Willem Moll takes this story seriously, which is derived from a *Vita* of Saint Frederick in the *Acta Sanctorum*. It may be factual, but the extreme unreliability of the sources for Utrecht in such an early period makes its validity very questionable.[20]

As with other forms of intellectual and religious activity, intellectual heresy declines in the late ninth and early tenth centuries. After the middle of the tenth century instances again occur. In a lenten sermon, Rather of Verona preached against heretics in his diocese, describing them as Anthropomorphites[21] who said that "it seems to us that God must be nothing at all if he has no head, eyes, ears, and feet." This crude materialism was supplemented by other peculiar doctrines, such as that on Tuesdays Saint Michael the Archangel says mass for God. Rather exclaimed over this ignorance and patiently explained that God is spiritual, like our minds, which do not possess hands or feet. One can only observe that this strange doctrine had a short life.

During the reign of Wolfgang of Regensburg (972–994) a heretic appeared who preached that the Word was not made flesh.[22] "If it is a word, it is not made," he said, "and if it is made, it is not a word." The heretic spoke with great eloquence and apparently was making some reputation for himself, so that the emperor Otto II called upon Wolfgang to refute him. Wolfgang at first demurred (from humility, his biographer tells us) but at length was prevailed upon to answer, and a dialogue between the bishop and the heretic ensued in which Wolfgang, relying upon reason buttressed by judicious quotations from authority, caused truth to triumph, and the shamed dissenter craved pardon for his error at the worthy bishop's feet. We may assume that this was the termination of this heresy; we are ignorant of its origins.

Writing early in the eleventh century the chronicler Radulf Glaber began his book with a section entitled *On the Divine Quaternity*. Much as one might want to leap at this, there is no connection with heresy.[23]

The Scholastics.

The definition of Scholasticism and the search for its origins have always posed complicated historical problems which it would not be well to explore here. Yet a few necessary observations must be made. The eleventh and twelfth centuries were a period of great change in Western thought. This change took place, roughly, in two stages. The first began with the eleventh century itself, its first standard-bearers being Gerbert of Aurillac and Fulbert of Chartres. This stage consisted in the revival of the dialectic, the orderly pursuit of truth in terms of *question, disputation,* and *conclusion.* In the creation of this dialectic, Berengar was a leading figure and may therefore be termed one of the first Scholastics. The second stage was the introduction of Aristotelian and Arab philosophical ideas through the medium of new translations; this stage began only long after the death of Berengar. But because of Berengar, the middle of the eleventh century is a watershed in the history of intellectual heresy. Before this period there were, as we have seen, conflicts over doctrine. But with the rise of Scholasticism these conflicts arose in part from attitudes and methods different from those of the past. The Scholastic was less ready to yield to authority and more willing to let pure reason be his guide. Whereas the Platonic dialogue had been in favor with many earlier thinkers, Eriugena for example, the Scholastics initiated and perfected the technique of the dialectic, and this very perfection made them the more willing to debate and defend their doctrines against arguments from traditional authority.

The Scholastic heretics have always attracted a great deal of attention, and their doctrines and careers need not be discussed at length. One of the transition figures between pre-Scholastic intellectual heresy and Scholastic heresy is Berengar of Tours,[24] whose denial of transubstantiation earned him condemnation at at least eleven synods. Though as long as he held to the Real Presence his position did not lack a long tradition, he received little support for doctrines that two hundred years earlier on the lips of Ratramnus and John the Scot had still commanded respect if not assent. The list of theologians supporting transubstantiation grew increasingly long and imposing during the twelfth century, Peter Lombard adding the weight of his influence against Berengar in his textbook *Sentences*. The question was finally resolved in 1215 when the Fourth Lateran Council proclaimed the doctrine of transubstantiation *de fide*. Thus it was legitimate, though questionable, to deny transubstantiation in the ninth century, and it was formally heretical to deny it after 1215. The individual who did most to precipitate this decision was the unfortunate Berengar, caught between loyalty to an old tradition and the as yet unclear formulations of dawning Scholasticism.

There has been some discussion of how broad the influence of Berengar was. Everyone agrees that there was no popular cult of Berengarism. His doctrine of the eucharist caused him to be connected by some of his contemporaries as well as some modern writers with the dualist denial of the reality of Christ's body, but this is not demonstrable. Neither is the interpretation that links Berengar to the

Reformist Patarini. Berengar was a relatively isolated intellectual connected with no popular group. Macdonald concluded that "it is improbable that Berengar's propaganda extended beyond the ranks of the educated clergy."[25] Even among the educated clergy his ideas gained no wide currency. The synod of Piacenza declared null any ordinations made by "Berengarians," among others, but who these may have been is not clear. Some of Berengar's eminent former students at the school of Tours, like Eusebius Bruno, bishop of Angers, attempted to shield him from the wrath of his enemies, but there is no indication that these students accepted his doctrines. None of the leading intellectual figures of the day did. Macdonald claimed that his influence extended to Normandy, Germany, and Liège, but much of the evidence is tenuous.[26] At the synod of Vercelli, a young Lombard and a young clerk of Tours supported Berengar with citations from Saint Augustine; both were arrested, and Leo IX was obliged to intervene to protect them from injury.[27]

The clearest specific indication of intellectual Berengarism does come from Liège, though not with the clarity that Macdonald supposed. One of the documents, a letter of Bishop Théoduin, which has been supposed to relate to Berengarism, is actually concerned with Reformists.[28] The sole remaining documents are a letter written by the scholasticus of Mainz, one Gozechin, to Walcher, his successor as scholasticus at Liège, and a letter of Adelmann, bishop of Brescia, to Berengar.[29] The letter of Adelmann, of uncertain date, indicates that Berengarian heresy had spread to Liège. The letter of Gozechin, written about 1060, a pedantic and turgid missive, complained that the young scholars of Liège no longer followed the road of correct doctrine and discipline but preferred to whore after the theology of Berengar, "that apostle of Satan." Drunk with the false vintage of this heresiarch, the scholars of Liège were like the plague, like scorpions, like petty kings of hell bursting forth from the underworld. They posed questions and expounded doctrines that were useless except to subvert those who heard from the true faith. Amidst all this bombast Gozechin did condescend finally to specify the scholars' error: it was that the eucharist was not truly the body of Christ but only its shadow. Gozechin knew Liège well enough not to have been mistaken, and the letter of Théoduin a decade earlier, though it does not prove the existence of Berengarism, does reveal that the bishop was particularly interested in the heresy, and this in turn is a sign that there really may have been Berengarism at Liège. The number and prestige of Berengar's opponents in the years following his death effectively prevented the formation of a school that would continue to support his position, however. There was little intellectual Berengarism, let alone a popular cult, and what there was was quickly dissipated before the strong winds beaten up by the defenders of transubstantiation.

Berengar was a transitional figure belonging wholly to neither time past nor time future, though he participated in the first stage of the development of Scholasticism. Now, in the early years of the twelfth century, the second stage was reached, bringing further change through the importation of the lost works of Aristotle, and Arabic commentaries on these works from the world of Islam. This had the effect of introducing new ideas (and of reintroducing old ones) to the West and, perhaps even more important, of popularizing a method, the syllogistic logic of Aristotle. Plato and Platonism, with their symbolic thought and language, yielded to Aristotle. The energies of philosophers were thenceforward devoted chiefly to assimilating the new ideas and to applying the new logic to both old and new problems. The discontinuity in the history of heresy is evident. The new intellectual heresies arose from disputes over method or over the definitions that the new logic came to debate. The disputes over heresy became at once more picayune, more precise, and more learned.

Already at the end of the eleventh century the great Scholastic controversies were foreshadowed by the beginning of the well-known quarrel over universals. Roscelin, a teacher of Abelard's, opposed the extreme realist position that held reality to exist in the world of ideas so that the individual was merely a "chance collection of characteristics." [30] He maintained that, to the contrary, individuals alone existed. A precise charge against Roscelin at the synod of Soissons was that when his antirealist doctrine was applied to the Trinity it implied that, though each person of the Trinity was real, the Godhead itself was merely a construction of our minds. The sources dealing with Roscelin are so fragmentary, and so little of his own work has been preserved, that it is impossible to say whether he was actually willing to go this far. It seems unlikely. As in the case of Berengar, the difficulty lay primarily in misunderstandings occasioned by the fact that terms and concepts were still undefined.[31]

Later in the century another philosopher was to be pursued by the orthodox for taking a position very different from Roscelin's. This was Gilbert de la Porrée,[32] who found himself in the midst of a raging controversy and was eventually censured at the council of Reims in 1148.[33] The so-called errors of Gilbert were extremely subtle, stemming primarily from the ultrarealist distinction between God and the divinity of God. The council did not formally condemn Gilbert, and so little was his reputation blemished that it was possible for a number of philosophers and theologians to follow his teachings to the extent that a school was formed which earned the name of "Porretan."[34] Scholars in this tradition included Radulfus Ardens and Alanus de Insulis.

Of all medieval heretics Peter Abelard is the most famous both in the history of philosophy and of romance,[35] but his position as a heretic has not yet been well defined. His chief difficulty, other than his personal arrogance, lay in his assertion of the duty of reason to challenge tradition and authority. Beyond this, he held a Pelagian doctrine on grace and free will.

There were numerous other Scholastic disputes in the twelfth century, but however important they may have been for the history of philosophy, they made little significant contribution to the history of dissent. The moral heresies of the Reformists were both more vital and more popular.

Judaizers.

The early Middle Ages was inclined to tolerate Jews, except in periods when popular madness got the better of Christian charity and incited vicious pogroms like those in Germany at the time of the Crusades. Jews were overt infidels to Christian eyes and in general kept apart from the Christian society in which they were imbedded like river rocks in a sandstone matrix; they were at an enormous personal and legal disadvantage in any dealings with Gentiles, but they were not actively persecuted. The cynical exploitation of the weakness of the Jews by Edward I, Philip IV, and other monarchs belongs to a later age that, more sophisticated, became more cruel.

Native Jews have no part in a history of dissent. That a Jew was a Jew was no more a protest against Christian society than that a Moslem was a Moslem. A man who was born a Jew and remained a Jew was but following his own religious tradition, and though he might live in France or Germany he was in fact a member of another society. But a man who was once a Christian but then converted to Judaism was very different: he was making the most extreme protest against Christian society. Having dwelt in the Christian community, he chose to reject it completely.[36]

Few are the reported examples of apostasy from Christianity to Judaism. Though the Pharisees might have scoured land and sea to make a convert, medieval Judaism had perforce to limit proselytizing, which was not tolerated in Christian Europe.[37] Though the door was left open to proselytes, there was no concerted attempt on the part of the Jews to woo Christians away from their faith; indeed, their pleasure over any such event would have been mixed with a fear of reprisals. On the other hand, no Christian was likely to turn to Judaism when this meant that he would be cut off from his society and sent in disgrace to a ghetto, at best despised by all his former associates, and at worst visited with dire punishment. It would have taken enormous courage to convert to Judaism, and every impulse of education and environment would militate against it.

It is therefore curious that there are any recorded cases at all of such conversion. A letter of Agobard of Lyon to King Louis I in 829 inveighed against three *missi dominici* who were purported to have leanings toward Judaism, though there is no question of conversion here; they had merely shown themselves harsh to Christians and merciful to Jews in their judgments. This is less likely to indicate a real sympathy with Judaism than an unwonted fairness in judgment that gave rise to complaints from irritated Christians who had lost their cases. Both the harsh Agobard and his successor Amulo (841–852) objected to the leniency of Louis I toward Jews. The court of the kindly emperor and his wife Judith not only showed mercy to Jews but actually encouraged the reading of Philo and Josephus and discussions of the relative merits of Christianity.[38]

This atmosphere was responsible for the first of the few instances of conversion to Judaism in the early Middle Ages of which we know anything. A priest of the court of Louis, a man with the good old Frankish name of Bodo, became strongly inclined in the course of his studies toward the Jewish religion. Setting out on a journey which he claimed had as its goal a visit to Rome and the fane of the Apostles, he went instead to Moslem Spain, where he settled in Zaragoza, induced his nephew to adopt Judaism as well, and took the Jewish name Eliezer.[39]

In the early years of the eleventh century another authentic example of conversion to Judaism comes to light. In the reign of Henry II of Germany (1002–1024), Duke Conrad of Bavaria had at his court a clerk who "consented to the errors of the Jews." [40] The news of the apostasy of this cleric, whose name was Wecelin, reached the king's ears, and the saintly Henry enlisted the aid of a Churchman of the same name to refute the terrible errors of this monster, whose writings revealed opinions about Christ and the saints that were considered blasphemous. The chronicler Albert fortunately preserves for us a bit of the writings of Wecelin himself, so that we have here the rare privilege of hearing the accused speak; less fortunately, this is followed by a much longer text, which is the letter of Henry the theologian refuting the errors of the Bavarian.

Wecelin based his rejection of Christianity upon his study of the Old Testament. According to the prophet Habbakuk, said Wecelin (the passage is actually from Malachi iii:6), God said, "I am one; I change not." But according to the Christian belief, God came to Mary and made her with child; this implies that God did change and must be false unless God lied in the Old Testament passage, which is ridiculous. In Exodus xxxiii:20 God said to Moses, "No man may see me and live"; this statement applies to any son of man, yet the Christians believe that Jesus the man is united in hypostatic union with the second person of the Trinity and even maintain that the saints look upon God in heaven. The Book of Psalms (cxlvi:3) says, "Put not your trust in princes, nor in the son of man, in whom there is no help." But the Christians do indeed put their trust in the Son of Man. Further, Ezekiel says (this is really Jeremiah xvii:5–6), "Cursed be the man that trusteth in man and maketh flesh his arm . . . he shall be like the heath in the desert, and shall not see when good cometh." What man is excluded from these prohibitions? Peter, John, or

Martin(!), whom the Christians call saints? Certainly not. They are not saints, but demons. Throughout the Old Testament one reads, "The Lord God of Israel," not "The God of the Gentiles." Are all the Christians mad? Does not David say in the Psalms (cv:8–9), "He hath remembered his covenant forever, the word which he commanded to a thousand generations, which convenant he made with Abraham, and his oath to Isaac"? This is the holy law and the circumcision that he gave to Moses his servant.

One would like to hear Wecelin at more length, but, alas, this is all the chronicler dared give us of his work. Was Wecelin a kind of proto-Abelard who recognized that there was a conflict between the teaching of the Old Testament and that of the New, was not afraid to face it, and who then, for some hidden reason, elected to put his trust in the Old Dispensation rather than the New? Was this an intellectual decision? There is Bodo's example, and in the later Middle Ages, too, there were occasional examples of intellectual conversion to Judaism.[41] Medieval scholars often had a predilection for Hebrew scholarship, possibly because, while to learn Greek they had to go to southern Italy or the East, they could make the acquaintance of the Hebrew tongue at the home of the local rabbi. Beryl Smalley cites the case of a monk writing to an anchoress in 1080, saying that the blessed in heaven would speak Hebrew. Scholars such as these, brought into close contact with Jewish people and Jewish thought, might occasionally have exchanged the religion of their fathers for an even older one.[42] Or, is it not more likely that Wecelin himself was a converted Jew who at last, through his study of Scriptures, which was not, by the way, very accurate, felt the pangs of conscience and returned to his earlier faith? Jews were often, when the mood for a good persecution came upon the community, forced to abjure their faith and adopt Christianity, as many sources testify.[43] That some of them should have remained Christians for a while and then lapsed is certain; one such instance is known from a Jewish source,[44] the annals of the later Spanish Inquisition are filled with such cases, and it may well be that Wecelin's was one such case half a millennium earlier.

In view of the enormous difficulties placed in the way of the apostate and of the fact that conversion is seldom wholly an intellectual matter, one would guess that some emotional attachment, either to memories of a Jewish childhood or to a Jewish friend to whom he was closely bound with ties of love, was likely to have been present. Wecelin's tone is highly emotional and full of anger: "What do you growl against these arguments, you animal?," he asks the Christian. Emotion certainly played a role in the third conversion to Judaism of which we hear in the early Middle Ages, that of an Englishwoman in the early years of the reign of Henry II, who abandoned Christianity after her marriage to Jurnet, a Jewish businessman of Norwich.[45] The long reply of Wecelin's adversary Henry gives us little more insight into Wecelin's situation. Henry answered the Jew by citing other texts of the Old Testament in opposition to those employed by Wecelin. The only items of interest in this long-winded letter of the medieval theologian is that he used the phrase "you Jews," evidence in favor of the theory that Wecelin was a lapsed convert. Had Wecelin been born a Christian, there might have been more of an attempt to lure him back to the fold, and his status as a Jew might not have been so readily accepted.

About the same time as Wecelin's apostasy, there were rumors from Sens, in northern France, where Count Rainard, a man of many ill qualities, was accused of favoring and aiding "the worthless Jews." What his precise intellectual position, if any, was, is not known, but Fulbert of Chartres, who was called upon for advice in the matter by the archbishop of Sens, dubbed him a heretic.[46]

Apart from these minor instances and others that probably occurred but are not reported in the sources, there is little to suggest that there was much concern with Judaizing. Abelard wrote a *Dialogue between a Philosopher, a Christian, and a Jew,* but this was no more than a didactic device, and though intellectual respect for Judaism continued and grew in the later Middle Ages, though the influence of Jewish thought increased with the translations of the late twelfth and thirteenth centuries, and though the thirteenth and later centuries counted some Christian converts to Judaism, such events were extremely rare at that time, and in the earlier Middle Ages were very unusual indeed.

Millenarianism.

Millenarian expectations were also uncommon in the early Middle Ages. It has been a long time since the explosion of the legend that medieval people thought the world was going to come to an end in 1000, and recent attempts to find examples of more sophisticated millenarianism in the early Middle Ages have tended to claim examples of chiliasm where none really existed.[47] The origins of millenarian expectation are to be found in the Book of Daniel, the twentieth chapter of the Book of Revelation, and the late Jewish apocryphal literature that pictured the triumph of the Son of Man and the dominion that would be bestowed upon him. This idea became entwined with that of the Parousia, or Second Coming of Christ, and has reappeared from time to time in the history of Christian speculation about the last things. Sometimes it was simplistically interpreted to mean that a thousand years from the Incarnation would bring the end of the world. Such speculation did not produce any millenarian movements in the early Middle Ages, but there were, in the tenth century, a few isolated examples of concern with imminent cataclysm. Abbo of Fleury wrote to Hugh Capet and his son Robert that in his youth he had heard preached in the church in Paris that after a thousand years the Antichrist would come and thereafter the Last Judgment. Abbo labored to refute this error with quotations from Scripture.[48] Around 960 a priest named Bernard, a hermit from the Thuringian March, appeared in Würzburg, teaching that God had revealed to him that the world was shortly to be consumed.[49] About 970 in Lorraine there was widespread belief that the world would be consumed that very year, since Good Friday fell on the Annunciation and people said that it was unbelievable that God would be conceived and die the same day.[50] These cases, of which there were doubtless a good many more that have been left unrecorded, betray no advanced millenarian thought but only a superstitious response to a misunderstood passage of the Scriptures. Millenarianism in the precise sense of expectation of a thousand-year reign of justice does not appear in the early Middle Ages.

These were the varieties of dissent in the early Middle Ages that played the supporting roles to the major part of moral and spiritual Reformist Dissidence.

7. General Condemnations

Among the references to dissent in the early Middle Ages are many that cannot readily be categorized, either because they are so general or because they do not provide sufficient information.

The eighth century.

General condemnations of heresy were common in the eighth century, owing in part to the great vigilance of Saint Boniface in these matters. Charlemagne was on several occasions aroused to the dangers of heresy. In a letter to various bishops of France, Germany, and Italy, he reported that heresy in regard to the Holy Spirit had appeared,[1] and in 774 Pope Hadrian I presented him with various canons condemning priests and other clergy involved in heterodox activities. Bishops, priests, and deacons praying with heretics were to be excommunicated and, if they had urged the heretics to take holy orders, condemned. Baptisms effected by heretics were, if improperly performed, to be deemed null and void. These canons, repeated from provisions made by the early Church, are no direct evidence of the existence of any particular heresy, but they show the concern of pope and king with the problem.[2] Pope Zachary had already written to Saint Boniface on July 1, 746, taking a moderate position in regard to baptism. If the form were improper owing to ignorance rather than malice, it was not to be considered heretical, and any baptism made in the name of the Trinity was to be considered valid.[3] An undated latter of Charlemagne,[4] noting points of doctrine to be inculcated with particular vigor, emphasized that Christ "truly suffered in the flesh," indicating that some sort of docetism may have existed at that time. A capitulary of 789 repeated Saint Paul's condemnation of the heresy of Simon Magus,[5] though this was probably merely a reference to simony. In 794 Paulinus of Aquileia condemned illiterate priests who through ignorance taught their flocks improper baptismal procedures.[6] The Saxon poet praised Charlemagne in verse for his action against heretics, though again no specific reference is given.[7]

Both the West and the East Franks experienced dissidence. In the west, in 781, Potho, abbot of Saint Vincent, was accused of heresy, though falsely.[8] Our knowledge of heresy among the East Franks is particularly great and Gregory III, writing in 731 to the bishops of Bavaria, warned of heretics and of the adulteration of Christianity with the rites of the heathen. He repeated this warning to the people of Germany as a whole that same year.[9] He exhorted all Christians to stand firm against paganism, against false priests and heretics, and against the false doctrines of the Irish, who had been immensely valuable in missionary and educational work, but, now that the papacy was strong enough to attempt to establish a unified and regular ecclesiastical organization, began to seem a hindrance.

The most important source of heresy and dissent among the Germans was the ignorance that was all too common in the period and was particularly widespread in a country only recently claimed from paganism. A letter of December 1, 722, of Gregory II to Boniface reveals the existence, on the eastern bank of the Rhine, of worshippers of idols passing under the name of Christians.[10] Ignorance and pagan practices combined to make Germany unusually susceptible to dissent. In the period 733–735, during a missionary visit to Bavaria in the time of Duke Hukbert, Boniface had to deal with Heremwulf, "a schismatic deceived by heresy," who had had considerable success in seducing the people. Boniface condemned him and expelled him from the Church, correcting those he had led astray and leading them back into the fold. Willibald, the saint's biographer, says that Heremwulf's error was "idolatry." [11] Willibald also refers to heresy in connection with Boniface's disputes with Duke Odilo of Bavaria,[12] accusing Odilo of actions injurious to the Church, and noting that people were improperly pretending to the priesthood and even the episcopal dignity. Willibald says that Boniface succeeded in leading the duke and his people away from the *injusta haereticae falsitatis secta,* but the actions of the Bavarians were clearly not in the nature of doctrinal heterodoxy. Willibald seems, like later writers during the great controversy between pope and emperor, to be using the term in the sense of schism.

Other German heretics obliged Gregory III to write another letter of warning[13] in 737–739, and Pope Zachary tells us of a heretical priest in Bavaria in 744.[14] A general council of the German clergy on April 21, 742, condemned "false priests" who were "deceiving the people," but it is not clear whether these clerics were guilty of heresy or of immorality. Elsewhere the council ordered the deposition of "false priests *and* deacons or clerks guilty of fornication or adultery," which distinction may indicate that heresy as well as immorality was involved.[15] In a letter from Pope Zachary to Boniface on April 1, 743, we hear of Frankish priests with "false beliefs." [16] Moral failings, such as sexual irregularity and violence, were indicated, but if the priests believed or maintained (*opinantur*) that such acts were legitimate, as seems to be implied, then they were moral heretics. In a letter of October 31, 745, Zachary praised Boniface for his work against false bishops, schismatics, and enemies who sowed the tares of heresy.[17] In 748 Boniface wrote the pope requesting advice on several points of discipline, and on May 1 of that year Zachary replied. His answer[18] revealed the dreadful state of the Frankish Church. False priests who had never been ordained by bishops, but who were yet more numerous than orthodox priests, wandered about administering the sacraments. Making a living by exploiting the people and demanding payment in money or in kind for their ministrations, they were nonetheless highly popular and protected by the people from the discipline of the authorities. They preached to the peasants, not in churches, but in the open fields. They baptized improperly and required no knowledge of the faith on the part of the catechumens. Zachary ordered Boniface to call a synod to rally the faithful against these activities, but that all efforts in this direction failed is clear from a letter of Boniface to the pope in 751.[19] Boniface had not only been unable to confine these popular heretics in monasteries, but he had encountered them everywhere, even at the Frankish court. Mindful of the rule that the excommunicated are to be shunned by the faithful, Boniface brooded over the fact that he was forced by circumstances to associate with them. Zachary's reply[20] indicates that the pope had also become less sanguine about the prospects of rooting out the evil. It was well, he replied, to avoid such people, but since this was impossible, Boniface was permitted the hope that by associating with them he might even succeed in saving their souls. Whether or not he was successful in his spiritual enterprise, his contemporaries and near-contemporaries praised his fight against the heretics. Archbishop Cuthbert of Canterbury, Othloh of Saint Emmeram, Liudger in his life of Gregory of Utrecht, and Eigil in his life of Sturmi, as well as Willibald himself, wrote testimony to Boniface's struggles against the dissenters.[21]

The corruption of Christianity by pagan practices in a newly converted land challenged Boniface in his first year as a missionary in Thuringia. Those Thuringians who had had the faith had "for the most part" lost it owing to men who preached a barbarously corrupted Christianity.[22] Sometime in his early missionary years, probably between 719 and 723, Boniface had to deal with a similar aberration on the part of royalty, the twin Saxon rulers Dettic and Deorulf, who practiced idolatrous rites "under the name of Christianity." These rulers had received a veneer of Christian teaching from some earlier, possibly Irish source, and then quickly reverted to paganism while retaining the name and some of the form of Christianity,[23] rather like an eighth-century Mau Mau.

At the end of the century, in 799(?) Alcuin cautioned the clergy of Salzburg to beware the spreading influence of heresy, warning them to fortify themselves against this plague by diligent application to Scripture.[24] In a little tract addressed to Rado, abbot of Saint Vaast, around the year 800, he inveighed against the danger of an increasing number of "pseudoprophets" in "these dangerous times." [25] Dangerous for the German Church the eighth century may have been; it was certainly not lacking in a variety of religious dissidence.

There are indications of dissent even in England and, horrible to say, in Ireland. The Penitential of Theodore, archbishop of Canterbury, a collection of canons Sir Frank Stenton called "a fundamental authority for the state of the church in Theodore's day," [26] contained detailed instructions for dealing with heretics. And in 790 the Irish Church warned against twisting the Fathers to obtain support for heretical doctrines, though it is not clear whether the documents refer to heretics in general or to heretics in Ireland itself.[27] Also, an Irish table of commutations mentions heresy along with lewdness, lying, and transgressions of order as something to be avoided.[28]

The ninth century.

A capitulary of Aachen in 802 specified that false martyrs were not to be venerated,[29] probably a reference to overenthusiasm on the part of denizens of certain localities for a favorite hero. Raban Maur, abbot of Fulda and a leading scholar of the reign of Louis the Pious, discussed heresy on several occasions. In the *Instruction of the Clergy,* written in 819, he listed heresies besetting the Church,[30] but all were ancient, an indication perhaps that contemporary heresy had not made much impression on him. Again, in *On the Universe* Raban touched on the question of heresy,[31] describing both Christian and Jewish sects, and then went on to list a few of the most important doctrines of the Church. This may indicate that he felt a need to emphasize these points against particular heretics. In the quarter of a century since he had written the *Instruction of the Clergy,* Raban may have become more aware of contemporary problems. He made it a point to insist that Christ was the Son of God "not by adoption," indicating that he had in mind the Adoptionist heresy that was still causing trouble in Spain. Again, his clear statement of the double procession of the Holy Spirit from both the Father and the Son was obviously aimed at bolstering the Western position against the unwillingness of the Eastern Church to accept the *Filioque* clause. Most of the other heresies he condemned under their ancient names. Was he merely shaking an academic stick at ancient errors, or was he condemning modern heresies under anachronistic names? A few of his remarks give food for thought. In the celebration of the eucharist, he tells us, it is proper to offer mixed wine and water, but improper to offer water alone. Were there ascetic dissenters who opposed the inclusion of wine in the consecrated elements? Again, he takes care to assert that the body is good in itself and condemns the Manichaeans for maintaining otherwise and for eschewing meat and legitimate marriage. This, too, might indicate the presence of overzealous ascetics, whose activities were not unknown elsewhere at the time.

Paschasius Radbert, a ninth-century theological light, mentioned the vice of heresy in a dialogue described in the *Vita* of Wala, abbot of Corbie, but this may betray nothing more than a pedantic familiarity with the problem.[32] In 827, Bishop Ansegis of Sens published capitularies aimed at correcting ignorant clergy and condemning superstitious practices, including the worship of uncanonical angels and the reverence for false writings and fraudulent letters from heaven.[33] Pope Nicholas I (858–867) dealt with heretics in his *decreta,* forbidding them to lodge accusations against orthodox bishops. Pope Formosus (891–896) wrote in 893 to Archbishop Hermann of Cologne complaining that the Church was being perturbed by "the artifices of pagans and false Christians," without specifying who these might be.[34] Formosus directed a similar missive to Archbishop Fulk of Reims (882–901), saying that heresies and schisms were to be found everywhere.[35] In 858 Walter Bishop of Orléans issued orders to the archdeacons of his diocese to investigate the doctrine of the clergy and enclosed a little creed to which they were to conform.[36] The recalcitrant young Bishop Hincmar of Laon and nephew of the great Hincmar of Reims not only was disobedient to metropolitan authority but was charged with several unorthodox practices that led his uncle to accuse him of heresy.[37]

In Germany and the Netherlands in the ninth century the situation was little different from that in France. The *Annales* of Xanten in the diocese of Utrecht report the appearance of an unknown heresy in 838 in a typical entry:

A rainy and extremely windy winter, and in January, on the 21st of the month, thunder was heard, and likewise in the month of February, on the 17th, loud thunder was heard, and an uncommon solar heat scorched the earth; and earthquakes occurred in many parts of the world; and a fire in the shape of a dragon was seen in the air. In the same year heresy arose. In the same year on the fifth night before Christmas loud thunder was heard, and lightning was seen, and in many ways the misery and wretchedness of mankind increased daily.[38]

The synod of Tribur in 895 was obliged to condemn again the idea that either water or wine alone ought to be offered at the consecration.[39] In the back country of the diocese of Utrecht, perhaps the wildest in Western Europe south of Scandinavia, rude heresy appeared among the half-savage inhabitants, including errors about the Trinity.[40]

In Italy, Padova was the scene of heretical preaching on the redemption about the middle of the century.[41] Pope John VIII wrote on August 28, 882, to the clergy of Ravenna ordering them to arrest one Maimberto, a disseminator of errors.[42] Heresy also appeared on the easternmost fringes of the Latin Church. John VIII wrote to Bishop Methodius of Pannonia (Bohemia-Moravia) in 879 summoning him to Rome to examine him about purported errors, involving for the most part liturgical innovations introduced during the conversion of that land.[43]

The tenth century.

The tenth century began in that period of unrest ushered in by the new barbarian invasions and the collapse of the Carolingian empire. Intellectual and spiritual life receded in these years, and reports of dissident activity are fewer in the later years of the century than in the earlier, and fewer yet in the first half of the tenth. Rather of Liège and Verona[44] and Atto of Vercelli[45] both attacked heresy in general terms, Atto remarking only that the error at which he aims is the equation of the faithful departed with the angels.

There were indications of dissent in Germany. On April 25, 989, Pope John XV sent a privilege of immunity to the monastery of Saint Gregory constructed under the orders of Bishop Gebhard II of Constance.[46] In granting the monastery the standard exemptions from episcopal authority, the pope included a caution not found in other comparable privileges, even those of John XV. "If indeed, which God forbid, the bishop of this holy diocese should be a heretic or a schismatic, the brothers of the aforementioned monastery shall have the power by authority of the apostolic see to investigate the ecclesiastical orders by which they know him to be a bishop lest he presume unjustly to do them harm." There is no question of Bishop Gebhard's orthodoxy, for John refers to him as "our best beloved brother," but it is possible that John had some other fear of heresy in that diocese. About 975, Bishop Pilgrim of Passau, on his accession to the episcopal dignity, wrote to Pope Benedict VII, making a confession of faith. This was required of any bishop upon his taking office, so the profession is in itself not unusual. But Pilgrim maintained that he had been unjustly accused of heresy. Unfortunately we can conclude nothing about the basis for the accusation.[47]

The eastern part of Germany then being gradually reclaimed from the Slavs revealed characteristics similar to those of western Germany in the eighth century. In 983, during one of the fierce Slavic risings against the German intruders, Bishop Wolcmer of Brandenburg was driven out of his see, the former bishop (Dodilo) exhumed and thrown to the dogs, and Christian worship replaced by "rites of demoniac heresy," namely, pagan practices. The relevant point is that not only the Slavic pagans, but also the superficially converted Christians in the area turned, like the children of Israel, to whore after strange gods.[48]

Just before the end of the century, dissent is attested by a poem composed as an epitaph for Bishop Notger (972–1008) of Liège. The poet affirms that Notger "instructed and replenished the clergy in Latin and the people in the vernacular with the great sweetness of his speech, a gentle milk that furnished a solid diet to the healthy. Heresies yielded readily beneath the blows of this stout knight of Christ. Fraud, feigned faith, and lies were put to flight, and when caught they trembled as if before the Judge of good and evil." It is possible that this is a mere topos, but the topos of heresy appears in epitaphs with extreme rarity. It is also possible that the eleventh-century author of the *Vita* was reading back the importance of heresy in his own day into Notger's time. The circumstances of the poem's composition, however, makes it unlikely, and it is probable that dissent did exist in Liège in the reign of Notger, though there is no indication of its variety.[49]

There is another passing reference to heresy in the Liégeois milieu at this time, again one from which little that is substantial can be deduced. Folcuin, author of the *Deeds of the Abbots of Lobbes,* mentioned heresy in dealing with an abbot of the eighth century.[50] This abbot, whose name was Abel, had the peculiar distinction of being archbishop of Reims (*ca.* 743–748) before becoming abbot of Lobbes. In that archdiocese in the eighth century it was customary to recite the names of each former prelate in commemoration masses for the dead. Abel, after he had resigned the archiepiscopal dignity, indignantly inquired why his name had been omitted from the catalog. Folcuin surmised that the omission was made in order to persuade Abel to return when the see again became vacant, but it seems more likely that the clergy of Reims simply saw no reason to include the name of a living man among those remembered in masses for the dead. The significance of this lies in Folcuin's reaction. In a rather confused passage, probably garbled by some subsequent scribe, Folcuin hastened to exonerate Abel of heresy, noting that the men of his day were ever eager to crush it. In this passage Folcuin attacked heresy with such vehemence that one may surmise that he had had personal experience with it.

Indications of nonconformity also appeared in France. Archbishop Hervé of Reims addressed the synod of Trosly (near Soissons) convening on June 26, 909, and observed that it had been impossible for many years to convene a synod owing to three problems, which he listed as the invasions of the barbarians, the political troubles of the kingdom, and "infestations of false Christians," which he proclaimed as punishment sent upon the people for their sins.[51] About 987, the famous abbot of Fleury, Abbo, wrote to the archbishop of Bourges to warn him against heresy, adding a bit of unusual advice to the prelate himself: "Never permit yourself to become a heretic in any way," the abbot warned, "for a person who errs from the faith that the Catholic Church holds from the holy Apostles does penance for his sins in vain." [52]

The chronicle of the abbey of Saint Bavo in Ghent relates a strange story for the year 969. An unidentified count was possessed by the devil; he was led before Pope John XIII that he might be bound to orthodoxy as once he had been bound by "deceitful clergy" to other doctrines. Our interest here is not in the purported possession, but in the reference to the deceitful clergy who may have been teaching false doctrines. The story is so fabulous, however, that it bears all the marks of unsubstantiated rumor.[53] At the end of the century, in the reign of Hugh Capet (987–996), abbot Abbo of Fleury addressed a little pamphlet to the king and his son Robert.[54] Defining heresy and posing it as a problem, Abbo requested the kings to imitate the examples set by the emperors of old in stamping out heresy: "Drive every heresy out of your kingdom, that God may keep you in eternal peace." Abbo's plea may have had some effect, for it was Robert to whom belongs the distinction of having been the first to order the official execution of heretics, at Orléans in 1022. On July 7, 997, Pope Gregory V wrote to archbishop John of Ravenna, bewailing all the heresies unhappily besetting the Church.[55]

The eleventh century.

With the increase in intellectual, political, and spiritual activity at the end of the time of troubles and the great increase in the amount of material available to the historian, the eleventh century stands out as the first in the Middle Ages for which the sources begin to be almost adequate. General concern over the problem of heresy increased, and the use of the term shifted somewhat after the inauguration of the reform papacy under Leo IX. The fervor of the reform program, especially under Gregory VII, caused a more promiscuous use of the term, with greater readiness than before to use it to describe deviations from the policies advocated by the papacy. General indications of dissent are many. Around 1079, Gregory VII wrote to Saint Anselm of Bec asking him to pray that the Church might be delivered from the heretics.[56] In a letter of January 25, 1075, to King Sweyn II of Denmark, Gregory complained that a rich province not far from Rome was in the possession of base and dastardly heretics; this reference is probably to the Normans, newly arrived in southern Italy, who treated Church property without great respect and with whom Gregory had yet to make an alliance. In 1075 Gregory was still militarily bound to the countess of Tuscany against Robert Guiscard, whom he doubtless considered the chief of the heretics.[57]

A heretical Armenian priest named Macharius, who had been condemned by Archbishop Gregory of Simas in Armenia, arrived in Italy, was examined by Gregory VII, and then went to live in Frigento, where the pope in 1080 asked the archbishop of Benevento to visit him and persuade him of the truth so that the heresy might not spread abroad. It seems an unusually lenient treatment of an acknowledged heretic; unfortunately the letter does not tell us what sort of doctrines Macharius had been preaching.[58] Later the same year[59] the pope wrote to Archbishop Gregory, probably as a result of his interview with Macharius, and condemned some of the practices of the Armenian Church, such as the confection of chrism out of butter rather than out of balsam, but these problems do not directly concern the Western Church. Eight canons of uncertain provenance, but dating from the 1070's or 1080's, caution that no one be allowed to preach unless approved by the bishop, "on account of the divers detestable errors taught by the uneducated." [60] The chronicler Bernold of Saint Blasien, writing about 1100, used an odd phrase in describing his sympathy for the reform program of Gregory VII, which could be interpreted as a statement that in his reign Gregory had to deal with a Church infested by heretics.[61] Many of the papalist writers in the latter part of the century mentioned heresy not infrequently, but in many cases, as in the books *Against the Simoniacs* by Humbert of Silva Candida, the simoniacs and schismatics are meant more often than doctrinal heretics.[62] In 1084, Gregory, like his polemicists, became somewhat violent against his enemies and accused them of heresy and plotting against Christ; the heightened tempers of Gregory's reign were conducive to the emotional use of pejorative language.

In France, an atrociously written piece of doggerel on theology addressed to the king by Adalbero of Laon speaks of heresy, and the author may have had dissenters in mind, but his leaden dullness both of pen and brain makes it unclear what he was thinking of.[63] A synod at Rouen in 1048 began the first of its published canons with the affirmation that "we must hold firmly to the creed of the Catholic and Apostolic Church," [64] and though no heretical doctrines were concerned, the council must have had dissent on the mind. The synod of Narbonne in 1056 condemned heresy in general,[65] and at Nevers in 1075 a man named Belinus and his comrades were put to death for an unspecified heresy.[66] In 1015 abbot Fulbert of Chartres wrote counts Gualeran and Gualtier praising the work of king Robert against the heretics. Fulbert noted that the archbishop of Sens had recently written him asking his advice as to how best to deal with Count Rainard of Sens, "a man favoring the worthless Jews." [67] In 1049 the province of Reims showed concern about dissent, when heresy was mentioned twice.[68] Again, in 1060, there is evidence of the existence of heretics at Sisteron in Provence; Nicholas II addressed a letter to the clergy and faithful of the town repeating an old eighth-century warning of Gregory II against the presence of Manichaeans, and it is difficult to imagine why he should have done this had there not been heretics in Provence at that time.[69] With the emergence of France as the intellectual center of Western Europe, intellectual heresy began to appear more frequently. The historian Radulf Glaber began his work with a chapter entitled *On the Divine Quaternity,* a literary coup not designed to quiet the suspicions of watchdogs of orthodoxy, and he was promptly accused of holding heterodox opinions on the Trinity. In fact, Radulf was merely amusing himself, as the ancients and medievals so often did, with the joys of numerology. There are four gospels, four elements, four virtues, and four senses, he observed, so that four must truly be a holy (*divina*) number. In this there was no real taint of heresy on the nature of the Godhead.[70]

In Germany, a Liégeois poem dating from 1010 to 1024 tells of dissent.[71] Entitled *On the Evils Originating in France,* it forms part of a collection of poetry known as the *Fecunda Ratis* (the *"Well-Laden Vessel"*), a collection of adages from the scriptures and the Fathers done into verse by a pedagogue for the edification of the young. Written by Egbert of Liège, it was presented to Bishop Adalbold of Utrecht.[72] The *Evils* warned its schoolboy audience of heretics who must, from the terms used and the immediacy conveyed,[73] really have been present in the diocese. Whether these dissenters may be identified with those vanquished by Notger or with the later heretics at Liège under Bishop Réginard cannot be ascertained from the text, which tells us merely that they arrived in the diocese of Liège from France and that they swore by Christ that they could not be killed. Egbert warned the people of Liège to lock and bolt their doors against the heretics, feeling that they were dangerous in the physical sense. It is hard from this to imagine what sort of heretics these were. Curiously, Egbert, in speaking of this heresy to the students, used the words "as you may remember," implying that they would have heard of it before reading the poem. Now, if Egbert were merely referring to heretics presently at Liège, he would not have said "may," as they certainly would have heard of those, nor would he have used the past tense when the latter part of the poem is a clear warning for the present. Finally, the words "of which you have heard of good deal" seem to refer to something the students would have dealt with in the classroom. The only writings on heresy that could possibly have been familiar to them were the anti-Manichaean writings of Saint Augustine. Egbert may have considered these heretics Manichaeans, then, but there is no other indication that they were, and the oaths by Lance, Cross, and Bowels of Christ, if they are to be taken at all seriously, preclude Catharist docetism, the doctrine that Christ's physical body was an illusion. As with so many of the other incidents of heresy at this time, the meager evidence resists further elucidation. Some general and vague indications of dissent in Italy in the eleventh century also exist. An Armenian named Simon was said to have been preaching heresy in Rome around 1016.[74] Leo IX wrote to Osimo in the diocese of Ancona attacking despoilers of churches as being worse even than heretics,[75] but the topical nature of this statement makes it dubious evidence for the existence of heretics. Urban II mentioned heresy on several occasions in writing to Italian correspondents. On April 17, 1097 (or 1098), he wrote Bishop Bernard of Bologna about certain brothers who had unknowingly allowed themselves to be ordained by heretics.[76] In an undated letter to the people of San Vincenzo on the Volturno, Urban affirmed, apparently in answer to a request for information, that sacraments administered by heretics and schismatics validly ordained were themselves valid, although for reasons of discipline the faithful ought to abstain from receiving them,[77] and in another undated letter to Lucius, prior of Saint Juventus in Pavia, he gave similar advice.[78]

The only hint of heresy in Scandinavia in the early Middle Ages appears in a passage by the famous historian Adam of Bremen, the leading early medieval authority on Scandinavia. Around 1050 King Anund Jakob of Sweden, a Christian, died, and his brother Emund succeeded him. Emund, though baptized, cared little for religion, and had in his entourage a certain Osmund or Asmund who had earlier been sent to the schools of Bremen to further his education. Emund appointed Osmund bishop. Afterward, going to Rome for his ordination, Osmund was unable to obtain the approval of the pope and in addition incurred the anger of the see of Hamburg-Bremen, which claimed jurisdiction over Sweden and resented the attempt to bypass it in the election and consecration of a Swedish bishop. Osmund wandered about for some time and finally obtained consecration from Archbishop Stephen I (*ca.* 1038–1058) of Gnesen in Poland. Returning to Sweden, Osmund passed himself off as having been consecrated by the pope and thenceforward ordered that the archiepiscopal cross should precede him in procession. Legates of the archbishop of Bremen arriving at the court of Emund heard that the purported archbishop was corrupting the newly converted barbarians with false doctrine. The Bremen legates doubtless exaggerated Osmund's supposed errors because of their political quarrel, and it is uncertain whether there was any truth in their claims. After unsuccessfully trying to discredit the legates, Osmund passes from our sight until 1070, at which date we learn that he died in exile in England. From this we may deduce that his errors, if there were any, were not allowed to gain currency in his homeland.[79]

Magic and superstition.

Superstitions and magical practices long persisted in Europe and are by no means dead yet. In the early Middle Ages they derived from three sources, the first being the tendency of the ignorant of all periods and climes to superstition, the second being the tradition of low Roman paganism, and the third being the tradition of Teutonic paganism. Superstition and magic were common throughout Europe, although strongest in those areas most recently converted to Christianity. Saint Boniface, for example, had great difficulties with pagans in newly converted Germany.

Superstition was often modified by Christianity or merely by the passage of time until it was rendered innocuous to the Church. The preservation of pagan practices in the cult of the saints is well known. Many pagan rites, like the dance around the maypole, were preserved long after their original significance had been lost. In literature, pagan motifs like the Grail story were used time and again by authors and for audiences who had little notion of their origin. Such phenomena are no indication of religious revolt.

Magic, on the other hand, persisted throughout the Middle Ages in open defiance of the Church.[80] Magic is a kind of prototypical science and technology, scientific in its highest forms in that it strives for understanding, and technological in its ordinary forms in that it strives to bring the forces of the universe under human control. The magic of the early Middle Ages, like the superstition, in part derives from Roman and Germanic antecedents and in part is autochthonous. Magic is colored by the particular society in which it exists, so that medieval magic acquired a Chrstian coloration while remaining in its nature and purpose non-Christian and even nonreligious. Magic can be considered neither heresy nor apostasy since it is in essence not religion at all. Because it was condemned by the Church, however, those who overtly and consciously practiced it or defended its practice were dissenters in the broad sense. The essential point is that the wide existence of magic indicates the breadth of indifference to the Christian view of life. Indications of magic in the period from the eighth to the twelfth centuries are so numerous as to defy citation, the most common practices being weather-witching, divinations, "diagnoses" and "cures," astrology, and the use of amulets.[81]

Witchcraft is essentially different from magic. Where magic is a prescientific or protoscientific attempt to control the universe through what were considered natural forces, witchcraft is a traffic with evil spirits. It usually involves the worship of these spirits and therefore is religious in nature; thus a member of the witch cult is clearly to be considered a heretic or even an apostate. Church authorities varied in their condemnations of wichcraft, some anathematizing only the practice of, others the mere belief in, the cult. Yet belief in demons was generally accepted as compatible with orthodoxy, and Satan has always occupied a firm place in Christian doctrine. It is certain that belief in evil spirits was ordinary in the early Middle Ages, and reports of cases of possession are not uncommon. But belief in demons and involuntary possession are not examples of witchcraft, and there is little evidence in this period of deliberate commerce with evil spirits. The witch cult seems to be a product of the later Middle Ages, and Margaret Murray's famous thesis of a continuity of a "Dianic religion" from ancient times has met with justified skepticism. References to "witches" (*stregae*) in early medieval documents usually mean *magicians* rather than witches in the sense we are using the term, and cases in which purported attempts were made to summon demons are dubious and isolated. The reasons for the eventual appearance of a true witch cult in the later period are beyond the scope of our present interest. It did not exist in the early Middle Ages.

Courtly love.

Courtly love has sometimes been counted a heresy.[82] Most would regard this an exaggeration of the seriousness of the matter and a stretching of the term out of proportion. Courtly love is not heresy in the strict sense. Yet if our interest is not merely in theological definitions but in broader areas of social response, the ethos of courtly love does represent, insofar as it was taken seriously, a revolt against the Church. Whatever its ultimate origins, and these have been hotly debated, courtly love subtly perverted many Christian attitudes and ideas. The exaltation of a finite creature to the highest altar of one's devotion, the use of a theological term like "adoration" in describing the lover's relationship to his lady, the replacement of faith by human love and of grace by human joy, are only the more evident examples of this perversion. The ideal of the knight of Christ is replaced by that of the knight of love, and the old Christian virtues of patience and submission are applied to another god than Jehovah. Though their theories may not always have been meant entirely in earnest, the courtly lovers quite evidently had "ultimate concern" for a devotion other than that of Christ.

Not a heresy in the formal sense, courtly love did represent disrespect for Christian principles and hostility or indifference to the Christian Church. As with superstition and magic, the wide currency of attitudes of courtly love in France and Germany of this period indicates that there was broad disaffection from Christian purposes to form the background of religious dissent.

8. The Problem of Dualism

Religious dualism is an attitude positing a warfare between two anti-pathetic cosmic forces as the chief dynamic underlying the phenomenal world. The two chief sources of religious dualism in the West are Persian dualism and Greek philosophical dualism. In the Persian variety, which flourished from the time of Zoroaster in the sixth century B.C., the principle of opposition is stated in its purest form: there is a god of goodness and light, and an autonomous, almost coequal god of darkness and evil; the two struggle incessantly with one another, though in the end Mazda, the god of light, will prevail. Greek dualism was also religious in origin, first appearing in Orphism, a cult arising in the eighth century B.C. Orphism taught a fundamental opposition of principles, one spiritual and the other material. The spiritual was equated with goodness. Man's position in this world was that of a spirit entrapped in a material body, the "prison of the soul," and his duty was to liberate himself from this confinement through the practice of the Orphic religion. The fundamental difference between Persian and Greek dualism is that while the former conceived of an opposition of principles, the latter supposed an opposition between spiritual and material, while crediting greater goodness and greater reality to the spiritual.

Whether Greek philosophical thought drew heavily upon Orphism, or whether both Greek philosophy and religion expressed an under-lying tendency to dualism, dualistic principles did take up residence in the central apartments of Greek speculative philosophy. There are innumerable varieties of metaphysical dualism, and Pythagoras looms large in its history, but it is Plato who stands out as the greatest of the philosophic dualists with his doctrine that the phenomenal world is a shadow world rendering only a pale suggestion of the real world of ideas.[1] What is most important to the history of the problem is that he equated the ideal with the good: what is ideal is rational and what is in accordance with right reason is good. The world of ideas is most good, and, by implication, matter is correspondingly least good.

Further steps might be taken. For the Orphics, matter was not only less good than was spirit, it was evil. For Plotinus, since evil was the lack of good, and matter of all things most lacked reality, matter, ergo, was evil. In Syria, the melting pot of the Hellenistic world, Greek and Persian dualism were now wed, and in the doctrine born of this union, the Greek evil matter was attributed to the Persian evil god, while the ideal world was reserved to the good god.

One effect of the new doctrine was to initiate the growth of dualistic religions and sects, but the other was to shape nascent Christianity itself. Christianity received the imprint of dualism from two distinct dies. First, Jesus and the primitive Christian community were influenced by the teachings of the Essenes, who in turn had come under the influence of Persian dualism. Second, as Christianity became progressively hellenized, Greek philosophical dualism made a deep and durable mark upon it. A basic ambivalence in the teachings of Jesus and of the early Church produced one of the most familiar tensions in Christianity, that between the Kingdom of God and the Kingdom of this world. Historians as well as theologians still debate the meaning of these terms, but it is certain that the opposition between them implies at least a modicum of dualism in the tension between the purely spiritual world of God and the phenomenal world here below.

Christianity is of course not purely, or even primarily, dualistic. If, influenced by the Essenes, Jesus taught the renunciation of the things of this world, he also, under the influence of traditional Judaism, taught that the world is God's creation and has value in itself. The best answer to the debate of whether Jesus was world-affirming or world-rejecting is that he was both, and this is precisely what has given Christianity the balance, sanity, and relevance that it has guarded through the centuries. In its teachings the tension between the two kingdoms is not expressed in the simple terms of spirit versus matter. The Kingdom of this world is a kingdom without God's grace; the Kingdom of God *is* God's grace.

If we live the life of grace, we are elevated above "the things of this world," but the material world is not as a whole either evil or unreal. It is the life of the Christian *in* the world, the way he uses it and acts in it, that is good or evil. Christianity is less a dualist, than an ethical, religion.

Yet the tension between this world and God's makes Christianity share many dualist attitudes. "For now we see through a glass, darkly; but then face to face," said Saint Paul. The real world is not the world in which we live our earthly lives, but the world of grace. Though the Christians said that the body was not the prison, but the temple, of the spirit, they knew that if it were used improperly, if material concerns were allowed to exceed their lawful limits, evil would be the result. When matter is abused it becomes, for the Christian as well as for the dualist, a heavy, weighty thing, pulling him down and away from God. Matter and the body are not evil in themselves, yet they lure the spirit from the path of perfect love, and they are obstacles to the Christian in his search for grace.

Dualism is present elsewhere in Christianity as well. Mysticism, whereby, as Dionysius the Areopagite said, we are "transported wholly out of ourselves and given unto God," is the most sublime and most complete method of perfecting true faith, which is abandon. In mysticism Christianity speaks a language similar to, though not identical with, dualism. The mystical soul, says Evelyn Underhill, will "deny the world in order that it may find reality." It recasts its character to conform with the "independent spiritual world." It seeks to escape from the "manifold illusions" in which it is immersed in order to eliminate the distance that separates it from God. It seeks to place a cloud of forgetfulness between itself and this world by the mortification of earthly desires, and with the arrow of love to pierce the cloud of unknowing that separates it from the divine reality. It is true that the Christian mystic loves the world that God has created, but he puts it away as a growing youth renounces the toys of a child. The allurements and entanglements of the world, insofar as they continue to attract, must be resisted, and in his resistance the attitude of the Christian begins to resemble that of the dualist. A later Christian mystic, unbridled by orthodoxy, lapsed into dualistic terminology: "O Lamb," said William Blake, "Assume the dark satanic body in the Virgin's womb!" Here the mystic has leaped the gate that separated orthodoxy from dualism, but the barrier was never high.[2]

In all Christian puritanism there is a touch of dualism. The puritan sees that the things of this world, which ought to be used in moderation, are used instead to excess, and in his revulsion he forgets that God is their creator. He sees their potential for evil more clearly than their potential for good, forgetting that the rot lies in the will of the man who abuses the thing rather than in the thing itself. In the fundamentalist rejection of wine, in the thinly veiled disgust for sex on the part of some puritans, there may linger more hatred of this world than love of God's, and this is dualism. The dedicated reformer in the Christian Church is usually touched by puritanism, and his puritanism is in turn touched by dualism. Simone Pétrement has precisely stated the inevitable association of dualism and reform:

Heresy . . . is dualist because it is heresy. The heretic wishes to make live again the moral teachings of the Gospel (that *separation* from the world and from the justice of the world) and what one may call the *method* of the Gospel (humility, mistrust of oneself and of one's own justice, hope in the higher light and in grace). This is enough recurrently to engender theories of grace, of the Spirit who descends, of the other world that judges this one, and, with the other world, the theory of the two principles. It is difficult not to see the links between all these ideas.[3]

The presence of dualist ideas in Christianity itself helps illuminate the central question of this chapter. Dualist ideas appeared in the early Middle Ages in the form of religious dissent. What was their origin? This question has long been debated and discussed by a great number of historians,[4] and a corresponding number of answers has been supplied. It has been suggested that gnostic ideas survived in western Europe from ancient times and that a more or less secret tradition of dualism existed in the West until it finally became explicit in the eleventh century. The idea that dualism was imported from the East has been accepted by the majority of scholars. It was long fashionable, and still is with some writers, to speak of the "Medieval Manichee," assuming that the ultimate derivation of medieval dualism is from ancient Manichaeism, but it is now thought more likely that gnosticism and the broad persistence of dualist ideas in the Near East, rather than Manichaeism in particular, were the foundry of these ideas. The classic interpretation, most recently presented by Sir Steven Runciman, traces a chain from primitive gnosticism to the Paulicians of Armenia, to the Bogomils of Bulgaria, to the Patarenes of Bosnia, and finally to the Catharists[5] (called Albigensians in the Midi) of western Europe. According to this interpretation, Eastern doctrines arrived in the Occident about the year 1000 or shortly before and reinforced tendencies to dualism that already existed there.

In the last decade, new perspectives have been gained. Père Antoine Dondaine has succeeded in showing beyond a doubt that dualism was introduced into the Occident by Bogomil missionaries.[6] This link in the chain is now firmly forged. But Père Dondaine's missionaries arrived, not in 1000, but in the 1140's. Many historians had already discovered that there was a great difference between the Catharism before the mid-twelfth century and that which flourished after that period, and Dondaine's discoveries have confirmed their knowledge. Some, however, continue to affirm the existence of Catharism for a century and a half before the arrival of the Balkan missionaries, explaining that the Bulgarians introduced an absolute, strict dualism into already existing Catharist circles and so transformed them from mitigated to absolute dualists. There is some truth in this interpretation, but it does not cut deep enough. For at least ten years now, Raffaello Morghen of the University of Rome[7] has suggested another solution. Morghen says that no dualism of any kind was imported from the East before the 1140's and that, further, no hidden tradition of gnosticism in the West can be adduced to explain the presence of dualism in the eleventh century. This Gordian knot is cut by the realization that *there is no firm evidence that Eastern dualism penetrated the West before the 1140's.*[8] The "Catharists" of the eleventh and early twelfth centuries were less exotic dualists then Reformists whose puritanism led them to exaggerate those elements of dualism inherent in Christianity itself.

The large number of purported cases of Catharist dualism in the West before 1160 will now bear reexamination.

In the latter days of the Roman Empire, real Manichaeans did of course exist in the West. We know from the career of Saint Augustine how numerous and persuasive they were. Diocletian felt obliged to persecute the Manichaeans as well as the Christians; under Valentinian

I and his successors the Manichaeans continued to be troublesome. Pope Leo I had to deal with them in 443, and the following year found them active in the provinces; Pope Gelasius I attempted to repress them, as did his successors Symmachus and Hormisdas. A Manichaean named Prosper was active around 526; Gregory of Tours mentioned heretics who may have been Manichaeans; Vincent of Lérins had found them in the south of Gaul, as had Pomoerius of Arles. A letter of Saint Gregory the Great to the Bishop of Brutium observes that they were still active in Africa and infecting southern Italy; at that time they were also in Sicily.[9] The council of Braga in Spain in 563 condemned Priscillianist doctrines that may bear the marks of Manichaeanism. What emerges from this summary is that Manichaeism indisputably existed in the Occident in the third, fourth, and fifth centuries. In the sixth century the Manichaeans likely continued to exist in North Afrca, Sicily, and southern Italy. The only purported case after the initial years of the century is that of the Priscillianists, but these were reform-oriented rather than dualist. It seems reasonable to suppose that Manichaeism became extinct in the West in the course of the sixth century, along with so many other ideas and attitudes of the ancient world.

The purported incidents of Manichaeism or Catharist dualism in the following centuries are much less impressive (the proponents of the continuity theory never say where the one leaves off and the other begins). The seventh century is devoid of surviving evidence, and the eighth almost so. Renato Esnault believed that a Manichaean interpretation could be placed on a passage of the antiphonary of the church of Lyon in this century,[10] but the only other crumb is the letter of Pope Gregory II to the Thuringians on December 1, 722.[11] In it the pope says that Saint Boniface has been instructed to reject Africans claiming to have orders because some are Manichaeans and others have been frequently baptized. It is conceivable that isolated African Manichaeans may have appeared in Germany at this time after fleeing the Moslem conquest of North Africa, but this is more than a little unlikely. The *pieds-noirs* settling in France in the 1960's insisted upon staying in the Midi, for they found the north of France uncongenial to their Mediterranean temperament, and it seems unlikely that their earlier counterparts would have journeyed to an even more remote province. Tangl, the editor of Boniface's letters, suggests that the terms *Afri* and *Manichaei* are only *topoi* drawn from earlier chancery documents,[12] and this seems the most likely explanation. Gregory may have been using *Manichaean* as a synonym for *heretic* in the same way that the German *Ketzer* came to be drawn from *Cathar*.

The ninth century has been thoroughly combed to yield more mysterious Catharist apparitions. The Spanish episcopate at the time of Charlemagne condemned "Manichees," but this must also be a *topos*.[13] A sacramentary of the eighth century shows Manichaean influence, probably largely derived from Augustine's anti-Manichaean writings. This curious text offers Christian amendments to Manichaean ideas and evinces, rather than an overt dualism, an uncritical mélange of undigested ideas.[14] More interesting is the capitulary of Aachen dating from 802 and entitled *De his qui dicuntur cataroe*.[15] This also proves to be a cliché derived from the council of Nicea of 325. No evidence of dualism at the court of Charlemagne, it does however indicate how the word *Catharist* came to be employed in the West. *Catharist* comes from the Greek *katharos*, "the pure," but the Occident first encountered the word, not upon the lips of Eastern missionaries, but in the familiar canon of the Nicene council that begins, "In regard to those who are called *Cathari*. . . ." These "Cathari" were the followers of Novatian, an ambitious priest of the third century, whose followers, owing to a real or a pretended rigor, called themselves "the Pure." Thus the term originally had not the slightest dualist connotation. Medieval men knew the passage well: both Peter Damian and Humbert of Silva Candida cite it,[16] and Landolfo the Elder used it in reference to the Patarini.[17] Therefore, the use of the term by medieval writers does not necessarily imply the influence of Eastern dualism.

Other attacks on dualist ideas in the ninth century also merely reproduced ancient condemnations. Thus the False Decretals copied the legislation of Martin of Braga, and Paschasius imitated Augustine.[18] A letter to Charlemagne on baptism lists a number of doctrines that a candidate must be taught, among which is that Christ "really suffered in the flesh." Jonas Bishop of Orléans (818–843) wrote a treatise (*De Institutione Laicali*) in which he took pains to defend the resurrection of the body.[19] However, in the absence of evidence more concrete than these passages, it is probable that these were little more than

THE PROBLEM OF DUALISM

topical allusions based upon a pedantic knowledge of ancient errors. The only document that is at all impressive as evidence for dualism is the commentary of Raban Maur on the Book of Joshua, which he wrote about 834.[20] In the course of this commentary, Raban reprimanded heretics whose interpretation of the Bible was unorthodox and who rejected the Old Testament. Raban used the present tense: "the heretics *are accustomed*. . . . those who *do* not receive the Old Testament." Though this may be nothing more than the historic present or the assumption that ancient heresy like ancient sin is immortal, it is at least evidence that cannot be rejected out of hand. But until the end of the tenth century there is no further suggestion of dualism.

The profession of faith made by Gerbert of Aurillac upon his election to the archbishopric of Reims in 991 contained an affirmation of the validity of marriage and the permissibility of eating meat, and this was once thought to be evidence that there were Catharists at Reims against whom the new prelate was obliged to uphold the orthodox faith.[21] The connection between the confession and heresy no longer seems clear. Aside from the certainty that the form of the profession was borrowed from earlier documents, the fact is that a synod held in Reims in 991 made no mention of any heretics Catharist or otherwise, scarcely likely if they were so powerful that a newly elected prelate was obliged to affirm on oath that he did not share their errors.[22] It is not necessary, however, to dismiss the profession as having no relevance whatever to the history of dissent. A number of standard confessions of faith circulated, and some had a long and interesting life. Small creeds were not infrequently issued by bishops or synods to enforce conformity in their dioceses,[23] and a creed was often included in statements made by a new prelate at his ordination. Hincmar of Reims,[24] Adalbert of Thérouanne,[25] Pilgrim of Passau,[26] and Bruno of Cologne[27] are known to have made such confessions, though these were substantially different from that made by Gerbert and did not include a specific defense of either marriage or meat. Gerbert's stands in a long tradition dating back as far as the sixth century. Its form is ultimately derived from the *Statuta ecclesiae antiqua* attributed to Caesarius of Arles,[28] whence it passed to the pseudo-Isidorean *Liber canonum* and the *Ordo Romanus antiquus,* which probably dates from the tenth century.[29] Gerbert used it in 991. Gauzlin, abbot of Fleury, who became archbishop of Bourges between 1014 and 1020, and whose predecessor had been warned against heresy by Abbo,[30] made essentially the same profession as Gerbert. More than a century later, the heresiarch Valdes, in attempting to demonstrate his orthodoxy to Archbishop Guichard of Lyon in 1180, made the profession of Gerbert with a number of additions,[31] after which it was developed into a common formula for the reconciliation of heretics.[32] It is therefore an unquestionable though curious fact that this confession, obviously drawn up as an attack upon heretical and probably dualist error, came again to be used as a direct weapon against heresy in the late twelfth and thirteenth centuries, while there is no clear indication that its use in the intervening years was anything more than a cliché. The long association of the confession with heresy justifies its mention in connection with Gerbert and Gauzlin, but, unless other evidence is forthcoming, their use of it cannot be taken as proof that heresy, not to mention Catharism, existed in their environment.[33]

The heresy that appeared at Liège in the reigns of Notger and Baldéric II could be supposed to have been Catharist if there were other firm indications of Catharism at the time, but since there are not, it is best not to make this conclusion. A whole structure of early Catharism has been erected in which one dubious case of dualism is confirmed by reference to other cases which, upon examination, prove to be equally dubious. No matter how impressive, a building is no stronger than its foundations.

At Châlons-sur-Marne around the year 1000, Leutard, the mad peasant of Vertu,[34] rejected the Old Testament, marriage, crucifixes and images, and tithes, which position might be Catharist but could as readily stem from anticlerical puritanism. Early in the century, Saint Gerhard, a missionary to Hungary and bishop of Czanád (1037–1046), reported that heresy was spreading from Greece into the Occident.[35] These heretics attacked the clergy and the authority of the Church; they rejected prayers for the dead and the resurrection of the body. Their doctrines could have derived from Bogomil dualism, but are also explicable in terms of exaggerated puritanism.

In 1012 Henry II "refuted the madness of the heretics" at Mainz.[36] These heretics have been supposed Catharists on the assumption that Catharism was widespread at the time, but this is precisely what is questionable. There is nothing in the very short notice given by the annals to indicate the nature of the heresy.

From 1018 to 1028 heretics were active in Aquitaine and around Toulouse.[37] The Aquitaine dissidents rejected marriage, images, the baptism of children, were ascetic in regard to food, were called "Manichaei," and were accused of having lustful orgies. In this case, the suspicious bits are the last two, and these may result from the pedantry and maliciousness of the chroniclers. Of the heretics at Toulouse in 1022 all we know is that they had hidden meetings, scarcely an incontrovertible proof of Catharism.

The dissenters burnt at Orléans in 1022 seem particularly suspicious.[38] If we accepted everything the chroniclers said of these dissidents, and drew all the applicable implications, we would be obliged to conclude that they were certainly more radical than ordinary Reformists. But the chroniclers differ in their reports and in some matters (whether the condemned abstained from meat or questioned the Trinity, for example) positively disagree with one another. Nearly every conceivable heresy, including the improbable belief in the eternity of the world, was attributed to them by their orthodox antagonists, and it would be credulous to imagine that they were guilty of all these errors. The doctrines most suspect of Catharism are a denial of the humanity and the passion of Christ (though one of the sources contradicts even this), a belief that the world was evil, and the practice of laying-on of hands on their members. While these doctrines (if they really were part of the dissidents' teaching) are certainly suspect, even they could originate in the New Testament: the apostles laid on hands, and the Prince of this world was surely the devil.

It has been supposed that the dissenters active in the dioceses of Liège and Arras[39] in 1024–1025 were Catharists. As usual, the evidence is contradictory, but their doctrines are best understood in the context of the Reform Movement and of apostolic piety. At Monteforte (ca. 1027) in Italy, the dissenters abstained from meat and marriage, claimed that they ended their lives in torment, and said that they had a pontiff "of their own." Only the last two points smack of Catharism, but the "pontiff" turns out to be the Holy Spirit, and the "torment" had nothing to do with the Catharist endura. The heretics of Monteforte explicitly affirmed the Old Testament and the humanity of Christ, which automatically precludes them from being Catharists. Heretics appeared at Charroux in Aquitaine about 1030, but the only hint of the nature of their heresy is the use of the name *Manichaei,* which can be explained as a *topos.*[40]

Warnings of heresy come from a letter of the clergy of Noyon-Tournai to the bishops of the province of Reims in 1030, but here there is no evidence at all of dualism.[41]

Between 1043 and 1048, Bishop Roger II of Châlons-sur-Marne wrote Bishop Wazo of Liège to ask his advice on the manner of dealing with heretics, and in the years 1048-1054 Leo IX was informed of heresy at Liège.[42] The dissenters of Châlons rejected marriage, abstained from meat, held secret meetings, laid on hands, and refused to kill animals. All these but the last can stem from Reformist puritanism, and the last was based, not on metempsychosis, but on the Old Testament, itself proof the dissidents were not dualists. The Liégeois present a problem, as they not only rejected marriage, baptism, and the eucharist, and denied the authority of the church, but they had their own hierarchy and were divided into *auditores* and *credentes.* They claimed that the body of Christ was only a shadow. The organization of the cult is similar to, but not identical with, the usual Catharist hierarchy. The docetism remains, though it is not an insuperable difficulty. It is possible that these particular heretics are of a later, twelfth-century date, and if so they might really be Catharists.

At this time, while Leo IX was in northern Europe, he presided over a council of Reims in 1049. At that assembly the fathers condemned the "new heretics" who had emerged in Gaul and who were now "pullulating in these parts." New heretics there certainly were and in great number, but unless they can in other cases be shown to have been Catharists, the implicit condemnation of Reims cannot serve as evidence in this cause.[43] In the same year Leo wrote on the subject of heresy to Bishop Peter of Antioch, but there is every reason to think of this letter as purely conventional.

The tale of purported Catharism in the eleventh century is told when we mention the trial at Goslar in 1051, the Patarini in Milan in the middle of the century, and a letter of Nicholas II to the clergy of Sisteron in Provence. The last can be rapidly dismissed, since it merely repeats the old letter that Gregory II had directed to the Thuringians in the eighth century, warning them about Manichaeans.[44] At Goslar, the name *Manichaei* was used, and the dissenters abstained from meat and refused to kill animals. It is likely that these heretics, who were supposed to have come from Lorraine, beyond which is Châlons, were connected with those of Châlons, and their refusal to kill animals need indicate Catharism no more than did the Frenchmen's. The Patarini were anticlerical and puritanical dissidents with no trace of any kind of Catharism to be found in their doctrines of apostolic poverty and rejection of the authority of the church.

The fact that there is a fifty-year gap between these cases and the next purported appearances of Catharism in the early twelfth century ought in itself to give pause to the proponents of the dualist theory. Though an argument from silence can prove nothing in medieval history, it is unlikely that a movement, imported from the East and powerful enough to have caused great disturbance already, should for more than half a century have ceased to obtain even a mention in any chronicle and then, inexplicably, have come to life again. What continuity there was, was a continuity of Reformist dissent, not of Catharism.

Under Archbishop Bruno (1102–1124) dissenters were found at Ivois near Trier, but their antisacramentalism in rejecting the eucharist and the baptism of infants is scarcely proof of Catharist affiliation. Henry the Monk and his associates Peter of Bruys and Ponnus have been misunderstood to be Catharists, and there is a supposed Catharist confession dating from the reign of Bishop Maurus of Cracow (1110–1118) in Poland. There are purported cases of Catharism at Soissons in 1114, Toulouse in 1119, Languedoc in 1123, and Trier, Utrecht,[45] and Liège in 1135. The Polish confession seems to imply a denial of the resurrection of the body and of prayers for the dead, but the same confession specifically affirms the reality of Christ's passion and therefore the physical nature of his body. The Toulousain dissidents attacked the authority of the Church and its clergy, disdained marriage, the baptism of children, and all the sacraments, as well as "feigning" apostolic holiness. Again, this is antisacramentalism rather than Catharism. The case of Soissons presents more difficulties, for besides these doctrines, they abstained from food generated *ex coitu*. The

Liégeois of 1135 rejected marriage, prayers for the dead, and the baptism of children; they too professed holiness. Again, puritanical zeal is more in evidence here than Catharism.

Two cases can be summarily dismissed. One concerned a priest named Herbert, convicted of heresy at Reims in 1136 and defrocked, but his beliefs are unspecified.[46] The other, the general condemnation issued by the Lateran Council in 1139,[47] merely repeated that of Toulouse in 1119.

In the 1130's or 1140's Hugh Metellus warned the bishop of Toul about heretics who may have been dualists. The general anathema issued by the council of Reims in 1148 may have included Catharists, but there is no specific evidence that this was so. Eudo of Brittany, who was condemned at this council, has been erroneously considered a Catharist by some writers. Heretics around Arras are mentioned in a letter of 1150–1153 sent by Eugenius III to Bishop Godescalc of that diocese, but again there is no specification of Catharism.[48] A book *Against the Heresies,* formerly erroneously attributed to Abelard was really written toward the end of the century by Ermengaud of Béziers, and so must be dismissed as evidence for the earlier period.[49]

These cases will now be examined as a whole to determine whether they bear real, or only imagined, traces of Catharism. In addition there are a few cases in the 1140's to 1160's which, because the evidence of Catharism here is not merely putative, will receive individual attention later. These latter are as follows: A priest named Evervinus found Catharists at Cologne in the 1140's; a council of Reims in 1157 attacked dualists under the name of "Manichaeans"; a clerk named Jonas was accused of Catharism at Cambrai in the 1150's; in about 1160 there were hints of Catharism at Liège in the shape of a sect called the "Colitiani," and at Cologne in a sect discovered by Eckbert of Schönau; at Oxford shortly after 1160, heresy made one of its rare appearances in England.

Since by the time of the council of Saint Félix of Caraman in 1167 it is beyond dispute that Eastern dualism was active in the Occident, it is the cases up to that time that must now be closely examined for traces of such beliefs. In summary, the list of possibilities is as follows: (1) the heretics attacked by Raban Maur in 834; (2) the mad peasant Leutard about 1000; (3) the heretics of Aquitaine (1018–1028); (4)

the heretics of Toulouse in 1022; (5) the affair at Orléans in 1022; (6) the dissenters of Liège and Arras in 1025; (7) the purported Catharists of Monteforte (1028–1045); (8) those of Charroux in 1030; (9) the heretics in Hungary (1037–1046); (10) those discussed by Roger II and Wazo (1043–1048), (11) the dissidents of Liège (1048–1054); (12) the incident at Goslar in 1051; (13) the Patarini; (14) the dissidents of Ivois (1102–1124); (15) Henry the Monk, Peter of Bruys, and Ponnus; (16) purported Catharism in Poland (1110–1119); (17) the heretics at Soissons in 1114; (18) those at Toulouse in 1119; (19) the dissenters of Liège in 1135; (20) those mentioned in the letter of Hugh Metellus; (21) those attacked by Evervinus of Cologne (1140's); (22) those condemned at the council of Reims in 1157; (23) Jonas of Cambrai (1150's); (24) the Colitiani at Liège around 1160; (25) the heretics condemned by Eckbert of Schönau (1163); and (26) the Oxford group (1166).

The question is whether these heretics were directly influenced by Eastern dualism. In establishing a relationship of affiliation or apparentation between ideas, two kinds of evidence have to be examined: the *external* evidence of physical contacts between Eastern dualists and Westerners that would permit the transmission of ideas, and the *internal* evidence that the Western ideas bear the marks of a bond with the East.

Any theory that holds that dualist heresy passed from the Balkans into Italy and thence into the West in the eleventh century runs afoul of at least four difficulties. The first is that of the twenty-six cases under consideration no less than twenty make no mention of the heresy's having been imported from without. In some instances such information is simply lacking; in many we know that the dissenters were indigenous. The other six cases are themselves not terribly revealing. The heresy at Orléans in 1022 was imported from Italy, that of Liège in 1025 at least in part from Italy, that of Liège in 1048–1054 from Champagne, that of Goslar in 1051 from Lorraine, and that described by Evervinus ultimately from Greece. The Oxford dissidents came from Germany. Of all these, only the Grecian and perhaps the Italian cases lend much weight to the Eastern argument. No clear picture of a gradual northwestward penetration of Eastern dualism emerges. Chronology does not permit us to make a neat geographical chain

—Greece-Italy-Orléans-Liège (Lorraine)-Cologne-Goslar-Oxford. It is true that a prima facie case for a general northward movement could be made. Correlating the geography with the chronology of the earlier cases, seven out of the eight earliest (excluding the dubious testimony of Raban Maur) either are southern or have southern origins: Aquitaine, Toulouse, Midi-Orléans, Italy-Liège, Monteforte, Charroux, and Czanád, the only exception being Leutard of Châlons. After the first eight cases, however, the distribution is random, and no northward movement can be discerned.

A second difficulty greatly adds to the weight of the first, for it is precisely these first eight cases that, with the exception of Orléans in 1022, bear the least resemblance to examples of true Eastern dualism. A third difficulty, already mentioned, is the half-century of silence between the trial of Goslar in 1051 and the reappearance of purported dualists at Ivois in the early twelfth century. Fourth and finally, there is no specific evidence that any missionaries from the Balkans arrived before the 1140's, and protests that trade routes between Italy and the Balkans were in existence, so that such intercourse was possible, must be admitted but dismissed as proving nothing.

The internal evidence is concerned with the similarities, or lack thereof, of these heretics' doctrines to those of the Eastern dualists, and proves no more hospitable to the theory than does the external evidence. After summarizing the doctrines of the unquestioned dualists of the thirteenth century,[50] we shall find those points upon which they seem to agree and then ask whether a Western Christian source for these doctrines is not also possible.

The fundamental supposition of the true dualists was that there are two opposing forces in the world, one good and one evil. Whether or not the power of evil was independent of the good God or one of his fallen angels was debated, but in either event it was he, rather than the good God, who created the world. The phenomenal world, having entrapped spirit in matter, was evil. The God of the Old Testament created the world and was the evil god. The Old Testament was therefore to be rejected, exception being sometimes made for the books of the prophets, who were believed to have predicted the coming of Christ. Man was in a difficult position: his soul was spiritual and therefore good; he must seek to liberate it from the flesh as effectively as he could.

By living the proper life (that is, by becoming a Catharist), one could escape the flesh; otherwise the spirit might be doomed to reincarnation. Purgatory was rejected in favor of metempsychosis, as was the resurrection of the dead. Water being corrupt and therefore impotent for good, baptism in the ordinary Christian sense was rejected. The baptism of infants was frowned upon in particular, for children were creatures in which spirit had been newly entrapped. No one could be saved until he had reached the age when initiation into the Catharist religion was permitted. Christ could not have had a true human body since the divine would not have clothed itself in a garment of evil flesh. His suffering on the cross was therefore an illusion, as was his resurrection. The Virgin Mary was often given little respect, for her fleshly body could not really have given birth to God. At most she was designated as an angel along with her son. Then, Jesus being an angel rather than very God, the doctrine of the Trinity was denied. Jesus' mission was not to redeem us through his passion, but rather to convey to us prisoners of the flesh instructions for effecting an escape from the body. Since Christ's body was an illusion and the eucharist matter, that sacrament was a delusion. The cross and all images were matter and therefore contemptible. The cult of the saints was rejected, as was the Christian sacrament of penance.

With all this, it was natural that the dualists denied the authority of the Catholic Church, which was an institution of the evil god designed to keep men enslaved to matter. In place of the Catholic hierarchy, the Catharists had bishops of their own, but no pope. Local Catharists were organized into groups in which a division was sharply drawn between the *perfecti* on the one hand and the *credentes* on the other. Admission to the sect was obtained through the rite known as the *convenientia*. This made one a *credens* and put one under the authority of the *perfecti*. In certain instances, particularly when they were suspected of having had doubts as to their belief, the *credentes* were obliged to adore the *perfecti*. After long instruction and practice in mortifying the flesh, including a year of exceptionally rigorous abstinence, the *consolamentum* was administered, and the *credens* became a *perfectus*. The rigors of this period were so great that it sometimes ended in death, which, if it occurred after the administration of the *consolamentum,* the great sacrament of the Catharists, was not to be regretted, since it meant the final liberation of soul from body. Later, and in certain areas, the *endura,* or fasting unto death, was occasionally administered, especially to children or to the sick, with the express purpose of effecting such a liberation. In these instances the *consolamentum* was administered at the end of the ordeal; then, if one survived, he became a *perfectus.* He was then a full initiate of the sect, wore special black clothing, and was expected to lead a life of utter purity, since the *consolamentum,* which filled the part of Catholic baptism, confirmation, extreme unction, and, in a way, holy orders as well, could not be repeated. This sacrament was bestowed by the laying-on of hands, the *perfecti* initiating a believer in a rite similar to the consecration of Catholic bishops.

The Catharists had other customs of a semisacramental nature. They had three long fasts annually. They performed public penance for public sin, private penance for private sin. Once a month they held a *servitium,* a service at which confessions of petty sins (the *perfecti* had no serious sins) were made and penances assigned. A resemblance to early Christianity is discernible, when sin after baptism was often considered unforgivable and many people for this reason put off the reception of the sacrament until late in life. An elaborate ritual feast was celebrated. The kiss of peace, a double kiss, was common between *perfecti.* The *melioramentum,* a special form of greeting between members of the sect, was also employed, usually between a *credens* and a *perfectus.*

The *perfecti* lived lives of ascetic rigor. They forbade the use of oaths. They rejected luxury and wealth (at least in theory; the nobles and bourgeois of Provence did not often abandon castle and house). They abstained from meat, partly because of their belief in metempsychosis. This same belief prohibited their killing most animals, particularly four-footed animals and birds, though snakes, insects, and other lowly creatures might be killed because they were purely evil and had no spirit within them. Meat was eschewed for the additional reason that it was a food engendered by procreation. The Catharists avoided other foods associated with generation, notably eggs, cheese, and milk. This aversion to procreation, as well as their attitude toward marriage and sex in general, stems from the fact that it is the sexual act that is responsible for imprisoning spirits in the flesh. Marriage was absolutely to be avoided; if it could not be, the spouses were at least to live in celibacy. Among the Catharists, it was less a feeling that sexual pleasure in itself was bad than an aversion to childbearing that determined their attitude. Promiscuity outside marriage was almost as bad as marriage itself, but it was the institutionalized wedded state that was particularly blameworthy. Two exceptions to this rule of sexual abstinence may have existed. Orthodox writers frequently condemned the Catharists for sexual laxity. This is a cliché in orthodox writing about heretics of all varieties: heresy is evil; a heretic is evil; ergo, he does all kinds of evil things. But where there is much smoke there may be some fire. The Catharist aversion to procreation would not have excluded sexual activities that could not result in conception, and the unnatural vices of which they were accused may not have existed entirely in the imaginations of their accusers. Psychoanalysis gives a hint as to the possible motivation of such deviations. Herbert Marcuse says of Orpheus, the founder (at least in myth) of Greek dualism, that, "Like Narcissus, he rejects the normal Eros, not for an ascetic ideal, but for a fuller Eros. Like Narcissus, he protests against the repressive order of procreative sexuality." [51] In addition, it must be remembered that the *credentes* were under no such compulsion to purity as were the *perfecti,* since the *consolamentum* always lay in their future, and they very likely indulged in excesses that their leaders would have eschewed.

This is a picture of the genuine dualism of the thirteenth century. Of these beliefs, which are found among the heretics of the eleventh and early twelfth centuries?

Many of the fundamental doctrines and practices of the dualists are not found at all before 1160. Among the purported dualists before that date, there is no trace of a belief in an equal, or almost equal power of the devil, nor in the inherent evil of the world, save in the case of the heretics burned at Orléans in 1022, and there the report comes from the pen of Radulf Glaber, an untrustworthy chronicler with an overcharged imagination. Radulf linked this doctrine with a belief that the world was eternal, an idea held neither by the Catharists nor by any other heretics I know of until the influence of Aristotle and the Arabs grew in the thirteenth century. Of metempsychosis there is no clear trace. The heretics of Goslar, like those of Châlons under Roger II, refused to kill animals, even a baby chick. This has the appearance of belief in transmigration, but according to Roger's letter to Wazo such was not true. His heretics abstained from killing animals because of the prohibition of the Old Testament to this effect. If he is correct, this means that they drew upon the ritual prohibitions of Leviticus and Deuteronomy and exaggerated them to the point of forbidding the slaying of any beast. It is also possible that the heretics were over-scrupulous in their interpretation of the commandment, "Thou shalt not kill." Anyway, here is an alternative to a dualist interpretation. There are many people today who have never heard of dualism but whom the taking of animal life offends. Further, if the dissidents of Châlons drew their ideas from the Pentateuch, they could not possibly have been dualists, for the latter held the Old Testament to have been inspired by Satan. The Goslar dissenters were almost certainly connected with those of Châlons.

There is no evidence that any of these early dissenters were disrespectful to the Blessed Virgin, though they commonly rejected the cult of saints in general. There is no indication that they denied the redemptive powers of Jesus in order to cast him in the role of a messenger of the divine. Though they condemned the authority of the Catholic hierarchy, they had none of their own. It has long been recognized that when the dissenters of Orléans denied the pope, declaring that "we have a pontiff of our own," they meant, not an earthly prelate, but the Holy Spirit himself. The heretics of Liège in 1048–1054 were supposed to have had their "faithful, their priests, and their prelates, *sicut et nos.*" It is possible that these heretics really date from the next century, and if they do, this might be a true Catharist hierarchy. On the other hand, they might be a group of madmen masquerading in a suppositious dignity; the lunatic Eudo of Brittany named his followers bishops. These same heretics of Liège are the only group before 1140 that bears traces of a Catharist division into *perfecti* and *credentes*. Yet at Liège the division was not between *perfecti* and *credentes,* but between *auditores* and *credentes,* a very different arrangement where the terms are not even equivalent to the Catharist ones. Here, the auditors were those who were being instructed in the doctrines of the group, while the believers were those who had "already been deceived," as the chronicler puts it, an arrangement similar to the division between catechumens and initiates in the early Church or to divisions in any number of religious sects.

In none of the instances of heresy under consideration is there mention of any of the typical Catharist rituals, the *convenientia,* the *consolamentum,* the special clothing of the *perfecti,* the adoration of the *perfecti,* or the *abstinentia* in either its preliminary or its fatal form. Among the heretics of Monteforte there was a practice vaguely reminiscent of the *endura:* under questioning, the heretics said that they "ended their life in torment." If they were put to death by wicked men, they rejoiced; and if one were about to die a natural death he called his neighbor to do him in. However, there is no evidence that death was to follow a period of fasting. Moreover, for the Catharists, natural death would suffice to free the soul from the body; they would have thought the violence unnecessary. Finally, the Monteforte dissenters gave a completely un-Catharist explanation of why they wished to die violently: they felt that through suffering on earth they might avoid punishment in the hereafter. Of the kiss of peace, the *melioramentum,* the ritual feast, or the three annual feasts there is no mention among any of our groups.

The major premises of the Catharists and their most characteristic customs were thus equally lacking among the heretics of the eleventh and early twelfth centuries. On the other hand, many doctrines held by these heretics were also held by the Catharists. For example: The Old Testament was rejected (Raban, Leutard, Petrobrusians). Purgatory and the efficacy of prayers for the dead were denied (Hungarians, Orléans, Liège of 1025, Petrobrusians, Liège of 1048–1054, Poland, Evervinus' first group, Eckbert). The heretics of Soissons did not separate their cemeteries from the fields, which may imply a belief that remembrance of the dead is useless. The baptism of children was rejected (Aquitaine, Orléans, Liège of 1025, Liège of 1048–1054, Ivois, Hugh Metellus, Henricians, Petrobrusians, Liège of 1135, Toulouse of 1119, Soissons, Evervinus' first and second groups, Eckbert, Oxford). The reality of Christ's body was denied (Orléans, Liège of 1048–1054, Soissons?, Eckbert), as was the fact that He suffered for man (Orléans). The resurrection of the body was rejected (Hungarians, Orléans, Poland). The Trinity may have been questioned (Orléans?, Monteforte?). The eucharist was held worthless (Orléans, Liège of 1025, Liège of 1048–1054, Ivois, Henricians, Petrobrusians, Ponnus, Toulouse of 1119, Soissons, Evervinus' first group, Eckbert, Oxford), and the cross and images were despised (Leutard, Aquitaine, Orléans, Liège of 1025, Petrobrusians, Ponnus). The cult of the saints was denied (Orléans, Liège of 1025, Petrobrusians, Poland, Evervinus' first group), as was the sacrament of penance (Orléans, Liège of 1025). The authority of the Church was rejected (Hungarians, Orléans, Liège of 1052, Liège of 1048–1054, Patarini, Henricians, Petrobrusians, Toulouse of 1119, Evervinus' first and second groups, Eckbert, Oxford).

The heretics were either extremely holy or, as their critics put it, "feigned holiness" (Orléans, Liège of 1025, Monteforte, Patarini, Ponnus, Henricians, Liège of 1135, Toulouse of 1119, Evervinus' second group, Eckbert, Oxford). They abstained from meat (Aquitaine, Orléans?, Monteforte, Châlons, Goslar, Ponnus, Soissons, Evervinus' second group, Eckbert). They rejected legitimate marriage (Aquitaine, Orléans, Liège of 1025, Monteforte, Châlons, Hugh Metellus, Liège of 1048–1054, Henricians, Liège of 1135, Toulouse of 1119, Soissons, Evervinus' first and second groups, Reims of 1157, Eckbert, Oxford). They were accused of indulging in sexual orgies (Aquitaine, Orléans, Châlons, Henricians, Liège of 1135, Soissons, Reims of 1157). They had hidden meetings (Toulouse of 1022, Orléans, Châlons, Ivois, Soissons, Eckbert) and desired esoteric knowledge (Orléans, Patarini?, Henricians, Evervinus' second group, Eckbert?). They had numerous followers (Leutard, Hungarians?, Aquitaine, Toulouse of 1022, Orléans, Liège of 1025, Monteforte, Charroux?, Châlons, Liège of 1048–1054, Goslar, Patarini, Ivois, Henricians, Petrobrusians, Soissons, Reims of 1157, Eckbert, Oxford). Occasionally they were called Manichaeans (Aquitaine, Orléans, Charroux, Châlons, Goslar, Reims of 1157, Eckbert) or Catharists (Trier of 1152–1156, Eckbert, Colitiani?) and Publicani (Oxford).

Since, however, there is no external evidence supporting a connection between these dissenters and Catharism, it is well to see whether there may not be another source of these doctrines, an alternative mine from which the heretics of the eleventh and early twelfth centuries extracted their beliefs. Such a mine did indeed exist, extremely large, well worked, and very close to home: the Great Reform Movement.

It is more plausible that medieval heretics would have drawn their beliefs from the communal well of reform, round which so many people were pressing, than that they would have sought a strange source in the East. If it can be shown that the doctrines professed by these dissenters may have derived from a reform source, then Ockham's razor should be applied and the simpler explanation accepted.

The Great Reform Movement was concerned with the restoration of the apostolic purity of the Church and drew its strength from the New Testament and the Fathers. One of the characteristics of the reformers was a concern for personal holiness, an asceticism that often became puritanical and was sometimes carried to unorthodox extremes.

There are other reasons for abstention from meat than a horror of procreation or a belief in metempsychosis. Days of abstinence when the orthodox refrained from meat were and are common in the Catholic Church, and it was usual in the monasteries to abstain at all times. Such abstinence was considered a mortification of the flesh conducive to piety, while some medieval writers offered the alternate reason that indulgence in meat provoked carnal lust. Concern with abstinence was common. Egbert of York spoke of "unclean meat" in the tradition of Leviticus and Deuteronomy, and it is not an inconceivable transition from considering some meats unclean to eschewing all.[52] Leo IV issued a letter on fasting and abstinence, entitling one of his paragraphs "On the Consumption of Meats."[53] Raban Maur took care to exhort Christians to limit their use of meats,[54] and the council of Ancyra in 314 was obliged to repudiate the exaggerated view that it was illicit to eat vegetables that had been cooked together with meat. It is no wonder that enthusiasts should have concluded that one of the marks of an apostolic life was totally to eschew meat. They preferred to resist the temptation to sell their birthright in heaven for a pork chop, no matter how succulent. Refusal to consume eggs, milk, or cheese, foods considered unobjectionable by orthodox Christians, is evidence of Catharism; but this was the practice only of the later heretics. Evervinus' second group abstained from cheese and milk, but this was after 1140. Saint Bernard's objections to these excesses seem less than fair, since he himself lived on a less than hearty diet of bread and water supplemented by boiled vegetables two times in the week. The heretics of Soissons felt a repugnance for foods generated *ex coitu*. This bears the marks of dualism, certainly, but it is a dualism that grotesquely magnifies that inherent in orthodoxy.

The horror of foods generated *ex coitu* is engendered by a horror of sexual intercourse itself, and many of these heretics condemned marriage. Now, there are three grounds for disliking the institution of matrimony. The first is that one prefers free love and orgies, and this is the interpretation put upon the matter by the heretics' orthodox opponents. The second is a Catharist belief that procreation serves only to entrap more souls in the bodily prison. The third is a puritanical exaggeration of Christian precepts. Christianity, influenced at its inception by primitive dualism, has sometimes been dubious in its approval of matrimony. The position of Saint Paul and many of the Fathers is well known: virginity is the holiest of states, followed by widowhood, while marriage is tolerated for those who cannot otherwise control their desires. There is, of course, a fundamental difference between Christian and Catharist doctrine on marriage, and that is that Christianity has even at its most puritanical at least accepted marriage for the purpose of generating children, while this is precisely the aspect of marriage the Catharists consider evil. "Marriage is good," says Raban Maur, "but on account of the children, not because the concupiscence of fornication is satisfied." [55] Eckbert of Schönau approvingly quoted the saint of Hippo to the effect that the sexual act, even in marriage, is at least venially sinful if not done for the specific purpose of procreation.[56] Sexual activity creates devotion to things other than the spiritual, so said the puritans; it deprives man of his rational faculties, and it blocks the spirit in its struggle to master the flesh. The tags and epigrams of orthodox puritans who found sex abhorrent have come down through the ages: "conceived in sin and born in corruption"; or *inter faeces et urinam nascitur*. This hatred of sex may often have had pathological as well as doctrinal roots; at any rate it was very common in the Christian Middle Ages. The enthusiasts simply went the last inch on the yardstick and condemned marriage altogether. That they condemned fornication even more than marriage is evidence in favor of puritanism and against dualism. There is no need to posit Catharist influence in either the matter of food or of sex.

Some of the dissenters rejected the Old Testament, but the majority did not. The heretics of Châlons and of Monteforte explicitly used it.

The heretics of Oxford rejected both the Old and the New Testaments because they received their illumination from the Holy Spirit within. In the case of Raban Maur's report of 834, his dissidents refused to accept the Old Testament, not because it was a work of the devil but because they objected to the morality of some of the patriarchs. Raban observes that they said that Joshua was utterly lacking in humility! Leutard rejected the Old Testament, except for certain of the prophets, as a source of revelation. It would be rash to assume Catharist influence in this lone case, when Leutard's motivation is entirely hidden. He was a simple peasant, and parts of the Old Testament may have seemed immoral to him. To the unlettered puritan, the peculiar activities of Lot's daughters or the coarse deceit of Jacob in his skins must have seemed of dubious edification.

Dissenters devoted to holiness and apostolic purity did not fail to note the discrepancy between the teaching of the Church and its practice. They came first to despise the clergy and then passed easily to contempt for the authority of the Church, reinforced by the lack of sympathy the authorities usually showed the enthusiasts. Since the heretics must implicitly have rejected the authority of the Church in the very fact of their heresy, no Catharism need be supposed here. Indeed, these dissenters usually rejected the idea of all organized Churches, giving no sign of substituting another hierarchy for that they left behind.

Such rejection of the authority of the Church was often accompanied by the rejection of the sacraments. Most of the sacraments are not indisputably to be found in the New Testament, and even baptism might be questioned—Saint Paul said that he had been sent to preach, not to baptize. The idea of a mediating clergy was repugnant to people who believed that the Holy Spirit dwelt among them. They were antisacramental, but not "other-sacramental," as were the Catharists. For baptism and the eucharist they did not substitute the *consolamentum* or the *abstinentia*. Their scorn of sacraments arose from their desire for individual communion with God. The eucharist was useless. The baptism of infants was rejected, but not on the Catharist grounds that water was evil or children loathsome, but because the child was unable to understand the meaning of what was done to him. For this attitude they had a precedent in that of the early Christians, who generally put off baptism until a time of life when its meaning could be comprehended. Like the early Christians they enjoined a perfect life after baptism and so felt that sin was inexpiable through the sacrament of penance. No act of penitence could save them; they were saved by their *justitia,* by their faith, by their relationship with God alone.

That they held hidden meetings is not remarkable, considering that the authorities were dedicated to suppressing their activities, and that they taught hidden doctrines is merely to say that they shared in that failing of all cultists and sectaries, the desire to feel superior to others by virtue of esoteric knowledge.

Their desire for a purely apostolic life led them to cut through practices and customs that they thought interfered between a man and his God. The cross and images were rejected because they obscured the contemplation of the ineffable. Earlier Iconoclasts in both East and West had rejected images, as the Protestant Reformers and Cromwell's men were to do later, this being a mark not of Eastern dualism, but of the latent dualism of Christianity which holds the spiritual to be more real than the material. The cult of the saints was dismissed as being absent from the New Testament and as standing in the way of man's relationship with God.

These heretics, like the later Protestants, rejected purgatory as unscriptural. Leutard also preached that his followers should refuse to pay tithes to the clergy, a corollary of his contempt for Church and hierarchy. The dissidents of Orléans maintained, according to Radulf Glaber, that good works were useless, a corollary of their belief that justification came from the Spirit within. All these doctrines can more easily be explained against a background of reform than against one of Eastern dualism.

Other points remain that present difficulties. Occasionally accusations of witchcraft were leveled against the dissenters we are considering, and some historians made a connection between this and the similar accusations made against the later Catharists. Since superstition was so common at the time, there may be some truth here, but it is almost certainly merely a cliché. In any event, Catharists were no more likely to be inclined to magic than were Reformists. More frequent were accusations of lust and orgiastic activity. Such activity is certainly incompatible with Reformism, while it is barely explainable in terms of the Catharist willingness to permit the *credentes* activities eschewed by the *perfecti*. But these indictments can, by and large, be discarded with those alluding to sorcery.

Historians of heresy have long been loath to believe all the accusations brought against the heretics, and when we read of conventicles where dissenters consumed the bodies of small boys we are reminded that medieval Christians also fancied that Jews ate children, that the Romans accused the early Christians of devouring infants, and that some backwoods evangelicals today believe that Catholics sacrifice Protestant babies in the mass. This peculiar notion seems to be deeply ingrained in the Occidental mind. The god Cronos ate his children; the Titans devoured the young Zagreus. One hesitates to contemplate what racial memory may lie behind these stories. Similarly, when we read of the heretics' wild orgies we are reminded that the Romans accused the Christians of sexual promiscuity in their secret meetings, and that almost every sect from the beginning of Christian history has been accused of some kind of lewdness. Accusations of lust and sorcery, while perhaps occasionally grounded in fact, should be taken with a peck, rather than a grain, of salt. They certainly do not constitute evidence in favor of Catharist influence, though they do demonstrate that the chroniclers had trite, as well as prurient, minds.

In many cases the dissidents were classified by the chroniclers as Manichaeans or Catharists. This difficulty is lessened by the fact that the term "Catharist" itself is not applied to any group before 1150, the exception being Landolfo's characterization of the Patarini as "Cathari," but Landolfo was simply following the well-known language of the First Nicene Council. The term "Manichaean" was applied to the heretics of Aquitaine, Orléans (by two of the chroniclers only), Charroux, and Goslar. In his letters from the south, Saint Bernard specifically stated that the heretics with whom he had to deal were *not* Manichaeans. As for the other cases, we need only mention the familiar fact that medieval chroniclers, men learned in books and not a little pedantic, delighted in pouring new wine into old bottles and assigning to modern heretics names and doctrines of ancient heresies derived from books. Medieval heretics were described as Montanists, Cataphrygians, or whatever ancient terms the pedants could conjure up from their musty texts. Saint Bernard called his opponents in the Midi "Arians." In the case of the dissidents of Châlons, the confusion is even more striking:

they were supposed to have said that Mani was the Holy Spirit, a doctrine unknown to the Manichaeans themselves, yet Wazo in his reply to Bishop Roger described them as "Arians." There is not the slightest reason to believe that any of these dissidents were influenced by Arianism, and anyone who deduced the existence of neo-Arian heresy in the early Middle Ages from this evidence would be verging on the preposterous. The designation "Manichaean" is therefore no more convincing; we have seen how Gregory II and others used it loosely. There remains the derivation of the term *Patarini* for the heretics of Milan in the eleventh century. It has been much disputed whether the name has an Eastern origin, and I do not presume to attempt to resolve the question;[57] but the use of the name cannot at this point be taken as compelling evidence of Eastern influence.

Evidence that these dissidents denied the Trinity is slight. Radulf Glaber tells us that the heretics of Orléans did so, but the *Miracula Sancti Benedicti* contradict him. The dissenters of Monteforte seem to have essayed a symbolical interpretation of the Trinity, but they did not openly deny the triune nature of the Godhead.

The most difficult problem remains the denial of the humanity of Christ and the corollary that he did not suffer for man on the cross. This was, however, not a common belief among the dissidents. The dissenters of Monteforte specifically maintained the humanity of Christ and his birth from the womb of the Virgin; the Polish creed affirmed that Christ really died. It is doubtful whether the heretics of Soissons denied it. Eckbert of Schönau's heretics denied Christ's humanity, but they are freely admitted to have been Catharists. We are left with Orléans, where the heretics probably held such a doctrine (though the *Miracula Sancti Benedicti* deny it) and where they explicitly refuted the reality of the passion. The heretics of 1048–1054 at Liège claimed that the body of Christ was nothing but a shadow. It cannot be denied that these doctrines are strikingly similar to the Catharist distrust of the flesh. Similarly, the denial of the resurrection of the body may indicate a dislike of the flesh. It must be remembered, however, that docetism existed in the early Church independent of Manichaeism or Eastern dualism. Ancient docetism derived from the inherent dualism in Christianity that made the spirit superior in worth to the flesh. How could God, the most real and spiritual of all beings, take on the unreal garment of flesh? It is not impossible or even improbable that the heretics of Liège and of Orléans arrived at docetist ideas independently of Eastern influences. It is even possible that (as in Plato's cave) they meant that Christ's body was a shadow even as all flesh, all matter, is a shadow and unreal in comparison with the reality of the spirit. But let us admit this problem as a difficulty, though it would be partially resolved if the Liégeois heretics were placed, as is possible, in the twelfth century.

In fine, there are no clear marks of Eastern dualism in the doctrines of Occidental heretics before the middle of the twelfth century, though in docetism and many other beliefs the dualism inherent in Christianity has been exaggerated to the point of heresy. Tending already in the direction of dualism, the Reformists were all the more ready to receive the Eastern missionaries who arrived in the West from the 1140's on.

It must finally be observed that the various dissidents under discussion did not form one group with even a relatively united body of doctrine. There is no clear correlation between the doctrines of the various groups: each was independent of the others,[58] a fact reinforcing the theory that they did not branch from a common Catharist trunk.

From the 1140's on, the increasing likelihood of Catharist influence requires a more lengthy examination of the particular cases.

Evervinus.

Three documents have been used as evidence regarding the dissidents whom Evervinus fought. The first is the *Annales Brunwilarenses* for the year 1143;[59] the second is a letter of Evervinus to Saint Bernard of Clairvaux[60]; the third is the sermons Bernard wrote in reply.[61]

The *Annales Brunwilarenses* simply state that in the year 1143 heretics were accused before Archbishop Arnold I in the church of Saint Peter in Cologne and that some purged themselves through the ordeal by water while others, having been found guilty, took to flight. Three were burned at Bonn by order of Count Otto of Rheineck. Manselli[62] and Aegerter[63] assumed, probably correctly, a connection between this document and that written by Evervinus. Although the laconic evidence of the *Annales* does not correspond in every particular with Evervinus' account, this discrepancy is not insurmountable in the light of the frequent inaccuracy of medieval reports. Further, the evidence supplied by Eckbert of Schönau in 1163 indicates that the Bonn group may have been associated with Evervinus' heretics.

Sermons 65 and 66 of Saint Bernard were written in reply to Evervinus' letter and were dated before Bernard's trip to the south in 1145,[64] so that the date of Evervinus' letter, and therefore of the activity of his heretics in Cologne, may be set at 1143–1145. Evervinus (Ebervin, Hervin) was a Premonstratensian canon of Steinfeld, and was prior of that house from 1121 to 1152. Born in France, he became count of Helfenstein. Entering the Church, he became a canon and later an energetic prior.[65] His vigor and aristocratic background brought him into contact with Saint Bernard, with whom he became good friends. It was therefore natural that he wrote the great Cistercian to ask his opinion concerning the dissenters.

In his letter, Evervinus distinguishes between two groups of heretics who had recently appeared at Cologne.[66] Some of the first group were captured. A number of these recanted and returned to the Church, but two, one of whom boasted the title of bishop, resisted and insisted upon debating their doctrines with the orthodox. When they failed to convince anyone, they asked for a delay so that they might produce learned men to defend their position. They said that if they were unable to convince the Catholics of the truth of what they preached they would choose death rather than recant. After three days of delay, in which Archbishop Arnold continually pleaded with them to reconsider, the mob went out of control, seized them, and consigned them to the flames, where they met their death with steadfast courage.[67]

The doctrines of these heretics derived in part from Reformist dissent but contained undeniable traces of real Catharist influence. The true Church, they maintained, was to be found not among the Catholics, but among themselves. They alone followed Christ properly, and they alone led the apostolic life. They followed a rule of poverty and accused the Catholics of worldliness, observing that even the monks, who claimed to possess nothing, held great stores of wealth in common. The Catholics loved this world; they, on the other hand, loved God's. They fasted, labored, and prayed night and day and therefore suffered persecution. The Catholics were pseudoapostolics; the Catholic Church had always been in error. So far there was nothing among these beliefs that might not have been Reformist rather than Catharist in origin, but of what now follows this is not true—for if the Catholic Church had always been in error, they said, the heretics and their fathers had always walked in the path of truth; their sect was therefore as ancient as Christ. For centuries it had been kept hidden *in Greece and other lands* but was now emerging in the West. The sectaries abstained from milk and from whatever food was engendered from procreation. They daily consecrated their bread and drink in a special fashion when they ate. The heretics denied the Catholic sacraments but baptized by the imposition of hands. Their group was divided into elect and listeners (*perfecti* and *credentes*). They condemned marriage.

From these heretics a second group was distinguished that was completely at odds with the former. Indeed, both groups had attracted the attention of the archbishop by the very fact that they were constantly at odds with each other. This second group professed purely Reformist doctrines.

From all this it is possible to deduce a train of events that must have repeated itself all over western Europe at this time. A group of indigenous Reformists existed at Cologne in the mid-twelfth century. Then ideas of Catharist dualism were introduced from east and south, these finding ready support from people who already subscribed to puritanism and a grotesque exaggeration of Christian principles. Some of the Reformists adopted the Catharist doctrine and organization while retaining most of their own doctrines; others rejected the novelties. The heretics then spilt into two groups and wrangled fiercely with each other, inspired with that bitter hatred that arises when brothers fall out. This scenario is conjectural, but if true it would explain a great deal. In any event, the existence of Catharist ideas at Cologne as early as 1143 must be accepted as definite.

Jonas of Cambrai.

Between 1164 and 1167,[68] Bishop Nicholas I of Cambrai (1136–1167) sat in judgment on a lawsuit brought before his court by a priest named Jonas, who was suing Abbot Hildebrand of the Augustinian house of Jette for possession of a church at Neder-Heembeek.[69] Nicholas had letters from his neighboring colleagues of Cologne, Trier, and Liège indicating that Jonas had been tried at least twice and found guilty of the *haeresis cattorum*. His heresy dated, evidently, from at least as early as 1151–1156. Upon receipt of this information, the bishop of Cambrai refused to hear Jonas' suit and confirmed the rights of Abbot Hildebrand to the church in perpetuity. We are unfortunately given no statement of Jonas' beliefs, but by the late date and the use of the term *cattorum* we may assume that Jonas was a genuine Catharist, and one who troubled to preach his doctrines in at least three dioceses.

The council of Reims of 1157.

Under Archbishop Samson (1140–1161), a council of Reims was convened on October 25, 1157, and published a decree against Manichaeans or *Piphili*, a name derived from a term, *Populicani* or *Publicani*, often applied to the Catharists.[70] The council cited no particular group of heretics but said that they roamed about the countryside in number and led the simple folk astray. Many of the heretics were "those vilest of people, the weavers." Though giving us to believe that the dissenters held many abominable doctrines, the council specifies only one, the rejection of legitimate marriage, and couples it with the usual accusations of profligate behavior. This is in itself no conclusive evidence of Catharism, but again the combination of the late date and the use of the name *Piphili* makes it probable that the condemned were indeed Catharists. The tone of the report and the fearsome penalties envisaged for those who were caught and refused to repent imply that Catharists were already quite troublesome in northern France by 1157.

The "Colitiani."

There is another vague reference indicating that Catharists were well known at Liège from the 1150's. Renier of Saint-Laurent, a Liégeois monk writing in that decade or shortly thereafter, produced a little tract entitled *De Ineptiis Cuiusdam Idiotae*[71] in which he rambled on about a number of things, but particularly about the great pride of his monastery, Rupert, later abbot of Deutz and a mystical theologian and commentator upon Scriptures. He tells us that Rupert wrote a tract upon the will of God in which he attacked the *heresim Colitianorum* which maintained that God had willed the creation of evil, and not merely the "evil of affliction" that punishes sins, but absolute evil. This tract was addressed to William of Champeaux, the bishop of Châlons, and to

Anselm of Laon, two of the greatest names in twelfth-century philosophy.

Now it is certainly true that Rupert did write a *De Voluntate Dei*[72] addressed to Anselm and William of Champeaux, but he did not mention any "Colitiani," nor indeed did the word *heresy* appear in the text. Rather, he reproached William and Anselm for lecturing in such a way that many of their students had misunderstood them and were teaching that God had willed Adam to fall. The students based this proposition on the thesis attributed to William and Anselm by Rupert: *Voluntas mali alia approbans, alia permittens.* The purpose of Rupert's little treatise was to show how the vagueness of this proposition attributed to God led to error. It is clear that Rupert was not accusing the philosophers of heresy, let alone of being "Colitiani." He did not assert that they or their students taught that God willed "absolute evil, the contrary of good and of virtue."

Since the accusation cannot be attributed to Rupert, it must have originated with Renier. Renier, living at Saint-Laurent, would have been familiar with the works of Rupert, but in this instance he appears not to have read the treatise in question with any great attention. Skimming it, his eye probably noted the introduction and certain phrases discussing evil and the will of God, and, not realizing that it was a question only of the age-old philosophical debate on the problem of evil, assumed that it was a question of a heresy, the heresy of the "Colitiani." We may not, then, assume that any "Colitiani" were active at the time Rupert wrote, for there is no evidence in his treatise one way or the other. But, since Renier so readily leaped to the conclusion that this was what Rupert meant, the heresy of the "Colitiani" must have been familiar to him. Renier was a man of parochial interests, whose writings all concern the local history of Liège and its inhabitants, so it is probable that the "Colitiani" were heretics with whom the Liégeois had had actual contact.

The date of the presence of these heretics at Liège depends, then, upon the date of the *De Ineptiis*. The date of Renier's death is unknown, but Sylvain Balau[73] has approximately dated several of his works. According to Balau, the *Vitae* of Eracle, Wolbodo, and Réginard were written around 1180, the *Triumphale Bulonicum* between 1153 and

1182, the *De Adventu Reliquiarum* before 1153. Renier probably died in the early 1180's. Thus the *De Ineptiis* was written about 1180 at the latest, and possibly around 1150 or even earlier. The "Colitiani" must have existed at Liège during this period.

Their name itself is bizarre and is found nowhere else than in the *De Ineptiis*. The doctrine that God willed to create absolute evil is clearly the dualist belief that the Creator-God was an evil demiurge. It is possible that Renier mistook the term *Cathari* for the term *Colitiani*, which he supplied from his own imagination. It is more likely that "Colitiani" was a scribal error for "Cathari." The only edition of the *De Ineptiis* that exists is that of Wilhelm Arndt, and the mystery will never be solved, for the only known manuscript of the work, in a twelfth-century codex at Louvain, was destroyed in 1914 during the German invasion.[74]

Eckbert of Schönau.

In 1163,[75] Eckbert, a priest and canon of Bonn, later abbot (1166 or 1167) of the Benedictine monastery of Schönau in the archdiocese of Trier, and the brother of the mystic Elizabeth of Schönau and himself the author of a number of works including *The Goad of Love,* wrote a book of thirteen sermons against the Catharists[76] and dedicated it to Archbishop Rainald of Cologne (1159–1167). The book was written not pedantically and from a distance, but by a man who had himself debated with the Catharists. His treatment of the heresy is nonetheless judicial and thorough, so that the book represents the earliest reliable source on the Catharists. It shows that the influence of Catharism in the northwest, first perceptible at Cologne at the time of Evervinus of Steinfeld, had by the 1160's become fully entrenched.

Eckbert says that a certain sort of heretic had frequently been remarked around Cologne in recent years and that these heretics had spread throughout all Christendom to such a degree that they constituted a real danger to the Church. They preached their doctrine fervently and crossed land and sea to make converts. They were fluent and clever in defense of their doctrines, so much so that they sometimes confounded their orthodox opponents and reduced them to silence. Some of them were well educated and learned in Scriptures. Some were of good family, though most were *rustici,* a term perhaps best translated as "bumpkins," in orthodox polemic more often a slur than an accurate description.

Eckbert harks back to the time when as a canon at Bonn he used to go with his friend Bertolf to observe and debate with the heretics. From his observations then and later he learned a great deal about the nature of their errors; some of his information was obtained from a man who had left the sect in disgust. It is unfortunate that Eckbert did not clearly distinguish the doctrines of the dissidents he observed in 1143 from those with whom he debated twenty years later, for if he had we might now have a detailed picture of how Catharist dualism penetrated and eventually took over Reformist dissent at Cologne. As it is, he tells us that the earlier heretics forbade marriage except when contracted between virgins, a Reformist position that the Catharists would emend to a total prohibition of matrimony. He made no distinction in name, however, between the earlier and the later groups, referring to all as Catharists, *Piphiles,* or Weavers (a sign of the increasing social implications of heresy).

On August 5, 1163, some of the Cologne group were tried and condemned by Archbishop Rainald and burned at the stake; these were overt and unabashed Catharists.[77] Between the time Eckbert saw heretics burned at Bonn and that when he saw them burned by the archbishop at Cologne in 1163 an evolution in their doctrines had occurred.

Some indication of this is given by Eckbert. At the time of Evervinus, there were two warring sects, one consisting of Reformists, the other infected with Catharism. Eckbert indicated that there was by 1163 only one group, though there was disagreement within it on matters of doctrine. The mass of the heretics held doctrines derived from Reformist dissent; these were openly preached and without dissimulation. But there were other doctrines secretly taught, or secret explanations given for openly taught beliefs, by an inner group that consisted of real Catharists. What must have happened is that the Reformist elements were slowly supplanted and assimilated to the ascendant Catharist creed. The Catharist leaders, to extend their influence, must have used the sect as a front organization, secretly preaching Catharism while offering their followers a diluted message that could easily be reconciled with the less radical Reformist dissent.

The Cologne heretics of the 1160's met in secret conventicles and had their *perfecti* who were, of course, members of the secret "in-group." Many of the dissenters were learned in the Scriptures, and all claimed to lead a holy life in accordance with apostolic teaching. Eckbert tells us that they did not celebrate Christian feasts but instead had a feast called *Malilosa,* which he identified with the *Bema* mentioned by Saint Augustine in his work against the Manichaeans. This identification was probably the product of Eckbert's imagination, stimulated by a pedantic knowledge of the ancient Manichaeans. It is difficult to say which Catharist ceremony he identified with this feast; perhaps he got the idea from their elaborate table ritual, or, as Borst perhaps too ingeniously suggests,[78] from the *consolamentum* itself, which might have been expressed in German as *Lösung des Makels* and then Latinized into *Malilosa.* Anyway, it is unlikely that the heretics had a Manichaean equivalent of the Christian Easter, as Eckbert would have it.

The heretics condemned marriage, permitting spouses to live together only if they practiced celibacy. Some of the heretics, however, permitted marriage between two virgins, an indication that these were of the outer group, still uninitiated into Catharism. The reason Eckbert attributed to the heretics for denying the legitimacy of matrimony is curious, for it had nothing to do with a fear of procreation and, further, it quoted the Book of Genesis, anathema to the Catharists, as its authority. (Elsewhere, Ezekiel and Ecclesiastes were also quoted by the heretics.) According to this explanation, the fruit Old Adam was forbidden to taste in the Garden of Eden was Eve herself: God meant to prohibit sexual intercourse altogether. This may well have been a rationalization presented to the front group by the inner core of Catharists, though it is hard to understand why they would have used one of the detested Books of Moses even for this purpose. Similarly, though they abstained from meat, the outer group did so for ascetic reasons, while the inner circle taught secretly that meat was forbidden because it derived from procreation. The inner circle seems certainly not to have retreated from the principles of dualism: the flesh and all matter were created by the devil, so they said. Christ was not really born of the Virgin, nor did he have human flesh (though Eckbert is not sure on this point), suffer, or rise from the dead. The souls of men were the very apostate spirits whom God cast out of heaven and who were now imprisoned in the flesh. Salvation from this fleshly prison was procured by good works, which, however, had validity only when performed by members of their sect.

It was this sect of theirs in which the truth was preserved and which had the "true priests," not the Catholic Church. Again, the reasons they gave for denying the Church were more Reformist than Catharist. Masses were invalid, they said, because of the immorality of the priests, and for this reason too the orders of the Church were invalid. "All those who have been called Roman pontiffs and cardinals," said the heretics, "have always been proud of avaricious men and for many reasons unworthy of the priesthood; for this reason we are certain that there is no true priesthood among the Catholics." A more avowedly Reformist position could not be imagined. Eckbert argued this point with the heretics, who then affirmed that even if the immorality of the Catholic hierarchy were not enough to make it invalid, it was proven by the fact that so many bishops from the beginning of the Church fell into heresy, an argument that the clever Eckbert did not hesitate to turn against his opponents.

As the sectaries denied the Church, so they denied its sacraments. Baptism was rejected, but on the Reformist grounds that children were ignorant of the meaning of the rite. This again seems to have been the argument offered by the outer circle, for we learn that the initiates said that all baptism with water was useless and performed "their own baptism" in the form of the Catharist *consolamentum*. According to Eckbert, this rite was performed as follows. The heretics assembled and locked themselves in a dark chamber where they could be sure of not being seen or overheard. In the midst of the group stood the man who was to receive the sacrament. The chief of the sect (*archicatharus*) stood before him with the appointed book in his hand. He placed his hands upon the candidate's head and blessed him. To fulfill the Scriptural call for baptism of spirit and fire, the rite was performed in the center of a circle of burning lamps.

They denied the validity of the eucharist, though they sometimes partook of it to divert suspicion. Eckbert ascribed to them a strange folly: when asked about their beliefs on the eucharist, they said that they denied the Catholic sacrament but that they "made the body of Christ" at their own table. By this they meant that their own bodies constituted the body of Christ, so that when they took nourishment they were adding to their own bodies and thereby "making the body of Christ." It is unlikely that real Catharists would have held such ideas; either Eckbert was mistaken, or the heretics said this in mockery of the Christian sacrament. They also denied the existence of purgatory, insisting that souls went directly either to heaven or hell at the moment of death.

The members of the inner group burned by the archbishop held unmitigated Catharist doctrines, including those of the creation of the world by an evil, secondary god; the nature of men as fallen spirits entrapped in matter; metempsychosis; and a docetic view of Christ's nature.

Eckbert's evidence presents us, then, with a clear notion of what happened in the middle years of the twelfth century when Catharist doctrines began taking over the movement of Reformist dissent that until then had dominated Occidental heresy. First, there was a purely Reformist group. Some of these were converted to Catharism, so there came to be two opposing groups. Finally the Reformist sect that had opposed the Catharists were infiltrated by the latter and gradually assimilated.

Oxford.

In 1166 [79] a group of dissidents who may have been connected with those of Cologne[80] were discovered in England. There were a good number of them, mostly foreigners, with one or two English converts. William of Newburgh, the chief source, says that the heresy had its origin in Gascony, but he is speaking of the origin of Catharism in general rather than of this group in particular. The heretics spoke an unspecified Germanic dialect, and it has been debated whether they were Flemish or Rhenish. Ralph of Coggeshall mentions Count Philippe of Flanders in relation to the heresy of the "Publicani," but he does not identify the heretics of Oxford with those Philippe prosecuted; moreover, there is a gap of twenty years between the events at Oxford and Philippe's activities in Flanders. There were commercial connections aplenty between England and both Flanders and the Rhineland,[81] and both had their share of dissent in the 1160's. We have already examined the heretics of Cologne, and a letter of Alexander III to Louis VII indicates that there were a number in Flanders at that time.[82]

Flemish or Rhenish, there were more than thirty of them, as many men as women, and at their head was one Gerard, whom all respected as their teacher and leader. All but Gerard, who knew his letters "a little," were illiterate. They had dwelt briefly in England and had attempted in peaceful fashion to convert a few of their neighbors to their beliefs, a task that was difficult in a country with no tradition of religious dissidence and whose language they could not have spoken fluently. The number of their known converts is limited to one, a woman who was impressed by some purported marvels that they performed and joined the sect. It does not seem likely that they were merchants, for several reasons. First, there were both men and women; second, they were illiterate; third, they relied trustingly upon their leader Gerard, in the manner of simple folk; fourth, William of Newburgh speaks of their being in *hiding*. A fifth reason is that it is difficult to explain what they were doing in Oxfordshire if they were merchants; the Rhenish and Flemish merchants congregated in London, where the citizens of Cologne kept a house. In answer to this last it may be objected that we are not in fact certain that they were found in Oxfordshire. They were tried at Oxford, but it is possible that they were haled there from elsewhere to suit the convenience of the prelates assembled at the council. In any event, they do not seem to have been merchants. What, then, were they doing in England? And why were they hiding? Any answer to this question is bound to be speculation, but it seems possible that they may have been refugees from the prosecution of the Catharists on the Continent. The fact that they wanted to hide may also have explained why they did not go about making converts with more enthusiasm; it may have been their rashness in making even one that betrayed them. At any rate, curious people began inquiring as to the nature of the strange sect and eventually informed the authorities, by whom the heretics were taken into custody.

They were brought before King Henry II, who wished to refrain from making judgment until they had been properly examined by the ecclesiastical authorities, whom he ordered to look into their case. It was decided that they should be heard at a council at Oxford. Since

Gerard was the only literate man among them, he was permitted to speak at the council for the others. When his arguments had been heard, they were condemned, and the council ordered the heretics to recant. They refused, and when threats were "piously" made, they continued to hold firm, saying that they were blessed of God and need fear no harm. To scotch the heresy without further ado, the bishops publicly proclaimed them heretics and turned them over the the secular arm. The king now had his answer and proceeded to take the proper measures against them. As the fires of vengeance were being prepared, their lone convert, the Englishwoman who had been impressed with their "marvels," lost hope and confessed her error, expressing her desire to return to the Church. This recantation was received with pleasure by the clergy, who decided that she "merited" reconciliation, since through fear of punishment she had deserted her friends. Her terror may merit more sympathy than the smugness of the chronicler in according it. The heretics were then led to the fire, rejoicing in the true spirit of martyrs as Gerard sang from the Beatitudes, "Blessed are you when men shall hate you." Each heretic was branded on the forehead, Gerard suffering a double branding in his capacity of leader. Their clothes were cut off as far as the waist, and they were whipped out of town "with resounding blows."

Ralph of Diceto tells us that they were then banished from the realm, but William of Newburgh tells a sadder story, and one that is confirmed by the assize of Clarendon in 1166, which ordered that no one in England should receive on his land, or in his house, or in his company, any of the sectaries who had been condemned at Oxford. If any one did so receive them, his house would be burned to the ground as a place contaminated. It was winter when the sectaries, both men and women, were whipped out of Oxford naked to the waist, and by order of the king no one was to take them in. So was fulfilled in the mind of the Christian king the injunction, "I was hungry, and you gave me meat: I was a stranger, and you took me in," or that of Saint Paul, "If thine enemy hunger, feed him; if he thirst, give him drink." Hungry and freezing, they died miserably of starvation and exposure, their agony being justified by what William of Newburgh called the "pious rigor" that succeeded in extirpating this "plague" and preventing any other from breaking out.

The teachings that occasioned such punishment bear a close resemblance to those preached on the Continent at that time, which is natural because of the Continental origin of the dissidents. They were of the kind of heretics called *Publicani,* William tells us, which immediately identifies them as Catharists, though their teachings betray the usual ambiguity between Catharist and Reformist teachings, another fact that may connect them with the ambiguous sect at Cologne with whom Eckbert of Schönau had to deal. They claimed to be Christians and said that they venerated apostolic-doctrine. They lived pious lives (or "claimed to"), and quoted the New Testament, particularly the Beatitudes, in support of their position. They contemned the Catholic Church and the Catholic sacraments, including baptism, the eucharist, and marriage. This is unfortunately the limit of our information, so that it is impossible to discern exactly what the respective proportions of Catharist and Reformist doctrines were in this sect. Indeed, it is possible that they may have been Reformists, though the date, their origins, and their name make this unlikely.[83]

If Eastern dualism had influence at Cologne in 1143, it is reasonable to suppose that it must have made its first appearance in the Occident no later than 1140. At the same time, the external evidence does not favor the theory that it arrived much earlier than this date and frowns severely upon the notion that it existed in the eleventh century. The internal evidence places almost its entire weight against an earlier date. We must therefore assign around 1140 as the date at which Catharist dualism first made an impression in the West. At any rate, it now seems probable that Eastern dualism penetrated the West in the mid-twelfth century rather than a hundred and fifty years earlier.

The chief single factor that led historians astray was one that involves what is admittedly an extraordinary coincidence. Medieval Catharism may or may not be a direct descendant of ancient Manichaeism, but it is certainly a descendant of ancient gnosticism and therefore closely related to ancient Manichaean doctrine. To call the medieval Catharists medieval Manichees is a distortion, but it is not a violent one. Historians knew, therefore, that heretics with historical and doctrinal connections with Manichaeism existed in Western Europe in the latter part of the twelfth and the thirteenth centuries. Then they read the chronicles of the earlier period, where they found mention of "Manichaean" heretics. What more natural conclusion than that these early heretics were the progenitors of the later Catharists? It was a simple step on the basis of this evidence to press the frontiers of Catharism back from the mid-twelfth to the beginning of the eleventh century. It was a simple step, but an errant one. The chroniclers did not call the earlier heretics Manichaeans because they were Manichaeans, but because the chroniclers, their perception dulled by the medieval respect for the authority of the ancients, consulted their Augustine and pedantically assigned the name "Manichaean" to dissidents who had no connection with Manichaeanism at all. It was an ironic coincidence that, after a century and a half of mistaken use of the word, there arrived in the West some Eastern dualists whose title to the name was, if not entirely clear, at least relatively valid.

If this were nothing but coincidence, it might be difficult to swallow, but there was here, as in many so-called coincidences, a rational connecting element. The Catharists of the thirteenth century were Eastern dualists. Dualism was the basic doctrine of the Manichaean religion. And it was precisely because they saw dualistic elements in the teaching of the eleventh-century heretics that the chroniclers and other contemporary writers used the pedantic "Manichaean" to describe them more often than, say, the pedantic "Arian," that and because it was Saint Augustine whom they knew the best. But this dualism they perceived in the teaching of the eleventh century heretics was not Manichaeanism or any form of Eastern dualism at all. It was the dualism inherent in Christianity itself, magnified and distorted. As a man looks into a fun-house mirror and fails to recognize his own image, so eleventh-century Christians failed to recognize their own images in the Reformists.

This ideological connection was translated into a human connection in the 1140's. It was precisely because Reformist dualism had so much in common with Eastern dualism that the Easterners had such an easy time getting control of Occidental heresy in the second half of the twelfth century. The Catharists seized the movement of Reformist dissent in much the same way as the Communists seized and took control of the Socialist left in central and eastern Europe in the twentieth century. From the mid-twelfth century on, imported dualism was at least as powerful a factor in medieval heresy as was native Reformism. But until then, in all the time emphasized in this study from the eighth century on, heresy was dominated by Reformist dissent, a movement of enthusiasm generated by the Great Reform Movement.

9. Conclusions

The dynamics of dissent.

The question of the dynamics of dissent is one of the relation of ideology to circumstance. History knows many instances of cooperation between ideology and circumstance in the causation of an event. It knows many instances in which ideology has been merely a rationalization for circumstance, as when Thomas Jefferson modified his belief in the strict interpretation of the Constitution upon becoming president or as when the enemy of papal prerogative, Gerbert of Aurillac, became its defender upon his elevation to the apostolic see. Was the ideology that produced medieval dissidence a product of the circumstances of its environment, and, if so, of what circumstances? Or was medieval dissidence essentially what it appears to be: a movement of religious enthusiasm?

Many recent historians have indicated the connection between religious revolt and the Great Reform Movement, and this interpretation has been in evidence throughout the present book. The question arises, however, whether this religious phenomenon was set in motion by social circumstances. Can the origins of medieval dissent be explained in purely religious terms or was the social element significantly present? Was the course of medieval dissidence, once established, significantly affected by social circumstances? To sum up, are the deepest dynamics of medieval dissent spiritual and intellectual, or are they economic and social?

These questions, neglected by historians of the nineteenth century, were raised first by Marxist historians, then by sociologists and historians with sociological interests who were provoked by the observations that Weber and Tawney made about the growth of Protestantism. The first insight into the problem was actually made much earlier by the skeptic Godfried Arnold, who in 1688 published an *Unbiased History of Church and Heresy*,[1] designed to embarrass Catholic and Protestant alike, in which he attributed the rise of heresy to discontent with ecclesiastical vested interests. The first Marxist suggestion that heresy had social roots came from Frederich Engels himself,[2] and Marxist writers from Engels through Karl Kautsky to the present day have adopted this position, the most energetic present writer of this school being Ernst Werner of the University of Leipzig.[3]

Non-Marxist writers in this century have also concerned themselves with the question.[4] Often the a priori assumption of social roots is made. Norman Cohn's *Pursuit of the Millennium*[5] adopts the social connection as one of its basic premises and ties this in with the idea that medieval heresies were basically millenarian movements that help explain the search for utopia in modern times. The difficulty is that the early medieval heresies of which he speaks were not millenarian; a further difficulty is that convincing evidence of the social connection of early medieval dissent does not appear in his pages. It is probably correct that there was a social element in the people's role in the first crusade, but dissent, and dissent of the Reform variety, existed long before the crusade. Similar assumptions were made by Antonino de Stefano, writing in 1938, who proffered the opinion that medieval dissent represented a social revolt against the influence of the Church in politics and that medieval heresies were heresies of the masses. "At bottom," he concluded, "the economic argument must have constituted, more than any dogmatic or religious discussions, the principal motive of the preaching of heresy."[6]

The most recent presentation of the sociological point of view is that of Gottfried Koch, whose *Frauenfrage und Ketzertum im Mittelalter* appeared in 1962.[7] Koch maintains that since the greatest power in the Middle Ages was the Catholic Church, class struggles tended naturally to assume religious forms. Medieval dissidents were, therefore, social rebels whose naïveté prevented them from understanding that their real demands must be political rather than doctrinal. Women participated in these movements to a disproportionate extent, for they were implicitly revolting against the domination of society by men.[8] Dissidence was incontrovertibly bound up with the great communal movement of the eleventh and twelfth centuries, when the towns revolted against their lords, who often were bishops. Koch admits that Grundmann has shown that the Catharists came from a variety of classes, but goes on to reaffirm the basic social motivation of Catharism, observing that it was not necessary that a movement be limited to the lower classes for it to be social in character. This is true, of course, but one would like more positive evidence that the movement was a social one. Koch admits that religious consideration always played a role in religious movements (one is grateful for this concession), but he affirms that the social and economic causes were not only more cogent but more real, ideological considerations being as it were merely the froth on the materialist brine. He then reviews the evidence for the social theory. Heretics were frequently identified with weavers. Women often appeared prominently among the heretics of the twelfth century. Peasants represented an overwhelming majority of the dissenters of that century. Among the Catharists, the division between the initiated "perfect" and the mere "believers" was based upon a class distinction. Except for the last point, for which there is no positive evidence, these observations will be of concern to us in the course of this chapter.

The contribution of the sociological school to the understanding of medieval dissent has been great. They have posed interesting questions and given new depth to our understanding of these movements. The eye of the historian can no longer skim scornfully over circumstance to light upon the platonic essence. Though most modern historians of medieval dissent are skeptical of fundamentally materialist interpretations, the historian who does not share the materialist interpretation would not now deny the importance of correlating religious revolt with economic and social circumstance.

It is evident that economic and social circumstance in the appearance of heresy merits attention. In previous considerations of the problem, however, there have been two assumptions that we cannot make here. The first is that the story of medieval dissent begins in the eleventh century. The second is that the evidence of social connections for dissent that comes from the twelfth or thirteenth (or even the sixteenth) century can be read back into the earlier history of dissent. The fact that, as we have shown, the origins of medieval dissent stretch back to the eighth century seriously weakens the effect of the discoveries of social circumstance surrounding heresy in later ages. No one would deny that this circumstance is significant in Marvin Becker's thirteenth-century Florence, but at the same time no one would or should imagine that because this is so, it must also be so in another time and another land.

With the ground cleared, we can look at early medieval dissent as a whole. To begin with, what might we expect to be true? In the first place, the doctrines of the dissenters seem to indicate an interest in social questions. They praised poverty. They attacked the pomp and vanity of the children of this world. They attacked the hierarchy and the clergy as a whole, and sometimes they specifically attacked the institution of tithing. In the second place, certain conditions seem conducive to a union of religious with social protest. Social protest is naturally directed against those who are most in evidence as instruments of social oppression. In the period under consideration these were most frequently members of the feudal nobility and very often of the feudal clergy. It seems natural that a bishop or an abbot who found his social and political authority under attack would very likely find his religious authority questioned as well. Indeed, it has long been observed that of all the feudal nobility the higher clergy were the most resistant to change, this being especially true in the rise of the communes, when bishops sometimes even went to their deaths struggling against the establishment of urban liberties. When the bishops so often allowed the distinction between their political and their religious authority to be blurred, and invoked religious sanctions against political enemies, it would not be strange if social and political rebels blurred the distinction and attacked the crozier as well as the sword. Thus, much rebellion "against the Church" was less a rebellion against the institution itself than an attack upon the bishop or priests who represented "the Church" in the eyes of the dissidents.

The popular nature of dissent, which seems to have drawn the bulk of its followers from among the poor, also seems significant. Again, we know that European society underwent a number of important social and economic changes from the ninth to the twelfth centuries: feudalism became a rigid hereditary system, commerce and industry were transformed, population grew more rapidly than before, towns grew in size and independence of spirit. Society became more variegated, and because of this the interests of various groups in society became more diverse. Finally, there are certain instances of dissent where the political elements are overt and obvious, as in the Iconoclastic controversy where hostility between East and West added to the rumor, or in the Adoptionist controversy motivated to a great extent by the conflict between particularist and Romanizing elements in Spain.

But there are certain other facts that might lead us a priori to place less emphasis upon social circumstance than might be expected. While it is true that the dissenters attacked the clergy and upheld the virtues of poverty, they in no instance (except for Arnold of Brescia and possibly the Patarini, who were not really dissenters) had anything like a social or political program. Even attacks upon tithes were not universal. The program of the Reformists and of their early Catharist successors was in fact precisely the opposite of a political or social program: they contemned the world and condemned matter. They looked, not to a wordly utopia in the future, or indeed to any future utopia, but to a return to the apostolic purity of pristine Christianity. Far from having a social program, their concern was with the enhancement of the purity of individuals. The Church as an institution was condemned, not because of its social role, but because its frequent state of corruption seemed to obstruct the individual's path to God. This is an ideal of holy poverty, not a trades-union program or a grange.

It is of course possible to press materialist interpretations farther and to maintain that though the program of the dissenters was explicitly religious it was implicitly social. The "real" motivations are social, the materialists say, but in their naïveté the dissenters could do no more than express their discontent in religious terms. These historians make an a priori philosophical assumption about what is "real," an assumption that may or may not be justified. And in this question of medieval dissent, the burden of proof lies with the materialists who, in almost gnostic fashion, seek the esoteric explanation in preference to the simple one.

More sophisticated sociological analyses of heretical behavior are possible following the principles of Neil Smelser in his *Theory of Collective Behavior* (London, 1962). Smelser suggests that collective movements can be understood through the "value-added process": certain components produce certain situations when they are added in the proper order. The first and most important of these determinants is structural conduciveness to change. This depends largely upon a situation of high "structural differentiation," in which the various sectors of society are separated so that change in religious thought, for example, can occur without being greatly checked by assumptions prevalent in other sectors of society. In the Middle Ages there was an unusually small degree of structural differentiation owing to the pervasiveness of the Catholic world view and to the notion of a unified Christian society, so that drastic change in any one sector of society was inhibited. This may help to explain why the dissenting movements seldom if ever attained the stature of what Smelser calls a "craze." They affected relatively few people. Smelser also distinguishes between "value-oriented" and "norm-oriented" movements, the former aiming at a deep transformation of the basic values of society and the latter aiming only at modifications of these values. Here again the basic homogeneity of medieval society was not conducive to the formation of "value-oriented" movements so that, with the possible exception of Catharism, medieval dissent was exclusively "norm-oriented." Nothing like the Protestant Reformation occurred in this period.

I leave suggestions as to the possibility of other kinds of inquiries into medieval dissent to those better qualified as sociologists. I am inclined to believe that the lack of data on the early Middle Ages limits both the use of sociological theory to explain the phenomena and the use of the phenomena to illustrate sociological theory.

A word must be said about medieval attitudes, though here one can be little more than subjective. Medieval people were concerned with money, with social position, and with power, as people have always been and probably will be for some time. But they also frequently had a concern just as deep as if not deeper than these, and that was with holiness. Whatever the concerns of the individual today, he must recognize that the ultimate concern of many medieval men was with the other world, not with this one. In a sense the dissent of the early Middle Ages was less influenced by considerations external to religion even than the earlier Church. Nationalism and class loyalty probably affected religious dissent in the earlier Church more than they did in our period.

Finally, in regard to the apparently natural correlation between religious and political revolt against the bishops, one fact appears curious: The connection between dissent and social revolt appears stronger in the late twelfth and thirteenth centuries when the bishops' power had already been seriously weakened by successful communal revolts, and when the struggles within the towns were more frequently struggles of artisan against wealthy merchant than of citizen against bishop. And this connection is correspondingly weaker in the earlier period when the bishops had more power.

These arguments show that we have no right facilely to assume, as some have done, that the social roots of dissidence are self-evident. Rather, the evidence must be carefully examined to determine what correlations there may be. I should like now to summarize the conclusions that seem to emerge.

First, the evidence is as a whole inconclusive because of its extreme sparseness. We have not the information on the medieval dissidents that we have, for example, on the members of the Long Parliament. We have only bits and pieces of the picture; from these we can sketch out the whole; but we must realize that had we the evidence that is missing we might be able to sketch a different picture. This limitation is especially severe when we speak of the class origins of the dissenters. Often the only indication of their place in life is the statement that they are clergy or that they were laymen, and this is not especially helpful. Beyond this, we have only rare information.

In those cases where information is available, peasants appear more often than any other group. Rather than define exactly what is meant by "peasant" it is best to leave the term vague, since the sources are themselves imprecise, speaking only of "unlettered rustics" or "simple country people" without telling us whether they are serfs, petty freemen, or something else. Peasants, then, in this general sense, appear prominently among dissidents throughout our period. In the eighth century, Aldebert's followers were peasants; in the ninth, the followers of Burgand at Bordeaux were peasants, as were the heretics of Utrecht and Mainz. Liutward was a man of humble origins who rose to a position of power. In the eleventh century, the heretics of Liège in 1025 were probably peasants; they were certainly illiterate. Those of Rennes and of Châlons were peasants. In the twelfth century, the two dissidents of Soissons were peasants, and so were the followers of Eudo of Brittany, though he himself may possibly have had noble origins, and so were the Eccentrics who persecuted the weavers at Sint Truiden. The Oxford heretics of 1166 were "simple." Now this is a good number, but if it be remembered that serfs and petty freeman taken together probably formed upward of 80 percent of the total population, and certainly more than 70 percent, a preponderance of peasants in dissenting movements is only to be expected. More than that, the ignorance and simplicity of most of the peasants, rather than hidden social motives, could explain some of the grosser errors into which they fell (Burgand, for example), though not their persistent attack upon ecclesiastical authority.

If we attempt to broaden our approach still further and speak of a general revolt of "lower classes," we are no better off, for in the years before 1160 there are only two cases where the lower urban classes seem to preponderate, one in that of the Patarini, which, again, is on only the borderline of dissent, and the other in that of the condemnation of the council of Reims in 1157, which attacked weavers as frequent participants in heretical movements.

If there were only very few indications of other groups being involved in dissent, there would remain a case for lower-class domination, but this is simply not so. The clergy were very frequently involved in dissent (though as it is usually impossible to tell what level of clergy this is a fact of no conclusive importance). Often, many groups were involved. Tanchelm and his lieutenants drew followers from various classes of town and countryside. The heretics at Orléans in the reign of King Robert included priests, canons and nuns, and other literate people as well as the simple; the same was true at Périgueux in the twelfth century. Arnold of Brescia was of noble birth and had followers of various classes. At Cologne in the time of Eckbert of Schönau some of the dissenters were peasants, but others were of good family. The heretics of Ivois were of different classes, as were the followers of Henry the Monk. Most of the town of Le Mans backed Henry, and we know that the whole castle of Monteforte in 1028, from the leading nobles on down, was in heresy. The role played by the aristocracy of southern France in courtly love and in Catharism is well known.

If the sources spoke more fully on the subject of class origins, we might be able to make a more positive judgment. But since they do not, and since it is highly unlikely that fuller sources will be discovered, we must be content with the limited evidence that we do have. This evidence reveals nothing that would allow us to ascribe a class basis for early medieval dissent.

Gottfried Koch maintained that women played a disproportionate role in the dissenting groups. Without presuming to speak for the later period, we may say that in our period there is no evidence for this. Women are specifically mentioned in only a few cases. At Orléans nuns were involved, and a woman was reputed to have introduced the doctrine there in the first place. At Périgueux nuns were involved as well as other people; at Monteforte the countess was involved along with the rest of the castle. At Oxford in 1166 women were among the condemned. Women are mentioned among the followers of Tanchelm and of Henry the Monk. We may presume with certainty that women were among the followers of Eudo, of Aldebert, and of others, but nowhere is there any indication that women were more frequently in heresy than one would naturally expect from the fact that they were half the population. In one case only, that of Theuda at Mainz in the ninth century, did a woman lead one of the groups.

The other way to approach the question is to see what correlations can be made between outbreaks of dissidence and other circumstances. I have investigated the possibility of correlations of dissidence with the following: political upheaval (this must be overt, like a communal insurrection), notable social movements (for example, unusual immigration), natural disasters and the ravages of war, commercial centers, industrial centers, proximity to major trade routes, intellectual centers, centers of religious reform, and areas under the direct control of ecclesiastical authority. Anyone who has attempted to draw up anything like a statistical table for the early Middle Ages knows how incomplete the materials are and how arbitrary classifications sometimes can be. If these correlations are necessarily ragged, however, they are at least not biased.

The first thing one notes is that there is a strong correlation of outbreaks of dissent with natural disasters. But this proves meaningless, for the chronicles of every region present almost every year in sober literal truth a picture of some kind of disaster. Thus, though many cases of dissent occurred when natural disasters were noted, there were many scores of years in which disasters were noted but in which no dissent that we know of occurred. Another fairly common correlation is that of reports of dissent with areas under the direct control of a bishop or abbot. This again is misleading, and for two reasons. The first is that population (and therefore the number of potential dissenters) is by definition greater in towns of importance. Such towns seldom lacked a resident bishop or abbot, and these, the bishops especially, usually possessed some political power. The second is that since heresy is clearly an ecclesiastical matter, reports of dissent are most frequently made to or by the bishop of a diocese. Thus the dissent frequently originated in an outlying area but had to be dealt with in the episcopal see for the simple reason that that is where the bishop's court sat. This was true—to name but three examples—of Leutard, Ramihrd, and the brothers of Soissons. But since every region of western Europe was under the ecclesiastical authority of a bishop in one way or another, this correlation is seen to be inconclusive.

There is no significant correlation between commercial and industrial centers and dissent. Before the latter part of the tenth century it is difficult to designate any such centers, but dissent is nearly as much in evidence before this period as after. When once they are established, the correlation is still not great enough to be significant, for, once again, these centers are also centers of population and, second, they are frequently the seats of episcopal government to which cases of dissent are referred. The most frequent assertion about medieval dissent in relation to social forces is that dissent often occurred at a time of social and political revolt, particularly in conjunction with communal agitation. This interpretation rested in part upon the erroneous belief that dissent commences to be important toward the end of the eleventh century, when the communal movement also becomes important. As we know, this belief is false.

Furthermore, the following facts appear: in the eighth century, out of thirty-eight indications of heresy, only eight coincide in even the most general fashion with political agitation. In the ninth century, the figure is two out of twenty-eight, and in the tenth century three out of twenty. But what of the eleventh and twelfth centuries, when social and political agitation are generally conceded to be more in evidence? The eleventh century offers six correlations out of fifty-three cases; the twelfth (up to 1160) eight out of about forty. Nor do the maps show a significant relationship between centers of dissent and trade-routes. To be sure, trade routes are roads upon which people travel, and the dissenters of Châlons, for example, went to Liège because there was a well-traveled route between the two cities. When dissent passed from one center to another it was obliged to go by road or river routes. But, as we have seen, many of the dissident groups were led by peasants or recruited by peasants, and there is no evidence whatever that in this period traveling merchants were in any large respect carriers of heretical ideas. The last gasp of the historian seeking social correlations will be to reply, good, then rural areas are those which bred dissent. More often than not this is true, but it is untrue to just the extent that makes even this generalization not very meaningful. Further, as the enormous majority of people lived in rural areas in the early Middle Ages, the preponderance of rural origins of heresy is not significant.

After the political troubles surrounding the Iconoclast and Adoptionist controversies, the first case in which social circumstance was prominent was that of Leutard of Châlons, who had such a success among the peasantry by preaching against the payment of tithes. Social circumstances were of utmost importance in the case of the Patarini in Milan in the eleventh century, where shifting political alliances among the classes and resentment of the archbishops' political power was conducive to religious instability. It is possible that the clergy's reaction to Ramihrd's criticisms would have been less violent had not the established order at Cambrai at that time been threatened by communal agitation. The two brothers of Soissons who attacked the clergy in 1114 did so at a time when that city was experiencing the most critical period of its struggle for communal liberties, the charter being granted only in 1116 after a long period of dissension. Henry the Monk's success at Le Mans must have been related to the long history of conflict there between townspeople and bishop over communal liberties, as indicated by the violence of the bishop's reception at the hands of his citizens when he returned from Rome. Heresy broke out at Cambrai in 1135 at a period of dissension between clergy and laity in that city, and it occurred at Liège the same year, in a period when that diocese had been torn by dissension and schism. Arnold of Brescia's native city suffered in his day from a dispute between bishop and people over the commune. In most of these cases the social element was present though not necessarily dominant. But these cases are the exceptions rather than the rule.

Moving from the political and social to the intellectual, it must first be admitted that the correlation between dissent and intellectual centers is equally weak. The intellectual dissidents were usually associated with places of intellectual activity, but this can hardly be considered exciting news, and aside from the intellectual dissenters there seems to be no correlation.

We are left with a correlation between dissent and the Great Reform Movement. Even here the congruence of circumstance is not as clear as one would like. But this does seem to be the only significant correlation, and it is most noticeable, as one would expect, in its connection with Reformist dissent. If we include the "Reactionary" dissenters, the correlation is even more frequent. They were not included because, first, their status as dissidents is somewhat marginal, and, second, any conclusions would be almost tautological: "Reactionaries" are those condemned as such by the reformers, so naturally the condemnations come from centers of reform.

The geography of dissent.

If we now stand back from the trees and look a bit at the forest, we may draw some geographical observations. Why did dissent appear in one place and not in another? The Rhineland, the Low Countries, and northern France were the center of religious dissent in the early Middle Ages. This area, which Sproemberg calls the *niederrheinische Raum,* and which was a "Fertile Triangle" in many respects, was a microcosm of dissent in which are represented all the varieties of heterodoxy that are typical of the period. This small triangle of lowlands in the northwestern corner of the Continent was the metropolis of heresy for a number of reasons. It was, along with northern Italy, the stage for the first developments in trade, commerce, and industry accompanying the economic revival of the eleventh century, and it was there that the towns first began slowly to spread outward from the castle wall, to burst the bounds of the cathedral enclosures, to germinate at bridgeheads and at places where roads forded rivers. It was there too that the middle classes first arose, the solid citizenry of these new towns, and stood up against bishop and feudal lord to demand town charters and municipal self government. Socially and economically the northwest was preeminent among all the lands of Europe.

But in this Fertile Triangle grew other rich crops as well, crops of an intellectual and spiritual nature. The territory between Paris and Cologne was trodden by many of the great thinkers of the period—Abelard, Hincmar, Gerbert, Raban Maur, and Hrotswitha, to name only a few. To the courts of Charlemagne, Louis the Pious, Charles the Bald, which these kings made centers of learning, came men like John Scotus Eriugena, Alcuin, Sedulius Scotus, and other ornaments of medieval culture. Under the Carolingians, Aachen, in the heart of Lorraine, the heart of the Fertile Triangle, was the rich center of intellectual as well as of political life; and after the fall of the Carolingians, the court of the French kings in Paris at one extremity of the Triangle, and the court of the German kings on the Rhine and just to the east, became the fruitful granaries of intellectual production as well as political control.

The spiritual wealth of those fields was even more a horn of plenty than the intellectual wealth. When Saint Boniface was finally assigned his permanent see, that see was established at Mainz, which, at the confluence of Main and Rhine, is on the border of the Triangle. From that time on, primed by the reform activities of the Carolingian monarchs and their Ottonian successors, Lorraine and its neighboring areas gave birth to one reform after another. Brogne, Saint Vanne, Gorze, the great centers of monastic reform, lay within the boundaries of the Triangle, and Hirsau and Cluny lay just outside, the latter to the south and the former to the east. Great men in the history of the reform movement, Bruno of Toul, Wazo of Liège, Rather of Verona but first of Liège, Humbert of Silva Candida but first of Lorraine, men high in the councils of reform in the north or at Rome, were all Lotharingians. Hildebrand himself, the great general of the reform movement, though an Italian, journeyed north at the exile of his friend Gregory VI in 1046 and sojourned among the reformers in Lorraine, from whence he returned filled with the spirit of reform. This Triangle, fertile in so much, was fertile also in the produtcion of religious dissent.

Though dissent centered in the Fertile Triangle, it existed elsewhere, too—in France, in northern Italy, which was second only to the Low Countries in the brilliance of its commerce and its culture, in the portions of Germany lying to the east of the Triangle, and on the Spanish marches. Certain areas of Europe were almost entirely untouched by dissent in the early Middle Ages, however, and this is a peculiar fact that requires some accounting for. Scandinavia produced no dissent, Scotland produced none, Ireland produced little, and England, most surprising of all in view of its close connections with the Continent, produced almost none. Each case is peculiar and requires separate consideration.

In Scandinavia, conversion to Christianity did not come until late. Norway and Iceland were converted under Saint Olaf Trygvesson (995–1000), Sweden under Olaf Skottkonung (993–1024), and Denmark under Canute the Great (1014–1035), but the process of conversion was only gradually completed, so that it was not until the end of the eleventh century that Scandinavia could really be considered Christian. Thus Scandinavia was behind the rest of Europe in the development of her Church, and, because of her great distance from the centers of European civilization, was always isolated from the cultural and intellectual movements of the Continent. Busy coping with paganism and later with the inroads of the Russians, whom the Swedes considered heretical after the schism of 1054, the Scandinavians did not have leisure or opportunity to pursue the kind of movements of intellectual and spiritual reform that produced heresy. Nonetheless, if Scandinavia in the eleventh century is compared with Germany in the eighth, when that country was in the process of conversion, it is striking that whereas heresy abounds in the German instance it is lacking in the Scandinavian. The explanation of this may lie partly in the relative poverty of the Scandinavian sources, for the Scandinavians had no Saint Boniface whose lengthy correspondence would put us on intimate terms with the process of conversion in the eleventh century. It may be partly explained also by the difficulty that the Scandinavian bishops experienced in administering their dioceses. Norway and Sweden were sparsely populated countries whose territories were fragmented by mountains, glaciers, fjords, lakes, and swamps, the sees were large compared with those of more southern regions, and the bishops of Trondheim and Skara found it impossible to visit their dioceses with the thoroughness and frequency of the bishops of Soissons or Parma. It is likely that heterodoxy of the sort that was common in Germany in the eighth century, Christianity adulterated with pagan practices or the eccentric perversities of ignorant men, also thrived in the hidden valleys of Norway or around the remote shores of Swedish lakes, but these nonconformists were safe in the obscurity of their wilderness and remained unknown to their bishops and certainly to us.

Ireland, equally remote from the centers of Western civilization, also complained very little of heresy, though her case is very different from that of Scandinavia. Ireland had been totally isolated from the rest of Christendom by the Anglo-Saxon conquest of Britain, which destroyed British Christianity. In the period when the Anglo-Saxon kingdoms were pagan and raised an effective barrier to commerce between Christian Ireland and the Christian Continent, the Irish in their isolation retained institutions that were being abandoned by the rest of Christendom and also developed new institutions of their own. The Irish monks wore a different tonsure from that of the Continental monks, the Irish Church celebrated Easter on a different date, and, most striking of all, the Irish Church was not divided into dioceses administered by bishops, but was administered instead by the abbots of the various monasteries, who filled episcopal functions. In the sixth century, the Irish sent missionaries such as Saint Columban to the Continent, and these missionaries performed enormous services to the Church in the erection of new monasteries and the spread of the learning in which Irish monks prided themselves. This commerce was strictly one way, however: the Irish taught the Continent much but did not learn from it. Missionaries seldom returned to their mist-shrouded isle from the sunny climes of the south, and what they learned of the new customs of the Continental Church was never disseminated in Ireland. When the conversion of the Anglo-Saxons began, at the end of the sixth century, it was conducted from two centers, Ireland and Rome. The northern Anglo-Saxon kingdoms were converted by the Irish and adopted the practices of the Celtic Church, while the southern kingdoms were converted through the efforts of Saint Augustine of Canterbury and his successors and conformed to the practices of the Roman Church. The two traditions proved incompatible, and when at the synod of Whitby in 663 the English Church decided as a whole to adopt Roman practice, the Irish missionaries returned to their island in high dudgeon. There they retreated into deeper isolation than before and continued to retain their peculiar institutions until the organization of the Roman Church was introduced in 1152.

Thus in the period from 716–1160 when early medieval heresy occurred, the Irish were almost totally isolated from the intellectual currents of the Continent and protected from the influence of Continental heresies. Moreover, they were so concerned with preserving the identity of their own Celtic Church against the Roman Church that they were particularly intolerant of the possibility of any heresy arising. The Irish Church therefore preserved its orthodoxy intact until the middle of the twelfth century, when the Romanization of Irish Christianity and the appearance of the English on Irish soil brought the Irish in closer touch with the main body of Christianity and exposed them to the danger of infection by heresy.

Scotland's immunity from heresy results in part from its participation in the defense of Celtic Christianity against Roman, a defense that, after Whitby, declined into defensiveness. In part it results from the same administrative difficulties that prevailed in Scandinavia. However, on Scottish moor and heath and in Scottish forest, strange beliefs and stranger rites might have long persisted unknown to bishop and chronicler.

The immunity of England is more difficult to explain. The English were converted to Christianity by the seventh century; their close connection with the Roman Church was established by 663 and seldom disturbed thereafter. English missionaries went to and came from the Continent in great numbers from the end of the seventh century, and it was Boniface the Englishman who not only completed the conversion of Germany but also reorganized the Frankish Church. The kings of Wessex were always in close contact with Rome, and the Anglo-Saxon Church was one of the most loyal supporters of the apostolic see. English monks such as Dunstan, Oswald, and Wulfstan were in close touch with Continental currents of reform in the tenth and eleventh centuries and instituted reforms of English monasticism on the model of Cluny and Fleury. Alfred the Great assembled Continental and Irish scholars at his court in imitation of Charlemagne, and England was never isolated from the intellectual currents of the Continent. This close connection was made closer when, from the reign of Edward the Confessor (1042–1066), Norman priests, prelates, and politicians began to flow into England in increasing numbers, and the connection was made fast in October of 1066 at the Battle of Hastings. The English Church was well organized and was blessed with many fine chroniclers, so that on account of neither isolation nor lack of informtaion can we explain the fact that England never boasted a heresy until the twelfth century.

The explanation I offer is in the nature of a hypothesis, but it is one that has the merit of helping to explain the Irish and Scandinavian problem as well. The hypothesis is this: heresy and dissent appeared in areas that were secure from physical and intellectual challenge from without, and failed to appear in areas and times where this challenge existed to a degree that its presence was repressive rather than stimulating. Scandinavia had to contend with paganism and with the Russian Orthodox on her borders. Hungary and Poland, while also bordering on Orthodox lands, were more concerned with resisting Catholic Germans than Orthodox Slavs, and therefore were free to develop heresies. Ireland and Scotland were, as we have seen, concerned with protecting Celtic Christianity against the challenge of a Roman Christianity so overpowering that it drove the Celts into helpless defensiveness. Southern Italy, exposed to both Byzantine Orthodox and Moslem threats, developed no heresy, while the protected north did. England was forced first to resist Celtic Christianity and then to defend herself against pagan Danes and Norwegians for nearly two hundred years. This threat subsided only after the middle of the eleventh century, and heresy appears in England for the first time in the twelfth. England later became a center of heresy in the fourteenth and fifteenth centuries, with Wyclif and the Lollards. The crusader kingdoms in the Near East, constantly on guard against Eastern Orthodox, Moslems, and Monophysites, produced no heresy.

The Fertile Triangle of reform and heresy was precisely that area of Europe—along with northern Italy, the secondary center of early medieval dissent—which was most protected. The Low Countries had their Viking and Hungarian invasions like the rest of Europe, to be sure, but their security was considerable compared with that of England, southern Italy, or even eastern Germany, which was constantly concerned with defense against pagan Slavs who were Christianized only in the course of the eleventh century. The Spanish March offers the one great exception to the rule. Here, in an area strongly challenged by Islam, the Adoptionist heresy arose in the eighth century, and not only in the marches but among the Christians in the south of Spain who were living under actual Moslem domination. With this exception, however, Spain was almost completely free of heresy until the end of the twelfth century, when dissent reappeared as the Moslem menace substantially retreated, and reappeared in that part of Spain, northern Aragon, which was farthest from the area of Moslem control.

The hypothesis is bolstered by chronological considerations. The latter part of the ninth century and the early part of the tenth form a period in which there are substantially fewer reports of heresy than in either the preceding or succeeding ages. This period is precisely when western Europe bore the brunt of the second barbarian invasions, when no town or village the length and breadth of the Continent was secure from the attack of Moslem, Viking, or Hungarian raiders.

The presence of external challenge can be a stimulation to new ideas, but if the challenge is too great, the opposite effect occurs, and the threatened retreat into defensiveness and rigidity to preserve their identity. This is the effect in operation in early medieval Europe: those areas protected from too strong a challenge developed heresies; those areas where the challenge was too severe did not.

The chronology of dissent.

From the eighth to the twelfth centuries medieval society experienced repeated cases of dissent. The history of dissent in this period is less one of filiation than of a community of similar responses to similar situations. The major element uniting the moral heresies of the period was the continual ferment of the Great Reform Movement.

Medieval dissidence began in the eighth, not the eleventh, century. Historians have neglected the earlier period, and many are skeptical that earlier dissent can properly be characterized as medieval. One justification for this attitude is the belief that the "popular" heresies (attracting followers from all classes, including the lowest) which are typical of the Middle Ages do not appear before that time. In this interpretation, the dissent of the eighth, ninth, and tenth centuries is more like that of the earlier Church, involving quarrels among priests and squabbles among intellectuals. However, as the large followings of Aldebert and Theuda testify, this was not true. Eighth-century heresy had already begun to exhibit the qualities of that of the eleventh and early twelfth.

Medieval dissent arose in the eighth century. It is perhaps as futile to seek the "causes" of this phenomenon as it is to seek the "causes" of the fall of Rome. There is no one cause of the appearance of medieval dissidence save that it first occurred at the time when Western Europe was acquiring its cultural identity. This was how medieval dissent came into being, if not why: it was part of the general creativity of a growing civilization.

From the eighth century onward, the number of cases of dissent does not vary greatly from century to century with one exception. The last years of the ninth and the first half of the tenth century, a time when the collapse of empire and papacy and the second wave of barbarian invasions created a hiatus in the advance of civilization, produced relatively little dissent. Of twenty cases in the tenth century, for example, only three occurred before 950. This observation fits the geographical evidence: dissent is associated with advanced areas and with advanced periods. Beyond this, there are somewhat more frequent reports of dissent in the eleventh and twelfth centuries than before, but this may very likely be the result of a greater wealth of sources for these centuries. At any rate, it is completely unjustified to assume that medieval dissent is not significant before the eleventh century.

Another chronological observation of importance is that the nature of dissent changes with the centuries. We have studied dissent from the eighth to the mid-twelfth century as a whole. I believe I have shown that it is legitimate, indeed necessary, to do so. But this is not to say that there were no variations or that the dissent of the early twelfth century was just like that of the eighth. A number of changes took place. As the intellectual level of society rose, intellectual heresies became at once more frequent and more refined. As the West grew away from the East, the westward flow of heretical ideas ceased until the last great influx, in the 1140's, in the form of Catharism. As Europe became more settled and the Church more firmly established, paganized heresies and crude sorcery became less common. And as the Great Reform Movement gathered momentum, the proportion of Reformist Dissidence grew.

The repression of dissent.

Medieval society responded to the challenge of dissent on two planes. On the theory level, the challenge aided in the development of doctrine by causing orthodoxy either to absorb it or to generate antibodies against it. On the human level, however, society reacted with intolerance and repression. In part, this repression arose from the general wish of societies to protect themselves and of orthodoxies to maintain themselves. Heretics, religious or otherwise, have never found general welcome. But the question cannot rest here for the Christian Middle Ages precisely because they were Christian. An institution that professes an exceptionally high standard of morality based upon love may reasonably be expected to present a more charitable record than do less spiritually ambitious institutions, and when it fails to do so the reason for its failure becomes interesting.

The basic reason for the repression of heretics was the honest rejection of heresies as untrue. Christianity is a unique religion in the enormous emphasis it has placed, since the time of Saint Paul and under the influence of Greek philosophy, upon abstract truth rather than upon the existential aspect of religion, the confrontation of man and God. The difference between these two emphases can be seen in the thought of Saint Paul and of Saint Augustine, where the word "faith" has two different connotations, one being personal trust in God and the other a firm assent to formulated propositions. The latter connotation of faith grew through the ages at the expense of the former, so that the mark of the Christian came to be less that ineffable relationship with God than assent to a body of doctrine. When assent to a body of doctrine becomes the criterion for membership in Christian society, a visible principle of exclusion is explicitly introduced: those who do not so assent are outside that society. Since the whole authority of society was placed behind this body of doctrine, dissent from a point of doctrine implied a direct challenge to the authority of society. It is a tribute to the courage of the dissenters that most of them did not hesitate to make this challenge explicit. Christian society acted as a whole to repress dissidence, and in this action both the ecclesiastical and the secular power participated.

Among the clergy, the will to suppress heresy stemmed in part from a genuine desire to protect orthodoxy and a secondary desire to maintain social peace. In part it sometimes arose from baser emotions, a fierce jealousy of political and social power and a more subtle fear of anything that presented a threat to things the way they ought to be. The tradition of the Church was unanimous in its condemnation of heresy. It offered, however, two answers to the question of its removal. One, perhaps the stronger, was the tradition of leniency. Tertullian, Cyprian, Lactantius, and other fathers, while vigorous in their denunciation of theological nonconformity, were usually less vigorous in their denunciations of the nonconformists. Augustine and Jerome could be very harsh at times, but their better feelings were more often expressed, as the following passage from the African indicates:[9]

For we are not to despair of anyone so long as the patience of God leadeth the ungodly to penance, and doth not seize him out of this life; for God doth not will that a sinner should die, but that he should be converted from his ways and live. He is a heathen to-day, but how knowest thou whether he may not believe in Christ to-morrow? He is a heretic to-day, but what if to-morrow he follow the Catholic truth?

The other, less fortunate tradition began when the "Peace of the Church" made the foundation of Christian society possible and when religious dissidence became a social crime. The first juridical execution for heresy was that of Priscillian in 385; Pope Leo I later approved this action, and popes and prelates were occasionally heard to urge the secular arm to do its duty in defending society against malingerers. Even Henry Charles Lea, however, in the course of his great diatribe against the medieval Church, admits that the Western Church was relatively tolerant of dissent until the later Middle Ages.[10] No juridical execution occurred in a case of heresy in the West after the death of Priscillian until the eleventh century, a period of more than six centuries when society did not strike down men who threatened its most cherished beliefs.

Though Lea observes that a measure of leniency continued into the thirteenth century, it is undeniable that the atmosphere began to change in the eleventh. No specific change of policy, no decree, no legislation heralded this change, but custom gradually and generally grew harsher. The Church came to tolerate and on occasion to approve the violent eradication of convinced heretics. Lea is correct in saying that to argue that the Church never executed heretics because it turned them over to the secular arm to do the job is casuistry: the ecclesiastical and secular powers cooperated in the repression. The question is why the atmosphere changed in the eleventh century. We do not know, but we can speculate. Though the union of Church and state and the concomitant secularization of the Church had existed from the time of Constantine and Theodosius, it may be that the increasing stability of society, in every respect, meant that it became at once easier to detect and hunt down dissent, and harder to tolerate it. The fact that dissent probably increased somewhat at this time may have something to do with it, though it is by no means certain that this purported increase was really very sginificant. Another explanation is the increasing attention paid by clergy and laity to their duty. The more conscientious a bishop was, the less he would be willing to tolerate dissent, a paradox similar to that in the history of early Christianity when it was often the "better" emperors like Diocletian who were the most severe in their persecution of the Christians. Lax emperors and lax bishops did not care or did not bother about dissenters; scrupulous ones did. The Great Reform Movement is in part responsible, then, not only for the fervor of the heretics but for the fervor of those who attacked them.

This increasing severity, as well as the large residue of leniency, is evident when we examine the Church's role in repression in the period we are studying. In the eighth and ninth centuries rigor was not much in evidence. Felix of Urgel, having been convicted of Adoptionism but then recanted, was restored to his see. Eriugena and Gottschalk were subjected to verbal attacks and some of their doctrines occasionally censured by synods, but neither of them, even the unpopular Gottschalk, suffered personal harm. Claudius, the Reformist bishop of Turin, also had to suffer no more than verbal slings. The wild men of Boniface's time, Aldebert and Clement, received scarcely harsher treatment. Aldebert was first patiently forbidden to preach; when he continued to do so a synod at Soissons formally condemned him and ordered him to burn the crosses he had erected throughout the countryside. He was taken into custody and suspended from the priesthood, to which office he may never have legitimately been entitled. Having escaped and continued to preach, he was condemned in absence at Rome, but here the only punishment assigned was an invitation to recant and a repetition of the order stripping him of his priestly dignity. Only if he continued to persist in his error was the punishment to go farther, and even then it was to stop at excommunication. The same synod of Rome was rather more harsh with Clement, who was excommunicated on the spot. When Aldebert and Clement refused to be moved by this evidence of papal attention and Saint Boniface demanded that stronger measures be taken, the pope replied only by suggesting that another synod be called and that this time both Aldebert and Clement be present. And if they there failed to recant, they should be sent to Rome for a personal interview with the pope. Eventually Aldebert may have been murdered by thieves, but at no time did he or Clement suffer at the hands of the Church, even though the latter was grossly and overtly immoral and the former had had success in preaching the most eccentric nonsense.

In two cases in the ninth century the ecclesiastical authorities were somewhat more severe. Theuda, the eccentric heresiarch of Mainz, was sentenced to public whipping by a synod convoked by the archbishop of Mainz, and Burgand and his followers, who had looted and sacked churches at Bordeaux, were sentenced to prison and a penance of seven years, after which they were to be readmitted to communion. It is difficult to imagine a society that lacked psychological insights treating nonconformists, including lunatics and vandals, with greater moderation than Christian society did the dissidents of these centuries.

Harsher times were to follow, but even in the eleventh century leniency prevailed more often than not. Said Peter Damian, "When the Saints have power, they do not even slay infidels." [11] It is said that the followers of Vilgard of Ravenna were hunted down and burned toward the end of the tenth century, but the chances are that the chronicler is confused with his facts. Leutard, the Eccentric of Châlons, was probably not even formally condemned, though he was certainly persuaded to recant and later committed suicide. His followers were still active a decade later; the heresy was eventually extinguished, but there is no mention of violence. At Liège in 1025 the heretics were jailed pending investigation by the bishop, but after they had been examined and had recanted they were set free. The heretics of 1048–1054 of that same city were saved by the clergy from the violence of the mob, and the Church extended its protection to the extent of lodging the intended victims in various religious houses until the fury of the people passed. The reply of Bishop Wazo of Liège to Roger II of Châlons is justly famous in the history of toleration. Excommunicate the heretics, Wazo said, and make it clear to your flock that they are to be shunned, lest others be contaminated—but harsher measures are not justified. One must hope, he continued, that the heretics will eventually see the light; it is for God to separate the wheat and the tares at the last judgment. Even the greatest persecutors of the truth have come later to be its greatest defenders, as witness the transformation of Saul into Paul. While not a plea for religious liberty, Wazo's letter is a fervent defense of mildness and justice.

Other cases in the eleventh century were less happy. In 1022 the bishop of Orléans and some of his colleagues passed judgment on a group of dissidents, and while ecclesiastical officers took pains to shield the heretics from the murderous instincts of the mob, they did nothing to inhibit their execution at the hands of the king. At Milan in 1028 the archbishop, having attempted to convert the heretics of Monteforte by reason and argument, at length lost patience and ordered a cross and a stake raised, asking the heretics to choose between them. Most chose the stake and perished in the flames. A number of bishops took part in the proceedings at Goslar in 1051 that ended in the hanging of dissidents.

Yet leniency was still to be found in the twelfth century. Tanchelm, one of the most troublesome of dissidents, was treated with remarkable moderation. Archbishop Frederick of Cologne had at one time briefly imprisoned him, but although his heresies were powerful in the Low Countries and known throughout Europe, no further measures were taken against his person, and Pope Paschal II never even issued a formal condemnation. In the midst of serious popular unrest and faced with a naked challenge to his authority, the most that the bishop of Le Mans did in the case of Henry the Monk was to send him on to make trouble in someone else's diocese. Henry was not prevented from preaching widely in the south of France before he was ultimately arrested and brought before the council of Pisa in 1135; before that date he was subjected to persecution no stronger than public debate. The end of Henry's career is somewhat obscure, but it seems that the council of Pisa confined itself to ordering him to return to his monastery and remain there, and it also seems possible that he avoided this restriction and came out to preach once again. The time and manner of his death are unknown. The only punishment Jonas of Cambrai is known to have received for his heresy was the loss of his lawsuit against Abbot Hildebrand. At Reims in 1136 the priest Herbert was defrocked but not personally harmed. Lambert le Bègue suffered no more than harrassment from his personal enemies.

Yet the Church's countenance grew ever harsher. Eudo of Brittany, the madman, was imprisoned for life, and many of his followers were hunted down and put to death. The heretics at Cologne in 1143 who would not recant were turned over to the secular arm for burning. One man was burned at Liège in 1135, though it is likely that this was done by the mob without the approval of the Church. The authority that condemned Arnold of Brescia to the fire is not known, but the pope ruled Rome and Arnold must have been tried by an ecclesiastical tribunal before being sent to his death. The archbishop of Cologne ordered the burning of the Catharists at Cologne in 1163, and the prelates assembled at Oxford in 1166 did not hesitate to turn over their dissenters to the secular arm. The council of Reims in 1157 officially spelled out the penalties for heresy: the leaders were to be sentenced to perpetual imprisonment, and their followers, unless they quickly recanted, were to be branded on the forehead with a hot iron.

It is fruitless to dispute whether Church or secular arm was the more responsible for the persecutions. Both represented Christian society. On the other hand, the state did not simply act as executioner for the Church, as lay rulers were often more eager than Churchmen to destroy the dissidents. In part the secular lords were concerned with the maintenance of social order, in part they supported orthodoxy because the Church supported their political ends, and occasionally, as with King Robert of France, whose marital difficulties had embroiled him with the pope, they may have wished to sign their loyalty to the Church in blood.

From the eighth to the tenth century the secular power did not often interfere, an exception being the essentially secular case of Liutward. In the eleventh century, the burnings at Orléans were ordered by King Robert and the hangings at Goslar by good Saint Henry III. In the twelfth century, the incinerations at Bonn in 1143 were under the charge of Count Otto of Rheineck, while the outrage of Oxford in 1166, when the heretics were whipped half-naked out into the winter countryside, was presided over by King Henry II, who added to his pious work by forbidding any of his subjects to take them in or give them shelter. It was the count of Louvain who finally dispersed the worshippers of the fools' ark at Sint Truiden. The interest of the secular power in dissent was not enormous, but when it acted it was on the side of harshness.

The third agent of repression was the people themselves, as individuals or together as a mob. Social circumstance played a role here: Ramihrd was lynched for very little because the clergy felt its position particularly threatened at that time, while Henry the Monk was not lynched at all. Occasionally the good citizenry was motivated by a self-righteous concern for the preservation of orthodoxy or for the good name of their city. Sometimes, as at Orléans, they were simply looking for diversion in the same spirit as that in which the Roman mob frequented the Coliseum. Ironically, the same fierce spirit of reform that inspired the Reformist Dissidents seems also to have encouraged the people's crusades, the pogroms, and the lynchings of dissidents.

The spirit of enthusiasm touched the masses most nearly in the eleventh and twelfth centuries, and before that period there is little evidence of lynching. Aldebert was slain by thieves, it is said, but this was probably not the result of his religious ideas. In the eleventh century, mob violence became more common. The outrageous murder of Ramihrd was perpetrated by the infuriated clergy over the protests of the bishop of Cambrai. At Orléans, the mob would have broken into the hall in which the heretics were being tried had not the king's men under the command of the formidable Queen Constance prevented them, and the good queen herself became excited enough to put out the dissenter Etienne's eye with her stick. At Liège in 1048–1054 the mob was prevented only by the efforts of the bishop from seizing and burning the heretics. In the same city in 1135, under similar circumstances,

255

the authorities rescued a number of heretics from the mob, who, however, succeeded in burning one. Tanchelm was slain by an angry priest who could not bear his taunts, Peter of Bruys was done to death by the mob of Saint-Gilles, and the brothers of Soissons were dispatched by the righteous people in the absence of their bishop. The heretics described by Evervinus of Cologne were snatched from the custody of the archbishop, who was using patience with them, and consigned to the flames. The priest Dominic William was killed, so says the chronicler, under similar circumstances.

Thus did the medieval laity participate with vigor in the affairs of the Church. The best epigram is provided in a later period by a condemned heretic himself. Bound on the rack, he observed that "he who was now binding him with the rope had a greater power of binding and loosing than our most blessed Lord himself." [12]

The story of Christian against Christian has been the great scandal in the history of the Church, a wretched spectacle that has excited the indignation of the sympathetic and the scorn of disbelievers since toleration first became a virtue. Even Julian the Apostate said that wild beasts did not treat one another with more cruelty than did the Christians. It is true that there is a certain injustice in these characterizations. In the history of any institution that has endured two millennia there will be ample material in human nature from which to extract the shocking and the brutal. It is easy to generalize from these cases and to forget the less publicized but more common instances of mildness and generosity. A people who establish for themselves enormously high standards by that very fact expose themselves to condemnation or ridicule when they fail to live up to them. These failures can be attributed to hypocrisy only by the most unfair critics: they are the result of human weakness. The failure of men to attain their ideals does not make the ideals less valuable or less necessary. Even in our period, which historians like Lea have painted so dark and wretched, leniency was more frequent than harshness. In many respects this period was brutal (though nothing could be more harsh or more cruel than nineteenth-century industrialism or twentieth-century war), but in comparison with the societies that preceded it it was unusually mild and just. With the imperial Rome of Sejanus, Nero, and the Coliseum, these centuries cannot be compared for inhumanity. Human society, taken in its entirety, was in those days inhumane, insensitive, and intolerant, and it is less surprising that the Church did not do more to reform it than it is elevating that the Church succeeded in transforming it as much as it did.

It is also true that medieval society lacked religious liberty. It was a closed society in the modern sense, but all societies until our modern Western one (and not excluding it in many respects) have been closed. Nor can the dissidents themselves escape responsibility. If the Church acted with lack of charity toward the dissidents, the dissidents acted with arrogance toward the Church. The injustices perpetrated against the dissidents cannot in justice be used as broadside attacks against the Church.

Yet when this is said and done, these injustices remain a terrible indictment of the wickedness of mankind as a whole and of the Christian Church in particular. For the Church does claim to speak for Jesus Christ and therefore has a responsibility for charity that greatly exceeds that of other institutions. The Church entered society to mitigate the harshness that was there, but was in turn itself soiled by the brutality it encountered. The union of Church and state was effective in mitigating the evil that was in the state, but it also diluted what was good in the Church. Compromise, moderation, and caution are not the most prominent marks of the true Church. The true Church is not static and complacent but dynamic and courageous. It does not shield men from the confrontation with reality, it ushers them into the presence of reality. It does not provide men with easy answers but with hard choices. Ordinary Christianity, like ordinary science, creates a world of security, but man's estate before God is essentially insecure. Christianity is the confrontation of awesome—and sometimes awful—reality, either in the austerity of nature or in the extremity of human need. Insofar as the Church fails to bring us into the presence of this reality it fails to bring us into the presence of Christ.

The true Christian is one who meets the challenge of reality with as much of his true being as possible. Often this is easiest for the truly committed and courageous heretic. "For you are not to suppose, brethren, that heresies could be produced through any little souls. None save great men have been the authors of heresies." [13] The drawback to heresy is that after its first vigor it creates a complacency or indifference to reality as great as or greater than that of the initial orthodoxy.

It will be argued that the success of the Church, and that not only in a worldly sense, has been the result of its inclusive, its catholic qualities. There has been room not only for the courageous and devoted but for the cowardly and indifferent. The ability to compromise distinguishes the wise man from the fanatic. But has this compromise not gone too far? Have silence and acquiescence to unbearable circumstances not been too common, even when all allowances for human weakness have been made? Has the ideal not too often been lost in the pursuit of the practical? To confront reality and to encourage others to confront reality is both difficult and impolitic. Yet it is the way of Christ and his apostles.

Appendixes

Appendix A
On the Sources

The sources present a number of problems. Some will object that much of the dissent cited in the earlier period consists of little more than bare references. It is true that the sources become increasingly spare as one moves back from the twelfth century, but this spareness itself may be an indication, if I may use a peculiar argument *contra silentium*, that there was more heresy in the early centuries of the Middle Ages than has been recorded. The silence of accounts in regard to heresy can hardly be regarded as significant when the same accounts fail to mention the barbarian invasions. No one can doubt that in the villages and mountains of France and Germany, not to mention more remote countries, many peculiar beliefs flourished that never found their way into written documents.

Yet it is beyond doubt that the student of the history of the eighth to the eleventh centuries labors under a serious disadvantage in regard to the sources. Europe was in the midst of a time of troubles, and there was much less historical and other writing in this period than there was later. Further, because of the unsettled conditions, less material was preserved. From my experience in the archives and the assurance of archivists I think it safe to say that the scholar is unlikely to find unpublished material on the history of early medieval heresy in the archives of northwestern Europe or the Vatican. I should like, by the way, to thank the archivists who helped me in my fruitless search for materials: though the search was vain, they were no less obliging for that fact. Monsieur Pierre Piétresson de Saint-Aubin, director of the services d'archives du Nord, Lille; Herr Doktor Friedrich-Wilhelm Oediger, director of the Hauptstaatsarchiv, Düsseldorf; Herr Professor Doktor Eugen Ewig, Universität Mainz; Dottore Germano Gualdo, Archivio segreto Vaticano; Monsieur E. T. Lemaire, Archiviste de la Ville de Reims; were particularly obliging in person or as correspondents.

There are relatively few records of any kind for the period in question. Why, beyond this, are there not more that record dissent? One of the primary reasons is a lack of interest in heresy on the part of the writers of the time. Charters relating to the possession of property not unnaturally concerned the individual churches more than debates over doctrine, and they preserved what interested them most. Society was too pressed by political and economic necessities to allow itself much time for the debate of abstract religious issues. The relatively liberal attitude of the authorities toward dissent, which prevailed into the eleventh century, demonstrates that people then were less concerned about dissidence than they came to be from the twelfth century on.

Finally, dissent was not the only subject the chroniclers tended to pass over. Most of the writers of the period were cloistered in monasteries, but this did not mean that they were all exceptionally religious men. On the contrary, many were younger sons sent off to make a career in the Church because their patrimony was exhausted. Many of the monastic chroniclers were, therefore, at least in their interests and their view of what was important, soldiers *manqués*. The chronicles and annals of the eighth to the eleventh centuries are full of tales of campaigns, princes, and popes. Even an outstanding historian like Flodoard was concerned primarily with politics and genealogies. When the annals do deal with religion, they speak of the relics possessed by their monastery or of miracles wrought by holy men in their locality. Interested in glorifying their own foundation, they are not likely to mention dissent unless one of their house had worked wonders in combating it. Good indication that dissent not reported by the sources did exist nonetheless comes from the later period, when the variety of sources available permits checking up. For example, one of the outstanding heretics of the twelfth century was Tanchelm, about whom we have considerable information from numerous sources. But two basic sources for the history of the diocese of Cambrai in the eleventh century, the *Annales Cameracenses* and the *Chronicon Sancti Bertini,* do not so much as mention his name. Had we only these two sources, were our knowledge of the twelfth century confined to as few sources as our knowledge of the tenth often is, we might erroneously conclude that there were no heretics in the diocese of Cambrai in the twelfth century.

Historians have long recognized that an argument from silence is valueless, and this is particularly true for ancient or medieval history, where the sources are few. To conclude that, because there are few mentions of heresy from the eighth to the eleventh centuries, there was little dissent in the period, would be improper.

It may be answered that an even more improper procedure would be to argue that, in spite of the silence, heresies must have existed. This objection would be well taken if there were in fact as little evidence as historians have assumed. But this is not so. If one tabulates the number of references to heresy in proportion to the number of documents available, one finds that there were, proportionately, *more* references to heresy before the eleventh century than after. For example, taking Jaffé's *Registers* of papal letters, we find that in the third and fourth centuries documents relating to heresy comprise about 15 percent of the total number, and for the fifth century the proportion rises to about 20 percent. The high proportion in the early centuries is probably owing in part to the particular fluidity of doctrine at that time, but also to the fact that the importance of heresy in that period would lead to the preservation of such material. In the sixth and seventh centuries the proportion falls to about 5 percent; in the eighth, thanks in part to the vigilance of Saint Boniface, it increases again to about 10 percent. In the ninth and tenth centuries it is true that the proportion is only 1 or 2 percent, but this proportion also holds true for the eleventh century, when medieval heresy is supposed by historians to be beginning, while in the twelfth century, the period when it is supposed to have burst into prominence, the proportion is less than 1 percent. No real conclusion as to the importance of heresy in each century can be drawn from evidence of such summary nature, but it does show that heterodoxy did not spring full-blown from Jove's brow in the eleventh century and that it cannot be assumed a priori that heresy did *not* exist in strength in the earlier period.

It must be admitted that the heretics of the eleventh and twelfth centuries are known in greater detail, because the sources increase in number and length. This does not make the study of earlier dissent less valuable: we are obliged to work with the materials we have, though we might wish to have a good many more. As W. H. Walsh has said (*An Introduction to the Philosophy of History* [London, 1951], p. 81), occasions arise when we are forced to make do with insufficient materials, but "that illustrates not the extent of the historian's trust in primary sources, but rather the poverty of the material in which he works." If the twelfth century is the rich summertime of medieval dissent, the springtime was the period from the eighth to the eleventh.

The problem of the reliability of the sources lays a more dangerous trap, for it can create a sense of security about facts that prove to be no facts at all. The carelessness or tendentiousness of medieval sources is well known. Following as they do the hagiographical tradition, which on the basis of the treasury of merits and the communion of saints saw nothing incorrect in ascribing to one saint the virtues of another, the medieval chroniclers are scarcely to be relied upon unquestioningly, yet often all the material we have on a subject comes from one pen. Medieval writers were fond of using *topoi,* stock phrases of praise or blame that they bandied about without much discretion, so that when a king was described as "defender of the Church," or, conversely, when purported heretics were accused of immoral orgies, it is sometimes impossible to know whether these are facts or *topoi.* Further, the bishops assembled in council—diligent students of the ecclesiastical past—often repeated canons issued in the distant past, so that it is difficult to tell whether they resurrected them out of concern with their current situation or simply out of vague piety. All these problems are exacerbated by the scarcity of sources which makes it impossible to check the accuracy of one by comparing it with another. Nor have a thousand years of war, fire, and natural decay been gentle with the historian's specimens.

Under these circumstances, the degree of certainty with which we can reconstruct the facts does not permit us to make categorical statements; the reader should assume, throughout the discussions of these and preceding pages, the phrase "insofar as the evidence goes."

Appendix B

Sources for Tanchelm's Heresy

(See p. 273 for list of abbreviations used in Appendix)

Some modern writers dealing with Tanchelm are Arno Borst, *Die Katharer* (Stuttgart, 1953), p. 84; Norman Cohn, *The Pursuit of the Millennium* (London, 1957), p. 53 (Cohn mistakenly views Tanchelm as an eschatologist); Henri Pirenne, "Tanchelin et le projet de démembrement du diocèse d'Utrecht vers 1100," *Académie Royale de Belgique, Bulletin de la Classe des Lettres,* ser. 5 XIII (1927). On this same question of the diocese of Utrecht see Josef-M. De Smet, "De monnik Tanchelm en de Utrechtse bisschopszetel in 1112–1114," *Scrinium Lovaniense, Mélanges historiques Etienne van Cauwenbergh* (Louvain, 1961). An excellent article, particularly on the sources, is L. J. M. Philippen, "De Heilige Norbertus en de strijd tegen het Tanchelmisme te Antwerpen," *Bijdragen tot de Geschiedenis,* XXV (1934). See also Walter Mohr, "Tanchelm van Antwerpen," *Annales Universitatis Saraviensis,* III (1954). For Saint Norbert and Tanchelm, see G. Madelaine, *Histoire de Saint Norbert* (Tongerlo, 1928); Anon., "St. Norbert et Tanchelin," AB, XII (1892); and P. Lefèvre, "L'Episode de la conversion de Saint Norbert et la tradition hagiographique de la 'Vita Norberti,'" RHE, LVI (1961), which is of the greatest use in the criticism of that particular source.

The Latin sources follow. I follow Philippen's numbering.

1) A letter of the cathedral chapter of Utrecht to Archbishop Frederick of Cologne, appearing in AASS, June, I, 830–832; Paul Fredericq, *Corpus documentorum inquisitionis* (Ghent and The Hague, 1889), I, 16; Leonard Ennen, *Quellen zur Geschichte der Stadt Köln* (Cologne, 1860–1879), I, 495–498; S. Ph. van den Bergh, *Oorkondenboek van Holland en Zeeland* (Amsterdam, 1866–1873), I, 66–67; Joseph Hartzheim, *Concilia Germaniae* (Cologne, 1759–1790), III, 763–766; and other editions given by Fredericq. Date: probably 1112–1114.

2) Peter Abelard, *Introductio ad Theologiam,* in MPL, CLXXVIII, 1056; Fredericq, *op. cit.,* I, 26; and Victor Cousin, *Petri Abaelardi opera omnia* (Paris, 1849), II, 83–84. Date: 1115–1121. Written after the death of Tanchelm (1115), it was condemned in 1121.

3) Hildolf, provost of the chapter at Antwerp, a diploma, in Fredericq, *op. cit.,* II, 5, and other editions cited by Fredericq. Date: 1124.

4) Burchard, bishop of Cambrai, a diploma, in Fredericq, *op. cit.,* II, 3, and other editions cited by Fredericq. Date: 1124.

5) Nicholas, bishop of Cambrai, a diploma, in P. J. Goetschalckx, *Oorkondenboek der Witheerenabdij van Sint-Michiels te Antwerpen,* I, 15, reproduced by Philippen, *op. cit.,* p. 251. Date: 1148.

6) *Vita Norberti* A in MGH SS, XII, 690–691, and in Fredericq, *op. cit.,* I, 22. Date: 1155 (according to Philippen).

7) *Vita Norberti* B, in *ibid.,* and in Fredericq, *op. cit.,* I, 23. Date: 1157–1161 (according to Philippen).

8) Robert de Monte, *Sigeberti Gemblacensis continuatio Praemonstratensis* in MGH SS, VI, 449; Fredericq, *op. cit.,* I, 25, and other editions listed by Fredericq. Date: 1155–1157. Philippen gives 1146–1155, but since Robert seems to have borrowed from the *Vita Norberti* B, the date must be set somewhat later. The first rescension of Robert's chronicle was completed about 1157.

9) *Sigeberti Gemblacensis continuatio Valcellensis,* in MGH SS, VI, 458, or Fredericq, *op. cit.,* I, 26–27. Date: Philippen gives 1114–1163.

In addition to the nine sources cited by Philippen, the following Latin sources exist. These are of later date and are not to be ranked in the strict sense with the primary sources.

10) *Vita Honorii II,* in Mansi, XXI, 320, drawn from *Chronicon Hirsaugense.* Date: twelfth century.

11) Baldwin of Ninove, *Chronicon,* in MGH SS, XXV, 528, and Fredericq, *op. cit.,* II, 3. Date: thirteenth century.

12) *Annales Veterocellenses,* MGH SS, XVI, 42, and Fredericq, *op. cit.,* II, 3. Date: twelfth century. A brief notice.

Finally, the following Latin sources of even later date exist. Fredericq included them in his *Corpus* because of the high repute of the authors, and since they sometimes bring something new (which conceivably could derive from an earlier source now lost to us), they may be included.

13) Johannes Trithemius, *Annales Hirsaugenses,* I, 387–388, in Fredericq, *op. cit.,* I, 27. Date: Trithemius died in 1516.

14) Meyerus, *Annales Flandriae,* in Fredericq, *op. cit.,* I, 23. Date: 1561.

15) Johannes Molanus, *Militia sacra ducum et principum Brabantiae,* in Fredericq, *op. cit.,* I, 28. Date: 1592.

Fredericq (*op. cit.,* I, 29) also includes a part of an eighteenth-century Flemish chronicle. But if items (13) through (15) above are of dubious value, this is of none.

Of particular importance is the question whether the *Vita Norberti* A really precedes the B, as its first editor, Wilmans, believed when he published it in the MGH. There seems to be little doubt that it does. The B is somewhat more detailed than the A and, as Lefèvre observed, hagiographers do not ordinarily shorten the lives of their heroes but are more inclined to embellish. The B is inclined to make Tanchelm more monstrous than the A, evidently with the intention of making Norbert's resistance the more heroic. Thus, while the A contents itself with a vague reference to immoral activities on the part of Tanchelm, itself probably no more than a topical gesture in the direction of conventional heresiography, the B luridly tells us that he ravished young girls in the very presence of their mothers. The author of B may be credited with imagination but not with historical reliability. As Philippen indicates (*op. cit.,* p. 255), a common source for both A and B is a likely possibility, but in its absence and until the thorough critique of the *Vita* suggested by Lefèvre is completed, A must in most instances be deemed more worthy of credence.

As far as the utility of the sources goes, the two most helpful are the letter of the canons and the *Vita* A. Robert de Monte is third, while the rest give us only slight help.

Serious attention must here be given to the arguments of Jozef-M. De Smet. De Smet has made a number of valuable contributions to our understanding of Tanchelm and for these I am, as the text indicates, in his debt. I am, however, unwilling to follow him in his major conclusions, to wit, that Count Robert had nothing to do with the Utrecht boundary dispute and, more important, that Tanchelm was not a heretic but a simple Gregorian reformer.

On the matter of Count Robert, De Smet argues as follows. The date of the letter of the canons of Utrecht is, as everyone admits, between 1112 and 1114. Tanchelm's activity at Rome could not have been known for long at the moment when the letter was composed. The undertaking to remove part of the diocese from the hands of the bishop of Utrecht must have occurred during a vacancy in that see, that is, after the death of Bishop Burchard on May 8, 1112. Now, since Count Robert died in 1111, he could scarcely have been responsible for the scheme. It is possible that De Smet's interpretation is correct, but there are a number of points that detract from the force of his argument. First, we are not obliged to admit that, simply because other such projects in regard to other dioceses occurred during episcopal vacancies, this project could not have been undertaken while Bishop Burchard was alive. The fact that the bishop was a staunch imperialist would perhaps have convinced Robert that Pope Paschal would have consented to taking these measures against him. One grants that the procedure would have been unusual, but, after all, Paschal did reject the scheme, and we cannot be sure that Robert would not have thought the plan worth trying. Or, again, it is possible that Count Robert would have sent emissaries to Rome to plan what steps to take when a vacancy should occur and opportunity present itself for action. Thus, to this point De Smet's arguments are powerful but not compelling. The rock upon which they founder is this: the letter of the canons mentions Tanchelm's heresies as being already well developed and says that he already had a group of followers known as "Tanchelmists." Now it is not possible that Robert or anyone else would have sent a well-known heretic to Rome to plead a case with the pope. The mission must therefore have taken place some years before the letter, probably about 1109 or 1110.

The only way De Smet can turn this argument is to maintain that Tanchelm was not a heretic at all, but an orthodox reformer. According to such an argument, all the evidence presented by the canons and by the lives of Saint Norbert, not to mention the chronicles, consists of calumnies circulated by Tanchelm's enemies. Thus Tanchelm would be the victim of a successful smear campaign. Certainly slander and libel are always possible—witness the case of Lambert le Bègue—and any fair critic is obliged to admit the probabililty that the reports of Tanchelm's activities presented by his opponents were grossly exaggerated. But why assume that Tanchelm was entirely orthodox when all the evidence is against it? The historian should not take a position contradicted by all the evidence unless there are compelling reasons for doing so, and I cannot see that they exist here. De Smet may be moved in part by a desire to vindicate the character of the Belgian preacher, but was heresy of the Reformist variety really so reprehensible? Behind the slurs of perversion and the like, the sources are very convincing in the doctrines they attribute to Tanchelm: they are typical of Reformist beliefs, and there is small likelihood that they were invented. As we have seen, there was a long tradition of Reformist dissent into which Tanchelm's case fits. That Tanchelm was a reformer is certain. It is not less admirable, and it is beyond reasonable doubt, that he was also a Reformist dissenter.

On the question of the diocese of Thérouanne, where I believe De Smet is entirely correct, he cites D. Bonenfant-Feytmens, "Tornacensis et Teruanensis," RBPH, VII (1928).

Notes

Notes

The sources for this book are in published editions of medieval works. Too diverse and piecemeal to be cited in a general bibliography, they are found, instead, in the notes. I was unable to find any unpublished materials from the period relative to this subject. An extensive bibliography of the secondary works may be found in my article, "Interpretations of the Origins of Medieval Heresy," MS, XXV (1963). A translation of many of the important documents dealing with medieval heresy is being prepared by Professor Walter Wakefield and will be published by Columbia University Press.

See also the appendixes for information on the sources—Appendix A for a commentary on the sources in general, and Appendix B for a list of the sources on Tanchelm's heresy.

I was unable to obtain in time the edition of a strange eleventh-century table of heresies published by M. Fornasari, "Collectio Canonum Barberiana," *Apollinaris,* XXXVI (1963).

ABBREVIATIONS USED IN NOTES

AASS: *Acta Sanctorum quotquot toto orbe coluntur.* Antwerp, 1643——. 70 vols.

AASSOSB: Jean Mabillon. *Acta Sanctorum Ordinis Sancti Benedicti.* Paris, 1668–1701. 9 vols.

AB: *Analecta Bollandiana*

AFP: *Archivium Fratrum Praedicatorum*

AHVNR: *Annalen des Historischen Vereins für den Niederrhein*

AKG: *Archiv für Kulturgeschichte*

BISIMEAM: *Bolletino dell'Istituto storico italiano per il medio evo e Achivio Muratoriano*

BCRH: *Bulletin de la Commission Royale d'Histoire*

Bouquet: Martin Bouquet *et al. Recueil des historiens des Gaules et de la France.* Paris, 1738–1904. 24 vols.

BSAHDL: *Bulletin de la Société d'Art et d'Histoire du Diocèse de Liège*

CCM: *Cahiers de civilisation médiévale*

CH: *Church History*

CHR: *Catholic Historical Review*

CQR: *Church Quarterly Review*

DTC: *Dictionnaire de théologie catholique*

Duchesne: André Duchesne. *Historiae Francorum scriptores coaetanei*. Paris, 1636–1649. 5 vols.

ETL: *Ephemerides theologicae Lovanienses*

Hef-L: Charles Hefele and H. Leclercq. *Histoire des Conciles*. Paris, 1907–1921. 10 vols.

HTR: *Harvard Theological Review*

Jaffé: Phillip Jaffé. *Regesta Pontificum Romanorum*. Leipzig, 1885. 2 vols.

JR: *Journal of Religion*

JTS: *Journal of Theological Studies*

MA: *Le moyen âge*

Mab. Vet. Analecta: Jean Mabillon. *Vetera Analecta*. Paris, 1723

Mansi: Giovanni Mansi, *Sacrorum conciliorum nova et amplissima collectio*. Florence, 1759–1798. 31 vols.

Max. Bibl. Vet. Pat.: *Maxima bibliotheca veterum patrum*. Lyon, 1677. 27 vols.

MGH Epp.: *Monumenta Germaniae Historica, Epistolae*

MGH Legg.: ———, *Leges*

MGH Lib. de Lit.: ———, *Libelli de Lite*

MGH SS: ———, *Scriptores*

MGH SS rer. Germ.: ———, *Scriptores rerum Germanicarum*

MPL: Jacques-Paul Migne. *Patrologiae cursus completus, series latina*. Paris, 1841–1864. 221 vols.

MRS: *Medieval and Renaissance Studies*

MS: *Medieval Studies*

Muratori: Lodovico Muratori. *Rerum italicarum scriptores*. Milan, 1723–1751. 25 vols.

NADADGK: *Neues Archiv der Gesellschaft für ältere Geschichtskunde*

RBén: *Revue bénedictine*

RBPH: *Revue belge de philologie et d'histoire*

REI: *Revue des études italiennes*

RHE: *Revue d'histoire ecclésiastique*

RHR: *Revue de l'histoire des religions*

RMAL: *Revue du moyen âge latin*

RQCAKG: *Römische Quartalschrift für christliche Altertumskunde und Kirchengeschichte*

RSCI: *Rivista di storia della Chiesa in Italia*

RSPT: *Revue des sciences philosophiques et théologiques*

RSRUS: *Revue des sciences religieuses de l'université de Strasbourg*

RTAM: *Recherches de théologie ancienne et médiévale*

RThom.: *Revue Thomisle*

TQS: *Theologische Quartalschrift*

ZFK: *Zeitschrift für Kirchengeschichte*

ZKT: *Zeitschrift für katholische Theologie*

CHAPTER I

[1] See Roland H. Bainton, "The Parable of the Tares as the Proof Text for Religious Liberty to the End of the Sixteenth Century," CH, I (1932).

[2] *Dynamics of Faith* (New York, 1957), p. 32.

[3] See my article, "Interpretations of the Origins of Medieval Heresy," MS XXV (1963), for a full account of the historiography of the problem.

[4] See Appendix A.

CHAPTER 2

[1] See my chapter, "Celt and Teuton," in Lynn White, ed., *The Transformation of the Roman World* (Berkeley and Los Angeles, [to be published in] 1966).

[2] Particularly relevant books on the history of intellectual and religious conditions in this area are: Rudolf Huysmans, *Wazo van Luik in den Ideeënstrijd zijner dagen* (Nijmegen, 1932); Etienne de Moreau, *Histoire de l'église en Belgique* (Brussels, 1947–1952); L. Brigué, *Alger de Liège* (Paris, 1936); Jacques Stiennon, "L'Etude des centres intellectuels de la Basse-Lotharingie, de la fin du Xe siècle au début du XIIe siècle. Problèmes et méthode," *Annales de la Fédération Archéologique,* 33d session, 1949; Josef Fleckenstein, "Königshof und Bischofsschule unter Otto dem Grossen," AKG, XXXVIII (1956); Alfred Cauchie, *La Querelle des Investitures dans les diocèses de Liège et de Cambrai* (Louvain, 1890–1891); *Milo Hendrik Koyen, De Prae-Gregoriaanse Hervorming te Kamerijk 1012–1067* (Tongerlo, 1953); Heinrich Sproemberg, *Beiträge zur belgisch-niederländischen Geschichte* (Berlin, 1959).

[3] Letter of Gregory VII to Countess Adèle of Flanders, Mansi, XX, 216–217.

[4] At the councils of Rome, 1050, 1059, 1063, and 1074; the council of Rouen, 1128; the council of Reims, 1131; the council of Liège, 1131.

[5] MPL, CLXXXII, 915.

[6] Gregory of Tours, *Historia Francorum,* X, 25.

[7] See chap. 4.

[8] Michael Tangl, *Die Briefe des heiligen Bonifatius* (Berlin, 1916), p. 128; Ephraim Emerton, *The Letters of Saint Boniface* (New York, 1940), p. 114.

[9] The Penitential of Theodore, in John T. McNeill and Helena M. Gamer, *Medieval Handbooks of Penance* (New York, 1938), pp. 188–189.

[10] Mansi, XII, 901–902; Hef-L, III, 985–992; MPL, XCVI, 859 ff.; DTC, X, 1720–1722; Emile Amann, *L'Epoque carolingienne* (Paris, 1947), pp. 130–132. See Hef-L, III, 985, for further bibliography.

[11] Letter of Hadrian I, Mansi XII, 814–819; MPL, XCVIII, 373–386.

[12] Amann, *op. cit.,* p. 131.

[13] Hef-L, III, 986.

[14] MGH Legg., I, 410; MPL, CXXXVIII, 579; Hef-L, IV, 191.

[15] The sources for Claudius are: Claudius, *Opera*, MPL, CIV, 609 ff., especially the *XXX Quaestiones super libros regum*, and the letter of Claudius to Theodemir; Dungal's reply to Claudius, *Responsa contra perversas Claudii Taurenensis sententias*, MPL, CV, 447 f.; Jonas of Orléans, *De cultu imaginum libri tres ad Carolum Regem*, MPL, CVI, 305 ff.; Hugh of Fleury, *Historia Francorum*, MGH SS, IX, 364. See also Carl Schmidt, "Claudius von Turin," *Zeitschrift für die historische Theologie*, pt. 2 (1843), pp. 39 ff.; Amann, *op. cit.*, p. 239; R. L. Poole, *Illustrations of the History of Medieval Thought and Learning* (2d ed.; New York, 1920), pp. 24–33.

[16] Agobard of Lyon, *Liber contra eorum superstitionem qui picturis et imaginibus sanctorum adorationis obsequium deferendum putant*, MPL, CIV, 199–228.

[17] See chap. 4.

[18] Edmond Martène and Ursin Durand, *Veterum Scriptorum* . . . (Paris, 1724–1733), I, 357–359. Martène and Durand found the letter in an old manuscript of the monastery of Deutz, where it was attached to the foot of the *Life* of Saint Heribert of Cologne, to whom they therefore supposed it was addressed. The letter names as addressee only the initial H. This H was, judged by the salutation, an archbishop. Of the three sees he might have ruled, Trier, Mainz, and Cologne, there was between 970 and 1142 no archbishop whose name began with H save Heribert. Further, the letter says that H was a monk, and Archbishop Heribert was a Benedictine. Martène and Durand seem, then, to have been justified in their identification of H as Heribert.

[19] Oscar D. Watkins, *A History of Penance* (London, 1920), I, 493 ff., 656 ff., 710 ff.; R. C. Mortimer, *The Origins of Private Penance in the Western Church* (Oxford, 1939), pp. 1–2; McNeill and Gamer, *op. cit., passim*.

[20] *Corrector*, no. 78, in McNeill and Gamer, *op. cit.*, p. 332.

[21] *Corrector*, no. 89.

[22] See my article, "A propos du synode d'Arras," RHE, LVII (1962).

[23] Hermann Theloe, *Die Ketzerverfolgung im 11. und 12. Jahrhundert* (Berlin and Leipzig, 1913), p. 8.

[24] There are many sources for the incident at Orléans, but their value differs considerably. The best contemporary sources are (1) Paul of Saint Père de Chartres, *Gesta synodi Aurelianensis*, written about 1022, which appears in Bouquet, X, 536–539, among others; (2) a diploma of King Robert, written about 1022, in Bouquet, X, 605–607; (3) a letter of Jean of Fleury to Oliba, abbot of Ripoll, written about 1022, in Bouquet, X, 498. Somewhat less reliable is a letter of Bishop Baldwin, of Thérouanne (*ca.* 989–1030), probably written between 1022 and 1025, because it mentions the heresies of Aquitaine but not those of Liège and Arras. It appears in the *Chronicon Morinense*, cited by O. Bled, *Régestes des évêques de Thérouanne* (Saint-Omer, 1904), no. 190,

and edited by Jacques Malbrancq, *De Morinis et Morinorum rebus* (Tournai, 1639–1654), II, 661–663. Again on a somewhat lower level is Adhémar of Chabannes, *Historiarum Libri Tres*, MGH SS, IV, 143, composed about 1028. The following medieval sources are of distinctly secondary value: (1) Radulf Glaber, *Historiarum libri quinque*, III, 8, ed. by Maurice Prou (Paris, 1886), pp. 74–81 (Radulf is derivative in part from Baldwin, and both Baldwin and Glaber confuse Stephen and Heribert in their narratives); (2) *Miracula Sancti Benedictini*, VI, 20; (3) *Chronicon Sancti Petri Vivi Senonensis*, Bouquet, X, 224; (4) *Vita Theoderici episcopi Aurelianensis*, AASSOSB, VI, pt. I, p. 175; (5) a fragment "Historiae Franciae," Bouquet, X, 211–212; (6) *Chronicon Turonense*, Bouquet, X, 284.

²⁵ It is generally agreed, by both the medieval sources and modern writers, that the synod at which the heretics were condemned took place at Christmas in 1022. It is possible, from the following information, to date the origins of the sect at Orléans as far back as 1015. First, the chantor Théodat, whose body was exhumed in 1022 because he had been a member of the sect, had been dead for three years, *viz.*, since 1019. Further, the sources tell us that the heresy had germinated for several years undetected. Hence, the origins of the group may be set somewhere about 1015.

²⁶ Letter of Jean of Fleury. (See note 24, above.)

²⁷ *Gesta synodi.*

²⁸ These doctrines are reported by Jean of Fleury. (See note 24, above.)

²⁹ The context is: "complures induxerant ad nuncium baptismo remittendum, signum Sanctae Crucis exterminandum, Divorum cultum exsibilandum, carnium esum quolibet tempore amplexandum." The use of *divorm* in the plural is unusual and might seem to indicate the pagan gods rather than the saints. *Divus* usually appears only in the singular when it means a saint, and then in conjunction with a proper name, as "Divus Paulus." On the other hand, the syntax informs us that these were things that the heretics were promoting, and it seems much more likely that one would *promote* mockery of the cult of the saints than that one would *promote* whispering about the pagan gods.

³⁰ For a similar conclusion see Raffaello Morghen, "Movimenti religiosi popolari nel periodo della riforma della chiesa," *Relazioni del X congresso internazionale di scienze storiche* (Florence, 1955), p. 316.

³¹ Adhémar, *Chronicle*, III, 49, ed. by Jules Chavanon (Paris, 1897), p. 173.

³² *Ibid.*, 69, p. 194.

³³ *Ibid.*, 59, p. 184. See Christian Pfister, *Etudes sur le règne de Robert le Pieux* (Paris, 1885), pp. 325–335.

³⁴ The two main sources are Radulf Glaber, IV, 2, in Bouquet, X, 45, and in Prou, *op. cit.*, 94–96; Landolfo Senior, *Historia Mediolanensis*, II, 27, in MGH SS, VIII, 65–66. Arno Borst, *Die Katharer* (Stuttgart, 1953), p. 77 n. 18, shows that the possible range of the date is 1024 to 1034. In the text, Borst says "around 1028," and I have followed him for the sake of uniformity. Of the

latest accounts, see particularly Morghen, *op. cit.*, and Raffaello Morghen, *Medioevo cristiano* (Bari, 1951), p. 238; Ilarino da Milano, "Le Eresie popolari del secolo XI," in G. B. Borino, *Studi gregoriani,* II (Rome, 1948), 68. Borst cites E. Wunderlich, *Aribert von Antemiano, Erzbischof von Mailand* (Halle, 1914), pp. 43 f., but I have found this unobtainable.

[35] See Borst, *op. cit.,* p. 78 n. 20, for the sources. Borst places the date shortly before the death of Saint Gerhard (bishop 1037–1046).

[36] Paul Fredericq, *Corpus documentorum inquisitionis* (Ghent and The Hague, 1889), I, 6–7. This letter comes to us as inserted by the chronicler Anselm into his *Gesta episcoporum Tungrensium, Traiectensium, et Leodiensium,* MGH SS, VII, 226. It also appears in the "altera rescensio" of Anselm, MGH SS, XIV, 117, and in Gilles of Orval, *Gesta episcoporum Leodiensium,* MGH SS, XXV, 73, although in this last it is in an abbreviated form clearly derived from Anselm. There are many editions of the letter in the context of the *Gesta* (Joannis Chapeaville, *Gesta Pontificum Leodiensium Scripserunt auctores praecipii*), I, 302–303; Martène and Durand, *op. cit.,* IV, 898 ff.; Bouquet, XI, 11 (a summary version of the letter is all that is offered by Martène and Durand and by Bouquet); MGH SS, VII, 226–228 (ed. by Rudolf Koepke); MPL, CXLII, 751–753; Fredericq, *op. cit.,* I, 6–7. The latest is that of Fredericq. Fredericq, however, drew his edition from that of Koepke in the MGH SS, so that Koepke's is the latest original edition. But there are three important manuscripts that Koepke did not utilize, and it is necessary to correct his readings with these. They are (1) a manuscript of the late twelfth or early thirteenth century from the abbey of Aulne, presently MS 3173 of the Bibliothèque de l'Université de Liège; (2) a seventeenth-century (1606) copy of the original MS, presently MS 1964 of the Bibliothèque de l'Université de Liège; and (3) another seventeenth-century copy, contemporaneous with (2) above, presently in the library of the abbey of Averbode. The two seventeenth-century copies, evidently related to each other, are closer to the original than is the twelfth-century copy or any of the sources that Koepke used. This is proved by the fact that there are two impossible readings in the letter as published by Koepke and as transcribed in the twelfth-century copy which do not appear in the seventeenth-century MSS.

The date of the letter was set by Koepke at 1048. To be fair to him, it is difficult to say from the placing of the date in the margin whether it is meant to apply to the letter or only to the paragraph before. Koepke probably meant the paragraph before, since he does not explain using the date 1048 to apply to the letter, but Fredericq took it to apply to the letter, and he followed this precision. It is a precision impossible to accept, since nothing either in the letter or in the context in which it is placed permits it. It is true that in Anselm's chronicle the letter follows an event known to have taken place in 1048, but this event is in turn followed by an account of 1047, then by events of 1046, then again by 1048. The only sure guideposts are the reigns of the two prelates involved. Wazo ruled from 1043 to 1048, Roger II from 1043 to 1062, and the letter must thus have been written between 1043 and Wazo's death on July 8, 1048.

In the letter, Wazo makes a passing reference to the independence of the spiritual sword from the temporal, noting that the spiritual sword is to be used to bring life, while the temporal sword is used to bring death. The offhand nature of this reference leads one to guess that the letter was probably written no earlier than 1046, for it was in the spring of that year that Wazo issued the first of his three famous dicta regarding the independence of the spiritual from the temporal power. The declarations of Wazo on this score were unique and exceptional in their time, so that the source of Wazo's statement in his letter to Roger could be none other than the thought of the Liégeois himself. If he had not already exposed his thought at least once in detail before the composition of the letter, he would not have mentioned the theory so lightly in passing. The date of the letter can thus be set probably between 1046 and summer 1048.

The edition of the letter by Fredericq is, to begin with, peculiar. He does not justify the insertion into his *Corpus* of material that deals, not with heresy in the Low Countries, but with heresy in the diocese of Châlons. There are, in fact, two justifications for treating the letter, but Fredericq was unaware of at least one of them. Moreover, and stranger still, he does not include in the *Corpus* the chronicler Anselm's introduction to the letter, which consists of a summary of the anterior letter of Roger. This summary (Anselm, MGH SS, VII, 226) provides us with the only indication we have of the doctrines of the heretics of whom Roger complained. We must be cautious in accepting it, however, for it is at the least third hand, reported to us by Anselm, who reports Roger, who in turn reports the heretics.

[37] Raoul Manselli, "Una Designazione dell'eresia catara: Ariana heresis," BISIMEAM (1956), pp. 233–246.

[38] Anselm, MGH SS, VII, 228.

[39] Roland H. Bainton, "The Parable of the Tares as the Proof Text for Religious Liberty to the End of the Sixteenth Century," CH, I (1932), 74–75.

[40] *Ibid.*

[41] For Wazo's intellectual importance, see Huysmans, *op. cit.*

[42] See my article, "Les Cathares de 1048-1054 à Liège," BSAHDL, XLIV (1961). At that time I mistook these heretics for Catharists.

[43] Editions in Mansi, XIX, 730, partial version in Fredericq, *op. cit.*, I, 8.

[44] Mansi, XIX, 742.

[45] *Ibid.*, p. 737.

[46] The primary sources are: Lampert of Hersfeld, *Annales,* ad ann. 1053, in MGH SS, V, 155; Hermann der Lahme of Reichenau, *Chronicon,* ad ann. 1054, MGH SS, V, 130; Anselm, MGH SS, VII, 228. Bernold, *Chronicon,* MGH SS, V, 426, derives from Hermann's account, as do the *Annales Mellicenses, Auctarium Zwetlense,* MGH SS, IX, 539. The Annalista Saxo, MGH SS, VI, 689, de-

rives his account from Lampert. On Goslar see Borst, *op. cit.*, p. 79. Also of use is Anton Joseph Krebs, "Heinrich's IV Entführung von Kaiserswerth nach Köln durch Erzbischof Anno II," AHVNR, IV (1857), 325-326. Wilhelm Herse, "Ketzer im Goslar im Jahre 1052," *Zeitschrift des Harzvereins für Geschichte und Altertumskunde*, LXVIII (1935), is useless. As for the date, Borst argues for 1051, and I do not dispute him. See Ernst Steindorff, *Jahrbücher des deutschen Reichs unter Heinrich*, III (Leipzig, 1881), 165.

[47] This connection is made by Borst, *op. cit.*, p. 79, Ilarino, *op. cit.*, p. 76, and Morghen, *Medioevo*, p. 238.

[48] Lampert, the only source that mentions Godfrey, is not without difficulties. The actual phrase used is, "Ibi (Goslariae) quoque per Gotefridum ducem heretici deprehensi sunt et suspensi." This may mean that the heretics were native to Goslar and that Henry ordered Godfrey to arrest them and take charge of their execution. The coincidence that would place both Godfrey and the heretics associated with Lorraine in Goslar at the same time makes this somewhat unlikely, though the idea of Godfrey's bringing heretics all the way from Lorraine to Goslar is also somewhat odd.

[49] The sources for Ramihrd are: *Chronicon Sancti Andreae Castri Cameracensis*, MGH SS, VII, 540, and Fredericq, *op. cit.*, I, 11-12; letter of Gregory VII to Geoffroi of Paris, Fredericq, *op. cit.*, II, 1, and Phillip Jaffé, *Bibliotheca rerum germanicarum* (Berlin, 1864-1873), II, 268.

[50] For the best recent study of the Patarini see Cinzio Violante, *La Pataria milanese e la riforma ecclesiastica* (Rome, 1955). See also S. M. Brown, "Movimenti politico-religiosi a Milano ai tempi della Pataria," *Archivio storico lombardo*, ser. 6, LVIII (1931); G. Miccoli, "Per la storia della pataria milanese," BISIMEAM, LXX (1958).

[51] Antoine Dondaine, "L'Hiérarchie cathare en Italie," AFP, XIX (1949), XX (1950). Alfonso Ricolfi, "La Setta dei catari a Firenze e la mandetta di Guido Cavalcanti," *Nuova rivista storica*, XIV (1930), errs when he says that Florence was a center of the Catharist heresy in the eleventh century.

[52] For example, *Tractatus pro clericorum connubio*, MGH Lib. de Lit., III, 594.

[53] Landolfo Senior, III, 26, in MGH SS, VIII, 92-93.

[54] For example, Ernst Werner, "Π αταρηνοί = patarini," in *Vom Mittelalter zur Neuzeit, Festschrift zum 65. Geburtstag von Heinrich Sproemberg* (Berlin, 1956), esp. p. 415. I do not think that the author has demonstrated gnostic influence.

[55] See Herbert Grundmann, *Religiöse Bewegungen im Mittelalter* (Berlin, 1935), p. 14. Se also P. Toubert, "Hérésies et réforme ecclésiastique en Italie au XIe et au XIIe s. A propos de deux études recentes," REI, n.s., VIII (1961), 58-71.

[56] Guibert of Nogent, *Autobiography*, ed. Georges Bourgin (Paris, 1907), I, vii.

[57] Agobard's works in MPL, CIV; Amulo's in MPL, CXVI; Rémy's in MPL, CXIX. For Agobard and the Jews, see J. Allen Cabaniss, *Agobard of Lyons*

(Amsterdam, 1954), pp. 58–63; James Parks, *The Jew in the Medieval Community* (London, 1938), chap. 2; A. L. Williams, *Adversus Judaeos* (Cambridge [Eng.], 1935); Malcolm Hay, *The Foot of Pride* (Boston, 1950).

[58] *Annales Quedlinburgenses*, MGH SS, III, 81. See also Albert Hauck, *Kirchengeschichte Deutschlands* (Leipzig, 1887–1906), III, 431.

[59] Adhémar, *op. cit.*, III, 52.

[60] Radulf Glaber, *op. cit.*, III, 7.

[61] Parkes has a good summary in his chapter 3. Jacob R. Marcus, *The Jew in the Medieval World* (New York, 1938), pp. 115–120, gives a translation of Solomon bar Samson's account of the massacre at Mainz on May 27, 1096.

[62] Saint Bernard, epistle 365, MPL, CLXXXII, 570.

CHAPTER 3

[1] Two documents relating to this heresy are reproduced by Paul Fredericq, *Corpus documentorum inquisitionis* (Ghent and The Hague, 1889), I, 20–22. The first is an excerpt from the *Gesta Trevirorum* (MGH SS, VIII, 193) and the second is an extract from Christian Brouwers' *Annales Trevirenses* (Brouwers and Masenius, *Antiquitatum et annalium Treverensium libri XXV*, II, 8–9). The second was composed at the beginning of the seventeenth century, and Christian Brouwers died in 1617 (Fredericq, *op. cit.*, I, 20), so that it is difficult to understand why Fredericq publishes it as a primary source. That Brouwers drew upon the *Gesta Trevirorum* is apparent in that his version of the apprehension of the heretics follows the same order of events as the *Gesta* and repeats the speeches of Archbishop Bruno almost verbatim. Moreover, he drew upon the *Gesta* exclusively, since he adds no new information other than his own lengthy paraphrases. When he speaks of the attack of the heresy upon Luxembourg, for example, he is noting only what we already know, that the diocese of Trier lay largely in Luxembourg. There is only one difference of fact between the two accounts: in the *Gesta* the bishop challenges the heretical priest at communion, while in Brouwers' version it is at the fraction of the host that this occurs. In short, the only legitimate source is the *Gesta,* which were written before 1150 (MGH SS, VIII, lll ff.).

Fredericq places the date of these events after 1112, postulating that the heretics were apprehended some time after the synod of Trier of that year (neither Mansi nor Hef-L gives any account of such a synod). There is really no reason to assume this. Although in the chronicle the event is placed among occurrences of the 1110's and 1120's, there is no other evidence for being more exact than affirming that the event took place between 1102 and 1124, the years of Bruno's reign.

[2] *Gesta Trevirorum,* MGH SS, VIII, 193.

[3] *Ibid.*

[4] Fredericq, *op. cit.*, I, 20.

[5] Pierre David, "Un Credo cathare?" RHE, XXXV (1939).

[6] Modern writers have variously used the spelling "Tanchelm" or forms of the spelling "Tanchelin." The sources themselves present a nice variety: Tanchelmus, Tandemus, Tanquelmus, Tankelmus, Tanchelinus, Tanszelinus, Fancellinus. Setting aside the fantastic Tanszelinus and Fancellinus and dismissing Tandemus as too far out of line with the rest, we have a formula: $Tan + k$ or $ch + in$ or m. The k or ch question need not concern us, as both represent approximately the same sound. The m or in question is one of interpretation of the scribal-book hand by modern editors. Since Tanchelm is a name known in other contexts and is also simpler than the alternative form, I have elected to follow the majority of writers in this spelling. The French have usually chosen "Tanchelin," owing to their difficulty in pronouncing the other form.

[7] See Appendix B.

[8] Jozef-M. De Smet, "De monnik Tanchelm en de Utrechtse bisschopszetel in 1112–1114," *Scrinium Lovaniense, Mélanges historiques Etienne van Cauwenbergh* (Louvain, 1961), p. 229.

[9] The difficulties with Tanchelm's dates are relatively slight. The *Annales Veterocellenses* (MGH SS, XVI, 42) tell us that he preached in 1112; the *Continuatio Valcellensis* (MGH SS, VI, 458) tells us that he died in 1115; and from the *Vitae Norberti* we know that by 1124 he had been dead a number of years. We may thus suppose him to have begun preaching around 1110 and to have died, as reported, in 1115.

The succession of events presented in the text is, I believe, the simplest that does not contradict the data given in the sources. The rationale is as follows:

1) Tanchelm as a native of Utrecht: It is conceivable that Tanchelm, as some historians have held, was a native of Flanders and went first to Utrecht after his mission. But this unlikely. Having approached the pope with a scheme against the diocese of Utrecht, he would hardly then make a first trip to the center of that diocese to form a religious guild among people he did not know.

2) His mission to Rome: He could not have engaged in heretical preaching before his mission to Rome, for Robert would not have sent a heretic to the pope.

3) His preaching in the islands and along the Meuse and Scheldt: His heresy must have dated, at least in its well-developed form, from his return from Rome. The letter of the canons of Utrecht tells us that he preached first in this area.

4) His arrest by Archbishop Frederick I: Tanchelm was arrested *before* he first preached heresy at Utrecht, for the chapter of Utrecht in their letter to the prelate congratulated him for having arrested Tanchelm on a previous occasion and pleaded with him to do it again.

5) His preaching at Utrecht: Here the excesses—if there really were such—of his cult began.

6) His preaching at Bruges and Louvain: That he preached in these cities is by no means certain, as it is only the sixteenth-century sources that mention

them. If Tanchelm did preach there, it must have been after he left Utrecht, which would be confirmed by Meyerus' date for the episode at Bruges.

7) His preaching at Antwerp: The *Vita Norberti* says that Tanchelm "came to" Antwerp but does not say from where. Since it was during his activities there that he met his death, this episode must obviously be placed at the end of the list. Arno Borst, *Die Katharer* (Stuttgart, 1953), p. 84, erred in taking the episode of the priest at Antwerp who fornicated with his niece as the event that impelled Tanchelm to preach against the clergy. The immorality of the priest may have prepared Tanchelm's way at Antwerp, but his heresy had long since been active.

[10] Borst, *op. cit.,* p. 85 n. 13.

[11] The career of Henry has always received considerable attention from historians of heresy, and I present here no more than a brief narrative account of his career. The best work on Henry and Peter is that of Raoul Manselli, *Studi sulle eresie del secolo XII* (Rome, 1953). The first chapter deals with the historiography of the problem, the second with Peter, and the third with Henry. Manselli gives a fine review of the sources, including a hitherto undiscussed debate between Henry and a monk named William. See also Manselli's "Il monaco Enrico e la sua eresia," BISIMEAM, LXV (1953), and his appendix to this article, which gives an edition of the debate with William. See also Watkin Williams, *Saint Bernard of Clairvaux* (Manchester, 1935), pp. 337–345. Of the complicated problem of the sources, this much must be said here for the sake of clarity. Saint Bernard's sermons 65 and 66 (MPL, CLXXXIII, 1088–1102), the so-called sermons on the Song of Songs, are *not* evidence for the Henricians but for the heretics opposed by Evervinus of Cologne. Saint Bernard's letters 241 and 242 *are* evidence for the Henricians and for them alone. There is no evidence for the common allegation that Henry rejected crucifixes. Peter and Ponnus did, but Henry was preceded by the cross on his entrance to Le Mans.

In addition to the letters of Bernard, the sources for Henry are: *Gesta pontificum Cenomannensium,* Bouquet, XII, 547–551; Alberic des Trois-Fontaines, *Chronicon,* MGH SS, XXIII, 839; Geoffrey of Clairvaux, *Vita Bernardi,* MPL, CLXXXV, 312–320; Geoffrey, *Epistola ad Archenfredum,* MPL, CLXXXV, 410–416; *Exordium magnum Cisterciense,* in *Vita Bernardi,* MPL, CLXXXV, 427–428; and the debate published by Manselli. The evidence of Peter the Venerable, *Tractatus contra Petrobrusianos,* MPL, CLXXXIX, 723, is not entirely trustworthy in regard to Henry, since it ties him too closely to Peter of Bruys.

[12] The assumption that he was from Lausanne rests upon an overeager reading of Saint Bernard's letter 241: "Inquire, si placet, vir nobilis, quomodo de Lausana civitate exierit, quomodo de Cenomannis, quomodo de Pictavi, quomodo de Burdegali. . . ." This means that Henry had preached in Lausanne before going to Le Mans but not that he was a native of the former city.

[13] *Vita Hildeberti* in Mab. Vet. Analecta.

[14] Josèphe Chartrou, *L'Anjou de 1109 à 1151* (Paris, 1928), pp. 165–166.

[15] This and most of the rest of my account of Henry's sojourn at Le Mans is taken from the *Vita Hildeberti*.

[16] MPL, CLXXI, 237.

[17] Manselli, *Studi,* chap. 2; Henry Charles Lea, *History of the Inquisition in the Middle Ages* (New York, 1888), I, 69; Borst, *op. cit.,* p. 3 n. 2, 83; Antoine Dondaine, "Aux Origines du valdéisme," AFP, XVI (1946), 226; J. C. Reagan, "Did the Petrobrusians Teach Salvation by Faith Alone," JR, VII (1927); Elphège Vacandard, *Vie de Saint Bernard, abbé de Clairvaux* (Paris, 1927), II, 226. See also Borst, *op. cit.,* p. 83 n. 10.

Contemporary sources for Peter are as follows. The fullest and most reliable is the *Tractatus adversus Petrobrusianos* of Peter the Venerable, in MPL, CLXXXIX, 719–850. This dates from the period 1131 to 1134, according to Manselli, *Studi,* pp. 28–29. For a bibliography on Peter's treatise, see Borst, *op. cit.,* p. 3 n. 2. In addition there are brief accounts or notices in the report of the Lateran council of 1139 in Mansi, XII, 524, in a *Vita Innocenti II* in Mansi, XXI, 391, and in the *Introductio ad theologiam* of Peter Abelard, II, 4, in MPL, CLXXVIII, 979–1112.

[18] Reagan, *op. cit.*

[19] For the date, see Manselli, *Studi,* p. 29. Borst, *op. cit.,* p. 83 n. 10, has 1126.

[20] Letter of Saint Bernard to Ildephonse, Count of Saint Gilles (epistle 241, in MPL, CLXXXII, 434–436: "Quippe speciem pietatis habens").

[21] Vacandard, *op. cit.,* II, 224-241.

[22] Lea, *op. cit.,* I, 72.

[23] The chief source concerning the Périgourdins is a letter of Heribert, a monk, possibly a Périgourdin himself, and possibly later archbishop of Torres in Sardinia. Slight variation is found in the account of the *Annales Marganenses* ad ann. 1163, ed. H. R. Luard, Rolls Series, XXXVI, pt. 1 (London, 1864), 15. See Borst, *op. cit.,* pp. 4–5; Herbert Grundmann, *Religiöse Bewegungen im Mittelalter* (Berlin, 1955), p. 18.

[24] Lea, *op. cit.,* I. 72.

[25] For Count John, and for Clement and Ebrard, see Borst, *op. cit.,* p. 84. The source for all this is Guilbert of Nogent, *Autobiography,* III, 17, ed. Bourgin (Paris, 1907), pp. 212 ff., or MPL, CLVI, 951–953.

[26] For the synod of Beauvais, see Mansi, XXI, 121–126; Hef-L, V, 548; Théodore Gousset, *Les Actes de la province ecclésiastique de Reims* (Reims, 1842–1844), II, 179.

[27] For the synod of Soissons, see Mansi, XXI, 127–130; Hef-L, V, 548; Gousset, *op. cit.,* II, 184–185.

[28] Georges Bourgin, *La Commune de Soissons, et le groupe communal soissonais* (Paris, 1908).

[29] Guibert of Nogent, *op. cit.*

[30] Gousset, *op. cit.,* II, 239–247.

[31] Synod of Toulouse, Mansi, XXI, 225–228. The date of the synod was July 8, 1119.

[32] *Gesta Nicholai episcopi Cameracensis,* MGH SS, XIV, 244.

[33] These are the *Annales Aquenses,* MGH SS, XVI, 685; MGH SS, XXIV, 37; and the *Annales Rodenses,* MGH SS, XVI, 711. The *Aquenses* give only one terse sentence, while the *Rodenses* offer a more extended account. These documents present no difficulties, as the date 1135 appears in both, and the two are nearly contemporary with the event yet are independent of each other.

[34] Jaffé, nos. 8774, 8814.

[35] Fredericq, *op. cit.,* I, 30.

[36] Charles Duplessis d'Argentré, *Collectio judiciorum de novis erroribus* (Paris, 1724–1736), I, 28, has the purported letter to Henry. Metellus wrote a better-authenticated letter to a monk named Gerard in regard to Berengar of Tours. It may be found in Mab. Vet. Analecta, p. 476.

[37] See chap. 6.

[38] Manselli, *Studi,* pp. 96 ff.

[39] See chap. 6.

[40] Synod of Reims, March 21, 1148, canons 17 and 18, in Mansi, XXI, 717–718.

[41] The source for Albero is the *Anonymi Libellus adversus errores Alberonis sacerdotis Merkensis,* published in Edmond Martène and Ursin Durand, *Amplissima Collectio* (Paris, 1724–1733), IX, 1252–1270. This pamphlet was written, according to Albert Hauck, *Kirchengeschichte Deutschlands* (Leipzig, 1887–1906), IV, 860, in the reign of the emperor Frederick I and before the year 1177, placing it between 1154 and 1177. Hauck dates it by the style, which he identifies as that used in Frederick's reign. The document itself is undated.

[42] Augustin Fliche, *La Réforme grégorienne et la reconquête chrétienne* (Paris, 1950), p. 266.

[43] Jaffé, no. 9688; Mansi, XXI, 689; MPL, CLXXX, 1579; Fredericq, *op. cit.,* I, 33.

[44] They are published together in Fredericq, *op. cit.,* II, 9–36, or separately in Jean d'Outremeuse, *Ly Myreur des histors,* ed. Stanislas Bormans (Brussels, 1864–1887), IV, 455, 461, 462, 465; Gilles d'Orval, *Gesta episciporum Leodiensium,* ed. Johann Heller, MGH SS, XXV, 110-112 (largely drawn from the *Vita Odilae* in AB, XIII, 197); Albéric des Trois-Fontaines, *Chronica,* ed. Paul Scheffer-Boicherst, MGH SS, XXIII, 631-950; Ulysse Robert, *Bullaire du pape Calixte II* (Paris, 1874), II, 293, 410 ff.; Joseph Daris, *Notices sur les églises du diocèse de Liège* (Louvain, 1867–1899), XVI, *passim.* There are seven chief documents: (1) the *Antigraphum Petri,* the work of Lambert himself (see end of note); (2) a first letter of Lambert to the antipope Calixtus III, whom Robert and others mistook for Calixtus II; (3) a letter of the friends of Lambert to Calixtus III; (4) a bull of Calixtus III regarding Lambert and directed to the bishop of Liège; (5) a second letter of Lambert to the antipope; (6) a letter of an adherent of Lambert to Calixtus; (7) a justification of himself written by Lambert and intended for the antipope. I use the chronological order suggested by Daris, *op. cit.,* XVI, 8–9. The *Antigraphum* is edited and discussed by Arnold Fayen,

"L'Antigraphum Petri et les lettres concernant Lambert le Bègue conservées dans le manuscrit de Glasgow," BCRH, LXVIII (1899), 255–356. Fayen also publishes the other documents in the same article.

[45] I cannot hope in these few pages to give a full account of Lambert's career and must disclaim any effort to explore the relationship of Lambert to the church of Saint-Christophe and other churches of Liège, or the much debated question of the significance of the term Bègue or whether Lambert was the founder of the Beguines. I wish here to discuss only briefly the question of whether Lambert was a heretic.

[46] Daris, op. cit., XVI, 10.

[47] Fredericq, op. cit., II, 24.

[48] Daris, op. cit., XVI, 12.

[49] Fredericq, op. cit., II, 12-13.

[50] Thus Daris, and Sylvain Balau, Etude critique des sources de l'histoire du Pays de Liège au Moyen Age (Brussels, 1903), pp. 328–330.

[51] His first letter to the antipope, in Fredericq, op. cit., II, 10.

[52] Their letter to the antipope, ibid., p. 12.

[53] Lambert's second letter to the antipope, ibid., p. 20.

[54] Daris, op. cit., XVI, 15.

[55] Lambert's final justification, Fredericq, op. cit., II, 28.

[56] Antigraphum, in Fayen, op. cit., pp. 272, 275, 285, 316.

[57] Lambert's final justification, Fredericq, op. cit., II, 28.

[58] Lambert's first letter to Calixtus, ibid., p. 10. If this unlikely accusation were true, it would be reminiscent of Visigothic practice in the seventh century.

[59] Lambert's second letter to Calixtus, Fredericq, op. cit., II, 20.

[60] Ibid.

[61] Lambert's first letter, in ibid., p. 10.

[62] Lambert's second letter, ibid., p. 20.

[63] First letter, ibid., p. 10.

[64] Second letter, ibid., p. 20.

[65] Final justification, ibid., p. 28.

[66] Final justification, ibid., p. 29.

[67] Ibid.

[68] Ibid., p. 30.

[69] Ibid., p. 31.

[70] Ibid., pp. 30–31.

[71] Ibid., p. 27; Antigraphum, in Fayen, op. cit., pp. 267 ff.

[72] Of Arnold's career, I offer a summary account only. The attention paid him has always been great. Some of the books and articles appearing in this century alone are: N. A. Bortnik, Arnold Breshianskii (Moscow, 1956); C. Carrodori, Arnaldo da Brescia, Riassunto storico biografico (Nerbini, 1928); Pietro Fedele, Fonti per la storia di Arnaldo da Brescia (Rome, 1938); Arsenio Frugoni, "Arnaldo da Brescia nelle fonti del secolo XII," Studi storichi, no. 8–9 (1954); George W. Greenaway, Arnold of Brescia (Cambridge, 1931); A. Ragazzoni,

Arnaldo da Brescia nella tradizione storica (Brescia, 1937); Antonino da Stefano, *Arnaldo da Brescia e i suoi tempi* (Rome, 1921); Antonio Suraci, *Arnaldo da Brescia* (Asti, 1952). Many of the general works on heresy discuss Arnold.

[73] Mansi, XXI, 525.

[74] Jaffé, no. 9281; Mansi, XXI, 628.

[75] *De Consideratione,* MPL, CLXXXII, 777.

CHAPTER 4

[1] See my article, "Saint Boniface and the Eccentrics," CH, XXXIII (1964).

[2] *Ibid.*

[3] For those councils, see *ibid.,* appendix.

[4] *Annales Fuldenses,* MGH SS, I, 365. The chronicler, Rudolf, was deemed worthy of respect by Pertz. He had a reputation as a historian throughout Germany and was a contemporary of the events he described. Sigebert of Gembloux, MGH SS, VI, 339, also mentions Theuda, but he drew from the *Fuldenses.*

[5] The *Annales* speak of bishops in the plural; Sigebert corrects this to archbishop, which seems sensible. It is unlikely, though possible, that a number of bishops were convened at the synod. More likely only the local clergy were present.

[6] Letter of Nicholas I to Frotaire of Bordeaux. Mansi, XV, 443–445; MPL, CXIX, 1124; Jaffé, no. 2840.

[7] *Annales Fuldenses,* MGH SS, I, 404. A contemporary source.

[8] Ilarino da Milano, "Le Eresie popolari del secolo XI," in G. B. Borino, *Studi gregoriani,* II, 88; Ignaz von Döllinger, *Beiträge zur Sektengeschichte des Mittelalters* (Munich, 1890), I, 60 ff.; Hermann Theloe, *Die Ketzerverfolgung im 11. und 12. Jahrhundert* (Berlin and Leipzig, 1913), p. 7; Radulf Glaber, *Historiarum libri quinque,* II, 12, ed. Maurice Prou (Paris, 1886), p. 50; Landulf, *Historia Mediolanensis,* MGH SS, VIII, 94. A kindred spirit, Anselm the Peripatetic, was accused of demonism. See R. L. Poole, *Illustrations of the History of Medieval Thought and Learning* (2d ed.; London, 1920), pp. 71–72.

[9] Henry Charles Lea, *History of the Inquisition in the Middle Ages* (New York, 1888), I, 108.

[10] Arno Borst, *Die Katharer* (Stuttgart, 1953), p. 74 n. 6.

[11] Further, the wording of the source makes it unclear whether the Sardinian heretics were followers of Vilgard or sectaries of another variety.

[12] See the letter of Roger II of Châlons to Wazo of Liège in Anselm, *Gesta episcoporum Tungrensium, Traiectensium, et Leodiensium,* MGH SS, VII, 226–227.

[13] Radulf Glaber, II, 11, in Prou, *op. cit.,* pp. 49–50.

[14] Christian Pfister, *Etudes sur le règne de Robert le Pieux* (Paris, 1885), p. 330; Borst, *op. cit.,* p. 73; Lea, *op. cit.,* I, 108.

[15] Among a great many others, see a capitulary of August, 829, MGH Legg.,

I, 350; the synod of Mainz, October 3, 851, MGH Legg., I, 411; a capitulary of February 4, 855, MGH Legg., I, 434; the constitutions of Otto I of 948, MGH Legg., II, 26; Jonas of Orléans, *De institutione laicali* MPL, CVI; Smaragdus, *Via Regia*, MPL, CII. A large proportion of synods contain some admonition that tithes are to be paid in the proper fashion.

[16] *Narratio de Alberico presbytero et ejus sceleribus,* in Edmond Martène and Ursin Durand, *Veterum scriptorum* . . . (Paris, 1724–33), I, 253–255. The narration was by Fulk, continued by Albert. Fulk was the eyewitness.

[17] This is probably what is meant by "foetido sanguine."

[18] Editions: MGH SS, X, 309–311; C. de Borman, *Chronique de l'Abbaye de Saint-Trond* (Liège, 1877), I, 84–86. Borman corrects some of the errors of the MGH edition. He notes that an interpolator of an unknown period has added the rubric 1135 to one of the manuscripts. The devastation of the country, mentioned by the chronicler at the end of the account, took place in 1136, so that the event must have taken place early in 1136 or late in 1135. The MGH places it between 1133 and 1136.

[19] Kervyn de Lettenhove, *Histoire de Flandre* (Bruges, 1874), I, 24.

[20] Paul Bonenfant, "L'episode de la nef des tisserands," *Etudes sur l'histoire du Pays mosane au moyen âge, Mélanges Félix Rousseau* (Brussels, 1958), pp. 101–102.

[21] Bonenfant, *op. cit.,* p. 104. The council of Reims of 1157 refers to weavers as "abjectissimi textores." See Mansi, XXI, 843. The Sint Truiden *Annales* themselves refer to a weaver as "rusticus textor et pauper."

[22] Bonenfant, *op. cit.,* pp. 107–108.

[23] On Eudo, see the council of Reims of 1148, Mansi, XXI, 720; Sigebert of Gembloux's *Gembloux Continuation,* MGH SS, VI, 389; *Premonstratensian Continuation,* MGH SS, VI, 454; chronicle of Robert de Monte, MGH SS, VI, 498; *Annales Parchenses,* ad ann. 1149, MGH SS, XVI, 605; *Annales Cameracenses,* MGH SS, XVI, 517; *Annales Magdeburgenses,* MGH SS, XVI, 190; *Annales Casinenses,* MGH SS, XIX, 310; Otto of Freising, *Gesta Friderici,* MGH SS rer. Germ., XLV (Berlin, 1912), I, 54–56; William of Newburgh, Rolls Series, LXXXII, pt. 1 (London, 1884–1885), I, 19; a Breton chronicle, Bouquet, XII, 558; Albéric des Trois-Fontaines, MGH SS, XXIII, 839; Baldwin of Ninove, *Recueil des chroniques de Flandre* (Brussels, 1837–1865), II, 706; Council of Reims, 1148, Mansi, XXI, 711 ff.; Théodore Gousset, *Les Actes de la province ecclésiastique de Reims* (Reims, 1842–1844), II, 231. Among the large number of secondary writers mentioning Eudo are Lea, *op. cit.,* I, 66; Borst, *op. cit.,* pp. 87–88.

The *Contra haereticos sui temporis* of Hugues, Archbishop of Rouen (MPL, CXCII, 1255–1298), may, according to Borst, *op. cit.,* p. 5 n. 10, be directed against Henry the Monk rather than against Eudo.

Of these sources, five are original and the rest derivative. The five original sources include two of basic importance, the Gembloux Continuation of Sigebert, and the Breton chronicle. The other three are the *Annales Parchenses,* the

Annales Cameracenses, and Hugues of Rouen. From the Gembloux Continuation derive Albéric, Baldwin, the Premonstratensian Continuation, and Robert de Monte. From the Breton chronicle derive the *Annales* of Magdeburg. Otto of Freising may be derivative or may have reported independently on the council of Reims. In any event, he is not a primary source for Eudo. Both the Gembloux Continuation and the Breton chronicle influenced William of Newburgh. William is the greatest problem in the historiography of Eudo, since part of what he offers is derivative from these two sources but part is original to him, so that he cannot be entirely dismissed. It is possible that he had another written source that has now been lost, so that what he reports independently may be of value. Further, William has long been recognized as one of the finest and most reliable of medieval historians. On the other hand, he did not begin his chronicle before 1196, nearly fifty years after Eudo's death, and as long as indications of what other sources he may have used are lacking, it is necessary to use caution. In some respects, notably in the question of Eudo's name, this is an important consideration.

[24] Eudes, Eudo, Eus, or Eys are the names bestowed by the majority of the sources, including the Breton chronicle and the *Annales Parchenses.* Unfortunately the Gembloux Continuation and the *Annales Cameracenses* have, respectively, Eunus and Eons. Norman Cohn (*The Pursuit of the Millennium* [London, 1957], pp. 38 ff.) uses Eudes, but most writers have followed Lea in calling the heretic Eon. To this tradition Borst has lent his weight. Both Lea and Borst, however, were influenced by the statement of William of Newburgh that the heretic identified himself with the Son of God in the passage "per *eum* qui venturus est." This would indicate that the name was indeed Eon. I have suggested, however, that caution should be used with William, and the earlier and certainly original source, the Gembloux Continuation, says that the madman made use of the phrase "per *eundem* Dominum nostrum." Here the *eundem* would fit better with Eudo or Eudes. One might simply assert Eudo or Eudes, at this point, were it not for the irritating fact that it is the Gembloux Continuation itself that calls the man Eun. Cohn assumed that he began his career as Eudes and later changed his name to Eon. This is possible and would permit us to imagine that he had first made the identification with *eundem* and later with *eum.* If this were true, it would have possible implications of gnostic influence, as discussed in the chapter on Catharism. Eudes is derived from Odo, so that Eudo is most likely the original spelling of the name. At any rate, it would have been a standard name, while Eon would have been, to say the least, unusual. Eun may be a Breton nickname, as suggested in the text. The agnomen De Stella assigned him by William of Newburgh may or may not be accurate, but its significance is certainly unknown.

[25] The sources vary as to the date under which they insert their information about Eudo, the earliest being 1145 and the latest 1149. This need not detain us long. We know that Eudo was active over a number of years, so that it is not necessary to opt for one year over the others. On the other hand, 1149 is too late

a date, since we know that Eudo was tried at the council of Reims in 1148. Giving him a few years to have built up his notoriety before being brought before the pope, we can assume that he began his preaching no later than 1145, and probably earlier.

[26] William of Newburgh says that the phrase was "per eum qui venturus est judicare vivos et mortuos et seculum per ignem," which Borst (*op. cit.,* p. 87 n. 20) points out is derived, not from the mass, but from an exorcism. William was probably improperly interpreting the phrase assigned Eudo by the Gembloux writer. Or it is perfectly possible that Eudo used both phrases, one at one time and the other before the council.

[27] See n. 24 above.

[28] This statement is even more curious in view of the fact that Alet ("episcopatus Aletensis") was not made a diocese till 1317.

[29] According to the *Annales Parchenses,* this tower was in the Porta Martis, one of the great gates of the city.

CHAPTER 5

[1] Humbert, *Adversus simoniacos,* I, 3, MGH Lib. de Lit., I. 107.

[2] Gerhoh of Reichersberg, *Liber de simoniacis,* MGH Lib. de Lit., III, 244. See also Yvo of Chartres, epistles 27 and 149, MPL, CLXII, 40, 155.

[3] Gregory the Great, epistle 106, MPL, LXXVII, 1030–1031.

[4] Acts viii:20.

[5] DTC, XIV, 2141 ff.; Atto of Vercelli, *De Pressuris ecclesiasticis,* MPL, CXXXIV, 74.

[6] N. A. Weber, *A History of Simony in the Christian Church* (Baltimore, 1909), p. 3.

[7] Augustin Fliche, *La Réforme grégorienne* (Louvain, 1924–1926), I, 23–24; decree of Nicholas I, Mansi, XV, 440.

[8] Abbo, *Apologeticus,* MPL, CXXXIX, 465 ff.

[9] Ephraim Emerton, *The Correspondence of Pope Gregory VII* (New York, 1932), p. xxx.

[10] November 5, 744, in Michael Tangl, *Die Briefe des heiligen Bonifatius* (Berlin, 1955, reprint of 1916 ed.), p. 105; Ephraim Emerton, *The Letters of Saint Boniface* (New York, 1940), p. 96.

[11] Jean Leclercq, "Simoniaca Heresis," in G. B. Borino, *Studi gregoriani* (Rome, 1947), I, 523–530.

[12] Gerhoh, *Ad Cardinales,* MGH Lib. de Lit., III, 404; Humbert, *op. cit.,* I, 7, MGH Lib. de Lit., I, 111.

[13] Opusculum xxx, MPL, CXLV, 523.

[14] *Adversus simoniacos,* I, 20, MGH Lib. de Lit., I, 134.

[15] *Ibid.,* I, 182, 185.

[16] MPL, CXCII, 908.

[17] Yvo, epistle xxvii, MPL, CLXII, 39–40.

[18] Aquinas, *Summa theologica*, II^a II^{ae} q. 100, art. 1, ad. 1; for Bonaventure and the other scholastics, see P. De Vooght, "La *simoniaca haeresis* selon les auteurs scholastiques," ETL, XXX (1954), 64–80. See also Leclercq, *op. cit.* An example of a modern historian's difficulty in dealing with "simoniac heresy" is that of Paul Fredericq, *Corpus documentorum inquisitionis* (Ghent and The Hague, 1889), where he sometimes includes references to simoniac heresy in his catalog but more often omits them, there being no apparent criterion for his choices.

[19] Fredericq (*op. cit.*, I, 14) cites for January 21, 1102, a bull of Paschal II against heretics led by a mysterious heresiarch named Henry. This Henry is the emperor and the heretics are the simoniac party that he leads.

[20] Jaffé, December 20, 1056.

[21] Jaffé, synod of Rome, February 13–March 24, 1073.

[22] Gerhoh of Reichersberg, *Opusculum de edificio Dei* (1126–1132), MGH Lib. de Lit., III, 142.

[23] I Nicea, canon 4, Hef-L, I, 539.

[24] Jaffé, June, 774.

[25] Hef-L, III, 778.

[26] September 1, 1073, Mansi, XX, 77.

[27] For example, Bruno of Segni, epistle 4, MGH Lib. de Lit., II, 565.

[28] *De simonia et investitura laicorum; quare utraque dicatur haeresis, opusculum iii*, MPL, CLVII, 218.

[29] *Magnum bullarium romanum* (Turin, 1857–1872), I, 468.

[30] Clement II to the church of Bamberg, September 24, 1047, Mansi, XIX, 622; MGH SS, IV, 799; Jaffé, no. 4149.

[31] *Annales Altahenses minores,* MGH SS, XX, 810–812.

[32] Bishops Liétard and Odo of Cambrai were so condemned. See *Gesta Pontificum Cameracensium,* MPL, CXLIX, 1 ff.

[33] Letter of Nicholas I to Emperor Michael, September 25, 860. Mansi, XV, 162; Jaffé, no. 2682.

[34] For example, *Annales Palidenses,* MGH SS, XVI, 70; *Annales Sancti Disibodi,* MGH SS, XVII, 8.

[35] John XII at the council of Rome, February 26, 964; Mansi, XVIII, 471–474. For the others, frequent references: see Mansi, XX, 639 (Wibert); Mansi, XXI, 283 (Burdinus); MGH SS, XVII, 381 (Pierleone).

[36] Goffredo and Tedaldo, archbishops of Milan, held the see against the reform candidate Ato in 1072–1075.

[37] Deusdedit, *Libellus,* MGH Lib. de Lit., II, 332.

[38] Mansi, XX, 1147. This condemnation was remodeled into an oath to which bishops and others suspected of supporting the imperial party were obliged to swear. Otbert, bishop of Liège, submitted such an oath in 1106: "I, Otbert, anathematize all heresies, especially that which is presently disturbing the state of the Church and that falsely teaches that anathema is to be de-

spised and that the bonds that unite the Church are to be set at naught. I condemn and anathematize this heresy with its authors and supporters. I promise obedience to Bishop Paschal of the see of Rome and to his successors, and I swear this by Christ and by the Church, affirming what the holy and universal Church affirms and condemning what it condemns. If I should attempt to deviate in any way from the profession I am now making, I will myself judge that the sentence of condemnation has been laid upon me." (MPL, CXLIII, 234.)

[39] MGH Lib. de Lit., epistle 4, II, 565; epistle 1, II, 563.

[40] Maurice Goguel, "Les Nicolaïtes," RHR, CXV (1937).

[41] See Henry Charles Lea, *History of Sacerdotal Celibacy in the Christian Church* (reprint; New York, 1957), pp. 47–60, for early legislation favoring celibacy.

[42] See Carl Mirbt, *Die Publizistik im Zeitalter Gregors VII* (Leipzig, 1894), pp. 239–342, for the struggle against the uxorati in the eleventh century.

[43] August 1, 1022, Mansi XIX, 343; MGH Legg., II, 561.

[44] Mansi, XIX, 907–910.

[45] Mansi, XXI, 457 ff., 475.

[46] See my article, "Saint Boniface and the Eccentrics," CH, XXXIII (1964).

[47] Peter Damian, opusculum v, MPL, CXLV, 90, 91, 95–96.

[48] Opusculum xxiv, MPL, CXLV, 481.

[49] MPL, CXLIII, 1314-1315; Mansi, XIX, 873–874.

[50] Letter of Gerhoh to Innocent II, 1131, MGH Lib. de Lit., III, 216–221. The term *heresy* applied to simony and nicolaitism is found throughout Gerhoh's work.

[51] Emerton, *Boniface,* p. 83; Tangl, *op. cit.,* p. 86.

[52] Théodore Gousset, *Les Actes de la province ecclésiastique de Reims* (Reims, 1842–1844), I, 535; a letter of Mancion to Fulk of Reims.

[53] Lea, *op. cit.,* pp. 118–121.

[54] *Ibid.,* p. 122; *Acta Pontificum Cameracensium,* MGH SS, VII, c. 29.

[55] Lea, *op. cit.,* pp. 161–163.

[56] Ulrich, *Rescriptum,* MGH Lib. de Lit., I, 254–260; Augustin Fliche, "Ulrich d'Imola. Etude sur l'herésie nicolaïte en Italie au milieu du XIe siècle," RSRUS, II (1922), esp. p. 130.

[57] Lea, *op. cit.,* p. 187.

[58] Mansi, XX, 437–438; Hef-L, V, 111.

[59] MGH Lib. de Lit., II, 436–448.

[60] Lea, *op. cit.,* p. 186.

[61] MGH Lib. de Lit., III, 573–578.

[62] *Ibid.,* III, 588–596.

[63] *Ibid.,* I, 254–260.

[64] *Ibid.,* III, 579–583.

[65] Mansi, XIX, 1037–1040; see also *Vita Alexandri II,* Mansi, XIX, 940.

[66] P. R. L. Brown, "Religious Dissent in the Later Roman Empire: the Case of North Africa," *History,* XLVI (1961), 93.

[67] Epistle of Hincmar of Reims to Odo of Beauvais, MPL, CXXVI, 93–94.
[68] Mansi, XIV, 421 ff.; Hef-L, IV, 43 ff.
[69] R. L. Poole, *Illustrations of the History of Medieval Thought and Learning* (2d ed.; London, 1920), p. 31; letter of Claudius to Abbot Theodemir, Max. Bibl. Vet. Pat., IV, ii, 151.
[70] See Ernst Dümmler, *Auxilius und Vulgarius—Quellen und Forschungen zur Geschichte des Papstthums im Anfänge des zehnten Jahrhunderts* (Leipzig, 1866); John J. Ryan, "Cardinal Humbert of Silva Candida and Auxilius, the 'Anonymous Adversary' of *Liber I Adversus Simoniacos*," MS, XIII (1951).
[71] Mansi, XVIII, 465; Hef-L, IV, 807; MPL, CXXXVI, 905.
[72] Gousset, *op. cit.*, I, 635 ff.; MGH SS, III, 658–686; Hef-L, IV, 844–866; Mansi, XIX, 107. See E. de Certain, "Arnoul, évêque d'Orléans," *Bibliothèque de l'Ecole des Chartes*, XIV (1852), 425–463; M. F. Lot, *Etude sur le règne de Hugues Capet* (Paris, 1903), chap. 2; E. Mourin, "Le Concile de Saint-Basle, récits du Xᵉ siècle," *Mémoires de la société académique de Marne et Loire*, XXIII (1868). See Mansi, XIX, 95, and Hef-L, IV, 841, for the synod of Senlis in 989 or 990.
[73] MGH SS, III, 686.
[74] Hef-L, IV, 874, from Richer, IV, 89, in MGH SS, III, 651.
[75] For example, the defiance of the pope by Willigis of Mainz (Thangmari, *Vita Bernwardi Episcopi*, MGH SS, IV, 754).
[76] Radulf Glaber, *Historiarum libri quinque*, II, 4, ed. Maurice Prou (Paris, 1886), p. 33. See also Augustin Fliche, *La Réforme grégorienne* (Louvain and Paris, 1924–1926), I, 14.
[77] Jaffé, no. 3959.
[78] MPL, CXL, 537 ff.
[79] Mansi, XIX, 423–424; Hef-L, IV, 938.
[80] MPL, CXLIX, 1422.
[81] MGH SS, XI, 672.
[82] Mansi, XX, 437–438; Hef-L, V, 111.
[83] MGH Legg., II, 44 ff.
[84] Jaffé, no. 5030.
[85] Wibert, in Mansi, XX, 600; MGH Lib. de Lit., I, 621–626; Mansi, XX, 599; Roman synod of 1089. Peter Crassus in MGH Lib. de Lit., I, 440; synod of Brixen in Mansi, XX, 547–548; synod of Mainz in MGH SS, V, 442; Wido of Ferrara in MGH SS, XII, 148 ff.
[86] *Ad Heinricum Imperatorem IV Libri VII*, MGH SS, XI, 591 ff.
[87] *Liber de utilitate ecclesiae conservanda*, MGH Lib. de Lit., II, 253–254. Other attacks upon Paschal as a promoter of heresy: letter of Sigebert to Paschal, Mansi, XX, 987–999; *Carmina in simoniam et Romanorum avaritiam*, MGH Lib. de Lit., III, 697–710. A similar attack on Urban II is in *Monachi cuiusdam exulis S. Laurentii de calamitatibus ecclesiae Leodiensis opusculum*, MGH Lib. de Lit., III, 622–641.
[88] Mansi, XXI, 151–152.

CHAPTER 6

[1] This point has been explored by Richard E. Sullivan, "Early Medieval Missionary Activity: A Comparative Study of Eastern and Western Methods," CH, XXIII (1954).

[2] On Iconoclasm, see Edward J. Martin, *A History of the Iconoclastic Controversy* (London, 1930); Louis Bréhier and René Aigrain, *Grégoire le Grand, les états barbares, et la conquête arabe* (Paris, 1947), pp. 431–470; Emile Amann, *L'Eglise au pouvoir des laïques* (Paris, 1947), pp. 107–128, 229–246; Norman H. Baynes, "The Icons before Iconoclasm," HTR, XLIV (1951); C. Bonner, "A Story of Iconoclastic Times," *Byzantion*, XXII (1952); Johannes Kollwitz, "Zur Frühgeschichte der Bilderverehrung," RQCAKG, XLVIII (1953); Ann Freeman, "Theodulf of Orléans and the *Libri Carolini*," *Speculum*, XXXII (1957); Liudpold Wallach, "The Unknown Author of the *Libri Carolini*," in *Didascaliae. Studies in Honor of Anselm M. Albareda* (New York, 1961); Wolfram von den Steinen, "Karl der Grosse und die *Libri Carolini*," NAGADGK, XLIX (1932); De Bruyne, "La Composition des *Libri Carolini*," RBén, XLIV (1932); Gerhart Ladner, "Origins and Significance of the Byzantine Iconoclastic Controversy," MS, II (1940). The concensus now seems to be that Alcuin, rather than Theodulf, was involved in the composition of the *Libri*.

[3] For Claudius, see chap. 2.

[4] On the Filioque, see Amann, *op. cit.*, pp. 173–184, 495. For Western reactions to the question, see Raban Maur, *De Universo*, MPL, CXI, 23–26; Ratramnus of Corbie, *Contra Graecorum opposita Romanam Ecclesiam infamantium libri quattuor*, MPL, CXXI, 223–346; Aeneas of Paris, *Liber adversus Graecos*, in Luc d'Achéry, *Spicilegium* (Paris, 1723), I, 113 f. All these writers of the ninth century assumed the validity of the doctrine of double procession and castigated the Greeks for resisting it.

[5] For survivals of Arianism, see Heinz Löwe, "Ein literarischer Widersacher des Bonifatius. Virgil von Salzburg und die Kosmologie des Aethicus Ister," *Abhandlungen der Akademie der Wissenschaften und der Literatur in Mainz*, no. 11 (1952), p. 60; see also Heinz Löwe in the *Rheinische Vierteljahrblätter*, XV (1950–1951), 105; B. F. Heiler, *Altkirchliche Autonomie und päpstlicher Zentralismus* (Munich, 1941), pp. 165–166; Kurt Schmidt, *Die Bekehrung der Ostgermanen zum Christentum* (Göttingen, 1939), p. 419. Romuald Bauerreis, *Kirchengeschichte Bayerns* (St. Ottilien, 1949), I, 26–28, maintains that there is no firm evidence permitting us to assume the existence of Arian survivals in Bavaria. Ignaz Zilbermayer, *Noricum, Baiern, und Oesterreich* (2d ed.; Horn, 1956), p. 86, also denies that the Bavarians were ever Arians.

[6] For Adoptionism, see Amann, *op. cit.*, pp. 129–152, for a full bibliography. See also Amann, "L'Adoptianisme espagnol du VIIIe siècle," RSRUS, XVI (1936). See Hef-L, III, 1001–1060, for councils dealing with Adoptionism. See H. Diepen,

NOTES

"L'Assumptus Homo à Chalcédoine," RThom, LIII (1953). There were many Frankish reactions: Paulinus of Aquileia, *Libellus sacrosyllabus contra Elipandum*, MPL, XCIX, 151–182; Paulinus, *Contra Felicem Urgellitanum libri tres*, MPL, XCIX, 343–468; Agobard of Lyon, *Liber adversus Felicem Urgellensem*, MPL, CIV, 29–70; Alcuin, letter to Felix, MPL, C, 144; Alcuin, *Scripta contra Felicem Urgellitanum et Elipandum Toletanum*, MPL, CI, 83–302; Alcuin (per Benedict of Aniane), *Adversus Felicis haeresim*, MPL, CIII, 1399–1411; *Epistolae variae dogmaticae ad pleniorem Adoptianismi historiam pertinentes*, MPL, CI, 1313–1359. For a letter of Charlemagne to the Spanish bishops, see Mansi, XIII, 899–906. Further: Alcuin, *De Fide Sanctae Trinitatis*, MPL, CI, 1–58, and another treatise by Alcuin in MPL, CI, 243–300.

[7] See especially A. M. Landgraf, *Dogmengeschichte der Frühscholastik* (Regensburg, 1952——).

[8] On Vergil, see Francis S. Betten, *St. Boniface and St. Virgil* (Washington, 1927); Philippe Gilbert, "Le Pape Zacharie et les antipodes," *Revue des questions scientifiques*, XII (1882); Montague Rhodes James in the *Cambridge Medieval History*, III, 513; Hermann Krabbo, "Bischof Virgil und seine kosmologische Ideen," *Mittheilungen des Instituts für oesterreichische Geschichtsforschung*, XXIV (1903); J.-R. Laurin, "Saint Boniface, Virgile, et le pape Zacharie," *Revue de l'Université d'Ottawa*, XXV (1955); Heinz Löwe, "Ein literarischer Widersacher"; G. Metlabe, "Saint Vergil the Geometer," *American Ecclesiastical Review*, LXIII (1920); Hermann Nottarp, *Die Bistumserrichtung in Deutschland im achten Jahrhundert* (Stuttgart, 1920), pp. 55–69; H. van der Linden, "Virgile de Salzbourg et les théories cosmologiques au huitième siècle," *Bulletin de la classe des lettres de l'Académie Royale de Belgique* (1914); Zilbermayer, *op. cit.*, pp. 185–192; M. Draak, "Virgil of Salzburg versus 'Aethicus Ister,'" *Opstellen aangeboden aan Prof. Dr. D. Th. Enklaar* (Groningen, 1959).

[9] Michael Tangl, *Die Briefe des heiligen Bonifatius und Lullius* (Berlin, 1916), p. 177; Ephraim Emerton, *The Letters of Saint Boniface* (New York, 1940), p. 146.

[10] Mansi, XII, 661; Hef-L, III, 950–951. The ultimate source for Volvic is the *Vita tertia Sancti Austremonii* in the AASS, November, I, pt. 1, p. 76.

[11] Letter of Hadrian I to Charlemagne, Mansi, XII, 793–794; Jaffé, no. 2472.

[12] Luc d'Achéry *Spicilegium* (Paris, 1723), I, 500.

[13] There are many works on Gottschalk. Among the more recent are Emmanuel Aegerter, "Gottschalk et le problème de prédestination au IX⁹ siècle," RHR, CXV (1937); Germain Morin, "Gottschalk retrouvé, RBén, XLIII (1931); Emile Amann, *L'Epoque carolingienne*, pp. 320–344; Hef-L, IV, 137–186. Works on Hincmar also deal with Gottschalk. The controversy produced numerous polemical books and letters, including two books by Amolo of Lyon, addressed to Gottschalk, MPL, CXVI, 97–106 (repeated under other names, CXIX, 95–102, and partly in CXXV, 57–59); Amolo, preface to a collection of Augustine, MPL, CXVI, 105–108; Eriugena, *De Praedestinatione*, MPL, CXXII, 347–440; Florus

of Lyon, *Sermo de Praedestinatione,* MPL, CXIX, 95-102; Florus, *Ecclesiae Lugdunensis adversus].* *Scoti erroneas definitiones liber,* MPL, CXIX, 101-250; Hincmar, *De Praedestinatione contra Gothescalcum,* MPL, CXXV, 49-56; Hincmar, *De Praedestinatione Dei,* MPL, CXXV, 65-474; Hincmar, *Ad reclusos et simplices,* ZFK, X (1889), 258-309; Hincmar, letters 2, 10, 13, MPL, CXXVI, 25, 71, 92; Servatus Lupus, *Liber de tribus quaestionibus,* MPL, CXIX, 621-648; Nicholas I to Prudentius of Troyes, Jaffé, no. 2680; Prudentius, *De Praedestinationem contra Erigenam,* MPL, CXV, 1009-1364; Raban Maur, letters 4, 5, 6, MPL, CXII, 1518, 1530, 1553; Ratramnus, *De Praedestinatione Dei, ad Carolum Calvum libri duo,* MPL, CXXI, 985-1068. Gottschalk's own works are in MPL, CXXI, 347-372, consisting of *Confessio, Confessio Prolixior,* and *Epistola Godeschalchi ad Ratramnum.*

¹⁴ Synod of Mainz, 848—Mansi, XIV, 913-915, Hef-L, IV, 137-149; synod of Quierzy, 849—Mansi, XIV, 919-921 (Hef-L [IV, 153] believe that the sentence against Gottschalk here as reported by Mansi is a later forgery); synod of Paris, 849—Mansi, XIV, 923-924, Hef-L, IV, 161-166; synod of Quierzy, 853—Mansi, XIV, 975, Hef-L, IV, 197-199; synod of Sens or Paris, 853—Mansi, XIV, 975, Hef-L, IV, 199-200; synod of Valence, 855—Mansi, XV, 1 ff., Hef-L, IV, 204-210; synod of Langres, 859—Mansi, XV, 546, Hef-L, IV, 216-220; synod of Savonnières, 859—Mansi, XV, 529, Hef-L, IV, 217-220; synod of Tuzey, 860—Mansi, XV, 557-590, Hef-L, IV, 227-232.

¹⁵ Eriugena's own works are *De Divisione Naturae,* written 865-870, in MPL, CXXII, 439-1022, and *Liber de Praedestinatione,* written 851, in MPL, CXXII, 347-440. Some recent works on Eriugena are C. Albanese, *Il Pensiero di Giovanni Erigena* (Messina, 1929); P. Baldini, "Scoto Erigena e la filosofia religiosa del IX⁰ secolo," *Rivista storica e critica delle scienze teologiche* (1906); Henry Bett, *Johannes Scotus Erigena* (Cambridge [Eng.], 1925); Giulio Bonafede, *Saggi sul pensiero di Scoto Erigena* (Palermo, 1950); Maieul Cappuyns, *Jean Scot Erigène. Sa vie, son oeuvre, sa pensée* (Louvain-Paris, 1933); Mario Dal Pra, *Scoto Eriugena* (Milan, 1951); Hermann Dörries, *Zur Geschichte der Mystik. Erigena und der Neoplatonismus* (Tübingen, 1925); Tullio Gregory, *Giovanni Scoto Erigena: Tre Studi* (Florence, 1963); Max Laistner *Thought and Letters in Western Europe, 500-900* (2d ed.; New York, 1957); W. N. Pittenger, "The Christian Philosophy of Eriugena," JR, XXIV (1944); Artur Schneider, *Die Erkenntnislehre des Johannes Erigena* (Berlin and Leipzig, 1921-1923). W. Turner, "Was John the Scot a Heretic?" *Irish Theological Quarterly,* V (1910), is not very helpful.

¹⁶ The most important works of Amalarius are the *De ecclesiasticis officiis libri quattuor,* MPL, CV, 985-1242; *De ordine antiphonarii,* MPL, CV, 1243-1316; and the letters, in MPL, CV, 1333-1340, and XCIX, 885-902. The debate as to whether there were two Amalarii (one at Trier and one at Metz) has long since been resolved in favor of the unitary position. The leading tracts against Amalarius are Agobard, *Contra libros quattuor Amalarii abbatis,* MPL, CIV, 339-350; the letter of Florus to the synod of Thionville, MPL, CXIX, 94-96

(see also Mansi, XIV, 657–664); Florus' third letter (attributed to Rémy of Lyon), MPL, CXXI, 1054–1055. For Amalarius' life and a bibliography, see Allen Cabaniss, *Amalarius of Metz* (Amsterdam, 1954). See also Conrad Albrecht Ley, *Kölnische Kirchengeschichte* (2d ed.; Essen, 1917), for possible influence of Amalarius. For further reference see Etienne Gilson, *History of Christian Philosophy in the Middle Ages* (New York, 1955), pp. 609–610.

[17] MPL, CV, 1336.

[18] Amann, *L'Eglise*, pp. 380–383; Mansi, XV, 649–660; Hef-L, IV, 312.

[19] Cesare Cantù, *Gli Eretichi d'Italia* (Turin, 1865), p. 75.

[20] AASS, June, II, 87 ff., 593; July, IV, 466. See Willem Moll, *Kerkgeschiedenis van Nederland vöor de Hervorming* (Utrecht, 1864–1871), I, 269.

[21] Rather, *Sermo II de Quadragesima*, MPL, CXXXVI, 706. See also Sigebert of Gembloux, *Chronicon*, MGH SS, VI, 348. The date is 946–965.

[22] Othloh, *Vita Sancti Wolfkangi*, MGH SS, IV, 537–538. Othloh wrote between 1037 and 1052. The place of the story in the text and the reference to "caesar otto," who must be Otto II, places the date of the alleged incident around 973–975. Its historicity is questionable.

[23] See chap. 7.

[24] Some of the better or more recent works among the vast body of material dealing with Berengar are O. Capitani, "Studi per Berengario di Tours," BISIMEAM, LXIX (1957); O. Capitani, "Per la storia dei rapporti tra Gregorio VII e Berengario di Tours," *Studi Gregoriani*, VI, 99–145; Jean Ebersholt, "Essai sur Bérenger de Tours et la controverse sacramentaire au XIᵉ siècle," RHR, XLVIII (1903); Carl Erdmann, "Gregor VII und Berengar von Tours," *Quellen und Forschungen aus italienischen Archiven und Bibliotheken*, XXVIII (1937–1938); J. R. Geiselmann, "Ein neuentdecktes Werk Berengars von Tours über das Abendmahl," TQS, CXVIII (1937); Raoul Heurtevent, *Durand de Troarn et les origines de l'hérésie bérengarienne* (Paris, 1912); Ludwig Hödl, "Die Confessio Berengarii von 1059," *Scholastik*, XXXVII (1962); Gerhart Ladner, *Theologie und Politik vor dem Investiturstreit* (Baden near Vienna, 1936); Allan J. Macdonald, *Berengar and the Reform of Sacramental Doctrine* (London, 1930), "Berengar and the Virgin Birth," JTS, XXX (1929), and "Berengariana," JTS, XXXIII (1932); P. Meyvaert, "Bérenger de Tours contre Albéric de Mont-Cassin," RBén, LXX (1960); Germain Morin, "Bérenger contre Bérenger. Un document inédit des luttes théologiques du XIᵉ siècle," RTAM, IV (1932); Charles E. Sheedy, *The Eucharistic Controversy of the Twelfth Century against the Background of Pre-Scholastic Theology* (Washington, 1946); R. W. Southern, "Lanfranc of Bec and Berengar of Tours," *Studies in Medieval History Presented to F. M. Powicke* (Oxford, 1948). see also Gilson, *op. cit.*, pp. 615–616.

[25] Macdonald, *Berengar and the Reform of Sacramental Doctrine*, p. 154.

[26] *Ibid.*, p. 120.

[27] *Ibid.*, p. 82.

[28] See my article, "Les Cathares de 1048–1054 à Liège," BSAHDL, XLIV (1961). I have since decided that these heretics were Reformists.

[29] Letter of Gozechin, Bouquet, XI, 500 ff.; Adelman, *Epistola ad Berengarium*, MPL, CXLIII, 1289–1296. The letter of Adelman, a native of Liège, adjures Berengar to forsake his heresy. Adelman was therefore not implicated in the heresy, nor does he speak of an infection of the schools of Liège. The uncertainty of the date makes it likely that the letter was written after Adelman became bishop of Brescia in 1048 and therefore it may have nothing to do with Liège at all. The letter of Gozechin has been dated by Ludwig Schwabe, *Studien zur Geschichte des zweiten Abendmahlstreites* (Cöthen, 1886), pp. 22 ff., as about 1069. I prefer the date assigned by the first editor, Mabillon, since the letter speaks of the recent migration "from these shadows" to the "true realm of light" of the emperor Henry and Archbishop Liutpold of Mainz. Since Henry III died in 1056 and Liutpold in 1059, the letter must date from about 1060.

[30] David Knowles, *The Evolution of Medieval Thought* (London, 1962), p. 111.

[31] Synod of Soissons, Mansi, XX, 741–744, Hef-L, V, 354–367. A report of the condemnation also appears in MGH SS, XVII, 15.

[32] Some of the better or more recent works on Gilbert are Auguste Berthaud, *Gilbert de la Porrée, évêque de Poitiers, et sa philosophie 1070–1154* (Poitiers, 1892); François J. Picavet, *Roscelin philosophe et théologien d'après la légende et d'après l'histoire* (Paris, 1911); Suitbert Gammersbach, *Gilbert von Poitiers* (Cologne, 1959); N. M. Haring, "The Case of Gilbert de la Porrée, 1142–1154," MS, XIII (1951); André Hayen, "Le Concile de Reims et l'erreur théologique de Gilbert de la Porrée," *Archives d'histoire doctrinale et littéraire du moyen âge* (1935–1936); P. H. Vicaire, "Les Porrétains et l'avicennisme avant 1215," RSPT, XXVI (1937); A. L. Lilley, "A Christological Controversy of the Twelfth Century," JTS, XXXIX (1938); A. M. Landgraf, "Untersuchungen zu der Eigenlehre Gilberts de la Porrée," ZKT (1930). Gilbert's own extant works are the *Liber de sex principiis* and commentaries on Boethius. The commentaries are found in MPL, LXIV, 1353–1412. The *Liber* is found in MPL, CLXXXVIII, 1257–1270, but a better edition is that of A. Heysse and D. van den Eynde (Münster, 1953). See Gilson, *op. cit.*, pp. 620–621, for further references. See also Jean Leclercq, "Textes sur St. Bernard et Gilbert de la Porrée," MS, XIV (1952).

[33] Mansi, XXI, 711–735; Hef-L, V, 812 ff.

[34] See P. H. Vicaire, *op. cit.*

[35] The bibliography on Abelard is enormous. One catalogue of the older books is in Hef-L, V, 593–598. A few of the best and most recent works are J. Ramsey McCallum, *Abelard's Christian Theology* (Oxford, 1948); G. Delagneau, "Le Concile de Sens de 1140. Abélard et Saint Bernard," *Revue apologétique*, LII (1931); M. L. N. d'Oliver, "Quelques lettres de Saint Bernard avant et après le concile de Sens," *Mélanges Saint Bernard* (Dijon, 1954); Etienne Gilson, *Héloïse et Abélard* (Paris, 1938); Raymond Klibansky, "Peter Abailard and Bernard of Clairvaux," MRS, V (1961); Jean Rivière, "Les capitula d'Abélard condamnés au concile de Sens," RTAM, V (1933); J. K. Sikes, *Peter Abelard* (Cambridge, 1932); J. Cottiaux, "La Conception de la théologie chez Abélard," RHE, XXXVIII

(1932); Arno Borst, "Abaelard und Bernhard," *Historische Zeitschrift,* CLXXXVI (1958); John Updike, "Faith in Search of Understanding," *New Yorker,* XXXIX, no. 34 (1963). Abelard's errors were inadequately summarized by Portalié in DTC, I, 45–48. I await with great expectations the completion of a dissertation on Abelard's heresies by Edward F. Little. Excellent work is currently being done on the sources by Heinrich Ostlender, Arthur Landgraf, and Frs. Buytaert and Van den Eynde, among others.

[36] Converts to Christianity from Judaism were also rebels in their way, but this involved the acceptance, rather than the rejection, of the prevalent doctrines of medieval society. It may be objected that it is arbitrary to define Western society in the Middle Ages as Christian, but since political power and social sanctions, as well as great numerical superiority, were on the side of the Christians, this arbitrary definition seems permissible for the purposes of this study.

[37] See the article, "Proselytes," in the *Jewish Encyclopedia;* William G. Braude, *Jewish Proselytizing in the First Five Centuries of the Common Era* (Providence, 1940); Guido Kisch, *The Jews in Medieval Germany* (Chicago, 1949); Solomon Katz, *The Jews in the Visigothic and Frankish Kingdoms of Spain and Gaul* (Cambridge [Mass.], 1937); Jacob Katz, *Exclusiveness and Tolerance: Studies in Jewish-Gentile Relations in Medieval and Modern Times* (Oxford, 1961), pp. 67–81.

[38] Mansi, XIV, 607–626; Jacob S. Raisin, *Gentile Reactions to Jewish Ideals* (New York, 1953), p. 442.

[39] Raisin, *op. cit.,* p. 445. Prudentius Trecensis, *Annales,* ad ann. 839, MGH SS, I, 433.

[40] Alpertus of Metz, *De Diversitate Temporum,* I, 7; MGH SS, IV, 704, 720–723. Alpertus was a contemporary of the event, writing in the years 1012–1018.

[41] Cecil Roth, *A History of the Jews in England* (Oxford, 1949), p. 41; Jacob Katz, *op. cit.,* pp. 78–79.

[42] Beryl Smalley, *The Study of the Bible in the Middle Ages* (2d ed.; Oxford, 1952), pp. 361–362.

[43] *Gesta Treverorum,* MGH SS, VIII, 190–192; James Parkes, *The Jew in the Medieval Community* (London, 1938), pp. 37–39.

[44] Katz, *op. cit.,* p. 76.

[45] Roth, *op. cit.,* p. 10.

[46] Fulbert's letter to counts Waleran and Walter, 1015. This is Fulbert's epistle 24 in Bouquet X, 452, or MPL, CXLI, 211.

[47] Eudo and Tanchelm were not Millennarians in any sense, despite the arguments of Norman Cohn, *The Pursuit of the Millennium* (London, 1957), pp. 33–40.

[48] MPL, CXXXIX, 471.

[49] Trithemius, *Annales Hirsaugenses,* ad ann. 960.

[50] MPL, CXXXIX, 471. Christian Pfister, *Etudes sur le règne de Robert le*

Pieux (Paris, 1885), pp. 321–322, explains why this should be dated 970 and not 992.

CHAPTER 7

[1] Mab. Vet. Analecta, pp. 74–75.

[2] Mansi, XII, 861.

[3] For Boniface, see K. D. Schmidt, "Boniface, Founder of Spiritual Unity in the West," CQR, CLIV (1953); Wilhelm Levison, *England and the Continent in the Eighth Century* (Oxford, 1946); Theodor Schieffer, *Winfred-Bonifatius und die christliche Grundlegung Europas* (Freiburg, 1954); Joseph Bernhart, *Bonifatius, Apostel der Deutschen* (Paderborn, 1950); *Sankt Bonifatius, Gedenkgabe zum 1200 Todestag* (Fulda, 1954); George W. Greenaway, *St. Boniface* (London, 1955); Joseph Lortz, *Bonifatius und die Grundlegung des Abendlandes* (Wiesbaden, 1954).

The best edition of the lives of Boniface is edited by Wilhelm Levison in MGH SS rer. Germ. Willibald's *Life of Boniface* is a nearly contemporary source, having been written shortly after the saint's death. Other lives are those of Othloh of St. Emmaram, Radbod, the Anonymous of Mainz, and the *Passio Sancti Bonifacii*. There are some translations in C. H. Talbot, *Anglo-Saxon Missionaries in Germany* (New York, 1954).

The best edition of the letters is Michael Tangl, *Die Briefe des heiligen Bonifatius und Lullius* (Berlin, 1916), of which the second edition (1955) is merely an offset of the first. Forty-eight of the letters appear in Talbot, in translation. Ephraim Emerton, *The Letters of Saint Boniface* (New York, 1940), gives a translation of the letters with a good introduction. See also A. C. Nielson, *De Brieven van Bonifatius* (Leyden, 1954).

[4] Edmond Martène and Ursin Durand, *Thesaurus novus anecdotorum* (Paris, 1717), I, 15–17. For the legislation on heresy in this period, see Carlo de Clercq, *La Législation franque de Clovis à Charlemagne* (Louvain, 1936).

[5] MGH Legg., I, 57; De Clercq, *op. cit.,* pp. 171–176.

[6] Mansi, XIII, 919–926.

[7] *Poeta Saxo* in Duchesne, II, 156, 157–158, 171, 173–174, 180–181.

[8] Mansi, XII, 796.

[9] *Ibid.,* pp. 280, 282.

[10] Tangl, *op. cit.,* p. 30; Emerton, *op. cit.,* p. 42.

[11] Willibald, *op. cit.,* chap. 8. Willibald gives no date, but we know that Hukbert ruled from 725 to 735/6 (see Schieffer, *op. cit.,* pp. 128, 139, 160, 169) and that Boniface made a missionary visit to Bavaria in 733–735 (*ibid.,* p. 169).

[12] Willibald's account (*op. cit.,* chap. 9) is confused. He speaks of the reorganization of the Bavarian diocese in 739 as if this were part of Boniface's program to crush the evils occasioned by the reign of Odilo; but Odilo himself invited Boniface to come at that time, and the hostility between the two dates

only from two years later. Moreover, Willibald would have us believe that Boniface secured the submission of Odilo on this occasion; again, the fact is that Odilo never submitted and that the reconciliation between Bavaria and the Frankish Church was the result of Pepin's show of force rather than of Boniface's persuasiveness.

¹³ Mansi, XII, 281.

¹⁴ Jaffé, no. 2271.

¹⁵ Mansi, XII, 365; Hef-L, III, 815 ff.

¹⁶ Tangl, *op. cit.*, p. 91; Emerton, *op. cit.*, p. 87.

¹⁷ Tangl, *op. cit.*, p. 120; Emerton, *op. cit.*, p. 107.

¹⁸ Tangl, *op. cit.*, p. 172; Emerton, *op. cit.*, p. 142.

¹⁹ Tangl, *op cit.*, p. 191; Emerton, *op. cit.*, p. 157.

²⁰ November 4, 751. Tangl, *op. cit.*, p. 194; Emerton, *op. cit.*, p. 159.

²¹ Cuthbert, in Tangl, *op. cit.*, p. 238; Emerton, *op. cit.*, p. 183. Othloh in Phillip Jaffé, *Bibliotheca rerum germanicarum* (Berlin, 1864), III, 484, 498. Liudger in MGH SS, XV, 70–71. Paul I to Pepin III in Mansi, XII, 597, 643–644. Canons of Angilramnus in MPL, XCVI, 1049. Willibald, *op. cit.*, chap. 10. Eigil in Talbot, *op. cit.*, p. 181.

²² Willibald, *op. cit.*, chap. 6.

²³ *Ibid.*, chap. 7.

²⁴ MPL, C, 297.

²⁵ MPL, CI, 666.

²⁶ *Anglo-Saxon England* (Oxford, 1947), p. 140. See H. J. Schmitz, *Die Buss-bücher und die Bussdisciplin der Kirche* (Mainz, 1883), II, 545–580; A. W. Haddan and William Stubbs, *Councils and Ecclesiastical Documents Relating to Great Britain and Ireland* (Oxford, 1869–1878), III, 173–204; John T. McNeill and Helena M. Gamer, *Medieval Handbooks of Penance* (New York, 1938), pp. 179–189.

²⁷ "Capitula selecta canonum Hibernensium," in Luc d'Achéry, *Spicilegium* (Paris, 1723), I, 500.

²⁸ McNeill and Gamer, *op. cit.*, p. 143.

²⁹ MGH Legg., I, 99.

³⁰ *De clericorum institutione,* MPL, CVII, 371–378.

³¹ *De universo,* IV, 8–10, in MPL, CXI, 94–104.

³² *Vita Walae,* in MGH SS, II, 550.

³³ MGH Legg., I, 108. Especially capp. I, 16, 66, 73.

³⁴ Jaffé, no. 3496.

³⁵ Flodoard *Annales,* ed. Philippe Lauer (Paris, 1905), IV, 2.

³⁶ Mansi, XV, 505.

³⁷ *Ibid.*, p. 824.

³⁸ *Annales Xantenses,* MGH SS, II, 226.

³⁹ Mansi, XVIII, 142.

⁴⁰ *Vita Frederici* (bishop of Utrecht), AASS, July, IV, 466.

[41] See Cesare Cantù, *Gli Eretici d'Italia* (Turin, 1865), p. 75.

[42] Mansi, XVII, 220; Jaffé, no. 3384.

[43] Mansi, XVII, 133; MPL, CXXVI, 850.

[44] Sermo II, in MPL, CXXXVI, 708.

[45] D'Achéry, *op. cit.*, I, 407.

[46] Mansi, XIX, 85; MPL, CXXXVII, 830–831; Jaffé, no. 3831.

[47] Mansi, XIX, 49–52.

[48] Thietmar of Merseburg, *Chronicon*, III, 10, in MGH SS, III, 764.

[49] This poem is inserted in Gilles d'Orval's *Gesta episcoporum Leodiensium,* but Godefroid Kurth (*Notger de Liège et la civilisation au Xe siècle* [Liège, 1905]) took the poem and its context out of Gilles and treated them as an eleventh-century life of Notger. The edition of the original in MGH SS, XXV, in which the poem is found on page 62, is the best. Jean d'Outremeuse also gives the poem in *Ly Myreur des Histors* (Brussels, 1864–1887), IV, 181. Jean, however, wrote in the fourteenth century and almost certainly took his text from Gilles d'Orval, as there is no difference in the text of the poem as given by Gilles and by Jean. Kurth, in his appendix to *Notger,* revised the portion of Heller's edition of Gilles that contains the Life of Notger.

In developing his argument for treating the Life as a separate source, Kurth established the high reliability of the text. The author was, according to Kurth, a Liégeois living some time after the great bishop's death. The date of the Life must, however, be before 1096, because the author mentions a gold cross that was melted down by Otbert at that date. The author is balanced and restrained, and there is every reason to credit his reliability. Yet since the Life dates from sixty to eighty years after Notger's death, it cannot be considered a primary source. But the poem, which is the part of the Life concerning heresy, is, Kurth maintained, more ancient. The author of the Life introduces the poem with the words, "unde scriptum est," and would scarcely have distributed it in bits and pieces throughout the text if he were himself the proud poet. The poem must therefore have been written before the Life, probably a good deal before. Indeed, it has all the markings of a funeral verse or epitaph. Such verses were commonly composed at the burial of a prelate, and since Notger's epitaph is unknown in any other form, this poem may well be his missing valediction. At any rate, it is clear that it is nearly contemporary with the death of the bishop and therefore valuable as a primary source.

[50] Folcuin, *Gesta Abbatum Lobiensium,* MGH SS, IV, 58–59.

[51] Théodore Gousset, *Les Actes de la province ecclésiastique de Reims* (Reims, 1842–1844), I, 563 ff.

[52] Bouquet, X, 333.

[53] *Chronicon Sancti Bavonis,* ad ann. 969, in *Recueil des chroniques de Flandre* (Brussels, 1837–1865), I, 527.

[54] Abbo, *Apologeticus ad Hugonem et Rodbertum Reges Francorum,* MPL, CXXXIX, 462.

⁵⁵ Mansi, XIX, 200–201; Jaffé, no. 3878.

⁵⁶ Mansi, XX, 619; Jaffé, no. 5149.

⁵⁷ Mansi, XX, 164; MPL, CXLVIII, 402; Jaffé, no. 4928.

⁵⁸ Mansi, XX, 310; MPL, CXLVIII, 570; Jaffé, no. 5171.

⁵⁹ June 6, 1080. Mansi, XX, 311; MPL, CXLVIII, 571; Erich Caspar, *Das Register Gregors VII* (Berlin, 1920), II, 510–514; Jaffé, no. 5172.

⁶⁰ Mansi, XX, 400.

⁶¹ MGH SS, V, 428. It probably means only that Gregory was hostile to heretics.

⁶² Humbert, *Adversus simoniacos*, II, xi-xiii, in MGH Lib. de Lit., I, 151–153.

⁶³ Christian Pfister, *Etudes sur le règne de Robert le Pieux* (Paris, 1885), p. 36 n. 5. This has been interpreted by Karl Erdmann, *Die Entstehung des Kreuzzugsgedankes* (Stuttgart, 1935).

⁶⁴ Misdated by Mansi, XIX, 751–754, as 1050. See Hef-L, IV, 993.

⁶⁵ Canon 13, in Mansi, XIX, 849; Hef-L, IV, 1123.

⁶⁶ MGH SS, XIII, 90.

⁶⁷ Epistle 24 of Fulbert of Chartres, in Bouquet, X, 452, and MPL, CXLI, 211. MPL incorrectly reads *Archiepiscopus Cenomanensis* (Archbishop of Le Mans).

⁶⁸ Mansi, XIX, 737, 742; Bouquet, XI, 523; Paul Fredericq, *Corpus documentorum inquisitionis* (Ghent and The Hague, 1889), I, 8.

⁶⁹ MPL, CXLIII, 1346; Bouquet, XI, 494; Ilarino da Milano, "Le Eresie popolari del secolo XI," in G. B. Borino, *Studi gregoriani*, II (1948), 78; Jaffé, no. 4442. Jaffé is no more precise in the dating than 1059–1061, the years of Nicholas II's reign.

⁷⁰ Radulf Glaber, *Historiarum libri quinque*, I, 1, ed. Maurice Prou (Paris, 1886), pp. 2–4. See S. Giet, "La divine quaternité de Raoul Glabre," RMAL, V (1949).

⁷¹ The only complete edition is that of Ernst Voigt, *Egberts von Lüttich "Fecunda Ratis"* (Halle, 1889).

⁷² In his introduction to the *Fecunda Ratis*, of which *De Malis Francigenis* is a part, Voigt (*op. cit.*) shows that the author was the Liégeois scholar Egbert. Kurth agreed with these conclusions in his "Egberts von Lüttich *Fecunda Ratis*," MA, III (1890), 78–80. Voigt's precise dating of the poem as between 1022 and 1024 is not convincing. The fact that the biography of Adalbold, known to have been written between 1018 and 1022, does not mention the work is no evidence that it had yet to be written; the tributes men of letters pay to public figures may go unnoticed more often than other literary men like to think. Further, Voigt's precision in saying that the heresy referred to must be that of Orléans in 1022 and that the poem must therefore date from 1022 or 1023 is unjustified, as we have shown that there was other heresy aplenty at the beginning of the century. All one can safely say is that the *Fecunda Ratis* was written by a Liégeois, Egbert, and presented to Bishop Adalbold between 1010 and 1024, and that it must therefore have been written either in this period or shortly before.

⁷³ The objection of Jeanne-Marie Noiroux, "Les Deux premiers documents

concernant l'hérésie aux Pays-Bas," RHE, XLIX (1954), 852–853, that the poem merely describes the appearance of heretics in France, is an unlikely reading of the text, which says "As storms usually come from the west, so *from that direction* has recently *arrived* a terrible heresy. . . ." For the Latin text, see Voigt, *op. cit.*, p. 205.

[74] Hermann Theloe, *Die Ketzerverfolgung im 11. und 12. Jahrhundert* (Berlin and Leipzig, 1913).

[75] Mansi, XIX, 672–673.

[76] MPL, CLI, 500; Jaffé, no. 5694.

[77] Mansi, XX, 714; Jaffé, no. 5745.

[78] Mansi, XX, 660; MPL, CLI, 529; Jaffé, no. 5743.

[79] Adam of Bremen, *Gesta Hammaburgensis ecclesiae pontificum*, III, 75, in MPL, CXLVI, 568–569; translated by Francis J. Tschan (New York, 1959), pp. 125–126. This Osmund is known to have gone to England and to have died in the monastery of Ely in 1070. See *Historia Eliensis*, II, 42, ed. Thomas Gale, *Historicae Britannicae . . . Scriptores* (Oxford, 1691), XV, 514. Adam's reliability as a source is open to question, and it is impossible to check him, as there are no other adequate sources for eleventh-century Sweden. The report in Adam's next chapter that a son of the king had visited the country of the Amazons does not fill us with confidence in the author. Berndt Gustafson, "Osmundus episcopus e Suedia," *Kyrkohistorisk Årsskrift*, LIX (1959), explains the vehemence of Adam's attack by the political implications of the tiff between Osmund and Bremen.

[80] To cite a few of the numerous sources from the early Middle Ages: Saint Agobard of Lyon, *Liber contra insulsam vulgi opinionem de grandine et tonitruis*, MPL, CIV, 147–148; capitulary at Aachen (802), cap. 21, MGH Legg., I, 99; capitulary of Ansegisius (827), capp. I, 16, 73, MGH Legg., I, 276, 281.

[81] Some of the more recent books on magic and witchcraft are Richard Bernheimer, *Wild Men in the Middle Ages* (Cambridge [Mass.], 1952); Maurice Bouisson, *Magic: Its History and Principal Rites* (New York, 1961); G. H. G. Grattan and Charles Singer, *Anglo-Saxon Magic and Medicine* (London, 1952); Pennethorne Hughes, *Witchcraft* (London, 1952); Bronislaw Malinowski, *Magic, Science, and Religion* (Boston, 1948); Henry Charles Lea, *Materials toward a History of Witchcraft*, ed. Arthur C. Howland (New York, 1957); Margaret Murray, *The Witch Cult in Western Europe* (Oxford, 1921), *The God of the Witches* (London, 1952), and *The Divine King in England* (London, 1954); Elliot Rose, *A Razor for a Goat: A Discussion of Certain Problems in the History of Witchcraft* (Toronto, 1962); Montague Summers, *The History of Witchcraft*, (2d ed.; New York, 1956); Lynn Thorndike, *A History of Magic and Experimental Science* (New York, 1923–1958); Hutton Webster, *Magic: A Sociological Study* (Stanford, 1948): Charles Williams, *Witchcraft* (London, 1941); Hugh Ross Williamson, *The Arrow and the Sword* (London, 1947). I must express my own opinion that the books of the Murray-Williamson school are largely nonsense.

[62] Notably by Alexander J. Denomy, *The Heresy of Courtly Love* (New York, 1947). See my article, "Courtly Love as Religious Dissent," CHR, LI (1965).

CHAPTER 8

[1] Simone Pétrement, *Le Dualisme chez Platon, les gnostiques, et les manichéens* (Paris, 1947), pp. 35 ff., offers a number of "myths and formulas of dualism in Plato": (1) God is not the cause of all things; (2) there is an "opposite of the good"; (3) there is another "God"; (4) God is absent in matter; (5) opposition between soul and body; (6) opposition between the limited and the unlimited. The predisposing factor (p. 32) was Plato's feeling of being "between two worlds." Pythagoras spoke of a large number of opposites (p. 121): the limit and the limitless, the divisible and the indivisible, the one and the many, right and left, male and female, repose and stationary, angular and curved, light and dark, good and evil, equal and inequal.

[2] Evelyn Underhill, *Mysticism* (New York, 1911), pp. 3, 106, 169, 333.

[3] Pétrement, *op. cit.,* p. 330.

[4] See my article, "Interpretations of the Origins of Medieval Heresy," MS, XXV (1963), and Daniel Walther, "A Survey of Recent Research on the Albigensian Cathari," CH, XXXIV (1965).

[5] I adopt this spelling instead of "Cathar." Strictly speaking, a Cathar (Catharus) is one of the perfecti, the elite of the Catharist sect, whereas the term "Catharist" may apply to any adherent of those doctrines.

[6] Antoine Dondaine: "Nouvelles sources de l'histoire doctrinale du néomanichéisme au moyen âge, RSPT, XXVIII (1939); "L'Hiérarchie cathare en Italie," AFP, XIX (1949), and XX (1950); and "L'Origine de l'hérésie médiévale," RSCI, VI (1952).

[7] Raffaello Morghen: *Medioevo Cristiano* (Bari, 1951); "Il Cosidetto neomanicheismo occidentale del secolo XI," in *Convegno di scienze morali, storiche, e filologiche: Oriente ed Occidente nel medio evo* (Rome, 1957); and "Movimenti religiosi popolari nel periodo della riforma della chiesa," *Relazioni del X congresso internazionale di scienze storiche*, III (Florence, 1955).

[8] Arno Borst, *Die Katharer* (Stuttgart, 1953), realized that true dualism does not appear till the 1140's. I had begun to suspect this while working with the documents of the eleventh century and, after reading Morghen, became convinced. Morghen was the first to enunciate the conclusion firmly; I mention my own study to give the argument further weight by indicating that independent observations on my part led to the same conclusion. The position was taken by Henri-Charles Puech in his "Catharisme médiévale et Bogomilisme," *Convegno di scienze morali, storiche, e filologiche, 1956* (Rome, 1957), pp. 56–84.

[9] Edmond Broeckx, *Le Catharisme* (Hoogstraten, 1916), pp. 16–18; Mansi, XX, 425; Johannes Lindeboom, *Stiefkinderen van het Christendom* (The Hague, 1929), p. 35; MPL, LXXVII, 729. See also Hans Söderberg, *La Religion des Cathares* (Uppsala, 1949).

[10] Renato Esnault, "Tracce ereticali nel medio evo francese," *Religio,* XIV (1938), p. 18.

[11] Michael Tangl, *Die Briefe des heiligen Bonifatius* (Berlin, 1916), p. 31; Ephraim Emerton, *The Letters of Saint Boniface* (New York, 1940), p. 114.

[12] Some of the editions bear a salutation to the Thuringians—for instance, Mansi, MPL, and Emerton. Others, notably Tangl, omit it. Whether or not the salutation is genuine, it is clear from the context that the letter is addressed to the Thuringians, whose missionary bishop Boniface had just become. Concerning these "Afros," see Léon Godard, "Quels sont les Africains que le pape Grégoire II défendit en 723, d'élever au sacerdoce," *Revue africaine,* V (1861), 49–53. "Afri" are mentioned in Gregory II's plan of Church organization in MGH Legg., III, 451, and the whole reference may be no more than a formula, as Tangl (*op. cit.,* p. 32) suggests. Gregory II wrote a general letter against Manichaeans later in his reign (Mansi, XII, 258), but in it he merely repeated the warnings contained in the earlier letter.

[13] Söderberg, *op. cit.,* p. 23.

[14] Otto Stegemüller, "Das manichäische Fundamentum in einem Sakramentar der frühen Karolingerzeit," ZKT, LXXIV (1952). Also see my article, "Saint Boniface and the Eccentrics," CH, XXXIII (1964).

[15] MGH Legg., I, 108, cap. 16.

[16] Peter Damian, *Liber gratissimus,* MGH Lib. de Lit., I, 49; Humbert, *Adversus simoniacos,* MGH Lib. de Lit., I, 104, 105, 112.

[17] MGH SS, VIII, 36, 88, 95, 98. See Borst, *op. cit.,* p. 82 n. 5.

[18] For the decretals, see Söderberg, *op. cit.,* p. 23; Esnault, *op. cit.,* p. 18; for Paschasius, see Esnault, *op cit.,* p. 18; Lindeboom, *op. cit.,* p. 35; MPL, CXX, 770.

[19] For the letter, see Edmond Martène and Ursin Durand, *Thesaurus novus anecdotorum* (Paris, 1717), I, 15–17; for Jonas, see Luc d'Achéry, *Spicilegium* (Paris, 1655–1677), I, 318–319.

[20] *In Librum Josue,* MPL, CVIII, 1041; Edmond Martène and Ursin Durand, *Veterum Scriptorum . . .* (Paris, 1724–1733), IX, 715.

[21] For the confession of Gerbert, see MPL, CXXXIX, 253. For a bibliography on the subject, see Hef-L, IV, 867.

[22] Concerning the synod, see Mansi, XIX, 107–153.

[23] Like that distributed to his archdeacons by Bishop Walter of Orléans. See chap. 7.

[24] Hincmar made his profession in 846 (MPL, CXXV, 1199).

[25] Adalbert made his profession in 870. Théodore Gousset, *Les Actes de la province ecclésiastique de Reims* (Reims, 1842–1844), I, 386–388.

[26] See chap. 7.

[27] *Ibid.*

[28] Dondaine, "L'Hierarchie cathare," p. 271. See also Germain Morin, "Les *Statuta ecclesiastica antiqua* sont-ils de Césaire d'Arles," RBén, XXX (1913), 334.

NOTES

[29] Max. Bibl. Vet. Pat., XIII, 708.

[30] See chap. 7. Also see P. Ewald, *"Vita Gauzlini abbatis Floriacensis* von Andreas von Fleury," NAGADGK, III (1878), 351–383, esp. p. 370.

[31] Antoine Dondaine, "Aux Origines du valdéisme," AFP, XVI (1946).

[32] *Ibid.* See, for example, MPL, CCXV, 1510–1513, and MPL, CCXVI, 289–293.

[33] M. Astier, "Etude sur un document relatif au pape Silvestre II—la lettre 180 de Gerbert et le premier canon du IVe concile de Carthage," *Bulletin historique et philosophique du comité des travaux historiques,* 1898.

[34] See chap. 4.

[35] Ilarino da Milano, "Le Eresie popolari del secolo XI," in G. B. Borino, *Studi gregoriani,* II (Rome, 1948), p. 50; Borst, *op. cit.,* p. 78 n. 20.

[36] *Annales Quedlinburgenses,* MGH SS, III, 81.

[37] See Borst, *op. cit.,* p. 74. Adhémar, *Chronicle,* III, 49, 59, ed. Jules Chavanon (Paris, 1897), pp. 173, 184–185.

[38] I will not give references here for the best-known cases. For bibliographical information, see chaps. 1, 2.

[39] Liège and not Châlons. See my article, "A propos du synode d'Arras en 1025," RHE, LVII (1962). For a discussion of these dissenters, see chap. 1.

[40] Adhémar, III, 69, in Chavanon, *op. cit.,* p. 194.

[41] Gousset, *op. cit.,* II, 48–49.

[42] I unite the letter of Pope L. with that of Théoduin. See my article, "Les Cathares de 1048–1054 à Liège," BSAHDL, XLIV (1961), and chap. 1 of this book. My dating has been questioned by Professor Hubert Silvestre (RHE, LVIII [1963], 979) and Professor Paul Bonenfant (MA, LXIX [1963]). As to Professor Bonenfant's arguments, the fact that there were Catharists in Lorraine in the 1140's is well known and does not demonstrate their identity with those of the purported letter of Lucius II. The crucial question remains the salutation of the letter, and I am not convinced that Adalbero's disgrace is the only possible explanation for the form of this salutation. Théoduin, too, was a weak bishop who had distinct difficulties with Gregory VII, toward the end of his reign. On the other side, some of the apparently Catharist beliefs of the heretics would be more easily explained if the later date were accepted. But since, from every other point of view, Leo IX is a much more likely candidate than Lucius II, I shall hold here to my original position while admitting that it is questionable.

[43] Mansi, XIX, 737, 742.

[44] MPL, CXLIII, 1346.

[45] Paul Fredericq, *Corpus documentorum inquisitionis* (Ghent and The Hague, 1889), I, 30.

[46] *Sigeberti continuatio Buraburgensis,* MGH SS, VI, 457.

[47] Mansi, XXI, 532.

[48] Fredericq, *op. cit.,* I, 33–34.

[49] Antoine Dondaine, "Durand de Huesca et la polémique anti-cathare," AFP, XXIX (1959), p. 250; Christine Thouzellier, "Le 'Liber antiheresis' de Durand

307

de Huesca et le 'Contra Haereticos' d'Ermengaud de Béziers," RHE, LV (1960), 130–141.

⁵⁰ The summary I give is of the generally held thirteenth-century doctrines; one must take into account variations of time and place.

⁵¹ Herbert Marcuse, *Eros and Civilization* (New York, 1962), p. 155.

⁵² Egbert, *Canons,* MPL, LXXXIX, 447.

⁵³ Jaffé, no. 2599.

⁵⁴ *De Universo,* IV, 10, in MPL, CXI, 102.

⁵⁵ *Ibid.,* in MPL, CXI, 101.

⁵⁶ Eckbert, *Sermons,* V, 5.

⁵⁷ Cinzio Violante, *La Pataria milanese e la Riforma ecclesiastica: le Premesse (1045–1057)* (Rome, 1955); Ernst Werner, "Παταρηνοί = patarini. Ein Beitrag zur Kirchen- und Sektengeschichte des XI Jahrhunderts," in *Vom Mittelalter zur Neuzeit, Festschrift zum 65. Geburtstag von Heinrich Sproemberg* (Berlin, 1956).

⁵⁸ A schematic tabulation of doctrines would make this apparent.

⁵⁹ Editions: MGH SS, XVI, 727; Joseph Hartzheim, *Concilia Germaniae* (Cologne, 1759–1790), III, 766 (Hartzheim falsely dates the account 1113 and supplies the name of Archbishop Frederick in place of that of Archbishop Arnold); see the reference of Richard Knipping, *Die Regesten der Erzbischöfe von Köln im Mittelalter* (Bonn, 1901), II, 69. Knipping gives the date March 5, 1153.

⁶⁰ MPL, CLXXXII, 676–679; Hartzheim, *op. cit.,* III, 353. The letter is translated by Samuel Roffey Maitland, *Facts and Documents Illustrative of the History, Doctrine, and Rites of the Ancient Albigenses and Waldenses* (London, 1832), pp. 343 ff.

⁶¹ Sermons 65 and 66 in MPL, CLXXXIII, 1087–1093.

⁶² Raoul Manselli, *Studi sulle eresie del secolo XII* (Rome, 1953), p. 90.

⁶³ Emmanuel Aegerter, *Les Hérésies du moyen âge* (Paris, 1939).

⁶⁴ For Saint Bernard's journey to the south, see Elphège Vacandard, *Vie de Saint Bernard* (Paris, 1895), II, 224 ff. Vacandard dates the journey in 1145, following a charter in *Gallia Christiana* (Paris, 1725), II, 814. Other writers have disagreed as to the date of Evervinus' letter, the estimates ranging from 1142 to 1149 (see Borst, *op. cit.,* p. 4 n. 4), but Borst himself is of the opinion that it is 1143 or 1144.

⁶⁵ Vacandard, *op. cit.,* II, 212; Theodor Paas, "Entstehung und Geschichte des Klosters Steinfeld als Propstei," AHVNR, XCIII (1912), 24.

⁶⁶ These heretics were neither Tanchelmists (as Paas, *op. cit.,* p. 51, suggests) nor Henricians (as Manselli, *op. cit.,* pp. 96 ff., suggests). There is no evidence for Henrician or Tanchelmist penetration of the Rhineland and no reason to suppose that the archdiocese of Cologne was unable to generate its own Reformist dissent. Evervinus implies that his heresies were home-nurtured.

⁶⁷ This is the discrepancy that suggests that the *Annales Brunwilarenses* might possibly refer to another incident. According to these annals, three heretics were

NOTES

murned at Bonn by Count Otto; according to Evervinus' letter, two were burned at Cologne by the people.

⁶⁸ For the date, see the argument of Paul Bonenfant, "Un Clerc cathare en Lotharingie au milieu du XIIᵉ siècle," MA, LXIX (1963).
⁶⁹ Hembeca or Hembecke minor.
⁷⁰ Mansi, XXI, 843; Gousset, *op. cit.*, II, 287; Fredericq, *op. cit.*, I, 35–36; Hef-L, V, 913–914.
⁷¹ MGH SS, XX, 593–602.
⁷² MPL, CLXX, 437 ff.
⁷³ Sylvain Balau, *Etude critique des sources de l'histoire du Pays de Liège au moyen âge* (Brussels, 1903), pp. 324, 351.
⁷⁴ MGH SS, XX, 559, gives the reference: "no. VI Ianssens Theol. profano, Codex bib. Lovaniensis universitatis membranaceus."
⁷⁵ Borst, *op. cit.*, p. 7 n. 4.
⁷⁶ MPL, CXCV, 11–96.
⁷⁷ MGH SS, XVI, 22, 686; *Chronica regia Coloniensis and Monumenta Erphesfurtensia* MGH SS, rer. Germ., XVIII, 114, and XLII, 71. Borst, *op. cit.*, p. 94.
⁷⁸ Borst, *op. cit.*, p. 220 n. 26.
⁷⁹ The date of the event is difficult to fix. The estimates of the original sources range from 1161 to 1166, and subsequent historians have, with apparent abandon, assigned dates ranging from 1154 to 1166. Of our two chief sources, Ralph of Diceto gives 1166, while William of Newburgh says, after referring to the death of Theobald of Canterbury on April 18, 1161, that the heretics were apprehended "iisdem diebus." After his report, he continues with the next event, which he dates April, 1162, with the introduction "eodem tempore." From this, many historians, including Borst (*op. cit.*, p. 94 n. 18), have concluded that the proper date is 1161 or 1162. Since William specifies that the events concerning the heretics took place in winter, the winter of 1161–1162 might seem the proper date.

This argument has, however, to contend with contradictory evidence. William says that the heretics, when apprehended, were summoned to appear before a council at Oxford. He gives no indication that any considerable time elapsed between the king's turning them over to the Church and the summoning of the council. Now, there is no record of a council's being held at Oxford between 1161 and 1166, though there was one in 1166. Hef-L, V, 949 f., argue that the council actually took place in 1160, which is no more helpful to our chronology. In all this quicksand there is one firm rock, and that is the date of the assize of Clarendon in 1166. This assize seems to suggest that the heretics had recently been condemned. What is certain is that it speaks of them as if they were still alive, since it forbids aiding them in any way. William of Newburgh, who implies that the date was 1161 or 1162, says that the heretics all died the same winter they were condemned; other chroniclers say that they were at least banished. Further, if the heretics were refugees in hiding, they would likely have been from Cologne, escapees from the persecution associated with Eckbert in 1163.

It seems most likely that the council of Oxford was in fact held in the winter of 1166. But a four year delay in dealing with the heretics would be inexplicable. It seems more probable that the whole sequence of events, therefore, took place in 1165–1166 rather than in 1161–1162.

[80] The sources are William of Newburgh, *Historia rerum Anglicarum*, Rolls Series, LXXXII, pt. 1 (London, 1884), 131 ff.; Ralph of Diceto, *Ymagines historiarum*, Rolls Series, LXVIII, pt. 1 (London, 1876), 318; Ralph of Coggeshall, *Chronicon Anglicanum*, Rolls Series, LXVI (London, 1875), 122; *Annals of Tewkesbury*, Rolls Series, XXXVI, pt. 1 (London, 1864), 49; Matthew Paris, *Historia Anglorum*, Rolls Series, XLIV, pt. 1 (London, 1866), 340; letter 113 of Peter of Blois to Geoffrey, Archbishop of York, MPL, CCVII, 340–341; article 21 of the assize of Clarendon, in William Stubbs, *Select Charters* (9th ed.; Oxford, 1913), p. 173; Walter Map, *De Nugis curialium*, ed. M. R. James (Oxford, 1914).

The material given by the *Annales* of Tewkesbury and the letter of Peter of Blois is little. The assize of Clarendon gives a not unambiguous notice. Walter Map and Ralph of Coggeshall wrote after the period and are derivative; Matthew Paris' account is taken from Ralph of Diceto. The two main sources are therefore the contemporary William of Newburgh and Ralph of Diceto, William's account being the fuller.

[81] Borst, *op. cit.*, p. 94 n. 18, opts for Cologne, as do I. Concerning merchants of Cologne in England, see Leonard Ennen, *Quellen zur Geschichte der Stadt Köln* (Cologne, 1860–1879), I, 544, 605; Henry II and Richard I granted privileges to citizens of that city.

[82] January 11, 1163. MPL, CC, 193; Jaffé, no. 10809.

[83] Everyone but H. J. Warner, *The Albigensian Heresy* (London, 1922–1928), I, 41, has accepted them as Catharists, including Borst, *op. cit.*, p. 94.

CHAPTER 9

[1] Godfried Arnold, *Unpartheyischen Kirchen- und Ketzer-Historie* (2d ed.; Schaffhausen, 1740–1742).

[2] Friedrich Engels, "Ludwig Feuerbach und der Ausgang der klassischen deutschen Philosophie," in Karl Marx and Friedrich Engels, *Ausgewählte Schriften*, II (Berlin, 1952), 373.

[3] See Ernst Werner, *Pauperes Christi* (Berlin, 1956).

[4] For a general study of the historiography of the problem, see my article, "Interpretations of the Origins of Medieval Heresy," MS, XXV (1963).

[5] London, 1957.

[6] Antonio de Stefano, *Riformatori ed eretici del medioevo* (Palermo, 1938), p. 368.

[7] Berlin, 1962.

[8] See Ernst Werner, "Die Stellung der Katharer zur Frau," *Studi medievali*,

II (1961). See also Heinrich Sproemberg, *Beiträge zur belgisch-niederländischen Geschichte* (Berlin, 1959), p. 290. Other reasonable views of material influences have been those of Austin P. Evans, "Social Aspects of Medieval Heresy," in *Persecution and Liberty, Essays in Honor of G. L. Burr* (New York, 1931), and, more recently, Marvin Becker, "Florentine Politics and the Diffusion of Heresy in the Trecento: a Socio-Economic Inquiry," *Speculum,* XXXIV (1959).

⁹ Saint Augustine, *Sermones de Scripturio Novi Testamenti,* LXXXI, iii, 21, in Eric Przywara, *An Augustine Synthesis* (New York, 1958), p. 276.

¹⁰ Henry Charles Lea, *A History of the Inquisition in the Middle Ages* (New York, 1955), I, 217; see also E. Jordan, "La Responsabilité de l'église dans la repression de l'hérésie au moyen âge," *Annales de philosophie chrétienne,* 4th ser., IV, VI, VIII, IX (Paris, 1907–1909); Léon-E. Halkin, "De l'excommunication au bûcher," *Hommage à Lucien Febvre* (Paris, 1954).

¹¹ Cited by A. H. Mathew, *The Life and Times of Hildebrand* (London, 1910), p. 10.

¹² F. Engel-Jánossi, "Die soziale Haltung der italienischen Häretiker im Zeitalter der Renaissance," *Vierteljahrschrift für Sozial- und Wirtschaftsgeschichte,* XXIV (1931), 400.

¹³ Saint Augustine, *Enarrationes in Psalmos,* CXXIV, 5, in Przywara, *op. cit.,* p. 272.

Index

Index